Para mi Tia & Tim,
I love you
This is my f
Forest Service.
I am working on
second book...

Saunders Meadow

A Place Without Fences,
A History of The Term Occupancy Permit Act of 1915

Gracias por
sus oraciones

Enjoy...
Dr. Roberto
antonio
Reyes

Saunders Meadow

A Place Without Fences

A History of

The Term Occupancy Permit Act of 1915

Celebrating 100 years

Dr. Robert A. Reyes

Mill City Press, Minneapolis

Mill City Press, Inc.
322 First Avenue N, 5th floor
Minneapolis, MN 55401
612.455.2293
www.millcitypublishing.com

ISBN-13: 978-1-63413-910-6
LCCN: 2016910508

Foreword provided by Historic Cabin Owners in our National Forests
Cover Design by Jaime Willems
Typeset by Jaime Willems

Printed in the United States of America

Contents

Acknowledgments ix

Foreword xi

Preface xiii

Introduction: There's No Place Like Home xv

A Summary of The Term Occupancy Permit Act of 1915 1

The Forest Service History 7

a. The Need for Wood
b. The Beginning of Permits and Special Use Summer Homes

First American-Born Forester, Gifford Pinchot, 1898–1910 13

a. Addressing Recreation

Implementing the Act 17

a. Consultant Frank A. Waugh, Landscape Architect
b. Landscape Engineer Arthur H. Carhart, 1919–1923

Permit Fees 33

Design and Development of Cabins and Tracts 41

a. Cabin Designs
b. Tract Designs
c. Lot Design
d. Landscape

Thirty-Year, Ninety-Nine-Year, One Hundred-Year Lease 55

Tract Associations 59

Term Occupancy Permit Act with Focus on California 61

Benefits of Term Occupancy Permit Act 67

a. First Benefit
b. Second Benefit
c. Third Benefit

Regions in the Forest Service 73

a. Northern Region 1: National Forest/Grasslands: Montana, Northern Idaho, Northwest South Dakota, and North Dakota
b. Rocky Mountain Region 2: Colorado, Wyoming, South Dakota, Nebraska, and Kansas
c. Southwestern Region 3: Arizona and New Mexico
d. Intermountain Region 4: Utah, Nevada, Southern Idaho, and Bridger-Teton National Forest in Wyoming
- Peavey Cabins
- Salmon Forest
e. Pacific Southwest Region 5: California and Hawaii
- Summer Homes
- In the Beginning
- The Early Years

Southern Forests: Cleveland, San Bernardino, Angeles, and Los Padres

Central Forests: Sierra, Stanislaus, Eldorado, Tahoe, Lake Tahoe Basin Management Unit, Inyo, and Sequoia

Northern Forests: Mendocino, Plumas, Lassen, Shasta-Trinity, Modoc, Six Rivers, and Klamath
- The Rest of the History

f. Pacific Northwest Region 6: Washington and Oregon
g. Region 7
h. Southern Region 8: Texas, Oklahoma, Arkansas, Louisiana, Mississippi, Alabama, Georgia, Florida, South Carolina, North Carolina, Tennessee, Kentucky, and Virginia
i. Eastern Region 9: Maine, New Hampshire, Vermont, West Virginia, Iowa, Illinois, Indiana, Ohio, Missouri, Michigan, Wisconsin, Minnesota, Pennsylvania
j. Region 10: Alaska Region

A Case Study of the Term Occupancy Permit Act of 1915: Tahquitz Special Use Summer Home Tract 145

a. Tahquitz Special Use Summer Home Tract
b. Saunders Meadow—A Place without Fences
c. In the Beginning
d. Loggers
e. Recreation

f. Tahquitz Tract, 1920–1925
g. Cabins
h. The Creation of Tahquitz Meadow Improvement Association and Further Tract and Water Development, 1926–1930
i. The Great Depression
j. Water Repairs, Development, and CCC, 1931–1940s
k. WWII
l. Water Conservation, 1942–1964
m. Land Exchange, 1965–1972
n. Lawsuit, Appointed Receiver, and Subdivision, 1972–1980
o. Annexation into Fern Valley Water District, 1981–1995
p. Termination of the Special Use Water Permit, 2013–2014
q. Present Day
r. Closure

Idyllwild, California, a Mountain Community Surrounded by the San Bernardino National Forest **233**

a. Area History
b. Homesteading
c. Idyllwild History
- Our San Jacinto-Idyllwild Forest Rangers
- Idyllwild Continues to Grow
- Civilian Conservation Corps
- Post-WWII Era, 1945
- Currently (2016)

Appendices **259**

a. National Register of Historic Places: Historic Cabin original Forest Service Lot 19, currently Lot 33—27160 Saunders Meadow Rd, Idyllwild, California—San Bernardino National Forest
b. Forest Service Timeline
c. Idyllwild Timeline
d. Saunders Meadow Timeline
e. Bibliographic References
f. About the Author
g. Index

Acknowledgments

This work would not have been possible without the contributions of many independent authors. One of those was Bill Sapp, archaeologist for the San Bernardino National Forest, who took the time to sit with me and answer my questions, as well as provide multiple studies, photographs, and maps. Another was the Idyllwild Area Historical Society located in the San Jacinto Mountains surrounded by the San Bernardino National Forest for their support and allowing me to use their vast photo collection and recorded Idyllwild history. I must also thank forest service ranger Heidi Hoggan in Idyllwild for all her time, information, and photos. Inspiration and background knowledge were provided by *The San Jacintos* by John W. Robinson and Bruce D. Risher and the informative *Idyllwild and the High San Jacintos* by Robert B. Smith. Without question, I am indebted to the United States Forest Service for responding so graciously. Rangers from every region of the country provided stories, documents, and photos. Also, many thanks to both the LSA Association, Inc. for allowing me to use their History Resource Survey and the US Department of the Interior, National Park Service, and National Register of Historic Places for all their help and information. Because of their guidance, this book is applicable to the sections on their historic registration application and serves as an example in the registration of historic cabins in relation to the 1915 Term Occupancy Permit Act. This book was based on interviews and partial documents (due to purging of original files), thus academic footnotes were not possible, but as the author, I have attempted to provide as many references as possible. Finally, much gratitude to my family and partner, Patrick Kennedy, for allowing me the alone time needed to accomplish the task at hand. And last but not least, my two dogs, Sara and Nana, who sat by my side at two o'clock in the morning while I researched and wrote, never leaving my sight.

Foreword

This is the first comprehensive collection of facts and details on the Term Occupancy Permit Act of 1915 available to those who desire to have their cabins registered as Historic Places. It is written in a manner that lends itself to be used directly on the National Register of Historic Places registration form. The entire collection can be used for the Statement of Significance section of the form. This body of work addresses the required Applicable National Register Criteria A, B, and C:

A. Property is associated with events that have made a significant contribution to the broad pattern of our history.
B. Property is associated with the lives of persons significant in our past.
C. Property embodies the distinctive characteristics of a type, period, or method of construction or represents the work of a master, or possesses high artistic value, or represents a significant and distinguishable entity whose components lack individual distinction.

The author also provides an example for the narrative description section by providing a narrative description of his cabin and a case study of the act's implementation by presenting the history and establishment of the Tahquitz Special Use Summer Home Tract, currently known as Saunders Meadow, located in Idyllwild, California. Also provided is the history of the area supporting the Tahquitz/Saunders Meadow Tract's significant contribution to the broader pattern of national forest history as an example for those who wish to have their tracts registered as a historic place.

The work is presented in a manner that allows the individual to read only the sections needed and of interest at the time by following the table of contents, hence the necessary repetition of historic details and facts. Any person interested in the topic will find this historic synopsis very helpful and useful in his or her own research.

Preface

Robert Reyes' *A Place Without Fences* provides a scholarly and well-researched background for a mountain community that previously knew very little about its history. His in-depth study and chronological timeline brings much-needed appreciation and understanding of the unique background of our Saunders Meadow legacy. We are fortunate that Robert had the zeal and personal interest to pursue this research after becoming the owner of one of the historic cabins in the Saunders Meadow tract in Idyllwild, California.

Connie Jones Pillsbury
Third-generation cabin owner, Saunders Meadow
Freelance writer
Atascadero, California

Introduction

There's no place like home

Nothing compares to sitting on your cabin deck at sunset. Your body goes limp like the local vinca plant welcoming the evening's cool breeze. The shadows of the ponderosa and Jeffrey pines make their way up your steps like an old friend visiting and wishing you a good night. The moonlight dimly reveals the road and trails, while the last of sounds are briefly heard from a barking dog and the laughter of children in a distant camp. When the good Lord looks down, Saunders Meadow is the view He loves the most.

We who came as visitors but stayed as residents can relate to every word. There is no place like Idyllwild, California. Surrounded by the San Bernardino National Forest, this nature lover's haven and spiritually minded artists' retreat will remain untouched by the ever-changing and complicated world. This small town can easily represent every mountaintop community found within the borders of our national forests. They are places cemented in an era when strangers could look each other in the eye, smile, and become friends. When neighbors were close as the native Manzanita trees and doors were left unlocked, always ready to welcome a stranger. Not only do we residents see it as a privilege to live within such serenity and beauty, we find it an honor.

This brief historic synopsis is our humble contribution to the affection we feel toward our community of Saunders Meadow—previously known as the Tahquitz Summer Home Tract, created in

1920 as a result of the 1915 congressional Term Occupancy Permit Act and our little town of Idyllwild, California—where the mayor is a doggie named Max Mueller. Our journey began with the purchase of our Forest Service summer home cabin built in 1921. While on our second visit to Idyllwild, we stumbled upon Village Properties on 54278 N. Circle Drive. One of the proprietors, Realtor Barbara G. Hunt, a true native "Idyllwildan" since birth, believed she had the right cabin for us. Almost apologetically, Barbara drove us to a cabin that had been unoccupied and on the market for over two years.

From the 243 Highway, we turned left onto Saunders Meadow Road, passing the Idyllwild Elementary School where logger Amasa Saunders built his home in 1880 and John and Mary Keen opened Keen House Hotel in 1890 using Saunders' home as one of the camp buildings. Across on the left was the original 1930s C. Selden Belden Pinecraft furniture building, which is now the Mile High Café, which used to specialize in sushi! Who would have known that Belden's Pinecraft furniture would become an expensive collectible that represented rustic American mountaintop craftsmanship. After ascending the hill to AstroCamp, we descended into a unique community resembling a National Park and Forest Service campground intentionally designed around a meadow. We noticed that it was a place without fences, where the cabins were strategically placed in a way as not to disturb the majestic pines.

These ancient trees had stories to tell of the 1400s Cahuilla tribe gathering acorns and grinding them in the mortars they created near Big Cedar Spring, stories of logging in the 1800s that caused them to be secondary growth, thanks to loggers like Anton Scherman, and stories of the 1925–28 Idyllwild/Mount San Jacinto Golf Club course built by Strong and Dickinson to compete with neighborhood developer Claudius Lee Emerson, which turned into Desert Sun School in 1935, renamed Elliott Pope

Preparatory School in 1983, turned AstroCamp in 1990, all located on the meadow. Tales of how the Civilian Conservation Corps built the now-forgotten firebreak surrounding the then Forest Service special use summer home community of Tahquitz tract now known as Saunders Meadow, Inc., and how Saunders Meadow Road was partly an unfinished CCC dirt trail first created by the Cahuilla tribe. If you slow down on your way to the town's collection center and take a little time to observe the area you just entered, your heart will leap and your soul will announce that you have entered a place preserved by forgotten national forest history.

As we rounded the bend, we spotted the old Forest Service special use summer home cabin designed by ranger and architect Coert Dubois. It had the original 1920s Forest Service greyish-blue painted trim. The Manzanita red siding had faded and cracked like my grandmother's face after ninety years of life. In a soft whisper, we could hear the cabin proclaim, "I have earned every line." All she needed now was a fresh coat of paint and gatekeepers to assure her another ninety years. Adding to her mystique was a grand 350-year-old California black oak—perhaps planted by the Cahuilla children—located by the deck that reached high, over, and around the cabin, lovingly shielding and protecting her, yet welcoming us to enter. The second Barbara opened the door, we knew we were home. We did not mind that the kitchen's original 1924 pine-panel cabinets with local Manzanita handles built by Hal "The Rustic Man" Holcomb, a well-known and respected rustic furniture maker, slanted to the right while the floor slanted to the left, or that there was only room for the original icebox.

The living room, with exposed rafters and log beams, had a massive fireplace made out of local granite stones in 1929 by Lem Poates, a renowned stonemason who would eventually supervise the construction of the future town hall in the 1940s. We were mesmerized by the authentic vintage state of this home. We had just walked into the past, into a museum. In the background, we heard Barbara say how easy it would be to remodel the kitchen. Blasphemy, I thought. This was a pearl, how was it possible that this treasure could stand abandoned and undesired for two long years? Regardless of reason, we were now the gatekeepers. The ugly duckling, the rustic bridesmaid, was finally selected, finally chosen.

We were so amazed and thrilled to have found such an old and authentic vintage place still standing, let alone unchanged. How in the world did it survive the human need to improve and upgrade? We soon discovered that all four prior owners, besides the Forest Service, were men and that the only woman related to the cabin was a good old American cowgirl, no frills needed here!

As we embarked on having this treasure listed as a State and National Historic Place, both application and research process had us include the history of the Forest Service, the area, Idyllwild, and Saunders Meadow. Truth be told, we found that the history of one could not be told without the other. If a true and full picture was to be painted of its historic significance, we would have to share a little of all four. Before we knew it, we had a quaint pocket-sized history guide, a case study, a synopsis of the Term Occupancy Permit Act of 1915 and our illustrious, if not tenacious, mountain community.

We hope that by the end you will appreciate how much American history is here within the shadow of our San Jacinto Mountains, within the walls of every cabin, and, of course, within each of our hearts here in Idyllwild and the 13,660 permittees in the Forest Service Special Use Summer Home Recreation Program who are fortunate enough to own cabins across our nation's national forests.

Enjoy. ~Dr. Robert Reyes and Patrick Kennedy

The author's historic Saunders Meadow cabin

A Summary of The Term Occupancy Permit Act of 1915

On March 4, 1915, with the prompting and support of the US Forest Service, Congress passed the Occupancy Act referred to as the Term Permit. This Special Use Permit Act allowed private citizens the opportunity to occupy national forest or public domain lands for a period of time. Congress gave Secretary of Agriculture David F. Houston power to set the terms and limits. Houston stated that a maximum total of five acres with a thirty-year permit would suffice. The land was to be used for family recreation summer homes, and secular and religious campgrounds, as well as resorts and stores.

After the announcement of the act, Chief Forester Henry S. Graves developed and presented "Instructions Regarding Term Occupancy Permits," a guide to assist all forest districts in their implementation of the new program. His guide recommended that less than one acre rather than five would meet most needs with a fifteen-year renewable term for a fee of five to twenty-five dollars a year, depending on use and structures built. Resorts and stores would run fifteen to two hundred dollars a year for eighty acres. Graves clearly stated in his booklet that the focus of the act and the agency would be on making the national forests more accessible to the recreation seeker, which at the time numbered over 1.5 million. The yearly updated and published "Forest Service Use Book" developed by past Chief Forester Gifford Pinchot back in 1905 as a Ranger Guide provided Graves thirteen stipulations for permittees to follow in its 1915 publication. Graves' terms in 1915 were:

A. The permittee will observe all regulations of the department of agriculture relating to the national forests;
B. Premises will be kept in a neat and orderly condition and the permittee will dispose of refuse and locate outhouses and cesspools as directed by the forest officers and observe such other sanitary requirements as may at any time appear necessary to protect public health;
C. Improvements will be constructed within a reasonable time and in accordance with plans and specifications filed with the forest officers, when required, and approved by them;
D. All reasonable caution will be taken to prevent forest fires;
E. Where the permit is for a business enterprise, permittee shall comply with the requirements of state laws and shall conduct his business in a legal and orderly manner;
F. Timber shall be removed only under permit from forest officers;
G. A fair annual rental will be paid for the use of the land occupied;
H. Structures will be removed within a reasonable time after the permit is terminated;
I. Permits may be transferred with the approval of the officer who granted it, or his successor, and hotels and resorts may also be sublet only with the approval of the district forester;
J. A right-of-way will be reserved for the free ingress and egress of forest officers and other users of national forest lands, as well as for the removal of products of the forest;
K. On the expiration of the permit, the permittee shall be considered the first applicant for a new permit to be granted subject to the conditions under which like permits are then granted;
L. As to public service enterprises, such as hotels or resorts, the permittee may be required to conform to such regulations respecting rates and services as the department may make should regulation be necessary in the interests of the public;
M. The permittee will agree to such special terms, as the conditions surrounding any particular case make necessary.

With these guidelines set, each of the six forest districts were allowed to survey tracts and design the layout of lots. Each tract was allowed 30 to 150 lots each; others tried to get permission to develop as many as 400 lots. Tracts were to be designed to flow and harmonize with the forest and natural features. Least disturbance of the environment was emphasized. Districts were allowed to add their own needed clauses to the terms. The additions were specific to region and terrain. Altitude mandated a certain roof: if an area experienced harsh winters, a higher pitched roof was required. Some districts only offered a five- to ten-year renewable permit, others fifteen years. All variations and program guidelines always focused and emphasized the safety, needs, and protection of both the public and the national forests. This program became extremely popular along the west coast.

Days after the passing of the act, District 5 surveyed tracts and designed lot layouts, followed by districts 6, 4, 2, and 1. These districts were located in western states, making them the leaders on the number of permits granted. In 1916, these districts developed some of the nation's original forms and guidelines for the management of the special use summer home tracts. These forms became standard and official Forest Service documents used across the nation. District 5 had many tracts, one was Tahquitz, located in Idyllwild, California. This tract was surveyed in 1920 and started organizing in 1923, becoming the Tahquitz Meadow Improvement Association in 1927. It is currently the only tract association in the nation that went through the exchange program offered by the Forest Service in the late 1960s that is still in existence and continues to follow the original Forest Service tract guidelines in order to maintain the natural beauty of the forest and community.

The United States Department of Agriculture archives reveal that there were close to 20,000 summer homes built throughout the one-hundred-year history of the act with an estimated 14,000 cabins still in the program. The 6,748-plus lost were destroyed by natural events such as fires, torrential rains, or mudslides and never rebuilt.

Summer Homes destroyed by floods in the 1930s

The rest were exchanged into private ownership or transferred to state and national parks. Many of the 13,660 cabins that have remained in their original state for the most part have been registered or are in the process of being registered as National and State Historic Places due to their value as an integral part of their local and regional history, and the national forest history. The special use summer homes not only officially opened the reserves to the public and established strong ties with mountaintop communities, but also solidified recreation as a legitimate use of our national forests, just as important as grazing and timber.

Men like architect Frank A. Waugh, landscape engineer Arthur H. Carhart, and both ranger and architect Coert Dubois, all influenced by the American Society of Landscape Architects (ASLA), helped promote and solidify the program's success. They produced a rustic charm that characterized and helped define the special use summer home cabin's architecture as the "American Campground" design. This look was first established in the parks by Waugh and the ASLA and at times was referred to as the "national park look."

Where the national parks switched to an elaborate and grander design, the Forest Service continued with this easily recognizable, rustic yet functional American look that continues to evoke the same elation now as when they were first built. They are grand and beautiful in their utilitarian simplicity so properly located in our nation's pristine forests and proud to have survived one hundred years of life. This is their story.

The Forest Service History

The history of the US Forest Service is, in part, connected to its relationship with small mountaintop communities such as Idyllwild. The recreation, social, and economic links between the two is unquestionable and sealed in their dependence on each other. These small towns relied on the protection provided by the rangers and recreation visitors to the national forests. In turn, these communities provided the guests what the Forest Service could not: places to stay, dine, and shop. To understand the development of both is to appreciate their Western tenacity and exemplary bravery that is admired and romanticized by the world.

The Need for Wood

Our country was built on wood. Since the discovery of fire, man has relied on trees. Wooden ships brought explorers to the New World. Colonists from Jamestown in 1607 to the Pilgrims landing on Plymouth Rock thirteen years later used lumber to build their shelters and forts and survive the freezing winters. The New World grew from this rich and abundant resource and a great nation was born.

Manifest Destiny was a widely held belief in the nineteenth century. Settlers believed that it was their divine calling to take, claim, and use all natural resources, which at times, sad to say, included "savages." These pioneers spread their virtues across the new and untamed American frontier. Hills and mountains were raped and cleared. It was the norm to overgraze as well as cut entire forests down leaving miles and miles of stumps and then move on to the next location, diminishing and destroying without any regard for the future. No need to think about preservation when there was an abundance of natural resources just ahead. Water, minerals, trees, and land would never end, yet as quickly as the nation conquered the West, our "frontier" came to an end. Painters, photographers, and writers called the nation to look back and reflect on the devastating effects of their actions and perhaps ponder the possibility of conservation.

The Beginning of Permits and Special Use Summer Homes

Before the creation of the Forest Reserves and as far back as the early 1800s, adventuresome individuals were visiting the wilderness and enjoying the forests across the country. In the West, it was common consent that this new frontier was free and available territory for the use and enjoyment by those who had the heart and courage to do so, and any form of government regulation was viewed as wrong, intrusive, and unwelcomed. But as the nation expanded, many fraudulent land deals were made, so in 1812, Congress created the General Land Office (GLO) to survey, regulate, and protect homesteaders, settlers, farmers, and miners. The GLO helped support Homestead Acts through land management.

The Homestead Act of 1862 allowed the westward-bound to claim public domain timberland. After providing timber to the government and railroads, these settlers were allowed to pay a minimal recording fee to the GLO in order to receive the deed to the land. They built cabins, fished, and hunted. As their numbers grew, so did the desire for recreation and preservation. Now that the forest was their home, they wanted to protect it. With this growing sentiment, in 1864, President Abraham Lincoln signed into existence the Yosemite Grant Act, protecting the wilderness in the Yosemite Valley and Mariposa Grove areas. This marked the first time the government specifically selected land for the sole purpose of preservation and public recreational use. Yellowstone Timberland Reserve followed as the nation's first national park in 1872. Later in 1890, Yosemite became a national park.

In 1873 the American Association for the Advancement of Science (AAAS) appointed Franklin B. Hough to conduct a study on the nation's natural resources. Hough researched and wrote convincing and compelling work. His paper in 1873, "On the Duty of Governments in the Preservation of Forests" was a complete contrast to the Manifest Destiny ideal and well received by Congress and the nation. The AAAS made Hough chair of the Federal Forestry Association, whose sole purpose was to influence and inform the government on forest protection. In 1876 Hough became the first federal forestry agent with a budget of $2,000 appropriated by Congress, marking the beginning of the American Forestry Service. As a result of Hough's effort and studies, Congress granted the president power to create forest reserves in 1891.

In 1897, Congress passed the Sundry Civil Appropriations Act in order to help manage and guide the new reserves. The act recognized prior recreational use of the forests by private individuals and thus established the practice of permit-regulated occupancy within them. Two years later, Congress approved the Mineral Springs Leasing Act, also known as the Terminable Permits Act of 1899, which allowed land leases and the building of tents or shacks "for the comfort and enjoyment of guests," establishing a precedent on recreational permits.

In the 1890s, the popularity of reserves for recreational use greatly increased. Thus the first rangers were assigned to the west, which had the highest number of visitors in 1898. With such interest from the public for recreation and the great outdoors, Congress authorized the GLO in 1902 to sanction the leasing of land and the building of private structures for both health and possible recreation activities. In 1905, summer homes were added to the 1902 list for permitted uses of the forest reserves. The trend continued with the Homestead Act of June 11, 1906. This act allowed living on forest reserve land that was no longer suitable for timber but deemed appropriate for agricultural use such as farming and grazing. These early homesteading ranching pioneers and farmers built homes, grazed their livestock, grew their crops, and enjoyed the great outdoors, once again reinforcing the idea of recreation and summer residence.

In 1905, the forest reserves were moved from the Department of the Interior to the Department of Agriculture. With the Transfer Act of 1905, the new Bureau of Forestry phased out homesteading. However, private citizens could continue to apply for a terminable permit with a yearly fee of five dollars. These permits, which originated in 1897, continued to allow the building of private structures such as hotels, cabins, and sanitariums on government land but had to be renewed yearly and could be terminated at the discretion of the forest supervisor at any given time.

In 1912, Forester Henry S. Graves reported that "much dissatisfaction existed with the 1901 provision . . . which authorized the revocation of permits at the discretion of the government." Renters of these lots could not justify spending large amounts of money on a home or business that could so easily be lost. That same year, the forester stated in his report, "if occupancy of lots wanted for summer camps, cottages and hotels for a period of years could be authorized, more substantial buildings than are now being erected would probably be put up." With such support and desire the building of summer cabins in the forest reserves continued to grow.

The annual Forester Report of 1913 showed 1.5 million visitors. Almost half a million were campers and visitors at hotels, cabins, and sanitariums. The report stated that the Angeles National Forest in Southern California had the highest percentage of visitors, with most requesting longer permit terms. In fact, permittees in California who had built summer cabins and resorts contacted Congressman John E. Raker and lobbied for legislation to secure property ownership rather than just longer terms. This request ended, in committee hearing, being denied.

Finally, in 1914, the House of Representatives Committee on Agriculture proposed a longer occupancy term permit for the benefit of the public's use of their national forests. Congress acted upon this Agriculture Appropriations Bill proposal with the approval of the Term Occupancy Permit Act on March 4, 1915, that allowed private citizens the right to obtain a lot for twenty-five dollars a year with a possible thirty-year permit. This permit was referred to as the Special Use Summer Home program.

Uncle Sam Has Choice Camp Sites for Rent—Summer Home at Big Bear Lake, San Bernardino National Forest, California, 1940s

First American-Born Forester, Gifford Pinchot, 1898–1910

Gifford Pinchot was a Yale graduate who had grown up privileged. His grandfather acquired a fortune in the logging industry, which at the time used the clear-cut method of logging. His parents, however, shared their concern for the depleting forests with their children. Even though the idea of forester as a profession was barely recognized in this country, let alone respected, Pinchot's father influenced him to study forestry. With the lack of such schools in America, he went to Europe to study in France, making him the first American-born forester.

As the first chief of the United States Forest Service, Gifford Pinchot faced the challenge of establishing a program that defined what it meant to care for the forests while serving and meeting the needs of both the nation and its people. Pinchot had to balance the voices of so-called experts, politicians, Congress, the states, and all who were to gain or lose financially from the use of these natural resources.

Addressing Recreation

Chief Pinchot knew there was money to be gained from responsible lumbering, yet, at the same time, he wanted to implement a form of conservation and address the growing needs for recreation. Pinchot's 1905 report stated that, "in the administration of the forest reserves it must be clearly borne in mind that all land is to be devoted to its most productive use for the permanent good of the whole people; and not for the temporary benefit of individuals or companies. All the resources of forest reserves are for use, and this use must be brought about in a thoroughly prompt and businesslike manner under such restrictions only as will ensure the permanence of these resources."

Pinchot's moral gauge for all decisions was in his belief in "the greatest good for the greatest number." The challenge faced by his bureau was keeping up with what this meant per era. Concurrently, the public's views continued to change and grow toward the enjoyment and protection of the forests. Painters and photographers showcased the nation's landscapes to the world. Environmentalists also expounded on experiencing the beauty of creation in its natural state. Naturalist and advocate of preservation John Muir wrote articles, research, and books such as *Our National Parks* that introduced the country to the beauty of Yellowstone and Yosemite in the California Sierras. The masses responded with the desire to visit, experience, and protect the nation's natural treasures. In 1898, Muir wrote, "God never made an ugly landscape. All that the sun shines on is beautiful, so long as it is wild." When early affluent forest adventurers first approached the exhausted and ravaged land, their outcry was loud and clear. They wanted certain sections of the forest preserved with complete protection and allowed to remain true wilderness, with the rest regulated and guarded from unbridled exploitation and only used for the recreational enjoyment of the public. Certain extremists simply wanted all reserves kept wild. As stated by John Muir in 1897, "God has cared for these trees . . . but he cannot save them from fools—only Uncle Sam can do that." A balance was needed.

Pinchot believed in responsible forestry; in 1905 he stated, "The vital importance of forest reserves to the great industries of the western states will be largely increased in the near future by the continued steady advance in settlement and development. The permanence of the resources of the reserves is therefore in-dispensable to continued prosperity, and the policy of this Department for their protection and use will invariably be guided by this fact, always bearing in mind that the conservative use of these resources in no way conflicts with their permanent value." Gifford's challenge was in balancing multiple views in the use of the forests. He had to protect them and yet meet the needs of the nation all at the same time.

These opposing views came to a head with the Hetch Hetchy Valley reservoir. Although Pinchot had been replaced by Henry Graves in 1910 due to Pinchot's public rebuke of President Taft's appointment of Richard Ballinger as US Secretary of the Interior, Pinchot remained the face of the Forest Service and his influence continued. Between 1901 and 1913, preservationists worked at protecting the Hetch Hetchy Valley and battled against Gifford, President Wilson, and Henry Graves. These three men supported the construction of a dam greatly needed in order to supply water to San Francisco. The issue took priority after the great San Francisco earthquake in 1906 when the city's inadequate water supply kept them from controlling the resulting fire. San Franciscan Congressman John E. Raker designed the needed legislation for the reservoir. In 1913, the Raker Act passed Congress with President Woodrow Wilson's signature permitting the dam. With the stroke of a pen, the magnificent Hetch Hetchy Valley in Yosemite National Park was destroyed, but the need of thousands of San Franciscans was met. National outcry against the Forest Service followed. The greatest good for the greatest number was met, but now the greatest number was crying out. The country now questioned the Forest Service's commitment to conservation, responsible forestry, and public service. As a result, the public switched their support and now favored the National Park Service, whose sole purpose was recreation, public use, and preservation in an elegant setting. This backlash caused the Forest Service to reevaluate and address the nation's concerns. As a result, the Forest Service presented the Term Occupancy Permit Act with a focus on the special use summer home program.

Hetch Hetchy Valley, early 1900s

Hetch Hetchy Reservoir, 1914

Implementing the Act

The Forest Service noticed that the National Park Service was generating revenue from the many visitors who were dazzled by the facilities that had been designed and built by the American Society of Landscape Architects (ASLA) and the prime locations with spectacular panoramic views within, ironically, the national forests. The Forest Service realized that they would need help in planning recreation facilities and properly implementing the Term Occupancy Permit Act in order to match the parks. In 1916, Forester E. A. Sherman said, "Great as is the economic importance of the National Forests as a source of timber supply, water supply, and forage production, it is not improbable that their value as playgrounds for the public will in time come to rank as one of the major resources. The Forest Service is giving due consideration to this fact. It has definitely aimed to foresee what the public needs in this respect will require, and to plan accordingly . . . " With such a supportive view and in order to compete with the national parks, the Forest Service found itself in need of a comprehensive plan and guidance in the implementation of the special use summer home program.

Consultant Frank A. Waugh, Landscape Architect

In 1917, the Forest Service hired ASLA's landscape architect Frank A. Waugh, who had worked for the National Parks Service, to assess and report on all current recreational facilities and survey possible future recreation sites across the nation's forests. Waugh found that the Forest Service only had old roads and trails leading to picnic grounds, defined by dilapidated tables, and small groups of unplanned summer cabins, consisting of shacks and tents. After his evaluation, Waugh presented guidelines and principles on the proper selection and implementation of recreation sites. He recommended the selection of the best sites possible, such as lakes, streams, and meadows. His main points were in keeping a highly natural style of design in order to harmonize all construction to the landscape. He believed in designing around the environment with very little interference. Waugh emphasized that summer home tracts and lots had to flow with natural paths around boulders and ancient trees as well as meander along streams, lakeshores, and meadows. The local topography—slopes, valleys, and creeks—had to dictate all tract and lot layout designs. In 1918, he stated, "the building of disreputable, unsightly structures which disfigure the natural landscape surroundings must not be allowed." His primary principles and guidelines for summer home tract design set the standard for all future development.

Waugh's report expounded that recreational use of the national forests was just as important as logging and that it could generate as much as $7.5 million annually if properly planned and managed. He emphasized the importance of hiring landscape engineers for every district to design recreation sites that would compare to those of their rivals, the national parks, and meet the needs of the people while protecting and preserving the pristine terrain.

1920s Automobile Camp, Southern California

Landscape Engineer Arthur H. Carhart, 1919–1923

In 1919, after serving in the US Army Medical Corps during WWI, landscape architect Arthur Hawthorne Carhart was hired by Assistant Forester E.A. Sherman as the Forest Service's first recreation engineer. Carhart worked to create an effective, comprehensive national recreation plan that would address the needs expressed by districts experiencing high numbers of visitors while implementing the Term Occupancy Permit Act. These recreational enthusiasts averaged 2.5 million in the early 1920s and were damaging the forest with their Ford Model T automobiles. Their "Tin Lizzies" trampled and crushed trees and shrubs. Carhart addressed this concern by designing the first automobile campgrounds.

Carhart warned that too much development would destroy and defeat the purpose of experiencing nature as true wilderness. He advised that development of summer home tracts and recreational campgrounds had to be well planned, concurring with Waugh. In fact, he eliminated summer home tracts built from 1915 to 1918 that he felt didn't follow Waugh's principles and encroached on nature. Many of these original tracts were truly improperly planned. The Forest Service, in 1915, had allowed plywood shacks and tents to be built until the required "improvement" amount of $250 was added to the permit stipulations in 1924.The Forest Service saw this amount as an investment for the construction of permanent and safe summer homes. These were a major improvement to the original lean-to temporary structures.

As a true advocate of wilderness preservation in 1920, Carhart lamented the winds of change: "Years ago there could easily be found open country where one could play, picnic, tramp, or camp at almost any turn of the road. A few years ago by going a small distance camping places, where nature was still supreme, could be found. But today, with man land-hungry, these places are fast disappearing." Older foresters in certain districts agreed with him and never quite accepted the summer home tract program or the recreational use of the reserves and thus hindered its evolution within their own districts.

Funding became an issue. In support of the nation's first landscape engineer, Assistant Forester of the Land Division Leon F. Kneipp suggested that Chief Forester Greeley request $50,000 from Congress in order to help Carhart. On October 4, 1920, Greeley approached Congress and stated that in order "to bring about the fullest use of the National Forests and contribute their proper quota to the Nation's health, there is needed a special fund of $50,000 for fiscal year 1922 for recreational development. This will permit the employment of several trained landscape engineers, more rapid and at the same time more careful development, the improvement of additional campgrounds and provision of other public facilities and conveniences, and enlarged cooperation with local communities." The American Society of Landscape Architects (ASLA) tried to help by supporting both the National Park Service and the Forest Service. They vowed to help the Forest Service further develop their recreation plan, even approaching the House Appropriations Committee in support of Chief Greeley. Unfortunately, the request was rejected. Only $10,000 was granted for the sole purpose of toilets and fire pits/safety and sanitation. Disheartened, Chief Greeley addressed his districts and reminded them that recreation was still a high priority.

One can surmise that Congress struggled with defining the differences and relationship between the Forest Service and the National Park Service. This may have caused Congress to shut down most funding. Their rivalry did not help either; both agencies wanted control over the other. National parks were seen as lavish and grand with one focus: providing enjoyment of nature in properly planned, "hoity-toity" recreational facilities that catered to the wealthy. In contrast, national forests were seen as wild, free, and rugged, aligned with American frontier spirit, inexpensive, and simple. The Forest Service believed that they alone understood forestry and the proper managing of its many natural resources and detested the notion of any facility being too showy. Gifford Pinchot's foresight on the importance of having both the National Park Service and the US Forest Service as one agency proved to be correct. In fact, if they had been, perhaps funding would have then been easily granted.

Forest Service ranger building, 1910

Glacier National Park Hotel Lobby, 1900s

In 1922, Carhart asked Congress for $45,000 for recreational grounds for fiscal year 1923 even after the rejection of Greeley's request. Carhart was granted a laughable $900. After five years of frustration, he resigned on December 31, 1922. With his resignation, the Forest Service stopped hiring landscape architects for a while. Instead, the Forest Service offered to train rangers in recreation design and summer home tract planning in order to meet increasing demand. A few districts participated and selected staff members to attend the two-week training. During this developmental era, recreation projects were kept simple and also focused on picnic areas, facilities, and auto camps.

Carhart proved to be ahead of his time, for two years later, in 1924, President Calvin Coolidge gave a speech in support of outdoor recreation and the responsibility of the government in meeting the public's growing desire for opportunities to visit and enjoy the national forests, whose numbers of visitors had grown to 4,660,389 that year. With such support from the president, one year later, Congress granted the Forest Service $37,631 toward recreational development. By 1929, the number of visitors jumped from four million-plus to 7,132,058, making the congressional funding inadequate to meet the public's recreational needs once again.

Under the leadership of Chief William B. Greeley, use of the summer home program greatly increased. Greeley and his assistant, Kneipp, allocated many acres of land for campgrounds, dormitories, cabins, recreational facilities, and summer home tracts while preserving primitive areas adjacent to the recreational locations. Forest districts that implemented the special use summer home program flourished. The program not only covered its own administrative expenses, but funded many public recreational projects from the collected permit fees. There were approximately 14,000 summer homes at this time with Region/District 5 reporting an estimated 6,000 permits.

A year later, in 1928, Robert Stuart replaced Greeley as chief. With demand for the program being so high, forest districts requested assistance. The Washington office answered the call through the production and distribution of the 1928 *National Forest Manual*, which contained summer home tract regulations and management guidelines in both special use and recreation development, all modeled after forest districts' successful programs. The manual stated that:

> . . . the use of national forests as places of residence should be especially encouraged if not in conflict with other more important uses or with good administration . . . In the discretion of the forest supervisor, intelligible plans and estimates of proposed buildings may be required of applicants. Design, rather than cost, will determine the acceptability of the plan. All structures within summer residential areas upon national forest land must harmonize with their environment. . . . Where tracts of land have been classified as suitable for residence purposes under the recreation plan, they may be surveyed, mapped, and laid out as lots, blocks, and groups of lots and blocks or both. Provisions should be made for roads, trails, water systems, proper sanitation, public camp grounds, and the location of stores, hotels, and other commercial enterprises, so as not to detract from residence value of other lots.

The increase of visitors kept the Forest Service busy with the summer home program and growing demand for public use. With more people visiting the national forests, the need began to shift from individual recreation to public use. In 1928, District 5 reported that "summer home site tracts were laid out years ago when the great increase in population and future use was not foreseen and some of the tracts are today needed for public use." In fact, San Bernardino National Forest stopped development of summer home tracts on prime locations around lakes and streams. It also stopped renewing permits when possible in order to use these pristine locations. As the popularity of public recreational use increased thanks to cars and better roads, the need for these sites became quite evident. During this time, the amount for new summer home construction required as an investment by the Forest Service was increased to $2,000. Every new permittee had to spend this amount on construction of his new summer home cabin.

In the late 1920s and early 1930s, congressional funding increased to $52,050 in order to match the growing number of visitors. This amount was stretched to cover the "basic needs" of all 150 national forests at the time. Once again the money was used for the building of small campgrounds, automobile campsites, toilets, and roads, and surveying summer home tracts. Chief Robert Y. Stuart allocated $150 to $200 per project, thus he was able to report that 1,493 out of the nation's 1,500 campsites were somewhat "properly" operational. Recreational facilities were not elaborate; they were kept simple and rugged. If you wanted grand, you would have to visit the national parks or build a privately funded resort as allowed by the Term Occupancy Permit Act.

In the mid-1930s, after requesting recreation development progress reports from the districts, now renamed "forest regions," the Forest Service recognized that the only way to have national uniformity and equity was to mandate that each region have a well-qualified recreation expert who would report to the Washington, DC office. Congress did not support this view due to both the lack of money and the fact that many regions in the central and eastern part of the country reported too little recreation activity and a desire to remain decentralized. In reality, they simply did not support the program. Regardless, Assistant Chief Forester Kneipp felt that a "centralized" national program within the department would force all districts to develop a strong, unified, and cohesive program.

The Roaring Twenties, with all its frolic and prosperity, attracted a whopping eight million adventure seekers to the national forests. The Forest Service and Congress responded with the building of roads, the addition of more summer home tracts, and simple public recreational facilities. Then in 1929, the stock market crashed and ushered in the Great Depression.

During this difficult era, recreation development funding was reduced by 25 percent. Extra funding came from the private sector and the summer home program fees. From 1932 to 1933, both the Forest Service and Congress recognized that the forests needed improvements and the nation needed jobs. Under the influence and prompting of Chief Robert Y. Stuart, Senator Royal S. Copeland called for a study of the nation's forests to "ensure all of the economic and social benefits which can and should be derived from productive forests by fully utilizing the forest land." The study produced, "A National Plan for American Forestry," which was referred to as the Copeland Report. This document led the government to see the national forests as a source of possible employment that could alleviate the current woes of the nation. Forester Earle Clapp supervised the study, and Forester Robert Marshall wrote the section on recreation. The 1,677-page report included projects such as the construction of roads, campgrounds, ranger stations, summer home tracts, dormitories, toilets, and lookout towers, as well as running telephone lines and creating trails and recreational facilities. Fortunately, President Franklin Delano Roosevelt provided the necessary support that would allow all of the Copeland Report's recommendations to be accomplished through his congressionally approved New Deal program. Hence, the National Industrial Recovery and Civil Works Administration Emergency Conservation Work Acts were approved, bringing relief, recovery, and reform to the nation during the Great Depression.

The Civilian Conservation Corps (CCC) program was a result of these acts, created to help unemployed and needy young men. The CCC created jobs for the conservation of natural resources on forest and public lands. The CCC's young men were well trained to work in both national forests and parks and provided the needed manpower to accomplish all the recommended Copeland Report projects. That same year, on October 23, 1933, Chief Robert Y. Stuart fell from his seventh-level office window in Washington, DC. It was speculated that his unfortunate death was due to the fatigue caused by the demands and pressures of a growing national program. Before his untimely death, Stuart wrote, "the importance of recreational use as a social force and influence must be met. Its potentialities as a service to the American people, as the basis for industry and commerce as the foundation of the future economic life of many communities, are definite and beyond question."

In 1933, Ferdinand A. Silcox became the new chief and helped all regions finally implement a national recreation program based on the principles first set by the successful special use summer home program.

Because programs under the New Deal focused on the public's welfare, the Forest Service's emphasis finally turned from the summer home program to public recreational facilities. In 1938, head of the Division of Recreation and Land Robert Marshall stated, "the recreation resource of the national forests will be managed for the fullest use of the general public and not for the exclusive use of individuals or small groups." In the midst of this change, the summer home tracts and resorts continued growing.

This was an amazing time—never in its history had the Forest Service seen such support. The special use summer home tract and resort program established recreation as a legitimate use of the national forests while generating needed funds. President Roosevelt put the country back to work by funding programs. The US Forest Service's infrastructure was set and ready to welcome the eighteen million people now visiting the 966 camps built by the CCC.

Unfortunately, on December 7, 1941, Japan attacked Pearl Harbor. The following day, the United States declared war on Japan, and on December 11, war was declared on both Germany and Italy. Funding for the Forest Service practically ended. Landscape architects were let go and recreation staff members were re-assigned or sent to war. In 1942, all recreation development ceased. Summer home tracts and resorts were no longer surveyed. Available lots continued to be leased due to private funding. Some national forests closed for lack of manpower. Regions with successful summer home tracts focused on fire prevention and the building of lookout towers just in case the enemy decided to attack the western region. The summer home tract permittees were welcomed year round at this time since they acted as guardians of the forest. Permit regulations were ignored due to the fact that the Forest Service now viewed cabin owners as helpers who kept a watchful eye on the mere six million visitors who could ignorantly start fires or cause damage to the forests. These visitors found the national forests an inexpensive retreat and a place for temporary rest from the stress of having their sons in battle.

After the war ended in 1945, the Forest Service returned its focus to recreation. The number of visitors crawled to 8.5 million. Citizens wanted to forget the last four years and they did so by going on recreational trips. Soldiers returned home with benefits. One was the ability to easily obtain a home. Another was access to an education or technical training. Prosperity was at hand and the economy flourished, creating a strong middle class that learned how to spend.

During this time, the Forest Service added more safety requirements to the original special use summer home guidelines in order to meet current demand and address higher contemporary safety and sanitary standards. Now, spark arrestors on chimney outlets were required, wastewater had to be properly dealt with, and all sanitary systems had to be pre-approved before installation. All upgrades, additions, and new construction had to be inspected and approved. New cabins had to be built within two years and permittees were required to spend $1,000 on construction improvements as opposed to the prior $2,000 established in 1928.

In 1946, the number of visitors to the national forests rapidly climbed to eighteen million. The Forest Service was able to accommodate such high numbers thanks to the CCC's work. The special use summer home tracts increased from 1946 to 1955 to nearly 18,000 permits, Region 5 had over 65 percent of the nation's tracts. Both soldiers and civilians took advantage of the low permit fees and inexpensive, easy to build, pre-cut, and pre-fab cabin and home kits. Even so, the special use program was no longer a Forest Service priority. In fact, Region 5's 1946 "Administrative Guide For Special Uses" deleted the entire section on how to design, layout, and survey tracts. At the same time, the Forest Service made permits and construction guidelines even more stringent. In the late 1940s to early 1950s, counties began requiring improvement permits as well.

Adding salt to the wound, in order to address the continuous increase in visitors and the further need of land for public recreational use, Region 5 added a clause to their guidelines in 1947 that stated:

> Occasionally good management or land use classification dictates the discontinuance of summer home use, and under the following conditions permits will be placed on a definite tenure in accordance with the policy for amortization of improvements:

A. Where land occupied by a summer home is needed for a higher use.

B. Where serious conflict exists with our roadside policy.

C. Where improvements are sub-standard and permittee will take no action to remedy conditions.

It was odd that the Forest Service would ever be in need of land since it only used a minute percent for recreation from the millions of acres it managed. Regardless, the summer home program peaked at this time with close to 20,000 permits. California, in Region 5, now accounted for 75 percent of all permits with 15,520. But things were about to change, as foreshadowed in 1947.

In 1955 all new tracts had to be approved by the Washington, DC, national office. Local regional supervisors were no longer allowed to survey without authority. The chief of forestry now required extensive documentation justifying need. The new stipulations made the development of tracts nearly impossible. The regions found the new process too expensive and time consuming, especially now that their attention was required on public recreation. Unfortunately, the program that had established recreation as a valid use of the national forests and had generated funds to support recreational development was now at the bottom of the totem pole, a dwindling starlet.

In the late 1950s, the recreational use of the national forests increased by 92 percent. In response, the United States Department of Agriculture initiated a five-year improvement program called "Operation Outdoors" on July 1, 1957. The objective was to repair the recreation areas built by the CCC and build new facilities to accommodate the masses, which now totaled 81,521,000 nationwide. Around the same time, the National Park Service also initiated a reparative recreational program called "Mission 66." The Park Service and other public lands were also included since they accounted for 1 percent of all summer home tracts, while the Forest

Service housed 99 percent of the cabins. At the end of the 1950s, all summer home guidelines were amended to reflect the Forest Service's new commitment to public use. Permittees were reminded that they were no longer allowed permanent year-round residence.

In 1959, Region 5's permit stated that there would no longer be new summer home lots. All new developed land would now be for public use. The program initiated by the Term Occupancy Permit Act of 1915, presented and welcomed with such fan fair, suddenly and quietly was put to rest twenty years later in 1979, ending all future development across the nation.

Permit Fees

Throughout the decades, special use fees arose as an issue, but not much changed. Original policy presented fees from $5 to $25 per year for summer homes and $25 to $200 for resorts and any other form of commercial use. It is appropriate to note that the original terminable-revocable permits begun in the 1800s were still available at a lower fee, but they came without the security of a set term and could be revoked at any given time. Permits for theaters, billiard halls, etc. would cost $75 for a term permit, but only $50 for a terminable-revocable permit. Hotels and resorts would be $200 for a term, but only $125 for a terminable. Stores and shops would run $75 for a term, but only $25 for a terminable. The Forest Service believed that the purpose of permits was serving the people and welcoming them to their land. Hence, increasing fees was the last thing on their minds, until the 1950s when Congress initiated a review.

As previously mentioned, during the 1930s the Forest Service started shifting its focus from individual recreation to public use. In the 1950s, the priority was no longer their star program—the special use summer home tracts—now the focus was on facilitating the masses visiting the national forests. So in 1959, Congress assigned an Outdoor Recreation Resource Review Commission (ORRRC) to evaluate and assess the nation's current and future recreational patterns and needs. In addition, Congress also presented an act amending the original 1915 Term Permit Act, no longer authorizing thirty-year permits. This amendment did not come with or give any specific terms or directives for the regions to follow, causing much uncertainty regarding the future of all cabin owners. In 1962, in order to address concerns, permittees and tract associations united across the country and joined the National Forest Recreation Association (NFRA), creating the Homeowners Division (HD). This move proved to be beneficial considering the ongoing congressional inquiry and coming changes.

In 1961, the ORRRC, after two years of reviewing programs, recommended charging fees for recreational use of all public sites. This would finance the development and maintenance of all outdoor facilities for the now 101,912,500 visitors to the national forests. Concurrently, the US General Accounting Office decided to assess and review summer home tract fees. Unfortunately, their 1963 Congressional report stated that the government had lost and was losing hundreds of thousands of dollars and would lose millions in the future, due to the Forest Service keeping fees below market value for almost a decade. The GAO specifically reported that they had assessed Region 5, and they found that in California, the camaraderie between permittees and the Forest Service had kept fees low. Region 5 stated that for the past forty-four years of the program, permittees, tract associations, and rangers had developed such a mutual relationship that raising fees would be like betraying a close friend. After all, wasn't the whole purpose of the program to bring people to their land? The GAO demanded change and a clear fee policy. Great confusion and unrest followed, but in 1969, as a result of the NFRA-Homeowners Division's efforts, Forest Service Chief Edward P. Cliff presented a plan to permittees. He would grant a twenty-year permit for an appraisal system to establish fees based on 5 percent of comparable private lot values.

A few years later, Congress decided to create the Public Land Law Review Commission to continue the study of public land uses and fees. Once again the focus was on Region 5 since it contained 75 percent of all national summer home tracts. Needless to say, the PLLRC found fees to be very low. When interviewed, Region 5 rangers stated that keeping up with the increasing California market was next to impossible and that the difference between the old and new fees would not only shock cabin owners but be too drastic for any permittee to afford. Regardless, the comptroller general of the United States advised Congress to raise the fees. In order to help permittees adjust to the higher amounts, the Forest Service phased in the higher rates over a five-year period. However, at the end of the term, fees were found to be below market value once again.

Concurrently, the Forest Service was updating their Forest Service Manual, which they planned to present in December of 1968. The Public Land Review Commission put in their two cents and recommended that they add the phrase "Future-Use Determination" as a clause. This meant that all permits were now to be under a new amendment that required "all tracts and lots to be studied and evaluated to determine weather to continue as tracts, be transferred into private ownership through land exchange or be taken back for public use." Not surprisingly, this created great stress and further disappointment on the part of all permittees. Again, tract associations intervened through the HD and put pressure on the government. At this time, rangers in charge of working with summer home tracts informed permittees and their associations of further coming changes. They encouraged tracts to study the possibility of going through the land exchange option that the Forest Service was offering. A few selected this rigorous option.

In 1970, after reviewing all financial documents, the private firm hired by the Public Land Law Review Commission back in 1965 recommended ending the special use summer home tract program, so, in 1976, the chief of the Forest Service issued a nationwide moratorium on all summer homes. He stated that no more lots would be developed or available within existing tracts. Then in 1979, he announced that no new tracts would be developed. Needless to say, a dark cloud covered the permittees nationwide.

In 1987, Dale Robertson, chief of the Forest Service and a good friend of cabin owners, worked with the new National Forest Homeowners organization in dealing with the new 1988 Summer Home Guidelines presented by Congress and the Future Use-Determination that continued to appear. Under Robertson's leadership, the Forest Service placed a moratorium on the clause for further study. A year later, much to the delight of cabin owners, a "Recreation Residence Policy" was published in the Federal Register. It presented new rights and benefits for cabin owners, all of which the NFH had been negotiating toward. Unfortunately, an appeal was made by an ignorant retired ranger trying to hold on to what little power he had and the new policy was placed on hold.

After a comment period, in which 7,793 concerns were reviewed, and two long years of frustration, the Forest Service published the final "Recreation Residence Policy." Much to the delight of cabin owners, the document stated, "Recreation residences are a valid use of National Forests . . . It is Forest Service policy to continue recreation residence use and to work in partnership with holders of these permits." No new tracts or lots would be developed, but the original ones would continue.

The next challenge for both the NFH and the Forest Service was the next appraisal scheduled for 1996. Values came in as high as $660,000 for a lot, resulting in annual fees of $33,000, other fees increased by 250 to 500 percent. Frustrated cabin owners contacted Representative Smith from Oregon, and Representative Helen Chenoweth from Idaho who presented a bill requiring a payment plan and twelve-month freeze for further study. During this waiting period, many arguments were heard on the problems with the appraisal process. As presented by the NFH:

> Appraisals assumed a theoretical unencumbered ownership estate, even though what is actually granted in the permit is a restricted possessory interest. Restrictions on use of these cabins under the policy are numerous. Year-round permanent residency is not allowed and use as a rental property is forbidden. Typical restrictions also include limitations on the square footage of the structure; types of vehicles that may be stored near the cabin. No recreation vehicles, boats or motor homes are allowed. Outbuildings and fencing are both prohibited. Garden cultivation and color of paint are under tight restrictions. Individual permits also contain additional restrictions reflecting unique local circumstances and management needs. None of which were taken into consideration during the appraisal.

Homeowner associations and cabin owners across the nation united in 1998 to form a coalition to find a solution. As stated by the NFH, "the coalition's focus was on congressional relief from the exorbitant increases in fees and the seemingly erratic application of appraisal methodology."

On its own initiative, the Forest Service contracted with The Appraisal Foundation for an assessment of the agency's appraisal program. The Foundation reported, "Based upon our review of the various materials, it is obvious that there have been significantly different interpretations of certain provisions from the Forest Service Handbook." Numerous permittees testified before three congressional hearings during the next three years. Richard Betts from Oakland, California, a highly qualified consultant appraiser, was hired by the coalition. After reviewing some sixteen sets of instructions to appraisers from various regions, the Forest Service

Washington Office, the coalition, and Rick Betts worked with the staff of Senator Craig (primarily Dan Whiting) to draft a bill that gave the Forest Service specific instructions on the appraisal process. It passed Congress and was signed by the president in October of 2000. Two years later, the Forest Service finalized detailed regulations in the implementation of the Cabin Users Fee Fairness Act of 2000 (CUFFA).

Fee determination under CUFFA was supposed to be based on the principle of better capturing the market value for use and occupancy of forestland. It was intended to do so by focusing on the adjustments to value that must be made to ensure that the lot being appraised was not overvalued. CUFFA was supposed to have remedied the fact that under the previous system adjustments for local or regional limitations on use had not been considered nor allowed. Many appraisals done under the old system used comparable sales that cabin owners believed were not equivalent to the cabin lot. Unfortunately, such practices continued. Subsequent appraisals performed under the Forest Service's interpretation of CUFFA were disappointing at the very least. Owners were once again shocked by high appraisal values. Perhaps market values had greatly increased, but even so, the focus had to change toward affordability.

A second coalition was thus formed to address the issues that arose from the appraisals performed the summer of 2007. Coalition 2 consisted of the National Forest Homeowners, American Land Rights Association, Washington State Forest Homeowners Association, Oregon Forest Homeowners Association, California Forest Homeowners, Sawtooth Forest Cabin Owners Association (Idaho), Priest Lake Association (Idaho), Lake Wenatchee Summer Home Association (Washington), and individual members in Wyoming, Arizona, Florida, and Tennessee. The new cabin owners coalition came together in late 2007 and grappled with the issues at hand and proposed a solution they believed had the best chance of resulting in fees for the recreation residence special use permit in an amount that would preserve the opportunity for individuals and families of ordinary means. The C2's effort, the Cabin Fee Act, was introduced in 2010. This legislation would cap the fees at around $5,500. Once these fees were set, they would only be adjusted in the future based on inflation. On December 19, 2013, after many decades of hard work, the Cabin Fee Act passed out of committee following a successful markup by the Senate Energy and Natural Resources Committee. On December 12, 2014, the US Senate passed the National Defense Authorization Act of 2015, which gave House Natural Resources Committee Chairman Doc Hastings authority to set a fair fee system for cabin owners in national forests. The National Forest Homeowners stated, "This milestone achievement coincides with the 100th anniversary of the Recreation Residence Program on National Forest lands. Passage of this act ensures continued economic support to local rural communities and enhances cabin owners' forest stewardship activities in partnership with the USDA Forest Service. We extend a special thank-you to Forest Service Chief Tom Tidwell for the US Forest Service's unwavering support of the legislation on behalf of the cabin community and the American public." At last a very important part of American Forest Service history is preserved, assuring the future of our land. After all, as so well stated by Char Miller, biographer of Gifford Pinchot, "The public lands become the way by which we know we are democratic, we own them."

Many thanks go to the National Forest Homeowners organization for their support and contribution to this section. Certain sections were used verbatim and all credit goes to their fine work (www.nationalforesthomeowners.org).

Design and Development of Cabins and Tracts

In 1908, President Teddy Roosevelt increased the national forests from 43 acres to 194 million. As a result, the San Jacinto Mountains in California were grouped and named part of the Cleveland National Forest in honor of President Cleveland. There, as well as across the nation, the public had been enjoying the forests since the 1800s, building lean-to fishing and hunting cabins. As a result of the needs of the public, Forester Gifford Pinchot added summer homes to the list of uses in 1905. In 1915, in order to better serve the public, Congress responded to the desires of the people as supported by the Forest Service and passed the Term Occupancy Permit Act. The act authorized David F. Houston, the secretary of agriculture, to set the terms and limits. He allowed the Forest Service to:

A. Permit the use and occupancy of suitable areas of land within the national forests, not exceeding eighty acres and for periods not exceeding thirty years, for the purpose of construction or maintaining hotels, resorts, and any other structure or facilities necessary or desirable for recreation, public convenience, or safety.

B. Permit the use and occupancy of suitable areas of land within the national forests, not exceeding five acres and for periods not exceeding thirty years, for the purpose of constructing or maintaining summer homes and stores.

C. Permit the use and occupancy of suitable areas of land within the national forests, not exceeding eighty acres and

> for periods not exceeding thirty years, for the purpose of constructing or maintaining buildings, structures, and facilities for industrial or commercial purpose, whenever such use is related to or consistent with other uses of the national forests.
>
> D. Permit any state or political subdivision thereof, or any public or nonprofit agency, to use and occupy suitable areas of land within the national forests, not exceeding eighty acres and for periods not exceeding thirty years, for the purpose of constructing or maintaining any buildings, structures, or facilities necessary or desirable for education or for any public use or in connection with any public activity. The authority for this paragraph shall be exercised in such manner as not to preclude the general public from full enjoyment of the natural, scenic, recreational, and other aspects of the national forests. (Occupancy Permits Act of March 4, 1915: Ch. 144, 38 Stat. 1089, as amended; 16 U.S.C. 497)

A few days after the passing of the Term Occupancy Permit Act, hundreds of permits were requested. During this era, western cities were growing rapidly. California, with many forests in close proximity to major cities, saw the greatest demand for permits. By 1917, hundreds of summer homes had been built. By June 30, 1920, a total of 1,329 permits for summer homes and resorts were granted in the Angeles National Forest. Region 5 wasted no time promoting the new special use summer home tracts. They used leaflets, brochures, forest maps, local newspapers, and national periodicals. All write-ups romanticized owning a cabin in the forest. California's Eldorado National Forest advertised their summer home program on a 1926 map that stated:

> For those who desire a permanent summer cabin, the Forest Service has surveyed and subdivided certain tracts into lots.

> Several hundred attractive cabins and houses have already been built for summer home permittees among the pines and firs along the main roads. The most popular sites are located along the Lincoln Highway, the Echo Lake Road, on the shores of Echo Lake, near Meyers, at Fallen Leaf Lake, and Glen Alpine . . . These sites can be leased from the Forest Service at a rental of $15 to $25 per year.

Many savvy businesses capitalized on this new opportunity by selling cabin kits, plans, and furniture. The Shevlin Pine Company made a fortune by offering both Shevlin pine log siding and designs using half-log siding. They ran ads in the LA newspaper clear through the 1920s. As early as 1915, the *Los Angeles Times* was running advertisements that offered land or cabins built on Forest Service lots. Some of the earliest cabin plans came from ranger and architect Coert Dubois. Dubois offered construction blue prints that he had designed between 1915 and 1927 for Forest Service use. His plans were for ranger cabins and stations but could easily be used for summer homes. Plans came with a list of materials and total cost including labor, making them very affordable. Many of the original cabins built reflected the Forest Service era's architectural styles. Cabin plans also came from many other sources.

According to Region 5's Forest Service "Final Inventory and Evaluation of . . . South Fork Recreation Residence Tract Study," plans were offered through *Popular Science Monthly*, a book titled *How to Build Cabins, Lodges and Bungalows*, and newspaper articles such as "Roomy Cabin Plans Shown" in the *Los Angeles Times*, July 15, 1934. The Los Angeles Small Home Plan Bureau also provided construction plans in local newspapers.

Articles such as "Exhibition of Cabins to Open" in the *LA Times* of April 26, 1931, expounded on how the consumer could build a cabin that blended in with the environment and not distract from the setting. It stated that cabins had to meet the basic needs for the occupants while only using 560 square feet and how roof pitch varied depending on the amount of snow in the area. Again, *LA Times* article "Roomy Cabin Plans Shown" of July 15, 1934 stated that storage was very important, since occupants needed space for food items, household goods, and outdoor equipment.

Ad of cabin plan in *LA Times*, May 20, 1928

These cabin plans came with bathrooms, but in most cases where plumbing was not available, the space was used for additional storage. Roomy cabin plans also included a large room with a large stone fireplace and adjoining porch. The porches were located under the main roof of the structure making the overall plans simple rectangles or squares. "Vacation Plan Type Featured" in the *LA Times* May 20, 1928, shared that board and batten over 2x4 studs were ideal as were exposed rafters and natural-finish siding; the color green or Manzanita red and browns were recommended when painting was required.

National magazines also wrote articles promoting the summer home program. *Sunset* in 1917 published many articles, such as "Vacations Made Easy: How Uncle Sam Invites the Family Out to His Place in the Country," "A Shop-Girl's Summer Home Even

Mother Had a Hand in the Building," and "Summer Homes." The *Saturday Evening Post* printed "Summer-Home Sites in the National Forests" in 1930. *House Beautiful* magazine wrote "A Kingdom for a Song." This article highlighted how a family could easily build their own forest home. In 1960, *Good Housekeeping* wrote, "Yes, a Summer Home in a National Forest."

The Craftsman Bungalow Company in the 1900s sold plans for customers of limited resources as well. Other companies such as Master-Craft Cabin Company of San Jose, CA, and Aladdin Readi-Cut Homes, the Diamond Match Company of Chino, and Sears all provided several home models to homebuilders with the needed plans and materials. Needless to say, summer home cabins became big business. In fact, they generated millions of dollars in Southern California alone.

Men like architect Frank A. Waugh, landscape architect Arthur H. Carhart, ranger and architect Coert Dubois, and ranger and recreation specialist Frederick William Cleator, along with a few others influenced by the American Society of Landscape Architects, established the summer home tract and cabin look that has been referred to by many names but is best described as the "American campground" look. It was first seen in the national parks. Tract layouts and cabin designs produced a rustic charm with simple rectangular buildings in Manzanita reds and brown hues that blended into the natural terrain and were strategically placed to not disturb the forest and provide a sense of privacy and isolation. This design replaced the original rustic lean-to shacks first built by permittees from the 1800s into the early 1900s. This new design was simple, practical, permanent, safe, and reflected the Forest Service philosophy of being utilitarian and cost effective. The rustic element was added when local natural materials were used as accents. As presented by Region 5 in the Strategy Evaluation of Recreation Residence Tracts report:

The Forest Service's commitment to a rustic style of architecture suited its own populist philosophy regarding construction of recreation facilities during its early years. It accused the Park Service of over development and fancy, elaborate, rustic lodges. The Forest Service generally fought this trend. This philosophy was intimately tied to the idea that forests' primary purposes were timber and watershed management, and recreation was incidental. Construction was always envisioned at the lowest level possible. Recreation facilities were always recommended to be inexpensive and simple.

If fancy was to be, it would be built by private funds.

Forest Service historian William Tweed provided the following list of characteristics that helped establish this Forest Service rustic, utilitarian, American campground look:

1. Buildings were constructed of natural, native materials and textures, such as stone, log, or wood shingles.
2. The proportions of a building were designed to fit the site and its surroundings.
3. Architectural elements were chosen for their utility, but also for their ability to blend with the geology or terrain.
4. Straight, harsh lines were avoided.
5. Vertical emphasis was to be avoided, particularly in the form of large, imposing roofs.
6. Buildings were designed to be viewed from all sides.
7. A central architectural theme was established for groups of buildings to create continuity. Where early buildings existed, these themes were to blend and not contrast sharply.
8. Natural colors were used to blend with the environment.

California included the following architectural features to the list:

1. Native materials were used to blend with the local, regional environment.
2. Exterior materials that visually complemented the natural setting were common, such as stones, log, or natural-wood siding.
3. Materials of different texture, size, and shape were used to enhance the overall appearance of the structure.
4. Exterior color scheme was used to enhance the structure's overall appearance. The use of natural colors was stressed: brown, reddish brown, green, gray. (Gray was often used at higher elevations to blend in with the native rock.)
5. High-pitched roofs for cabins located 5,000 feet above sea level were used due to harsh snowstorms.
6. Gable, hipped, and gambrel roof shapes were commonly used.
7. Shutters were used for window embellishment as well as for security.
8. Chimneys and fireplaces were the principal means of heating the structure. Chimney design varied widely between forests and regions, but native stone was a common building material.
9. Multi-paned windows, both sash and casement, were common.
10. Decks and porch railings reflected the purpose of summer homes and often served as an extension of the living space, allowing the owners to enjoy the natural setting. Porch railings formed an enclosure for the deck, which were commonly used as sleeping porches when screened in.

Cabin Designs

As stated by Region 5's South Fork Recreation Residence

Tract report, "the diverse geology, terrains, and climates in California created a wide variety of building form modifications as a response to these environments." All summer home cabins shared the characteristics that helped define the rustic American campground look; their architectural designs varied according to local terrain, trends, era, personal style, and Forest Service regional architecture. In regards to the East Coast summer homes, they were either small one- to two-room cabins or mansions built by the rich and politically influential. One must note that most cabins on the East Coast started on private lands later re-acquired by the Forest Service and incorporated into national forest, hence their elaborate designs.

All summer homes fall into one of the following plans

1. Forest Service Rectangular Plan was an efficient and utilitarian cabin with a gable or hip roof. It could be a side-gable or gable-front cabin. Some of these cabins included a very small loft used for storage or sleeping. This plan was common from 1917 to 1927 and, in Region 5, was developed by Coert Dubois who designed them as Forest Service ranger structures. The plans were given to permittees who found the plans useful as one- to two-room summer homes. This plan replaced the original rustic lean-to shacks that were common in the early years.
2. Log Cabin was a very traditional and regional style. Examples of this design go back to the 1800s and are still currently very popular.
3. L Plan or Gable-ELL Plan had a cross-gable roof. The floor plan was L-shaped, but could also take the shape of a T. This design was common from 1930 to the 1940s.
4. Rectangular Plan had modified gable roof due to larger loft area and was very popular in the 1940s to the early 1950s.

This design started replacing many of the original cabins from 1925 during remodels and upgrades. By the 1930s, the rustic style was no longer desirable. Many found the rectangular plan cost effective and easier to build.

5. Stone Plan was regional, very rare, and only found where stones were in abundance. Common from 1900 to the 1930s.

6. Irregular Plan with a shed roof was the beginning of the "modern" look common from the mid-1950s to mid-1970s.

7. A-Frame Plan was the beginning of the end, common from the mid-1960s to mid-1970s.

8. Contemporary Two-Story Plan replaced the last of the original Forest Service cabins. Common from the late 1960s to the present, it can range from modest to elaborate.

Rectangular Cabin Plan, Tahquitz Saunders Meadow Tract

Log Cabin Plan, Idaho Panhandle National Forest

L or Gable ELL Cabin Plan, Idaho Panhandle National Forest

Rectangular Cabin Plan, Lewis and Clark National Forest

Stone Cabin Plan, Graystone San Jose Tract

Irregular Cabin Plan, Idaho Panhandle National Forest

A-Frame Cabin Plan, Alaska

Contemporary Two-Story Cabin Plan, Flathead National Forest

Credit goes to John R. Grosvenor's *A History of the Architecture of the USDA Forest Service* for plans and Region 1 for providing photos of tract layout designs, cabin styles, and descriptions. Kirkwood Lake Tract in Eldorado National Forest, CA, provided cabin photos, Tahquitz-Saunders Meadow Tract in San Bernardino National Forest, Idyllwild, CA, also provided cabin photos, and South Fork Tract and San Juan Tract, CA, provided tract layouts, and Region 10 in Alaska provided cabin photos.

Tract Designs

All tract designs were created to blend with the local terrain and natural features. The focus was always on having the least possible disturbance and destruction of nature. The following are layout patterns created for all summer home tracts.

1. **Linear Pattern Tracts** were located by rivers and lakes and referred to as Lakeshore Tracts as well. These tracts followed the contour of a body of water and were developed by the Forest Service prior to the passing of the "U" regulations that prohibited placement of private recreation residences within view of public attractions. Summer homes could not block access or water feature views from the public. There had to be a section made available for all to use and enjoy.
2. **Grid Pattern Tracts** were used around road systems or flat sites. Lots were located on both sides of trails curving in accordance with terrain and natural features such as meadows and valleys. This design was also referred to as Ridgeline or Rectilinear Pattern and used on mountain ridges, terraces, or steeply sloped areas. Lots were laid out in rough parallel lines, at times resembling a neighborhood.
3. **Dendritic, Branching, or Radial Pattern Tracts** were commonly used on ridges and canyons where trails branched out and continued to do so into smaller branches and trails leading to more cabins.
4. **Curvilinear Pattern Tracts** were placed along winding trails with cabins facing the road.
5. **Gridiron Pattern Tracts** were typical twentieth century suburban neighborhoods and not very common. This plan never really blended into nature so was usually combined with other tract patterns.

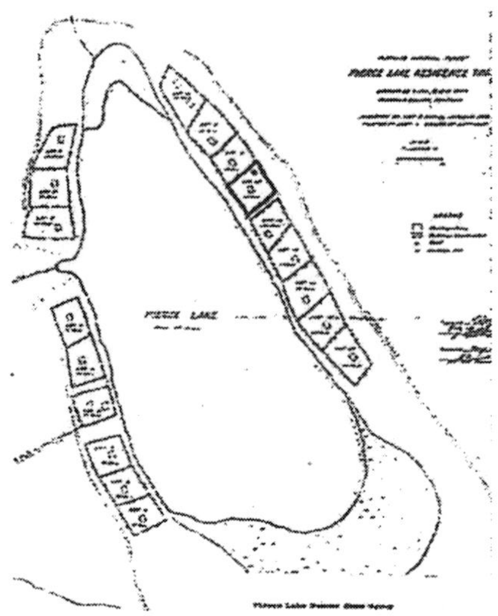

Linear Pattern/Lakeshore Tract, Region 1

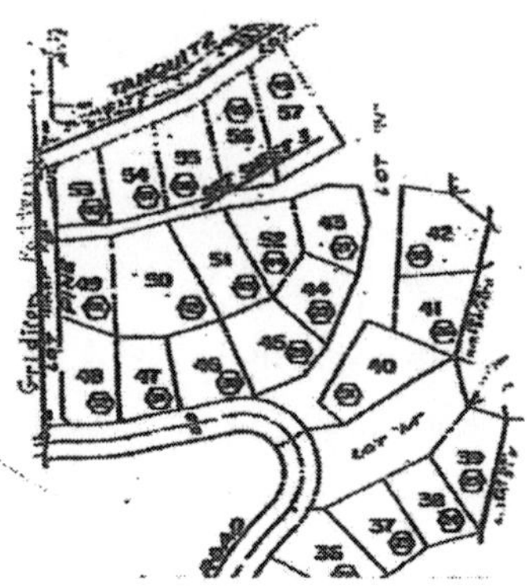

Gridiron Pattern Tract, Tahquitz 1920 Tract, San Bernardino National Forest

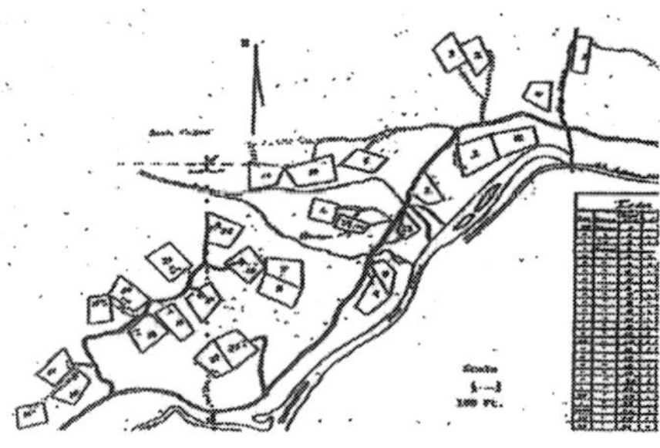

Dendritic, Branching-Radial Pattern Tract, Custer National Forest

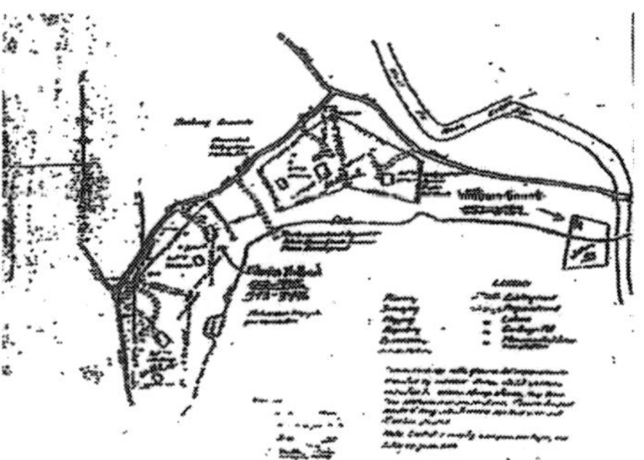

Curvilinear Pattern Tract, Custer National Forest

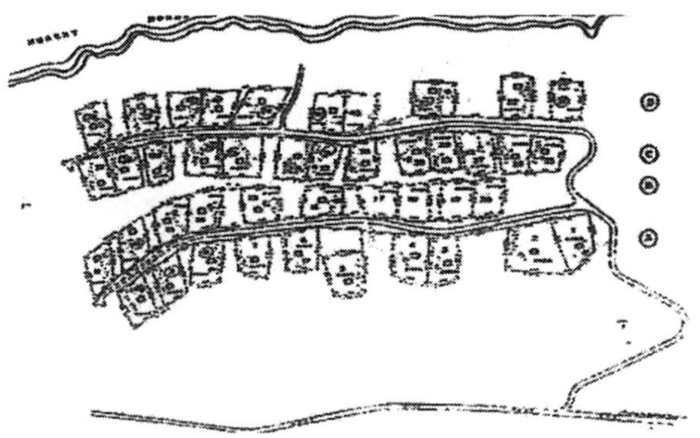

Grid or Ridgeline/Rectilinear Pattern Tract, Flathead National Forest

Lot Design

Originally, lots were found to be over one acre in size, but due to the high demand in the early 1920s, parcels were reduced to between one quarter to three quarters of an acre, with most averaging one quarter of an acre. This practice of lot design continued up to the 1960s, when tract development practically ceased. Lots could be rectangular, triangular, or trapezoidal in shape. The shape of a lot and location of a cabin were based on the terrain and natural features found within the lot and tract. Natural features included meadows, rock formations, slopes, arroyos, ridges, and lakes. Cabins and other structures, such as water pump sheds, were situated in the center of the lot away from others to provide privacy. Garages were not permitted. In regards to outhouses, they were located away from the main structure and located far from any water source. All additional structures were required to match the color and style of the main house.

Landscape

The landscape was to be kept natural. Man-made elements such as birdbaths, fountains, and gnomes were not allowed. The integrity of the forest was a priority. Water was scarce, so landscaping was not encouraged. If gardening was allowed, all plants to be integrated had to be native and only used to replace damaged foliage. The tract had to maintain its natural appearance. Needless to say, fences were not allowed.

Thirty-Year, Ninety-Nine-Year, One Hundred-Year Lease

The 1915 terms and limitations set by Secretary of Agriculture David F. Houston clearly stated multiple times that terms would "not exceed thirty years." Yet research proves otherwise. There have been permits extended to sixty, ninety, and even one hundred years. Perhaps this practice can be attributed to the words of Forest Service Chief Graves that "priority to extend permit terms would go to current permittees." Did he mean above and beyond the stated thirty years? Regardless, there were factors that reinforced a ninety-nine-year practice.

First, the Forest Service's original responsibility was to serve and meet the needs of the people by welcoming them into their forests and catering to their desires. Secondly, the agency had a philosophy of decentralized management. Each region was allowed to decide what was best for their constituents as long as it was safe and did not interfere with the other forest uses.

Thirdly, it was common practice in the late 1800s to the 1900s for privately owned land adjacent to or located within the forest reserves to be leased for ninety-nine years. Fourthly, government terminable permits that were started in the same era were renewable without a cancellation date. Even though they could be terminated at the reserve's supervisor's discretion, they could also be renewed for one hundred years, or into eternity for that matter. These terminable permittees whose government-leased lots were located within the vicinity of these private ninety-nine-year lots falsely believed that they too were entitle to the same length of time. This presumption transferred to the new Term Occupancy Permit Act of 1915 participants. In fact, many falsely referred to their permits as ninety-nine- or one hundred-year leases.

Ironically, some permittee families found a way, or were simply allowed by their local region rangers, to renew their summer home permits for additional thirty-year increments. In 1970, original summer homes built in 1924 were found to belong to the same families after forty-six years. In 2014, the years of total ownership of 1924 cabins to the same families increased to ninety years with permits still being renewed for additional years. Again, this may have reflected the Forest Service belief that priority to renew would be given to the original or current permit holder.

Permittees also found another way to maintain further ownership. Before the original thirty-year lease ended, the original permittee would sell or give the summer home to his son or daughter who would sign a new lease with the Forest Service, which gave preference to family members. After another thirty years, the son's children would inherit or buy the summer home from Dad and sign another fifteen- to thirty-year lease, again reinforcing the one hundred-year lease myth. Currently, there are families whose cabins have been in their ownership for ninety-nine years and will reach the one hundred-year mark in 2015, abolishing the myth!

There are a few families that can trace their cabin ownership to the late 1800s under the old original terminable permits that were grandfathered into the term occupancy tracts in 1915. Others boast full and private ownership of both cabin and ex-national forest land. In the late 1960s and early 1970s, the Forest Service encouraged many tracts to participate in a temporary land exchange process. If the tract association members acquired land that the Forest Service was interested in acquiring and found it to be of equal or greater value to the land the cabins were on, there would be an exchange, granting the deed to all permittees. Not only would they own their cabins, but the land as well.

Tract Associations

In the early years, between 1915 and 1927, the Forest Service highly recommended summer home owners to organize into tract associations in order to deal with their sanitary issues. The associations would then manage concerns such as water, sewer, and fire safety as well as addressing the need for trails, bridges, and roads. The tracts worked hand in hand with the Forest Service, creating a positive camaraderie that not only relieved rangers from the burden of extra administrative, tract-related work, but benefited the permittees with needed association bylaws support.

Early summer home permit regulations required all new permittees to become members of the tract associations and sign the bylaws before finalizing the permit: "the holder of this permit agrees to be subject to all rules and regulations of such association . . ." (U.S. Department of Agriculture, Forest Service, California District 1924:49). The lot permits would only be finalized by the Forest Service after the association presented written proof that the applicant had signed the tract agreement and paid dues in full. Membership in the association helped create a good sense of community. This relationship was beneficial since original summer homes were rustic and assistance was always required and needed. Original cabin owners either used oil lamps or candles for light, they cooked outdoors, and those who could afford to built outhouses. Eventually tracts saw the turning of trails into better roads, outdoor cooking replaced by wood-burning stoves, the welcoming of the icebox, electricity, and telephones as well as running water in the late 1930s and early 1940s, all thanks to their associations' hard work and good standing with the Forest Service.

Rangers and associations worked well together handling the logistics and management of tracts. The first associations to be documented were found in Region 5: California's Pinecrest Lower Strawberry Lake Tract Home Owners in the Stanislaus National Forest united in 1922, Lake Arrowhead in the San Bernardino National Forest in 1923, and Tahquitz in Saunders Meadow in Idyllwild in the San Bernardino National Forest in 1924 to 1927. All three associations individually organized in order to secure Forest Service permits for domestic water use per the Sundry Civil Appropriations Act of 1897, which allowed water privileges for a fee. Other tracts in the Idyllwild, California, area were Fuller Creek, adjacent to the current Pinewood subdivision, Keen Camp, and Fern Valley. Lily Creek also organized into associations in the San Jacinto Mountains of the San Bernardino National Forest between 1921 and 1927 in order to acquire special use water permits as well.

Other tracts organized in order to accomplish other tasks. The cabin owners of the Deadman's Flat Tract in the Stanislaus National Forest created their improvement association in order to obtain special permission to build a bridge using member fees and special assessment dues. There was the 1923 Big Santa Anita Canyon Improvement Association and the 1924 American River Summer Home Owners Association in Eldorado National Forest, which formed in order to provide security and water docks. As these associations and those across the western regions grew, they organized into the National Forest Permittees group, then the Homeowners Division under the National Forest Recreation Association, eventually becoming the current National Forest Homeowners organization.

Term Occupancy Permit Act with Focus on California

Region 5 of the United States Department of Agriculture Forest Service, also known as the Pacific Southwest, accounted for the most special use summer home permits granted. Forest Service archives show that the Golden State had over 300 tracts with a total sum of 15,520 permits at the program's peak, making Region 5 the leader in recreation and home ownership among all national forests.

Californians, with their progressive views and interest in conservation, gladly welcomed the opportunity to live within their beautiful national lands. In the early years, the demand was so high that over 299 lots were claimed within a few days of the act's implementation. The most popular and sought after land was by lakes, streams, meadows, or in any location with a panoramic view. As soon as these locations were surveyed and tracts designed, their lots were instantly claimed. Most applicants came from metropolitan areas such as Sacramento, Stockton, San Francisco, and Los Angeles and lived within a 100- to 150-mile radius from their summer homes. Others came from rural agricultural communities adjacent to the reserves such as San Jacinto and Hemet.

In California, as across the nation, national forests were a great and inexpensive place of refuge during WWI and the Great Depression. In fact, the 1920s saw great growth among summer home tracts with 2,000-plus permits requested. The Angeles National Forest reported that they had granted over 1,300 permits due to Angelinos' love of nature and recreation and, of course, proximity to their many national forests. In fact, where else did summer last as long and could one have breakfast at the beach, lunch in a national forest, and dinner in the desert all on the same day? It was no wonder that Region 5 had over 70 percent of all national permits during this time.

Southern California was booming in the 1920s. The "talkies" were big business, attracting hundreds of wannabe stars—Walt Disney even moved to LA during this era. In fact, the great city of Los Angeles, as it was sprawling and growing through tourism, Hollywood filming, and oil drilling, saw the need to accommodate her citizens by building a campground with over sixty cabins on twenty-three acres at Seely Creed Flats in the San Bernardino National Forest just so they could get away from the pressures of modern urban life. The Auto Club of Southern California and Los Angeles County Department of Health also installed twenty-four chemical toilets on the Angeles National Forest for the comfort and sanitary safety of guests. For the first time, public campgrounds had toilets. There were over a million motorists camping out across the West and the Automobile Club of Southern California capitalized on this opportunity by promoting car campers, which were campgrounds for autos, and by funding the required facilities in the local national forests. Region 5 reported that the showers and bathrooms built in 1922 and 1923 at Willian Kent campground on Lake Tahoe in Tahoe National Forest were greatly needed and welcomed. In the Bay Area of San Francisco, the Association of Car Dealers provided funds in order to construct an automobile campground as well.

Car Campground, 1920s–30s

Angeles National Forest Summer Homes built by the city of Los Angeles in 1916

In the San Bernardino National Forest in the San Jacinto Mountains, five special use summer home tracts with 151 lots were also established. Three were located in Idyllwild, the largest being the Tahquitz or Saunders Meadow tract with fifty-nine lots, which exists to this day. Cleveland National Forest laid out twenty summer home tracts. Unlike snowbound regions, Region 5 tracts were available year-round, and with new government roads, once-remote summer homes were now easy to access. In fact, all eighteen Region 5 forests had tracts.

In the 1930s, the Forest Service reported that Region 5 gained $150,000 from summer home fees. Additional funds were projected based on the many requests for additional permits, making it the most successful source of recreational income during the Depression era. In fact, not only did the summer home program pay for itself, it provided funding for other public projects such as roads and schools.

During this era, Region 5 reported 8,000 permits with many more steadily coming in. In 1933, the Civilian Conservation Corps (CCC), also known as the "forest conservation army," helped continue this public recreational boom. Funding abounded from the National Industrial Recovery Act and the Civil Works Administration, which provided $200 million per month and provided 4 million jobs for 4 million unemployed individuals. With so much support, recreation facilities were built and used by many, making recreation a normal part of life, not only in Region 5 but all across the States. As stated by William C. Tweed, "National Forest recreation has become a part of life for tens of millions of Americans, and an important, if somewhat secondary, fact of National Forest administrations." During this time, California saw most, if not all, of the Copeland Report projects implemented in its forests thanks to the CCC.

WWII brought a halt to all Forest Service activities across the nation. Tract development was also put on hold. With the lack of rangers, summer home permittees were welcomed by the Forest Service to act as keepers of the land clear through the winter months. They helped foresters with safety issues. The year-round residents were also welcomed by small mountaintop communities during those hard and tumultuous times. The summer home permittees' spending on provisions helped maintain the local economy throughout the entire year. Enforcement of permit regulations and guidelines were lax during the war. As long as there were no safety concerns or rowdy behavior and permittees continued helping by guarding the forests, the Forest Service looked the other way and welcomed the extra watchful, protective eyes.

By the end of the war, recreation activities resurged. The US Forest Service files recorded 8.5 million recreational visits in 1945. This number increased to 18,240,677 visits in just one year. Requests for permits for both summer homes and resorts in Region 5 overwhelmed rangers, making it almost impossible to meet all needs. Region 5 reported 3,913,000 visitors in 1946. In fact, California had 75 percent of all permits nationwide during this era. With such an increase in visitors, the Forest Service began to switch their focus to large group facilities rather than individual summer home tracts by the end of the 1950s. The change was evident when only sixteen tracts were added, limiting the number of available special use permits. Yet compared to the rest of the nation, these numbers were still high.

At this time, Washington, DC, decided to take the power from regions to approve new summer home tracts. This move slowed down development and marked the beginning of the end for summer home tracts. In fact, the last recorded tract surveyed and developed was in California in 1959 with the last of its lots finally leased in the late 1960s. Concurrently, rangers encouraged their special use summer home tract associations to look into the possibility of participating in the land exchange program that the Forest Service was offering. Finally, in 1979, the Forest Service announced that no new special use summer home tracts would be developed nationwide.

In 1987, Region 5 reported having 7,063 permits. That number dropped to 6,314 in 1998. Currently, in 2015, California has 40 percent of the nation's total, with an estimated 5,857 permits on 253 tracts. Nationally, there are a total of 13,660 permits.

Benefits of Term Occupancy Permit Act

The Forest Service found the implementation of the 1915 Occupancy Act beneficial in three areas: meeting and satisfying the public's recreation needs, an increase in manpower for the protection of the forest, and the opportunity for financial gain from permit fees.

First Benefit

For years before the Forest Reserves were created and the Term Occupancy Permit Act implemented, local folks were already visiting the forest for recreation and spiritual purposes.

After the early era of the General Land Office administration, the public asked for recreational opportunities and the Forest Service responded by providing permits.

In 1912, Forester Henry S. Graves stated that:

> At the close of the fiscal year there were in effect 13,810 permits authorizing the occupancy of small tracts of forestlands . . . stockmen obtain them for pastures for stock, cabins and lumber mills and camps. With the construction of new roads and trails the forests are visited more and more for recreation purpose, and in consequence the demand is growing rapidly for sites on which summer camps, cottages, and hotels may be located . . . In some of the most accessible and desirable localities the land has been divided into suitable lots of 1 to 5 acres.

In his 1913 report to Secretary of Agriculture David F. Houston, Graves stated that:

At the close of the year 15,649 permits were in effect authorizing the occupancy of small areas of land for miscellaneous uses. These are principally either for purposes incidental to some other form of business use or to provide for recreation use of the forests. Of the first class are permits to stockmen for pastures, corrals, water tanks, dipping vats, etc., and to lumber operators for mill and campsites. Of the second are permits for the construction of hotels, pleasure resorts, boathouses, etc., but most of all for cottage and permanent summer campsites. Transient camps are, of course pitched wherever the recreation seeker chooses to wander, without permits, restrictions, or formalities of any kind; but persons who wish to use regularly the same piece of land and to construct some improvements for their greater comfort are assured exclusive possession of such land as they need through a Special Use permit . . . recreational use of the forests is growing very rapidly especially on forests near cities of considerable size. Hundreds of canyons and lakeshores are now dotted with camps and cottages built on land use of which is obtained through permits of the Forest Service. This is a highly important form of use of the Forests by the public, and it is recognized and facilitated by adjusting commercial use of the forests, when necessary, to the situation created by the needs of the recreation seekers. Examples of such adjustment are the exclusion of stock from localities where they would interfere with such a summer population, or the prohibition of use of certain canyons for driveways, and provision in timber sales for very light cutting, or not cutting at all, close to lakes and elsewhere where it is desirable to preserve the natural beauty of the location unmarred, for the enjoyment of the public.

Regardless of any political motive behind the creation of the Term Occupancy Permit Act related to the Hetch Hetchy Valley reservoir, a higher altruistic reason was followed by the Forest Service.

Second Benefit

Those with a vested interest in the forest, being that it was now their second home, provided an extra and greatly needed watchful eye on the lookout for trespassers, illegal grazing, logging, and fires. The Forest Service Recreation Residence Policy Report prepared by Region 5 stated that, "residence permittees were seen as people with a stake in the proper management of the national forests." In 1917, hired consultant and landscape architect Frank Waugh reported that "contrary to common expectations, the presence of campers and summer home permittees assisted positively in fire protection." Furthermore, in 1926 the Forest Service stated that "a residence occupied under the restrictions imposed by a permit not only reduces the fire risks as compared to transient camping, but makes of the permittee a volunteer fire fighter whose interest in forest problems is increased by reason of close contact with them and financial investment in a forest." These extra helpers were greatly welcomed during WWII. While rangers fought in the war, permittees kept watch over the reserves year round, paying their yearly fees faithfully and consistently.

Third Benefit

On June 30, 1916, Forester Henry S. Graves reported that:

> The outstanding features of the year in national forest administration were: a marked increase in receipts, which were greater by $342,071.36 than in 1915 totaled $2,823,540.71 and occupancy for other special uses was $85,235.30, an increase of $7,177.98.

> The business of the national forest is on a thoroughly sound basis. An efficient organization has been built up to handle the work of protection of the forests and of developing the resources. The rapidly increasing use of the forests points not only to the public, but also to increased financial returns. While the underlying purpose of the national forests is in no sense a financial one, and while the general public benefits resulting from the forests would in themselves justify every cent that it costs to maintain them, nevertheless they already are producing a very substantial revenue and it should be possible in the not distant future to cover not only the costs of administration and protection, but also the costs of improvement, betterments, and other expenses incidental to this constructive forest enterprise.

States and local communities benefited from these receipts as well. As presented by Graves in 1916, "under existing law, besides 10 percent of the receipts which is made available for expenditures by the Secretary of Agriculture in building roads and trails for the benefit of the public, another 25 percent of the receipts is paid to the states by the Federal Government for the benefit of the county schools and roads." The amounts available under both the 10 percent and 25 percent clauses of the law during the fiscal year of 1916 were $610,797.75 for schools and $244,319.10 for roads and trails.

Forester Graves continued to report that:

> Permits for the occupancy of National Forest lands for various uses other than waterpower were issued during the year as follows: pay permits totaled 19,289 of which 4,270 were for pastures and 2,118 for residence sites. These are the leading forms of occupancy in point of numbers and are generally paid for. Through occupancy permits the needs of the public for summer home sites within the Forests now are met adequately, since the law gives authority to the Service to

issue term leases. Increasing use of the forests for recreation is bringing a rapid development in the demand for such leases.

In 1917, hired consultant and landscape architect Frank Waugh's report and plan calculated a possible recreation return of $7,500,000 annually due to Americans' love of nature and their desire for special use summer homes.

Regions in the Forest Service

As the biographer of Gifford Pinchot, Char Miller, so well stated, "That a nation would decide that some lands would never be given away that they would be held in the hands of the people is a remarkable step for a nation to make," especially when the country's original attitude was to get rid of land as fast as possible.

On December 1, 1908, Chief Forester Gifford Pinchot established the forest districts. It was the Forest Service's original philosophy that safety and the proper fiscal management of the nation's resources were both top priority. The creation of districts, which became regions in the 1930s, helped manage and meet the individual needs specific to the populace of every area. One of these needs was recreation, and every region had its own unique process and history in developing their programs. As Edgar Brannon, the director of Grey Towers National Historic Landmark for the Forest Service so clearly stated in 2005, "National forests exist not for the benefit of the government, but for the benefit of the people."

In 2012, all regions were contacted and asked for information that rangers felt was an important and relevant part of their special use recreation program's history. All responded by providing an abundance of data, research, and documents above and beyond the requirements offered through the Freedom of Information Act (FOIA).

All credit goes to them and their staff. This collection of their work is based on their belief that we have a heritage worth remembering. Due to the purging of files, information may not be complete but can serve as an introduction for further research.

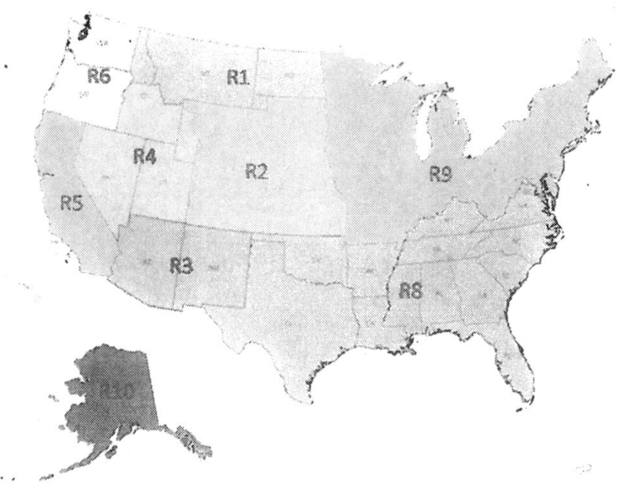

Forest Service Regions

Northern Region 1: National Forest/Grasslands: Montana, Northern Idaho, Northwest South Dakota, and North Dakota

Region 1 staff provided the following information. Special thanks goes to both Brandon Schulze, public affairs specialist for the USFS, and Brandon Smith, manager of land uses and recreation residences, for providing data and a copy of an original summer home brochure as well as their Recreation Residence Historic Context For Eight National Forests in USDA-Region 1 prepared by HHM Inc. Austin, TX. Information used was verbatim with minor editing and credit goes to their fine work.

> For much of the early twentieth century, District 1 brought visitors to their national forests through marketing efforts and by allowing private businesses to cater to local and out-of-state visitors by running dude ranch and summer resort businesses. Recognizing the numerous recreation opportunities their

forests had to offer, District 1's Office of Engineering prepared (Recreation Realm) maps in 1920 highlighting all recreation possibilities within Montana and northern Idaho. The marketing maps were displayed in local hotels and businesses across the district's states.

During the 1920s, District 1 national forests relied on special permits and the high level of interest in summer homes as the primary source of fees and recreation development. By 1929, Region 1 had made substantial progress in developing new recreation residence tracts across their forests. During the New Deal era in the 1930s, summer home interest among the public diminished. Region 1, however, continued to experience growth in summer home development, albeit on a much smaller scale than in the 1920s.

As recreation visits to area forests increased in the postwar years, so too did public interest in summer homes. Region 1 was initially unable to match the increased demand. Assistant Regional Forester R.U. Harmon attributed the delay in development to two factors: "The lack of both building materials and equipment following the war affected not only family home construction, but also the building of summer homes. The second factor limiting summer home construction was the region's inability to provide enough sites to accommodate the numerous applications for special use permits." Because the Forest Service in the 1930s began setting aside increasing amounts of land for public use, new sites for summer home developments decreased. In addition, new Forest Service recreation regulations excluded summer homes from certain areas such as lakeshores, streams, roadside zones, and scenic strips. As a result, applications for summer homes in Region 1 by 1948 were significantly delayed, with over 1,000 applications waiting to be approved.

By the early 1950s, Region 1 recreation planners began making progress in surveying and setting aside new residence tracts for summer homes. Nevertheless, in the late 1950s, Forest Service resistance against expanding the program grew due to the growing costs associated with the residences and the fact that Washington had taken over tract development approval. Snow removal, sanitation, and road construction all contributed to higher costs, the majority of which were not covered by permit fees. To compensate, the regional office raised summer home fees during this period. In addition, intermittent Forest Service oversight of special use permits caused the decline of summer home design standards and administration. As a result, the Forest Service began to greatly limit the expansion of the program. By 1960, applications for new permits in Region 1 significantly decreased given the limited development of new sites and tracts. National policy directives in the late 1960s and early 1970s ended further summer home tract development.

Currently, Region 1 has 102 tracts with 854 summer home permits. It also has one summer homeowners tract association:

Priest Lake Permittee's Association in the Idaho Panhandle National Forest

Region 1 also submitted the following information:

1. A copy of a 1919 to 1930s circular put out by Region 1 informing the public of the summer home program titled *Suggestions*.
2. Tract Planning, 1935
3. General Construction Standards, 1934
4. Forest Service Summer Home Policy, 1941

SUGGESTIONS

TO THOSE DESIRING TO OCCUPY LOTS FOR COTTAGE AND SUMMER RESORT PURPOSES WITHIN THE KANIKSU NATIONAL FOREST AT PRIEST LAKE, IDAHO AND OTHER LAKES WITHIN THE FOREST : : : : : :

NEWPORT MINER PRINT
NEWPORT, WASHINGTON

2127

SUGGESTIONS

to those desiring to Occupy Lots for Cottage and Summer Resort Purposes within the Kaniksu National Forest.

The Kaniksu National Forest, lying in the extreme northern part of Idaho and northeastern Washington, contains within its borders all of Priest Lake, which is a body of water some 25 miles long by 4 miles wide, as well as numerous other smaller lakes, among which the most important are Upper Priest Lake, Sullivan Lake, Bead Lake and Brown's Lake. All these lakes, particularly Priest Lake, afford excellent sites for summer cottages, as well as for camping and other recreation purposes. The use of this land is encouraged by the Government in every possible way, and recently all the suitable Government land on the shores of Priest Lake was surveyed and marked off into lots, there being over 600 lots available for special-use permits on this one lake alone. Other lakes in the Forest

2

are being surveyed as rapidly as possible, and will very shortly be open for use under Forest Service regulations. Where surveyed, the lots are marked off by large stakes, numbered to correspond with the number of the lot, so that the identification of the lots on the ground is a simple matter. Furthermore, plats of the lots, with full descriptions, are on file in the office of the Forest Supervisor at Newport, Washington, and at Coolin, Idaho, where they may be consulted at any time. Priest Lake is reached by stage from Priest River, Idaho, a station on the Great Northern, or from Newport, Washington, on the Great Northern and the Idaho & Washington Northern railroads, while Sullivan Lake is reached from Metaline Falls, the present terminus of the I. & W. N. R. R. Bead Lake and Brown's Lake can be reached from Newport, or from Cusick, Washington.

The following outline is given for the guidance of those who desire to apply for permits for cottage lots within the Kaniksu National Forest:

1. Applications for permits to secure lots for cottage or summer resort purposes within the Kaniksu National Forest shall be submitted on Form F, which may be secured from any Forest officer. On this Form the lots desired must be so described, either by number or by reference to well-known objects, as to be easily identified by the Forest officers. Anyone may apply for lots, but not more than one permit will be issued to any one person, nor will more than one application by the same person be placed on record. Priority of application will be determined according to the time of receipt at the office of the Forest Supervisor. No application will be considered and recorded unless submitted on Form F, or by letter containing all the information required on Form F.

3

2. A formal application may be withdrawn and a second application made, providing that the permit has not been issued, but not more than two withdrawals will be accepted from any one individual within the current calendar year, and no transfer of applications prior to the issuance of permits from one party to another will be permitted. Any number of applications by different individuals for the same lot may be filed, but the permit will be issued to the one having the prior right, as established under 1. Conflicting applications will remain of record at the option of the applicant until construction work under the permit issued has been completed, when all conflicting applications will be canceled and no further application for the same lot will be accepted except as provided under 7.

3. The minimum annual charge for lots used for non-commercial cottage or summer resort purposes is $10.00, payable in advance. This fee is entirely nominal, and is made so for the purpose of encouraging the non-commercial use of the lots. Commercial use, however, is not discouraged, but will be required to pay a reasonable annual fee, depending upon the character of the use. All permits provide that payment of the annual fee must be made within 30 days from the date of the permit, and that failure to make payment within the specified time makes the permit null and void. Payments are made directly by the permittee to the Western Mon-

tana National Bank at Missoula, Montana, and must be made in the form of postal or express money orders, or National bank drafts, made payable to the above mentioned bank. Personal checks will not be accepted. All payments must be accompanied by a letter of transmittal, Form 861-M, which is furnished by the Forest Supervisor when notice that payment is due is sent out. Directions for making payments are contained on the back of this Form. Such notices are sent out with each permit as it is issued, and annually thereafter one month in advance of the date upon which payment is due. If payment is not made when due, second notice is sent to the permittees, notifying them that the permit will be canceled unless payment is made within 30 days. All calls for payments are sent to the address of record of the permittee, and all permittees are requested to keep the Forest Supervisor informed of their address in case any changes occur. Failure to receive notice of payments due, resulting in cancellation of permit for the reason that notices were sent to the wrong address will not constitute a valid reason for renewal of permit unless the new address of permittee had been filed with the Forest Supervisor.

4. All permits shall be issued calling for construction work under the permit within a reasonable length of time. This period is always set so that construction shall be commenced and completed during the field season following the date of the permit. "Field Season" in construed to mean opening in the Spring and closing in the late fall. Failure to comply with the requirement as to construction involves cancellation of the permit unless the written consent of the Forest Supervisor for extension of time is

secured. No specific character of construction is required under the permits, but the buildings erected must be of a permanent and habitable character, and attempts to hold cottage lots under permit by a pretense of construction will not be allowed. In case of dispute as to the intent of the permittee in his construction, the decision of the District Forester shall be final.

5. All permits shall require the permittees to fight fire free of charge to the Forest Service when called upon by Forest officers, when such fire either threatens the improvements of the permittees or property adjacent thereto, or for which the permittee is responsible. Permittees are not called upon to fight fire at remote points unless they desire to do so. The assistance of permittees is appreciated in case of emergency, and the usual Forest Service wages are paid where the fire neither threatens the property of the permittee, nor is one for which the permittee is responsible.

6. All permits shall specify that the use shall be exercised at least 15 days each year, but this regulation shall be interpreted to mean that there shall be bona fide use of the lot for summer resort purposes and shall not be held to strictly unless it appears that the lot is being held for speculative purposes and not in good faith.

7. All permits are made non-transferable, and no transfer of a permit from one individual to another between the date of issuance of the permit and the date set for construction will be permitted. In case a permittee is dissatisfied with his lot before beginning construction he may relinquish and apply for a second lot, but no second application for the lot which he has relinquished will be considered for at least one year, except at the discretion of the

Forest Supervisor. Two withdrawals will be accepted from the same person, but in case a second withdrawal is submitted no application will be received from the person submitting such a withdrawal for at least one year from the date of the last withdrawal, except in the discretion of the Forest Supervisor. Parties wishing to transfer their improvements may secure permission to do so by submitting to the Forest Supervisor a certified contract of sale or other evidence of transfer of title, together with a request for cancellation of the permit covering the lot on which the improvements are located. This should include: (A) A certified contract of sale; (B) Request to cancel the permit signed by the permittee: (C) An application for permit on Form F covering the same lot signed by the transferree.

8. Permits shall provide that timber for construction purposes shall be secured either under free-use or by purchase. As long as dead timber is available it will be granted free under free-use permits, subject to the regulations governing the use of the National Forests, as contained in the Use Book. No green timber will be granted under free-use permits while available dead timber remains. Green timber for construction purposes or for fire wood may be secured by purchase under the usual regulations governing timber sales on National Forests. All Rangers are authorized to make sales up to a value of $50 on the stump, and parties desiring to purchase timber should apply to the nearest District Ranger. Free-use permits are also issued by District Rangers, and should be obtained before timber is cut from Government land.

9. All permits shall be issued with a provision requiring that the permittees shall clear the

premises of all inflammable brush and refuse, and shall bury in a suitable place all tin cans, garbage and other unsightly articles. It is expected that the premises shall be kept neat, and especially that every reasonable effort shall be made to guard against the setting of fires. No pollution of streams or springs will be countenanced, and no one is permitted to monopolize any stream or spring situated on his lot or to obstruct any trail or road or the use of the beach as a highway.

10. All permits shall be issued subject to the right of the Forest Service to authorize the raising of the level of the lake or lakes for the storage of water for any purpose authorized by statute. Wherever the raising of a lake is contemplated, the greatest height to which the water can be raised will be indicated on each lot by a suitable stake, so that permittees may place their improvements above any possible high water level. On Sullivan Lake a permit has been issued authorizing the raising of the water to 40 feet above normal water level, and the maximum water line has been plainly marked out all round the lake. On Priest Lake an application to raise the water 1[illegible] feet above low water mark is being considered, and this line is also marked so that permittees can place their improvements above the proposed water level.

11. For sufficient cause permits may be revoked by the District Forester on recommendation of the Forest Supervisor. The Forest Supervisor may in his discretion reject an application from a permittee whose application or permit within the current calendar year has been rejected or canceled for cause. Applications for permits the following year will be considered on their merits.

12. All permits shall be issued subject to all

prior existing valid claims. Permits are not issued for lands covered by claims initiated under any of the United States Land laws, or on lands covered by any prior permit without the consent of the claimants or the permittees. Where permits are issued on claims the permittees are barred from interfering with the rights of the claimants to develop the claim in accordance with the law under which the claim was entered; and the Forest Service has no jurisdiction in cases of dispute between permittees and claimants, nor does the Forest Service permit grant the permittees any rights as against the claimants.

13. In all cases where dispute arises as to the location of boundaries between lots the Forest Service will survey and mark the lot boundary on application by the permittees, providing an officer of the Forest Service can be spared for the work at the time.

APPLICATIONS BY ASSOCIATIONS.

In addition to giving special-use permits for the use of lots by individuals, permits are also issued to associations, clubs, etc., for the use of groups of lots for club purposes. At Priest Lake four groups of lots, which are particularly suited for use by associations, are reserved for this purpose. In order to secure lots associations or clubs should proceed in accordance with the following suggestions:

14. Applications by associations shall be made on Form F, and shall be signed by the secretary of the association and be accompanied by (a) A

certified copy of the constitution and bylaws of the association, or of the articles of incorporation in case the association is incorporated: (b) The names and addresses of all the members of the association in good standing; and (c) A list of the officers of the association, with their addresses.

15. The maximum number of lots which any association may hold under permit as an association for club purposes shall not exceed four. This requirement, however, shall not be interpreted to mean that the individuals comprising the association are barred from applying for lots as individuals under the regulations governing applications by individuals, and lots held by the individual members of the club may be adjacent to the club property or separate therefrom.

16. The selection of lots for a clubhouse within one of the reserved club site locations where the entire club site is not applied for by the association shall be made subject to the approval of the Forest Supervisor. This selection of clubhouse lots under the circumstances described above must be made so that the use of the remainder of the club site by other parties, either individuals or associations, shall not be handicapped. This requirement, however, shall not be interpreted to mean that in case an association applies for lots within a reserved club site, and the members of the association apply as individuals for the remainder of the lots, that the association will be instructed in any way as to which lots shall be used for club purposes and which shall be used for individual cottages.

17. Payments for lots by associations shall be at the same rate per lot as established for individual permittees, and shall be made subject

to the same rules as previously described under (8).

18. All requirements pertaining to individual cottage lots shall also apply to association lots, except that the erection of one clubhouse will constitute the improvements required on the entire group of lots held by the association under the name of the club or association holding the permit. This requirement, however, shall not be interpreted as exempting club members holding lots as individuals from the necessity of erecting cottages on their lots subject to the same requirements as other individual lot holders.

CAMPING RESERVES.

The use of the lakes within the Kaniksu National Forest for camping purposes is encouraged in every possible way. In no case is the entire lake shore surveyed into cottage lots, but all lakes have large stretches of shore line exempted entirely from use for summer cottage purposes, and reserved strictly for the use of camping parties. This is particularly true at Priest Lake, where a number of the finest beaches on the lake are held from special-use permits as camping reserves. No permits are required to camp on these reserves, or on any of the unoccupied surveyed lots. Camping parties are particularly requested to observe the requirements contained on the camping notices posted at all camp grounds, and to be especially careful in the handling of fires in the dry season. They are

also requested to dispose of all refuse and maintain camp grounds in a neat and attractive condition. For the description and locations of the camp reserves on the lakes within the Kaniksu National Forest the plats and notes on file in the office of the Forest Supervisor, or at the office of the District Ranger, within whose district the lake is located, should be consulted.

Under certain circumstances permits for the exclusive use of a camp ground will be issued. Such permits will only be issued to schools or charitable institutions desiring to secure a camp ground to which they can be guaranteed the exclusive right for a term of years. These permits will be issued free, and to secure the same, application by letter should be made to the Forest Supervisor of the Kaniksu National Forest, who has discretionary power to issue such permits and will furnish complete instructions as to the methods of procedure to be followed in making application for such a privilege.

COMMERCIAL USES.

In anticipation of the extensive use of Priest Lake and the other lakes within the Forest for summer resort purposes, lots which are particularly suited for hotels or other commercial enterprises will be reserved for this purpose. Parties desiring information in regard to such locations should communicate with the Forest Supervisor

12

of the Kaniksu National Forest at Newport, Washington, who will be glad to furnish all information available in regard to such opportunities. Special regulations and special fees shall be applied to all commercial uses of lots on the lakes, depending upon the iircumstances in each case. All permits for commercial establishments shall contain a clause prohibiting the sale of intoxicating liquors on the premises, whether the same is permitted by the laws of the state or not.

1919–1930s circular in Region 1 informing the public of the summer home program

Residence Tract Planning, ca. 1935

Residence Tract Planning
(From Linthacum's Copy, "Tract and Site Planning)

1. Don't subdivide an area into lots mechanically like cutting a cake or pie.

2. Pick best sites for main residence building and plat these with the idea of laying out a lot use area around it.

3. Lots should have a max. of 125 feet frontage under average cover conditions. They should not be over an acre.

4. Have good screening between the main bldgs. and adjacent lots to give separation and some privacy.

5. Have a policy for each tract as to what facilities will be allowed for each lot, i.e., garages, guest cabins, boat wharfs and shelters, etc.

6. Lots should not be jouned in long, unbrokens strings. Have right of way break every fourth or fith lot as manimum.

7. Lot lines back form lake or stream enough to allow free community or public passage, usually minimum of 50 feet.

8. All structures on lots back far enough or well screened aut of view from lakes or public roads. General practices (R-4) under current policy to be at least roadside and waterfront zone distance 200 feet on principle roads and public waters.

9. Don't put a lot out on a prominent point in a lake or other water or in such relation to its approach as to interfere with community access to it. Likewise a single lot should not command monopoly of a bay suitable for a community use wharf or other facility.

10. Don't lay out a lot across any stream, however small. Keep lot lines clear so all permitties may have equal priviliges in the stream.

11. Select and desiginate area for community playgrounds orother purposes as needed or possible. Community wharfs desirable to reduce numbers.

12. Make tentative location of trunk services road and spur entrances to let. Entrances roads curve enough not to open view to buildings.

13. Have approved policy for kinds of structures and developments that will be allowed on the tract; i.e., garages, guest cabins, boat wharf and shelter, ice-house, storage building, etc,. On each lot stake location for all improvements and structures which it is porposed ever to allow on that lot.

14. Some adjustments or shifting of tentative road and building locations probally necessary to get best layout.

15. The trunk or entrance road should not pass through any lot to reach another.

16. When ald roads and other improvements staked in final locations, establish corners of lots to give a balanced use area around the residence building. Suggent trees for corners with scribed stunp blazed facing center of lot. (Corner # over lot #, 1/2 is corner 1 of lot 2)

Residence Tract Planning Guide, circa 1935

General Construction Standards, 1934

GENERAL CONSTRUCTION STANDARDS FOR SUMMER HOMES

UNDER NATIONAL FOREST PERMIT.

REGION ONE.

Foreword:

As evidences of man increase in the forests, so decrease many of the attractions sought by those visiting the forests for recreation. In developments on recreational areas, the Forest Service seeks to save these attractions, - to preserve an environment as nearly natural as possible.

Towards these aims, the guides or standards below are designed. They do not demand any one specific treatment applicable to all cases, nor are they intended to restrict individual tastes. Instead they are a guide indicating the kinds of construction and development that are to be avoided or cannot be condoned.

Location of Structures and their Number

One prerequisite for natural conditions is that man-made structures be inconspicuously located; another, that their number be held to a minimum.

Structures must be set back from main highways and other public travel routes, lake shores and streams, - the distance back depending on configuration of the ground and available tree and shrubbery screening. Similar screening is necessary between adjoining permittees, to insure privacy and seclusion. In most cases, the Forest Service sets the limits within which structures may be placed on any lot, at the time of its survey.

A few moderate-sized buildings are better than a greater number of small ones. Less attention is attracted, thus retaining more of natural appearances, and the fewer buildings are more easily designed and located to blend with natural surroundings. (Incidentally there is greater convenience for the occupants, and usually greater economy in construction and maintenance.

Adaptation to Site

Buildings should be adapted to the site, harmonize with the setting, "fit the ground."

High foundations must be avoided; on a sloping site the foundation may be kept lower by a little excavating on the uphill site and terracing of the location for the building. Noticeable variation in height of foundation of buildings on

1

the same site is undesirable.

The bungalow type of residence is preferable. Tall buildings rarely "fit" the forest; low structures are best.

Building Materials

Building materials should be suitable to the forest, and those native to the locality are preferable.

Log houses will harmonize with nearly all forest settings and landscapes; variations are obtainable with peeled, sawed or hewed logs.

Lumber buildings may be made quite suitable in some cases. Unplaned lumber will finish or weather with a more "natural" appearance than planed lumber.

A neutral-toned stain or oil finish is less artificial than paint, although painting is acceptable if neutral colors are used. Do not use bright or gaudy color schemes which clash with the natural forest scheme; sienna browns, nature greens or battleship grays are best.

Construction of natural stone will be satisfactory where rock is plentiful naturally on the site, if startling design and finish are avoided. Bright-colored mortar in masonry work is out of place in the usual scheme of forest color.

Brick, cement, stucco and similar materials for structures are inappropriate and not permissible.

Building Design and Architecture

1. Foundations should be kept as inconspicuous as possible. They may be partially hidden or screened with natural growth or foundation plantings of shrubs, vines, ferns, et cetera. Plants native to the locality are best.

Buildings on slopes may not have an opening left underneath where they are off the ground on the lower side; nor may porches be open between the floor and the ground. Such construction appears unfinished. The space may be logged up or latticed with pillar type of foundation, or the foundation itself extended.

Pillars are inferior to a wall foundation, and where used should be ample in number and substantially made.

Where exposed to view, foundations should preferably be rock masonry than cement, but the latter is not objected to.

2. Walls should present clean, pleasing surfaces, and the various wall areas of a building should keep some geometrical

-2-

relation to each other.

No wall or portion of a wall of a building should be so placed in relation to the others or be of such a marked difference in shape or dimensions that a portion of the building appears to have been "stuck on".

3. Windows and doors should be of uniform shape and should be placed with relation to each other so that the result will be balanced and pleasing.

The sizes of doors and windows should ordinarily be fairly uniform throughout the building, but this may necessarily have to be varied a little to maintain "balance" in the appearance of a wall. A large door and large window in a small wall surface are not good, and a very small window and door (or none at all) in a large wall are not pleasing.

Large, blank wall surfaces should be broken up, if possible, with windows, a door or a fireplace.

Round, diamond-shaped or other odd windows must not be used with the usual building design in the forest.

4. Roofs should present a simple and pleasing pattern.

Slopes of various roof areas on a building or on several buildings on the same site should be consistent.

Roofs should not be too much broken up. Broken ridges and valleys should be avoided. Combinations of a hip-and-boxcar roof or roofs of different pitches on the same building or on two or more buildings associated in a group are not good.

Shingles or shakes are most suitable for roofs in the forest. Slate or sand-surfaced composition roofings are satisfactory if of subdued green or other harmonizing color.

5. Porches should fit the house. Preferably they should be integral with the building. An appearance of being "stuck on" is not good; an example is a log porch on a frame building, or vice versa. If the house would look as well or better with the porch removed, the design is not good.

All porches should be substantially constructed. A flimsy porch might spoil an otherwise satisfactory building. The foundation of the porch is as important as that of the house.

6. Chimneys must be fire-safe and as substantial as circumstances permit. A stovepipe through the roof is unsightly as well as dangerous.

Native stone material is preferred as most natural. Cement or neutral-colored tile is acceptable. Brick chimneys are least appropriate.

-3-

7. Fireplaces of as rustic construction as possible often may be made to add considerably to the appearance in a forest setting. They should be safe and substantially made.

Stone is most suitable and fitting. Cement is acceptable, especially if it is made pleasing with rubble work. Brick is less adaptable to natural settings.

Lines of the fireplace on building exteriors should be simple, without swellings and bumps, and angular construction.

8. Decorations, if any, on the building should be very simple. "Doodads", scroll work or curlicues of any kind are unsuited to a forest residence.

9. In general, simplicity is the keynote of good design. Proper proportions, a feeling of naturalness and an air of simple dignity are the essentials. Things ornate, elaborate, pretentious, showy, tricky, fussy or peculiar are bad.

Plans and Specifications

Elaborate or expensive plans made by an architect are not required, though a prospective summer-home builder will often find benefit in referring to one or to suggested plans of which many are published in lumber trade journals or home and garden magazines or the like, or can be furnished by lumber retailers.

Simple plans definitely showing that no undesirable features are contemplated, and putting emphasis on the "layout" of structures, - their location, relationship and number, - and on their dimensions and exteriors, are adequate. Interior floor plans are not needed.

Landscaping

To preserve naturalistic conditions, landscaping is best along informal, natural lines rather than of formal character foreign to the specific locality, and should contemplate moderate rather than extreme results. Simplicity and as close as possible approach to the way Nature would establish its components on any area are the keynote to most desirable effects and to the most pleasing, permanent and increasing returns for ~~the effort. Landscaping effects should aim at directing atten-~~tion to the natural conditions on any site, and to obscure so far as possible the evidences of artificiality due to occupancy.

1. The fine litter and humus cover on the ground must not be removed; not only is the bare, unnatural ground unsightly, but also in many locations it increases dust and reduces fertility of the soil.

2. Existing trees, shrubbery, vines, et cetera, must be preserved so far as practicable. They must not be cut, trimmed or pruned, except in making space for structures or unless approved by the local Forest officers. Blazing, carving or

otherwise defacing trees is prohibited. Buildings should be adjusted or adapted to the terrain and the native rocks and trees, rather than altering these to fit the structures.

3. Plantings when required would obviously fit in far better with the surrounding growth if of trees, plants, vines, ferns, et cetera, native to the locality, or when that is not feasible, of a selection of foreign plants resembling the native as closely as possible. Bright-colored plants in exaggeration of what may naturally be found manifestly clash with the natural.

4. Just as flowers do not occur naturally in artificial beds, so, plainly, flowers in artificial beds at forest residences depart from natural conditions. Naturalistic rock gardens of native plants or cultivation of wild flowers are preferable, and even those would be better - since breaking away from the natural - if not too conspicuous.

5. Fences and gates should be avoided if possible. When necessary, they should be of native materials and of utmost simplicity. They must be inconspicuous, screened with natural shrubbery growth wherever possible. A painted fence, especially white or bright color, is startlingly artificial in an otherwise natural background.

6. Roads, walks, paths and trails, when necessary, preferably should be gently curving or winding, not crooked, rather than straight. A straight-line clearing for a road is more unnaturally conspicuous than one that is curved.

Flagstones or gravel or sand are best for walks or paths. Brick walks and cement walks do not fit in a forest atmosphere, although irregular cement blocks - neutral stained, in imitation of flagstones - may be found compatible.

7. Decoration of the grounds with whitewashed or painted rocks or stones or by whitewashing tree trunks, even though neatly done, is not permissible. Fancy or elaborate rock work on fountains, or ornate rustic or garishly-colored furniture and yard fixtures, are not desirable in good landscaping as in other good architecture.

General Construction Standards, 1934

Forest Service Summer Home Policy, 1941

M-1531-R1

FOREST SERVICE
United States Department of Agriculture

U
USES
General

February 1941

FOREST SERVICE SUMMER HOME POLICY

The national forests are public property and are managed for "the greatest good to the greatest number in the long run."

Since a summer home is an exclusive use of national forest land it naturally and properly must not be allowed to interfere with public or semipublic uses. Summer homes may only be permitted on areas which because of topography or location are unsuited for public use or on areas which, as far as can be seen, will not be required for present or future public needs and where the presence of summer homes will not interfere with public enjoyment of other areas.

Areas to be designated for summer homes are selected by experienced forest officers in accordance with the above principles. Fortunately, summer homes do not require a large area and places can be found which are very satisfactory for summer homes and yet do not interfere with public use. Such areas are surveyed into individual lots of one-half to one acre in size. As a general rule, it is both impracticable and undesirable to permit single summer homes in isolated, scattered locations. Several lots usually are surveyed in a group, with adequate spacing between the individual summer homes for separation and privacy.

In order to prevent unnecessary intrusion into the forest scene and interference with general public use, summer homes are not permitted within sight of highways, on lake shores, along the frontage of fishing streams, near public-use areas, or within areas of scenic natural features and attractions. However, the objective is to locate them in places which are suitable for summer home use and in attractive country with good forest cover, and they may often be within convenient distance of fine recreation areas.

The location and plotting of summer home areas is just one of the many things which the men charged with administration of the national forests have to do, so it is not possible to have a large supply of sites ready at any one time. Persons desiring a summer home should get in touch with the forest supervisor of the particular national forest in which they are interested. If summer home sites are available on that forest, the forest supervisor will arrange for an inspection of available tracts so the prospective summer home permittee may select a site from the unoccupied surveyed lots available. If no summer home sites are available on that national forest, the forest supervisor will, if practicable, direct the summer home applicant to another national forest on which lots may be available.

When a person has selected a summer home lot he is issued a special-use permit for the area, which grants him exclusive use with certain restrictions. The fee for a summer home lot is generally from $15 to $25 a year. The permit is renewable each year by payment of the annual fee, if its conditions and requirements have been complied with, but in case the Government has need of the area for higher use the permit may be canceled after giving the owner due notice and a reasonable time to amortize his investment. Since summer home sites are now so carefully selected, this would happen only under unusual and unforeseeable conditions.

Forest Service Summer Home Policy, 1941

Rocky Mountain Region 2: Colorado, Wyoming, South Dakota, Nebraska, and Kansas

Region 2 staff provided the following information. Special thanks goes to Paul E. Cruz, USFS regional recreation business program manager, and Diane Hitchings, USFS recreation special use program manager, for providing data and resources. All information presented came from the following Region 2 materials:

1. The 1928 circular *The National Forests of Colorado*
2. John R. Grosvenor's 1999 *A History Of The Architecture Of The USDA Forest Service*
3. Forest Service historian William C. Tweed's "A History of Outdoor Recreation Development In National Forests 1891–1941"
4. Dana, S.T.'s, "Forest and Ranger Policy: Its Development in the U.S." from 1956
5. Shoemaker, T. Jr.'s, "Improvement for the Public. Minutes of Supervisor's Meeting, District 2, Jan. 29 – Feb. 3, 1917"
6. Reini, G.H.'s, "A History of the National Forests in Colorado" from 1931

Information used was verbatim with minor editing and credit goes to their fine work.

Congress authorized the Secretary of Agriculture to issue permits to persons and associations for the construction and use of recreational structures in 1915. But it wasn't until mobility was enhanced by the increased access to automobiles, the development of roads and trails, as well as leisure time, that the need for recreation management by the Forest Service was realized in District 2. At a meeting in 1917 of forest supervisors in Denver, Theodore Shoemaker, supervisor of the Pike, stated,

"The tide has just set in, and people from all over the country are coming in increased numbers to claim the use of their property..." Shoemaker acknowledged that non-governmental funding and entrepreneurial undertakings would fill the need for hotels and rental cabins, and he emphasized that the Forest Service was in a position to encourage these developments as well as to regulate them. Within the next two years, the Forest Service developed its first recreation plan, with the help of Arthur Carhart, the region's newly hired recreation engineer. The plan was a result of the fact that Colorado national forests were becoming America's playground.

On April 1919, Arthur Carhart designed the first foot trail for tourist use on Pike's Peak. The following month he traveled to the San Isabel National Forest in south-central Colorado to begin work on other recreation plans for the region's many forests. During 1919 and 1920, Carhart worked at Trappers Lake, Colorado. He focused on summer home tracts . . . in 1928, Region 2 reported that an ever-increasing number of recreational visitors were finding their way into the region's national forests. A regional forest map stated, "provision is made for free camping, and in many cases through cooperation with local organizations campgrounds are being located and equipped. Where there is any demand, summer home sites are surveyed and offered at a nominal fee to those who want permanent summer quarters in the forests. Under the same arrangement, lodges and clubhouses for organizations may be established. Permits for commercial resorts also are issued where they will help in making the national forest more readily available for human use." Region 2 also granted special use permits for a number of dude ranches, resorts, gasoline stations, and stores. Special use permits for "Big Game" hunting, fishing, horseback riding, hiking, and skiing were also provided. (Dana)

In 1936, Region 2 hired its first professional architect, S.A. Axtens. According to Grosvenor,

> . . . he gave the region a style that was more rustic than any other; it included uncoursed local stone and brick, walls of peeled or shaved logs or wide clapboard siding, and moderately pitched roofs with wood shingles or shakes. The use of wood as a construction material was perhaps the ultimate expression of Forest Service values, and designers took every opportunity to use it. Timber reflected the pioneer architectural traditions of Rocky Mountain architecture. Rustic style was especially appropriate for the mountains, where wood shakes, native stone, and logs were cheap and readily available.
>
> Forest Service personnel took great pride in their buildings. Extensive construction records document the extraordinary care taken by rangers in making sure their buildings were as well built as possible. This rustic architecture used a strong horizontal emphasis, complementary colors, extensive use of wood and stone, and lower overall massing to harmonize with the environment.

Currently, Region 2 has 287 tracts with 1,250 summer home permits. Region 2 also has four permittee summer home tract associations registered as members of the National Forest Homeowners organization. They are:

- Happy Top Summer Homes in Pike National Forest, Colorado
- Herman Gulch Homeowners Association in Arapaho National Forest, Colorado

- Homestake Valley Tract in White River National Forest, Colorado
- Brooklyn Lake in Medicine Bow National Forest, Wyoming

The following information was provided by Region 2 and the Forest History Society website:

1. Sanitation and Health List
2. National Forest of Routt Circular, 1941

SANITATION AND HEALTH

1. Mountain streams will not purify themselves in a few hundred feet. Boil or chlorinate all suspected water.

2. Burn all paper, old clothing, or rubbish. Bury or place in pits or receptacles provided all garbage, tin cans, bottles, and other refuse.

3. Do not wash soiled clothing or utensils or bathe in springs, streams, or lakes. Use a container and throw dirty water where it cannot get into the water supply without first filtering through the ground.

4. Use the sanitation facilities provided by the Forest Service on campgrounds and elsewhere.

5. Observe the rules of sanitation and protect yourself and others. Report all insanitary conditions to the nearest health or forest officer.

6. Obey the posted "Rules for the use of improved campgrounds."

Sanitation and Health List

UNITED STATES DEPARTMENT OF AGRICULTURE
FOREST SERVICE

ROCKY MOUNTAIN REGION
DENVER, COLORADO

National Forest Circular, 1941

Southwestern Region 3: Arizona and New Mexico

Region 3 staff provided the following. Special thanks goes to Melissa Dean, USDA Forest Service public affairs, and Karen O'Leary, recreation special uses coordinator, for providing data, resources, and references. All presented information and photos are from the 1988 *Timeless Heritage: A History of the Forest Service in the Southwest* by Robert D. Baker, Robert S. Maxwell, Victor H. Treat, and Henry C. Dethloff. Again information was used verbatim with minor editing and credit goes to their fine work. All courtesy of the Forest Service.

> Recreation became a factor in the 1920s, when automobiles made the forests more accessible. Roads, recreation facilities, and opportunities expanded significantly in the 1930s, with assistance from the Civilian Conservation Corps and other New Deal agencies. After World War II, recreation exceeded timber, grazing, or mining in economic impact upon the Southwest and became the major area of Forest Service involvement with the public. People were using the forests for year-round experiences, for relief from the summer heat, and for physical and scenic alternatives to the urban lifestyles. The forests became the public's summer retreats and their winter playgrounds. The forest was a place to simply enjoy for its own natural beauty.
>
> Hence, the region's main focus became the preservation of wilderness areas. Over 2.7 million acres have been set aside in the Southwest for wilderness management thanks to Aldo Leopold's hard work. In 1924, the establishment of the 750,000-acre Gila Wilderness gave birth to the National Wilderness Preservation System. Before 1920, the public and the Forest Service perception of forest recreation generally included

hunting, fishing, hiking, camping, picnicking, and sightseeing. Forest recreation was regarded as primitive, individualistic, and very personal. The attitude was reflected in a 1937 recreation study which explained, "we should contribute information in regard to everything that has to do with forest recreation, that is, with the close contact between people and the quiet, restful spots of the natural forest where they can digest the chaotic items of their lives and see themselves in the correct relation to both civilization and nature." Thus "progress"—in the form of automobiles, railroads, snowmobiles, lodges, summer homes, ski lifts, off-road vehicles, bicycles, motorcycles, recreational vehicles, and electric generators—was strongly seen as intrusive upon the silence and beauty of the national forest in the Southwest.

Needless to say, there was some apathy, or ambivalence if not antipathy, in the Forest Service in the Southwest at first toward the summer home program as a legitimate use of forest resources. Regardless, recreation plans were established to encourage the allocation of suitable forest areas for summer homes, camping areas, hotels, and voluntary agency camps. The region prepared public information folders titled "Recreation in the Southwest" and "Sunshine Recreation of a Nation."

Structure design was very unique in Region 3. Grosvenor stated that, "a distinctive style identified this region. A bungalow type with low-pitched gable roofs sheathed with asphalt shingles became common. Rafter ends were exposed under wide eaves. Exterior chimneys were prominent. This style was popular for Arizona national forests. A Spanish type with flat roofs with parapeted walls also emerged. In New Mexico, buildings were designed using a pueblo style. Also having flat roofs with parapeted walls, the parapets were stepped in a line using a regular pattern. Standard plans used vigas projecting in front and rear. Wood lintels were installed over windows and entrees but not exposed. Construction materials were limited to adobe with stucco veneer." All these designs reflected the region's native cultural style.

Currently, Region 3 has 44 tracts with 684 summer home permits. Region 3 has four summer home tract associations registered as members of the National Forest Homeowners organization. They are:

- Columbine in the Coronado National Forest, Arizona
- Turkey Flat in the Coronado National Forest, Arizona
- Willow Canyon Homeowners Association in the Coronado National Forest, Arizona
- Holy Ghost Canyon in the Santa Fe National Forest, New Mexico

The following are photos and vintage postcards representing Region 3, courtesy of the Forest Service and friends of the forest.

Cibola National Forest, 1920s

1920s Summer Home in Santa Fe National Forest

Lincoln National Forest, Ruidoso, New Mexico

Intermountain Region 4: Utah, Nevada, Southern Idaho, and Bridger-Teton National Forest in Wyoming

Region 4 staff provided the following information. Special thanks goes to Kathleen Moore, recreation special uses program leader, and Melissa Hearst, land special use program manager, for providing the following:

1. Forest Service telegraph announcing permits
2. Information on the summer home special use "Peavey Cabins"
3. A "History of the Intermountain Region" by the USDA Forest Service
4. Thomas G.Alexander's *The Rise of Multiple-Use Management in the Intermountain West: A History of Region 4 of the Forest Service*
5. Ruth Clayton's *The History of Recreation Residence Building in Logan Canyon*

Information was used verbatim with minor editing and credit goes to the mentioned.

American Indians had located themselves in the area long before the arrival of Euro-American settlers. The majority of aborigines of the Intermountain Region were Shoshonean-speaking peoples belonging to the broad tribes of Shoshoni, Ute, Bannock, Paiute, and Goshute. At the time of the Euro-American penetration, a rich diversity of lush foothill and mountain meadows, tall timber, and sagebrush covered or peppered the mountains and valleys of the Intermountain Region. Early diaries indicate that wildlife was also spread over the eastern and northeastern portions of the area. Numerous herds of buffalo and elk and a great many beaver were documented as well as grizzly bears.

In the 1800s, Utah businessmen earned their fortunes from

lumber operations. Reports indicated that sawmills and logging operations used "very destructive methods." Loggers would burn the Scoffield side hills during the heat of the summer to kill the timber and remove the undergrowth. Later in the year they would move in to the "high-grade" and "harvest only the choicest trees," leaving the rest of the trees and downed timber to rot. The burning made it easier and cheaper to get the best timber out and easier to move the raw lumber to the sawmills, but the ecological devastation was a high price to pay. Operations like these left the forests devastated after the loggers moved out. Slash and litter covered the ground, leaving wasted wood and fire hazards. The emptiness and lack of trees in some of the areas logged this way is still evident today.

According to Ruth Clayton, in 1908, "special use permits were granted for telephone lines, canal rights-of-way, stores, mills, hotels, and other such facilities. Region 4 also started granting permits for recreation facilities. That same year, the service set aside a tract in Logan Canyon for construction of summer homes. Applications for the use of lots in such tracts were made to the forest supervisors, investigated by a forest officer and, if accepted, approved by the chief of the Forest Service.

Peavey Cabins

In the late 1920s, the Peavey historic cabins were built. The Peavey family owned four cabins for approximately sixty years. Various members of the family were involved in state and national political positions. The Peavey family also owned one of the largest livestock companies in southern Idaho, The Flattop Sheep Company, established in the early 1920s. The Peavy (Peavey) cabins are located on the south shore of Pettit Lake in the Sawtooth National

Recreation Area in central Idaho. The scenic mountainous area in which Pettit Lake is located endured over one hundred years of debate concerning its preservation and use. In 1972 the Sawtooth Nation Recreation Area was finally created as part of the National Park Service, no longer a part of the Sawtooth National Forest.

Before the preservation change, A.J. Peavey leased lot 1 on Pettit Lake on July 1, 1926. Construction began in the summer of 1927. The other three lots and cabins were leased in 1928,1929, and 1930. Timber for the cabins was not cut from the site, but was dead standing lodge pole pine that the Forest Service allowed to be cut from the area. The Peavey family maintained a special use permit on Pettit Lake until about 1985 when the cabins were sold. Since 1985, a series of owners have leased the property.

Salmon Forest

In 1910, supervisor James Ryan estimated that 500 people use the Salmon Forest for recreation, with about one-third coming from eastern states, and the remainder coming from areas adjacent to the forest. Ryan felt that after the completion of the railroad in 1910, the number of people coming to the Salmon Forest for recreation, or any another forest in the region for that matter, would greatly increase. The records for 1931 estimate 2,500 visitors to the North Fork, 400 visitors to Hughes Creek, 1,000 hunters going through Shoup, and about 150 visitors to the Idaho Primitive Area via Salmon Forest.

In 1939, supervisor Godden recommended the building of simple campsites for hunters and fishermen, for fire protection and sanitation, possibly at the mouth of Dry Gulch, and other sites along Middle Fork and Camas Creek. Inspector Anderson in 1939 reported that the Salmon Forest did not have intensive recreational use, but he did recommend development of campgrounds along the

Middle Fork in the Primitive Area because of increased use there. One of the land use problems on the Salmon Forest reported in 1943 was the taking up of mineral claims as a subterfuge for other uses. This resulted in practically no requests for summer home special use permits on the Salmon National Forest and a great variety of low standard buildings along the Panther Creek and Salmon River roads.

Original tracts were located in prime locations. In some cases, summer homes conflicted with public recreation used. On Fish Lake, for instance, the forest officers had considerable difficulty in keeping houses away from the shores so the general public could have access to the lake. Finally, a grandfather clause was established, allowing existing owners to keep their cabins near the lake but requiring their successors to move. This led to the "U" regulation that prohibited the placement of private summer homes completed around public attractions. There had to be a section open to the public to enjoy the lake.

Currently, Region 4 has 100 tracts with 1,388 summer home permit lots. Region 4 has five summer home tract associations registered as members of the National Forest Homeowners organization. They are:

- Thomas Canyon Cabin Owners Association, Inc. in the Humboldt National Forest, California
- Bridgeport Forest Homeowners Association in the Humboldt Toiyabe National Forest, Nevada
- Kyle Canyon Summer Homes Association in Nevada
- Rainbow Canyon in the Humboldt in the Toiyabe National Forest, Nevada
- Porter Fork in the Wasatch-Cache National Forest, Utah

Region 4 also provided the following information:

1. A 1915–1920, *Salt Lake Telegram*, "Uncle Sam Has Choice

Camp Sites for Rent in Mountains of Utah"
All information is courtesy of the Forest Service.

Uncle Sam Has Choice Camp Sites for Rent in Mountains of Utah

HOW would you like to own a beautiful little summer cottage up in the mountains, where the air is pure with health giving odors of the pines, and where a gurgling mountain stream, filled with gamey trout that leap into the air after flies, is engaged in gurgling its way to the Great Salt lake right past your cabin, luring you to try your angling luck by day and to sweet dreams by night?

Sounds fine, doesn't it? Also, it sounds strangely like real estate literature. That's exactly what it is—only Uncle Sam's the agent.

Also, Uncle Sam is the landlord of this property and he has it to rent. He hasn't the cottages, but he has the places to put them, and they are alongside the well known gurgling streams. Hurry up, folks; there are only a few desirable sites left. These are in Big Cottonwood canyon, a few in Mill Creek canyon and a number in American Fork canyon.

In finding out which of these sites you want you must hire a rig or automobile and go give them the up and down. Up and down is good, they being on the mountainsides. The government as a real estate agent differs from the regular realty persons, in that it has no soft springed touring cars, with softer spoken salesmen, to point out the beauties of the sites. If you want them, you have to go get them yourself.

Here are the terms upon which forest lands will be leased:

a. That the permittee observe all regulations of the department of agriculture relating to the national forests;

b. That premises be kept in a neat and orderly condition and that the permittee dispose of refuse and locate outhouses and cesspools as directed by the forest officers and observe such other sanitary requirements as may at any time appear necessary to protect the public health;

c. That improvements be constructed within a reasonable time and in accordance with plans and specifications filed with the forest officers, when required, and approved by them;

d. That all reasonable caution be taken to prevent forest fires;

e. That where the permit is for a business enterprise the permittee shall comply with the requirements of state laws and shall conduct his business in a legal and orderly manner;

f That timber shall be removed only under permit from forest officers.

g. That a fair annual rental be paid for the use of the land occupied;

h. That structures may be removed within a reasonable time after the permit is terminated;

i. That the permit may be transferred with the approval of the officer who granted it, or his successor; that hotels and resorts may be sublet only with the approval of the district forester;

j. That a right of way be reserved for the free ingress and egress of forest officers and other users of national forest lands, as well as for the removal of products of the forest;

k. That on the expiration of the permit the permittee shall be considered the first applicant for a new permit to be granted sub-

Leasing Authorized.

The act of March 4 of this year, authorizes the secretary of agriculture upon such terms as he may deem proper, to allow the occupancy of national forest lands for any period not exceeding thirty years where the lands are to be used for summer homes, hotels, stores, or other structures needed for recreation or public convenience, but no person may be allowed to use more than five acres.

The purpose of the act is to make the national forests more available than hitherto for recreation uses. Prior to its enactment national forest lands could not be occupied for the various purposes mentioned in the new law, but only under permits which were revocable at the discretion of the department.

Users of national forest lands have expressed an unwillingness to make substantial improvements where they are to occupy lands under a permit subject to revocation, at any time. Where, however, inexpensive structures are contemplated no difficulty has been experienced in meeting the wants of users by granting such a permit.

It is expected, therefore, that in the future, as in the past, the needs of persons who do not expect to occupy the land for more than a few years will be met by the ordinary special use permit. But when prospective permittees contemplate the erection of structures involving expenditures valued at a considerable amount, and, therefore, expect to occupy the land for several years, they should be given the right to occupy for a definite period under the new law, if they so desire.

Surveys Planned.

Although there is no information available at the local office of the Wasatch national forest just now, as to where these sites are located, it is planned by W. F. Bruins, forest supervisor, to have surveys made later in the year. Topographical maps will then be made, showing all the available sites and persons may visit the forest office and lease their lots from a plat map.

These sites are not numerous in the Wasatch forest, it was stated today, for the reason that much of the best land—that located along the banks of streams—has been taken up as state selections. Most of it is owned either by the city of Salt Lake or

ject to the conditions under which like permits are then granted;

l. That as to public service enterprises, such as hotels or resorts, the permittee may be required to conform to such regulations respecting rates and services as the department may make should regulations be necessary in the interests of the public;

m. That the permittee agree to such special terms as the conditions surrounding any particular case make necessary.

2

by private individuals. This is true of Big Cottonwood, Little Cottonwood, Parleys, Emigration and City Creek canyons. However, there are a number of excellent sites, one in particular, at the mouth of Silver fork in Big Cottonwood, three miles above Brighton* and a mile and a quarter above the Wasatch nursery.

Land Limited.

The amount of land which any person may be allowed to use is limited to five acres. For ordinary summer home uses it is believed that an area considerably less than this amount will be sufficient to meet the needs of most persons, since such an area will be large enough to include all structures which it is probable will be erected. Ordinaritly, one acre, or even less, would suffice. Great care should be taken to prevent a few persons getting control of the best sites where it would be possible to suitably accommodate many others.

It is not expected that permittees will be placed close together unless there is such a demand for building sites in any particular locality that users must be placed near together in order to meet the reasonable needs of all.

Permittees can be assured that while they are allowed to occupy only a restricted area, nevertheless it will be the policy of the department not to allow other persons to use lands immediately adjoining unless justified by reasonable necessity.

Rates Are Low.

The government is not a high priced landlord, either, as witness this scale of annual rates:

Summer homes, $10 to $75.
Stores, $15 to $100.
Resorts, $15 to $200.
Hotels, $15 to $200.

These rates may be modified when warranted by special conditions. The rates for special use permits issued for indefinite periods may be as low as $5 per annum for summer homes.

District foresters are authorized to grant permits where the permittee does not wish to make expenditures in excess of $1000 nor to obtain a permit for a great period than fifteen years. All other permits will be approved by the forester.

3

Pacific Southwest Region 5: California and Hawaii

Region 5 staff provided the following information and data. Special thanks goes to Bill Sapp, the San Bernardino National Forest archaeologist, for providing the following:

1. "Contextual History For Recreation Residences In The Pacific Southwest Region – November 1987" by Dana E. Supernowicz and Lamonte Richford
2. Pacific Southwest Region, USDA Forest Service "Strategy Evaluation of Recreation Residence Tracts In The National Forests of California From 1906 to 1959" by Heritage Program Region 5, Linda Lux, Judy Rose, Dana Supernowicz, Mike McIntyre, Pam Conners, Jon Brady, Jan Cutts, Joan Bradoff-Kerr, Steve NcNeil, and Susan Lassell
3. "Final Inventory and Evaluation of National Register of History Places Eligibility South Fork Recreation Residence Tract USDA Forest Service, San Bernardino National Forest Pacific Southwest Region" by Lauren Weiss Bricker, Michaela Elizabeth Baker, Anita Anyi Jen, and Bill Sapp
4. Photographs

Again information was used verbatim with minor editing and credit goes to their fine work, courtesy of the Forest Service.

Summer Homes

Recreation residences are a public lands phenomenon essentially peculiar to the Forest Service. Few other federal agencies have established recreation residence programs. The Army Corps of Engineers permitted about 1,400 vacation cottages, primarily in the Midwest, along reservoir projects in the Missouri and Mississippi drainages. At one time, the Bureau of Land Management leased cabin tracts, primarily in California's southern desert country; but it eventually sold those tracts to the lessees. The National Park Service had several summer home tracts, some resulting from a short-lived program at Grand Coulee and Lake Mead National Recreation Area, and others resulting from residences existing prior to park establishments.

In California, the National Park Service reluctantly managed recreation residences at Lassen Volcanic National Park and at Mineral King in Sequoia & Kings Canyon National Parks. At Lassen, the residences existed prior to park authorization. At Sequoia, the residences resulted from incorporation of former Forest Service permits when Mineral King was transferred from Forest Service to National Park Service control.

In the Beginning

In the beginning, controversy over public domain and states' rights over land in the west plagued the government. The popular thought of the day was that "the great frontier was free for the taking," so when Congress started regulating and controlling public land through the General Land Office and forest reserves, the public and states got up in arms.

The creation of forest reserves in 1891, and the subsequent increase in government control, were seen by the west as major infringements on private and states' rights. Western states thought they were witnessing the beginning of a generation of revenue-generating landlordism. What used to be free—grazing and recreation—were now securing revenue through permit fees.

Perhaps the passing of the Term Occupancy Permit Act of 1915 was in part due to the so-called Western States Opposition and the agency trying to appease the public and states by offering them land through tracts and lots and as many opportunities for them to use public domain land through very low permit fees.

The Early Years

The earliest recreation residences in California date to 1906. These early, unplanned, and scattered cabins were later incorporated into surveyed tracts in 1915, following the implementation of the Term Occupancy Permit Act. Over the succeeding year, tracts were added and changed throughout the eighteen southern, central, and northern forests of California.

Southern Forests: Cleveland, San Bernardino, Angeles, and Los Padres

The situation in Southern California was somewhat unique. Because income from timber sales and grazing was low, forest officials saw summer home owners as a means to help subsidize many other administrative activities. Also, with Southern California's rapidly expanding population, the desire for recreation opportunities away from one's permanent residence grew. The main factors that led to the extensive development of summer homes in Southern California were the development of the automobile and an outdoor movement beginning in the early 1900s. In 1914 the forest supervisor of the Angeles National Forest encouraged the construction of a public highway up Santa Ana or San Antonio Canyon to fuel recreational development. After completion of the highway, the district office was flooded with applications. Forest roads made access easy to some tracts, while others, such as Big Santa Anita Canyon and Winter Creed, required packing construction materials in by mule.

The Cleveland National Forest in San Diego County was slower in developing summer homes than the other southern forests, largely because it was farther from metropolitan areas and, therefore, less accessible. Most tracts opened between 1917 and 1924, but filling those tracts took much longer. Yet, this area had the most demand for summer homes nationwide.

Central Forests: Sierra, Stanislaus, Eldorado, Tahoe, Lake Tahoe Basin Management Unit, Inyo, and Sequoia

Summer home use in the central forests evolved from local ranchers taking their families into the mountains after harvest for fishing and hunting trips. Others homesteaded and built summer cabins as part of dairy operations or private hunting lodges from 1906 to 1915 when Congress approved the summer home tract program.

Summer homes developed and spread from main routes of the newly created state and federal highway system. Better highways meant easier access to national forests, particularly from metropolitan areas, such as Stockton and Sacramento. The Lincoln Highway 50, the nation's first transcontinental highway, bisected both the Eldorado and Tahoe National Forests and created two routes over the Sierra Nevada. In the Stanislaus National Forest, improvements along present-day Highway 4 and Highway 108 made the areas around Pinecrest and the Calaveras Big Trees more accessible.

Demand for summer homes grew rapidly in the Lake Tahoe area during the 1920s. Soon after a tract opened, it was filled. Two tracts were located on the lake, one on the north shore and one on the south, and are now privately owned. Most of the other tracts were developed around Echo Lake, Fallen Leaf Lake, along the Upper and Lower Truckee River, along Glen Alpine Creek, and on Lily Lake.

Northern Forests: Mendocino, Plumas, Lassen, Shasta-Trinity, Modoc, Six Rivers, and Klamath

Summer home development in the northern forests of

California generally evolved more slowly than in the southern and central forests. The lack of demand for such homes can be attributed to the remoteness of the northern forests. In the northern forests, such as the Modoc, Klamath, and Six Rivers, fewer tracts were selected, many of which were developed after WWII. Because more restrictions were placed on tract selection after 1940, these tracts were isolated and farther from popular recreations areas. For this reason, permittees tended to spend less money on their improvements than their predecessors had in the 1920s and 1930s. After the 1940s, recreation opportunities such as fishing, hunting, and backpacking took the place of the summer home tracts.

In fact, in 1945 the Forest Service issued a prospectus inviting proposals from private developers for a recreation project in northern Central California, but to no avail. In 1965, the Forest Service tried again and issued a second prospectus and selected Walt Disney Enterprises' proposal. Disney's master plan was for a 300- acre resort in the northern part of the state. The resort would accommodate 8,000 people per day. The plan showed restaurants, gondolas, ski lifts, a conference center, and stores. Unfortunately, the Sierra Club filed a lawsuit and took it to the supreme court. Disney later dropped the project. One can only imagine the billions of dollars the state and county could have benefited from, now knowing how socially and environmentally responsible this company conducts business. The rest is history.

The Rest of the History

In the early years of recreation development, Region 5 had James N. Gibson who worked with other collaborators as the region's recreation specialist. Gibson and his team introduced the use of log rails and log ground barriers along roads and trails in order to keep automobiles and people from destroying nature. They oversaw work on the Angeles and Cleveland National Forests, which included the land now recognized as the San Bernardino National Forest. These recreation specialists also worked on concrete fireplaces and picnic tables in order to define proper recreation areas while protecting the wildlife. In 1917, the region had ranger and architect Dubois designing cabins and ranger structures. Dubois would gladly provide his Forest Service construction plans to summer home permittees with clear and understandable instructions as well as a list of materials required for the building of one of his clean and simple Forest Service structures that could be used as a cabin for the total cost of $250 on materials and $112 for labor at $4 per day.

He emphasized the use of local native materials in order for cabins to blend into the natural surroundings. This was of great help since plywood shacks and tents were no longer allowed and those grandfathered in had to upgrade to the new standards. Dubois also worked with San Bernardino National Forest Supervisor Steven A. Nash-Boulden on developing tracts and fire prevention. Many tracts were located around the Big Bear and Arrow Head areas. Five other tracts were located in the Idyllwild area, Tahquitz being the largest with fifty-nine lots.

In the 1930s, the Forest Service hired the private firm of architects Norman Blanchard and Edward J. Maher to form the Region 5 architectural unit. All their buildings were constructed in 1938. As presented by Grosvenor in the *California Ranger* magazine dated June 16, 1933, Chief of Lands L.A. Barrett said that the new architects would bring a renaissance in Forest Service ranger station architecture:

> The firm has been engaged for the purpose to create an "All-American" style. Old World influences are barred and Uncle Sam's new ranger stations will represent only the best

of the U.S.A. Not only will the lines of our ranger stations be revamped, but the color scheme will be improved. The green roof will be retained, but the French-battleship gray paint . . . will be changed to a brown stain to blend appropriately with the colors of the forest.

Blanchard and Maher described what their architectural style was to be as a "Mother Lodge" style, later known as "California Ranch House."

In 1987, Region 5 reported having 7,063 summer home permits, that number dropped to 6,314 in 1998.

Currently, California has 40 percent of the nation's permits with an estimated 5,870 lots on 253 tracts. In the peak of the program, Region 5 had 15,520 permits, over 70 percent of the nation's total. Region 5 also has 43 summer home tract associations registered as members of the "National Forest Homeowners" organization. They are:

- Almanor Improvement Association in the Lassen Volcanic National Forest
- Barton Flats Cabin Owners Association in the San Bernardino National Forest
- Big Santa Anita Canyon Permittees Association in the Angeles National Forest
- Bridge Tract Cabin Owners Association in the Eldorado National Forest
- Bumble Bee Summer Home Association in the Stanislaus National Forest
- Camp Mcclellan Improvement Association in the Angeles National Forest
- Camp Sierra Improvement Association in the Sierra National Forest

- Casa Loma Recreational Homeowners Association in the Tahoe National Forest
- Crystal Crag Water & Development Association/Lake Mary in the Inyo National Forest
- Eagles Nest in the Lassen National Forest
- East Lakeview Water Association in the San Bernardino National Forest
- East Shore Silver Lake Improvement Association in the Inyo National Forest
- East Silver Lake Improvement Association in the Eldorado National Forest
- Echo Lakes Association in the Eldorado National Forest
- Echo Summit Permittees Association in the Eldorado National Forest
- Falls Tract in the San Bernardino National Forest
- Hume Lake in the Sequoia National Forest
- Huntington Lake in the Sierra National Forest
- Ice House Canyon in the Angeles National Forest
- June Lake Permittees Association in the Inyo National Forest
- Lake Alpine Improvement Association in the Stanislaus National Forest
- Lake Kirkwood Association in the Eldorado National Forest
- Lakeview Water Improvement Tract in the San Bernardino National Forest
- Layman Association in the Plumas National Forest
- Lower Emerald Bay in the Eldorado National Forest
- Metcalf Cabin Owners Association in the San Bernardino National Forest
- Mt. Laguna Improvement Association in the Cleveland National Forest

- Pine Creek Tract Improvement Association in the Cleveland National Forest
- Pinecrest Permittees Association in the Stanislaus National Forest
- Polique Canyon Association in the San Bernardino National Forest
- Prairie Creek Homeowners Association in the Tahoe National Forest
- Salt Creek Summer Homes, Shasta, in the Trinity National Forest
- Santa Ana River Cabin Association in the San Bernardino National Forest
- Santa Lucia Improvement Association in the Los Padres National Forest
- Seven Pines Cabin Owners Association in the Inyo National Forest
- Silver Lake Homeowners Association in the Lassen National Forest
- Snowcrest Heights Improvement Association in the Angeles National Forest
- South Silver Lake Homeowners Association in the Eldorado National Forest
- Spring Creek Tract Association, Inc. in the Eldorado National Forest
- Upper Emerald Bay Cabinowners Association in the Eldorado National Forest
- Upper Truckee Tract Association in the Eldorado National Forest
- Whitney Portal in the Inyo National Forest
- Wrights Lake Summer Home Association in the Eldorado National Forest

All associations and forests are located in California.

Region 5 staff and friends of the forest also provided the following:

1. Copy of original Forest Service letter to future permittee in the Cleveland National Forest, San Juan Summer Home Tract
2. Special Use Application for lot on San Juan Tract

(All courtesy of the Forest Service)

(Sleeper Collection)

UNITED STATES DEPARTMENT OF AGRICULTURE
FOREST SERVICE
CLEVELAND NATIONAL FOREST

L
Uses
Cleveland

Corona, Calif.,
January 30, 1929.

Mr. W.D. Coleman,
924 Cypress Ave.,
Santa Ana, Calif.

Dear Mr. Coleman;

Enclosed please find a sketch of the vacant lots in San Juan Canyon, and a number of application blanks for cabin sites in that Tract. I trust that you will be able to find a desirable lot in that group, as they are all that we have left.

Very truly yours,

J.K. Munhall
J.K.MUNHALL,
District Ranger.

P.S. Send applications to me at Corona.

Our building restrictions call for at least a $500.00 cabin and also a chemical toilet. Plans of building must be sent Forest Supervisor and approved before any work is started.

1929 Forest Service letter to future permittee, Cleveland National Forest, San Juan Summer Home Tract

(Ogden—4-7-24—1,000)

UNITED STATES DEPARTMENT OF AGRICULTURE

FOREST SERVICE

SPECIAL-USE APPLICATION AND REPORT

Application is hereby made for Lot No.................., ... (Name of tract)

for the purpose of maintaining a ....

Signature..

P. O. Address ....

RANGER'S REPORT

1. Acreage.................................... Date....................................

2. Additional description if necessary ....

....

3. If transferred, from whom..

4. Charges ....

5. Recommendations and stipulations ....

....

....

....

Approved.................................... (Date) ....

.... Forest Supervisor

Case closed.................................... (Date) ....for non-payment. Lot released.

.... Forest Supervisor

Special Use Application

Pacific Northwest Region 6: Washington and Oregon

Region 6 staff provided the following information. Special thanks goes to James Sauser for providing data and resources such as *The U.S. Forest Service in the Pacific Northwest, A History* by Gerald W. Williams and "The History of the Recreation Residence Program on the Deschutes National Forest" by Rachel Vora and a copy of the original "Summer Homes in The National Forests Of Oregon and Washington" by Fred W. Cleator. All information was used verbatim with minor editing and credit goes to their fine work. All courtesy of the Forest Service.

The first summer homes in Region 6 were built in 1916 on the west side of the Metolius River across the river from Camp Sherman. Five years later, Fred Cleator, C. J. Buck, and Perry South completed a land use survey of the Metolius River summer home tract. Summer homes, encouraged by the Forest Service to get support from people recreating on the national forests, proved popular. The Washington Office believed that their popularity showed that the national forests, rather than national parks, should be the prime recreation lands for the people.

Mt. Baker Lodge, a summer resort with stunning views of Mt. Shuksan across Sunrise Lake, was constructed in 1927 on the Mt. Baker NF. Winter snow skiing in the mountain area near the lodge was tried in 1929. The lodge burned to the ground in 1931. Region 6, with its beautiful national forest, lakes, and mountains, attracted the second largest number of summer home permittees in the nation. Ranger Cleator created recreation plans and summer home tracts across the region. Frederick William Cleator was trained as a recreation development specialist among other things after Carhart's resignation. Cleator developed guidelines for summer home tracts as well. He surveyed and created sites for tracts and lots. He wrote the "Summer Homes in the National Forest of Oregon and Washington" brochure in 1932. Cleator stated, "we backed the home sites away from the highways, out of the dust . . . plats fit river and shorelines providing isolation, but not too much of it. I found that persons who thought they wanted to get way from everyone soon got too much of being alone. I made it so they could see a light in the distance."

Frederick W. Cleator also established high building and land use standards. Cleator stated, "future needs are planned for, in so far as they can be foreseen, and the land is subdivided into parcels for free camp grounds, picnic parks, and playgrounds; resorts, hotels, and commercial enterprises which foster recreation usage; organization sites and summer homes sites and it is the intention of the Government that permittees shall have all the liberties and privileges that they might enjoy on their own land, provided the rights and liberties of others are not infringed upon." Cleator also developed codes of conduct, "Good Manners in the Forest" and " A Smokers Code," all included in his brochure.

Currently, Region 6 has approximately 2,053 summer home permits on 110 tracts. That's 20 percent of all permits nationwide. This makes Region 6 the second highest in the number of cabins, just behind California.

There are eighteen summer home tract associations registered as members of the National Forest Homeowners organization. They are:

- Anthony Lakes Homeowners Association in the Wallowa-Whitman National Forest, Oregon
- Crescent Lake Homeowners Association in the Deschutes

National Forest, Oregon

- Diamond Lake Homeowners Association in the Umpqua National Forest, Oregon
- Lake Of The Woods in the Fremont-Winema National Forest, Oregon
- Marion Forks Summer Homes in the Willamette National Forest, Oregon
- Metolius River Forest Homeowners Association in the Deschutes National Forest, Oregon
- Odell Lake Homeowners Association in the Deschutes National Forest, Oregon
- Stahlman Summer Home Association in the Rogue River National Forest, Oregon
- Upper Rogue River Cabinowners Association in the Rogue River National Forest, Oregon
- Chinook Pass in the Okanogan-Wenatchee National Forest, Washington
- Govt Mineral Springs Cabin Association in the Gifford Pinchot National Forest, Washington
- Lake Quinault in the Olympic National Forest, Washington
- Lake Wenatchee SummerHomes in the Okanogan-Wenatchee National Forest, Washington
- Rimrock Cabin Owners Assoc. in the Okanogan-Wenatchee National Forest, Washington
- Teanaway Recreational Tract Association in the Okanogan-Wenatchee National Forest, Washington
- White River Recreation Association in the Mt. Baker-Snoqualmie National Forest, Washington

Region 6 staff and friends also provided the following:

1. "Summer Homes in The National Forests of Oregon and Washington"

Brochure on Summer Homes

NATIONAL FORESTS AND HEADQUARTERS

OREGON

Forest	Location	Post Office
Cascade	West-central Oregon	Eugene, Oreg.
Crater	Southern Oregon	Medford, Oreg.
Deschutes	South-central Oregon	Bend, Oreg.
Fremont	Southern Oregon	Lakeview, Oreg.
Malheur	Eastern Oregon	John Day, Oreg.
Mount Hood	Northwestern Oregon	Portland, Oreg.
Ochoco	East-central Oregon	Prineville, Oreg.
Santiam	West-central Oregon	Albany, Oreg.
Siskiyou	Southwestern Oregon and northwestern California.	Grants Pass, Oreg.
Siuslaw	West coast of Oregon	Eugene, Oreg.
Umatilla	Eastern Oregon and Washington	Pendleton, Oreg.
Umpqua	Southwestern Oregon	Roseburg, Oreg.
Wallowa	Northeastern Oregon	Wallowa, Oreg.
Whitman	Eastern Oregon	Baker, Oreg.

WASHINGTON

Forest	Location	Post Office
Chelan	Northern Washington	Okanogan, Wash.
Columbia	Southern Washington	Vancouver, Wash.
Colville	Northeastern Washington	Republic, Wash.
Mount Baker	Northwestern Washington	Bellingham, Wash.
Olympic	Far-western Washington	Olympia, Wash.
Rainier	West-central, Washington	Tacoma, Wash.
Snoqualmie	Northwestern Washington	Seattle, Wash.
Wenatchee	North-central Washington	Wenatchee, Wash.

HOW TO PUT OUT YOUR CAMP FIRE

Stir the coals while soaking them with water. Turn small sticks and drench both sides. Wet the ground thoroughly around the fire. Drown out every spark. Then—
Pour on several more buckets of water!

SUMMER HOMES IN THE NATIONAL FORESTS OF OREGON AND WASHINGTON

By Fred W. Cleator, *Assistant Inspector, Region 6, Forest Service*

CONTENTS

	Page		Page
National forests and headquarters	11	Costs—payments—refunds	8
Introduction	1	Renewals and transfers	9
Recreation plans	1	General regulations	9
Where to find a summer home	2	Good manners in the forest	10
How to get a summer-home permit	3	Helpful suggestions	10
Who is eligible?	4	Smoker's code	11
Buildings and other improvements	4	Sample special-use permit	13
Landscaping	6	National-forest map folders	14
Lot descriptions	7		

INTRODUCTION

The object of this publication is to tell where and how permits may be secured for summer-home sites on the national forests in the north Pacific region. It will answer general questions and also give certain information as to what the summer-home permittee may expect from the Forest Service and what the Forest Service will require of the permittee. It will endeavor also to explain standards of construction and improvement that will safeguard the property of the permittee and the adjoining property of other individuals or of the Government from fire, insanitary conditions, or other hazards. It will tell also how to preserve and promote the scenic and recreational values which are inherent in the national forests.

RECREATION PLANS

In preparing recreation areas or units for the use of the public the ground is first carefully examined, mapped, and classified, and a detailed plan of usage decided upon. Future needs are planned for, in so far as they can be foreseen, and the land subdivided into parcels for free camp grounds, picnic parks, and playgrounds; resorts, hotels, and commercial enterprises which foster recreation usage; organization sites and summer-home sites. The fact that the Government has much timber and forage to harvest also requires that provision be made not to hamper unnecessarily the coordinated use of these resources. The plan seeks to safeguard and protect high recreation and scenic values and sometimes must modify commercial exploitation of other resources. Ranger stations, road-maintenance camps, fish-hatchery sites, and many other administrative tracts which are more or less the by-product of recreational usage must be given a place in the general scheme. (See map p. 12.)

Public camps and picnic parks are generously supplied and selected in naturally safe convenient locations; commercial sites are very conservatively selected to fit actual public need; summer-home sites and clubs are almost always located to afford seclusion—away from dust, noise, and dangerous traffic of highways.

There are hazards from fire, snow slides, and surcharged streams which require certain restrictions of location which may not be readily understood by the applicant.

WHERE TO FIND A SUMMER HOME

There are 22 national forests within the States of Oregon and Washington. Each of these forests has opportunities for supplying the summer-home demand. These forests are located almost entirely

F-218705

A simple and attractive little summer home. Mount Hood National Forest

in mountainous country, which varies from spectacular, rough, and rugged to friendly, gentle types of land.

In the Pacific Northwest there is not only abundant timber and brush for shade and as a setting to frame the summer-home picture, but there is abundance of water in different forms. Water of some kind is practically always a part of the picture and fulfills the greatest need of the vacationist. If the seeker for a mountain summer home desires to be near a lake, a river, a creek, a hot spring, a mineral spring, a cold spring, or a falls, he can be satisfied within reason if he will but inquire.

The angler, the hunter, the hiker, the photographer, the mountain climber, the water-sports lover has but to make inquiries, and in all probability he will find a suitable place.

The Cascade Range, forming the backbone of the two States, furnishes the principle vantage ground for the summer-home seeker. He may, if he wishes, find space in the Olympics of far western Washington or in the Coast Range or the Siskiyous of Oregon, or he may prefer the pine country of the Blue Mountains, or a location in one of the dozen or so minor mountain ranges of the two States.

At the back of this publication is a list of the national forests of the Pacific Northwest, or what is known as the north Pacific region. It gives the location of the forests and the headquarters of the forest supervisors. Maps and information are available from these offices or from those of many forest rangers scattered through the forests.

HOW TO GET A SUMMER-HOME PERMIT

A summer-home permit is a written permission from the Forest Service to build a home for summer use on a certain piece of Government land. The land or building lot is not sold by the Government but is merely leased to the occupant. The recipient of the permit must construct at his own expense the buildings he wants.

F-44201A

A beautiful setting for a summer home. Olympic National Forest

Application for a summer-home permit may be made verbally or in writing. Term-permit applications must be in writing and should state the character and approximate cost of the improvements contemplated. A formal application blank is not needed. The application may be made to a forest ranger or through any Federal forest officer, but preferably to one of the forest supervisors on the abovementioned list. A letter addressed to the forest supervisor at the city indicated will reach him.

Those who want general information may write to the regional forester, Portland, Oreg., who has jurisdiction over all of the national forests in the Pacific Northwest.

Ordinarily the interested person should see the ground before he makes application. Dependence on the judgment of other people is seldom satisfactory, and application made from hearsay may result in much inconvenience. If the summer-home seeker is making a selection on a popular summer-home ground it is well to note second and third choices in the event the first may have been disposed of.

While the Government desires to please the applicant and supply his needs so far as possible, obviously no guaranty can be given to fulfill the wishes of everybody. (See Recreation Plans, p. 1.)

WHO IS ELIGIBLE?

The Forest Service does not discriminate among individuals so long as the permittee obeys the laws and regulations of the United States, the State, and county in which the land is located and the rules of any local governing body, which are determined by a majority of the users in any community or recreation unit.

F-206003

Unusual but good-looking type of construction. Deschutes National Forest

Permits will be issued to a family, a club of two or more individuals or families, or to a large organization, such as the Boy Scouts or Young Womens' Christian Association, or even to a city for a community health camp.

Associations of summer-home and recreation users for handling local community business, water developments, fire protection, sanitation, etc., are welcomed by the Forest Service and are mutually beneficial.

BUILDINGS AND OTHER IMPROVEMENTS

Improvements must not be placed on ground not under specific permit except by special authority.

Construction plans must fully satisfy the Forest Service with regard to fire menace, sanitation, and appearance. It is mainly required with buildings that they be put up in a workmanlike manner with substantial roofs, floors, doors, windows, brick or masonry chimneys, fly-proof toilets and garbage containers; and that the setback of residence and general ensemble be not out of harmony with the neighborhood. Plans and locations of improvements must be approved by the Forest Service before construction begins. This does not mean that buildings must be uniform in character, but it will usually mean that they shall be of a generally accepted rustic style, and attractive in appearance. Glaring colors are not permitted.

In large colonies it may become necessary to install chemical toilets or septic-tank disposal, a piped water system, or other improvements to safeguard life and the health of the community.

Should there exist, or subsequently be organized in a summer-home colony, a cooperative public-service organization composed of a majority of the permittees, holders of individual permits must agree to be subject to all rules and regulations of such association or organization.

If house logs are available and desired for building they may be purchased, and application for cutting should be made to the nearest forest officer. Although the stumpage price of this material is very low, it should be understood that the cost of log construction usually runs considerably higher than frame, except where lumber is inaccessible. Bark left on logs, except cedar, invites insects. Barbed wire should not be used in fence construction.

F-220281

Poor construction—stovepipe too near roof and gable—apt to cause fire

Toilets, chemical or pit, septic tanks, and garbage pits must be built at least 100 feet away from a possible source of drinking-water supply and must be securely screened against insects and animals, and placed out of sight wherever possible. In the natural growth of the community, stricter sanitation measures may be necessary for the safety of the public.

The ordinary summer-home lot is surveyed for one residence only. Any attempt at evasion of this principle, such as construction of an extra building for subrental, may result in cancellation of the permit. It will at least mean increasing the fee proportionately. Summer-home permits are not intended for commercial use. Club and organization permits allow of more buildings.

LANDSCAPING

Trees and brush screens should be given proper consideration. Any tree which is a menace to life and property or impairs the view or

F–218791

Good taste in both house and grounds

shuts off desirable breezes may be cut, but not without prior approval of the forest officer in charge.

F–204559

Rustic porch frame and native stone for chimney

Houses should be well braced in areas of heavy snowfall and should not be built under leaning or dead trees.

In landscaping the lots, it is expected that a natural appearance will be kept. Small trees should not be "limbed up," but only the dead material should be removed.

Groups or clumps of trees and bushes should be encouraged between houses and especially between the house and roads or streams. Occasional vistas or glimpses of the roads or water are desirable and are preferred to a steady open view.

The slashing and removal of trees and brush is permitted only after obtaining the consent of a forest officer.

If summer-home lots are adjacent to public-travel routes, appearance of premises will be the subject of close supervision by the Forest Service. This means that signs, fences, gates, clearing, and other individual improvement efforts must be sufficiently conservative to retain the effect of natural roadside beauty, which is one of the principal aims of the Government in treatment of scenic highways. Signs giving lot numbers or names of permittees are always

F-170120

A clubhouse on the east side of Rainier National Forest

allowable, but conservative standardization may be necessary. Simple rustic signs are suggested.

Advertising signs are not permitted on the national forest except by special authority.

LOT DESCRIPTIONS

A summer-home lot runs from one-fifth to one-half acre, according to roughness of land, timber and brush cover, and other features. It will average from three to five times the size of the ordinary city residence lot, and be all that the ordinary family wishes to care for. It is intended to be so located as to give seclusion and a taste of the wilderness. Lots are practically always surveyed in colonies, which gives that feeling of safety desirable where women and children are so much in the majority.

The lots are surveyed along landscaping principles with the idea of obtaining vistas, building sites, and safety. No attempt is made to square up the lots. They are made to fit the streams, the slopes, the roads, and other features. The corners may be stakes, rocks, or living trees, but they are official surveyors' markings and should be carefully preserved in place to avoid complications.

Lots for large organizations may go up to 10 or 20 acres in size, and may sometimes include large playgrounds or athletic fields. Sometimes it is possible to set off a local park and playground to go with a colony of summer homes. Very often a generous strip of natural park is left between the lots and a lake or stream, to be used and handled by the community.

COSTS—PAYMENTS—REFUNDS

The fee charged for a summer-home permit is between $10 and $25 per year; the average is $15. For permanent family residences

F-224418

A simple, inexpensive, yet attractive, little summer cabin

and for clubs and organizations using larger and more valuable lands the fees may be larger. Character-building organizations, such as the Camp Fire Girls and the Epworth League, are charged a low fee, even though the lands may be very valuable for recreation use.

Exclusive use of land is the basis for these charges. Of the gross national-forest annual receipts, 25 per cent is returned directly to the State for schools and roads, another 10 per cent is spent for construction and maintenance of roads and trails by the Government; the remainder is covered into the United States Treasury to offset costs of forest administration. Some counties levy a special tax on summer homes on Government ground, but it should be understood that they have no authority to levy a tax on the land, which is federally owned.

After initial deposit is made, annual payments become due on January 1 each year. Money not due the Government or paid on account of a permit canceled through no fault of the permittee will be refunded.

RENEWALS AND TRANSFERS

The special-use permit is automatically renewed each year upon payment of the fee and satisfactory compliance with the terms of the permit. A 10-year lease or term permit at increased fee is obtainable unless there are special complications. This is renewable so long as terms are complied with. Either of these forms is satisfactory, and ordinarily there is no advantage in one over the other.

A permit may be transferred, with the approval of the officer by whom issued or his successor, to the purchaser of the improvements on the site. A letter or bill of sale authorizing such a transfer must

A summer home of logs in heavy Douglas fir, Rainier National Forest F-192881

be presented to the forest supervisor before transfer can be completed.

GENERAL REGULATIONS

It is the intention of the Government that permittees shall have all the liberties and privileges that they might enjoy on their own land, provided the rights and liberties of others are not infringed upon. Local summer-home-association rules and regulations obviously must not interfere with Federal or State laws or regulations.

All summer homes and premises are subject to at least one, usually more, official annual inspection by the Forest Service. This is intended as principally advisory, but in case of infraction of fire or sanitation rules, drastic action must occasionally be taken in order to safeguard the general public. Continued negligence or intentional disregard of common-sense rules of safety will subject the permit to cancellation. Local forest officers have standard plans satisfactory for summer-home sanitation and protection which are free for the asking.

Permittees may use dead or down timber on the permit area for firewood so long as the use is confined to family and guests, and so far as it comes within the free-use regulations of the Forest Service. Such material can not be sold.

Keeping of chickens, cattle, sheep, or other farm animals is not permitted unless special authority is obtained.

Improper location of toilet—in too exposed a site and too near the road F–182481

GOOD MANNERS IN THE FOREST

A good sportsman, camper, or tourist when he goes into the national forest—

- First obtains a camp-fire permit.
- Carries a shovel, an ax, and a bucket.
- Follows the smoker's code.
- Appreciates and protects forest signs.
- Puts out his camp fire with water.
- Leaves a clean and sanitary camp.
- Observes the State fish and game laws.
- Cooperates with the forest rangers in reporting and suppressing fires.
- Practices what he preaches.

HELPFUL SUGGESTIONS

Practically all summer-home fires are caused by leaving unattended débris piles, by defective flues, or by wooden sills under fireplaces. A burned house wrecks the surroundings. Valuables and foodstuffs should not be left in summer homes over the winter or unused season.

Springs are intended for public use, and ways to them should be left open.

Fishing is permitted on national forests to those holding a State fishing license. Be a sportsman, and there will always be fish and game for all. It is not good forest manners to clean fish on the shores of lakes and streams; or to throw wash water, cans, and débris where they will be noticed by callers or travelers.

F-220289

Corner of log house at Diamond Lake, Umpqua National Forest

There are strict rules against picking wild flowers and digging up shrubs and plants on or near highways and recreation areas. By exercise of judgment, people may often make use of these wildings to beautify home and garden, but unless moderately done the waste of a great scenic beauty is inevitable. Please do not take wild flowers or shrubs growing within a hundred yards of travel routes.

Spur roads are often intended only for summer routes and may be subject to damage if traveled when wet. Much trouble will be saved by getting proper and prior authority for making any improvements outside the permitted lot boundaries.

SMOKER'S CODE

(For the dry season)

DANGEROUS TO SMOKE WHILE TRAVELING ON FOREST, BRUSH, OR GRASS LANDS

Smoke only—
- While stopping in a safe place clear of all inflammable material, or
- Outside of areas closed to smoking by State law or Federal order, or
- Inside a vehicle on 2-way highways, or
- Above timber line, and

After smoking
- Put out all lighted material.

Federal regulations prohibit smoking on Government-owned lands within the national forests of Oregon and Washington while traveling in timber, brush, or grass areas (except on paved or surfaced highways) from July 1 until the close of the fire season, as declared by the regional forester, but not later than September 30.

The law prohibits throwing away any burning matches or tobacco, or other lighted materials in a forest region.

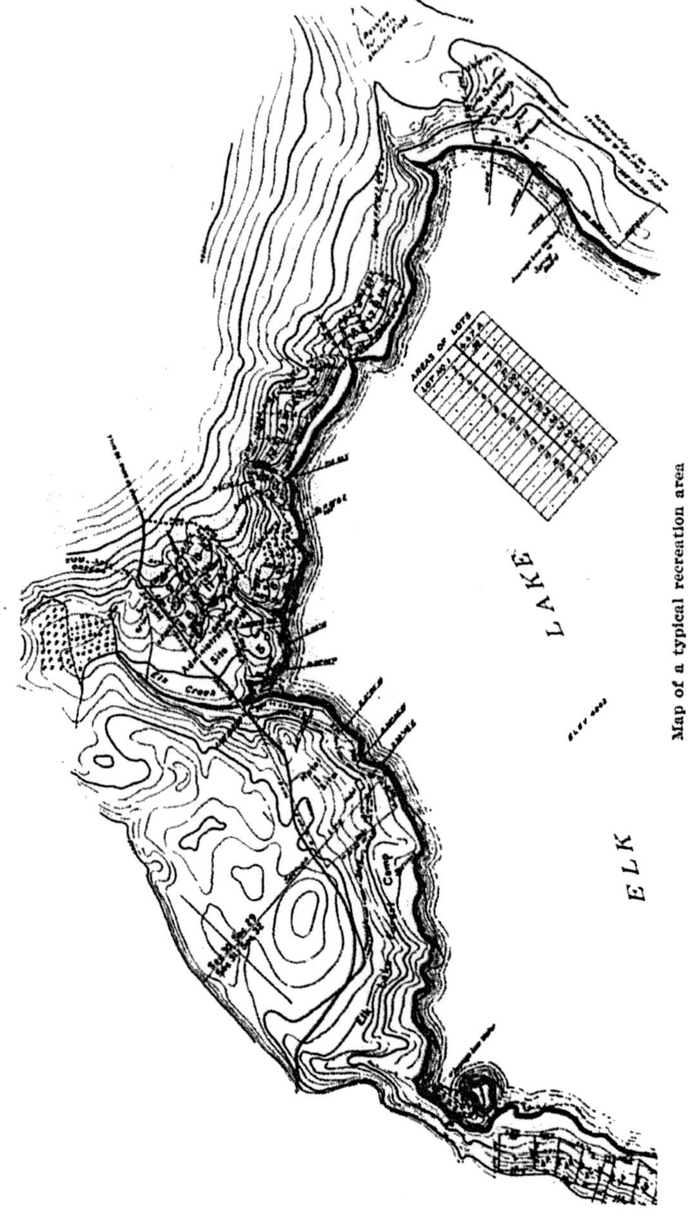

Map of a typical recreation area

SPECIAL-USE PERMIT

(Sample)

(Case designation.)

Permission is hereby granted to____
of____
to use the following-described lands:______________________________________
(Describe the lands to be occupied, if
____
unsurveyed, by metes and bounds, with reference to a road or stream or well-known
____
landmark, right of way by terminal points, direction, and lands occupied.)
____
for the purpose of____
(Briefly but clearly describe the use, giving area of inclosures,
____
length and width of right of way, etc.)
____
subject to the following conditions:

1. The permittee shall pay to the____
Bank of____
(United States depository), to be placed to the credit of the Treasurer of the United States in consideration for this use, the sum of______________________
____dollars ($_____________)
for the period from____, 19____,
to December 31, 19____, and thereafter annually, on January 1,_______________
____dollars ($______________).

2. The permittee shall comply with the regulations of the Department of Agriculture governing the national forest, shall observe all sanitary laws and regulations applicable to the premises, and shall keep the premises in a neat and orderly condition and dispose of all refuse, and locate outhouses and cesspools as required by the forest officers.

3. This permit is subject to all valid claims.

4. The permittee shall take all reasonable precautions to prevent and suppress forest fires.

5. The permittee, if engaged in business, shall conduct same in an orderly manner and in accordance with all requirements of the laws of the State of __________________________________ as well as the laws of the United States.

6. The permittee shall pay the United States for any damage to its property resulting from this use.

7. The permittee shall fully repair all damage, other than ordinary wear and tear, to roads and trails in the national forests caused by the permittee in the exercise of the privilege granted by this permit.

8. Construction work (or occupancy and use) under this permit shall begin within____________months, be completed within_____________years from the date of the permit, and this use shall be actually exercised at least____________ days each year, unless the time is extended or shortened.

9. In case of change of address, permittee shall immediately notify the forest supervisor.

10. The charges for this use may be readjusted whenever necessary to place this permit on a basis consistent with the charge to other permittees for like privileges. A general readjustment will be made at the end of five years from the date of issuance of permit and at the end of each 5-year period thereafter.

11. No national forest timber may be cut or destroyed without first obtaining a permit from the forest supervisor.

12. Upon the abandonment, termination, or revocation of this permit, and in the absence of an agreement to the contrary, the permittee, if all the rental charges due the Government have been paid, may, within a reasonable period, to be determined by the issuing officer, remove all structures which have been placed on the premises by him, except where the material was furnished by the Forest Service, but upon failure to remove the structures within that period they shall become the property of the United States.

13. This permit may be transferred with the approval of the officer by whom it was given or his successor, subject to such conditions as may be imposed at the time of transfer. It shall terminate upon breach of any of the conditions herein or at the discretion of the regional forester or the Forester.

14. The permittee shall provide, whenever requested by the forest officers, a way across the land covered by this permit for the free ingress or egress of forest officers and for users of national forest land and purchasers of national forest products.

15. The permittee shall keep the premises in a clean and sanitary condition and clear and keep same clear of all inflammable material.

16. The permittee shall construct a substantial building of permanent character in accordance with the plans and specifications filed with the forest supervisor and shall install a sanitary system approved by the Forest Service, before using these premises.

17. The proposed location of all buildings must be approved by a forest officer.

18. The permittee shall use this tract for noncommercial purposes only and not to exceed 10 gallons of volatile liquid (which shall be securely stoppered in air-tight containers) shall be kept on these premises outside the tanks of automobiles.

19. Should there now exist, or subsequently be organized, a cooperative public-service organization or association composed of a majority of the special-use permittees located on this tract, the holder of this permit agrees to be subject to all rules and regulations of such association or organization.

20. Flues must be constructed of brick, masonry, or poured concrete with a lining of terra cotta or cement tile. Standard brick or masonry flues constructed by a reliable mason will be accepted. Terra cotta or tin flues are prohibited.

---------------------------- (Date)

---------------------------- (Signature of officer issuing permit)

---------------------------- (Title)

NATIONAL-FOREST MAP FOLDERS

There are available from the forest supervisor or the district ranger detailed map folders for each of the 22 national forests in Oregon and Washington. These are the so-called ranger maps which

Portal entrance to a group of summer-home lots, Mount Hood National Forest

show streams, roads, trails, section and township lines, and other data. On the backs of these maps are data on the resources, use, and improvements of the particular national forest, as well as information on camping places, trail trips, etc. There are also available road map folders for each State and special folders and leaflets on the Oregon Caves, Oregon Skyline Trail, Mount Hood Loop Highway, Mount Baker Highway, and Naches Highway Logs.

U. S. GOVERNMENT PRINTING OFFICE: 1932

Region 7

Region 7 was divided between Regions 8 and 9 in 1965.

Southern Region 8: Texas, Oklahoma, Arkansas, Louisiana, Mississippi, Alabama, Georgia, Florida, South Carolina, North Carolina, Tennessee, Kentucky, and Virginia

Region 8 provided the following information. Special thanks goes to Jim Twaroski, special uses program manager for the USDA Forest Service.

Regions 7, 8, and 9 had sacrificed their land and natural resources from the 1800s to the early 1900s for the growth, expansion, and industrialization of the nation. While the western forests were enjoying growth and recreational development, the eastern regions were re-acquiring land that had been sacrificed and granted into private ownership through the many government homesteading and land grant congressional acts that encouraged westward expansion and agriculture development. All this land that the eastern regions were purchasing had been destroyed through overuse. Regions 7, 8, and 9 now had to focus on reforesting, proper management, and protection of the newly reacquired forests.

As stated by Jim Twaroski, "in regards to summer homes in Region 8, tract development dates from the 1930s to 1960s as much as the Southern Region was derived from lands acquired through the Weeks Act of 1911. There was a large amount of land purchased from private individuals during the 1930s through the 1950s using the authority of this act, so many of the tracts simply were not in Federal ownership." Hence many of the summer homes in the eastern regions were mansions on private land grandfathered in. Twaroski continued with, "if any summer home tracts date from 1915–1924, it would possibly be in those forests designated early in the history of the Forest Service such as the Ocala National Forest in Florida, the National Forests in North Carolina, or the Ozark-St. Francis National Forests in Arkansas."

Currently, Region 8 has 33 tracts with 434 individual permits on eight forests:

- El Yunque National Forest,
- Chattahoochee-Oconee National Forest,
- Cherokee National Forest,
- Daniel Boone National Forest,
- Kistachie National Forest in Florida,
- National Forests in North Carolina, and
- the Ozark-St. Francis National Forest.

Region 8 has one summer home tract association registered as a member of the National Forest Homeowners organization:

- Bear Creek Lake in the Ozark-St. Francis National Forests, Arkansas

Eastern Region 9: Maine, New Hampshire, Vermont, West Virginia, Iowa, Illinois, Indiana, Ohio, Missouri, Michigan, Wisconsin, Minnesota, and Pennsylvania

Region 9 staff provided the following information. Special thanks goes to Laura Hise, recreation residence permit manager, for providing data and all necessary resources and reference. Again, information was used verbatim with minor editing and credit goes to their fine work.

The eastern region of the Forest Service was created in 1965 when Region 7 was divided between regions 8 and 9. In the early years of their history, due to the automobile and train, regions 8 and 9 received a greater influx of new recreationists than any other region. These regions concentrated most of their recreational development efforts almost entirely on providing camping and picnic areas and facilities for winter sports. They perceived no need to develop new facilities since their part of the country was adequately supplied with private resorts. Likewise, there was no summer home development in Region 7 and very little in Region 9. Those surveyed catered to the affluent and politically influential or had been grandfathered in from private lands. In Region 9, the Great Lakes area was known as a summer vacation retreat because of the cool climate, but by 1940, it became a playground for winter sports enthusiasts.

The history of Region 9 was a result of the "two-century war" between the white settlers and the Indian tribes who occupied the land. It is a story of encroachment of white settlements, Indian resistance, wars, and campaigns by the United States Army to repress the Indians and eventually remove them to places farther west through a process of forced treaties. In the end, what was called "the Indian problem" was solved to the satisfaction of the new population by taking the Indians' lands away from them and putting them on small, out-of-the-way reservations, where many of them remain today. Natural resources such as wood, iron, coal, and oil were used to welcome the industrialization of the country into the modern era of steel and world power.

Just like Region 8, most of Region 9's forestland had been transferred into private ownership through the Homestead and Land Grant Acts. Now the depleted land had to be purchased back by the government and given to the Forest Service to manage. Because of this, eastern region national forests are a patchwork of public and private ownership where the government owns about 20 to 50 percent of the land within its boundaries.

Farms, cities, and broad highways now intersect the beautiful land and "seas of trees" in the eastern region. There are 162.4 million acres of forestlands—but major parts of what was once a vast empire of hardwood forest have been replaced through development of cities and towns. Of the remaining forests, only 8.49 million acres are today in national forests. A similar situation exists with the 1.8 million acres of rangeland, mostly in Missouri, where only about 65,000 acres are in national forests. While the west was enjoying recreation and the summer home program, the east was rebuilding its forests, which had been originally used to build a nation.

Currently, Region 9 has 719 summer home permits. It also has one summer home tract association registered as a member of the National Forest Homeowners organization:

- East Mcvity Bay Summer Homes in the Chippewa National Forest, Minnesota

Alaska Region 10: Alaska

Region 10 staff provided the following information, data, and resources such as "Everyone's Cabin in the Woods: Historical Context for Public Recreation Cabins in the Alaska Region 1960–1970" by K. Nicole Lantz and "Forest Service Memories: Past Lives and Times in the United States Forest Service" by Gilbert W. Davies and Florice M. Frank. Again, information was used verbatim with minor editing and credit goes to their fine work.

> Alaska became a United States territory in 1912 and a state on January 3, 1959. Region 10 has summer home cabins, but most fall under The Dingell-Johnson Act, also referred to as the Federal Aid in Sport Fish Restoration Act of 1950, and not the Term Occupancy Permit Act of 1915. Yet as a territory, it did benefit from this congressional act and encouraged its implementation.
>
> In 1915, special use permits for private recreation cabins

and tent platforms were issued. Large-scale construction of hotels was planned but never came to fruition. In 1917, ranger Rudo L. Fromme was sent to Alaska to see about a possible transfer to replace retiring supervisor Bill Weigle. While there, Fromme visited the Tongass and Chugach forests. Both men looked at a housing tract, which happened to be just outside the city limits of Anchorage, but just within the boundary of the national forest. It definitely looked like a special use case. The tract consisted of two double rows of small one- to three-room huts facing each other across a dirt street. There seemed to be about thirty of these batten board buildings laid out in a strict geometric lineup, a good representation of the gridiron tract pattern, as though established by a city or ranger surveyor. One of the cabins had a sign that read, "Irish Rose." Rose came out and asked what the men were doing. Ranger Fromme told her that his wife wanted pictures of houses that would likely appeal to her on their relocation to Alaska. Fromme stated, "It looks to me as though this little abode might ring the bell. This looks like a nice quiet neighborhood." "Phony-baloney," snapped Rose, jerking her neck and slamming down the window. A Forest Service special use permit would not be issued due to the fact that the tract turned out to be a very busy "red light district."

Currently, the Alaska region provides a broad range of recreation opportunities where a visitor will inevitably face inclement weather. Shelter is, at times, much appreciated. There are currently 206 cabins available for nightly rentals to the public. Cabins are available to rent through the National Recreation Reservation Service. Public recreation cabins are maintained at the district level throughout the Alaska region. They are most often located in remote locations on saltwater beaches, inland lakes, rivers, and glacial forelands and have become an integral part of recreation for residents and visitors in Alaska.

From 1897 to 1927, Alaska had one recreation cabin. From 1930 to 1941, seven more were added. Between 1942 and 1959, three more were built. Between 1960 and 1971, ninety-one more cabins were added. Then, from 1972 to 2009, another 104 were built. The first eleven cabins were under the original Term Occupancy Permit Congressional Act of 1915. The rest of the cabins were built under the Dingell-Johnson Act. According to the Forest Service, there are currently only fourteen permits on their records.

Region 10 does not have any tracts, "Irish Rose" is long gone, and all other cabins are now under the ownership of the region and managed by the National Recreation Reservation Service. The following information was provided by Region 10 and comes from "Everyone's Cabin in the Woods: Historic Context for Public Recreation Cabin in the Alaska Region 1960–1970" by K. Nicole Lantz, courtesy of the Forest Service.

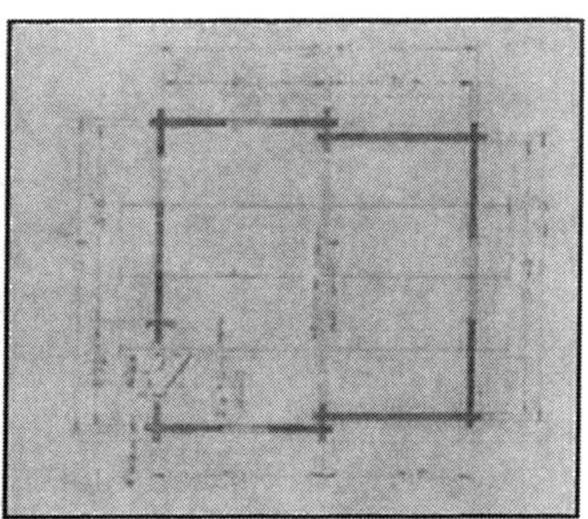

Top: Outlying Cabin Plate 29B 1963: Front elevation detail and floor plan. 2 x 14 x 13½, not including porch. Has a jog in the side wall where the floor cantilevers out over the foundation allowing the front half of the floor plan to be larger than the rear.

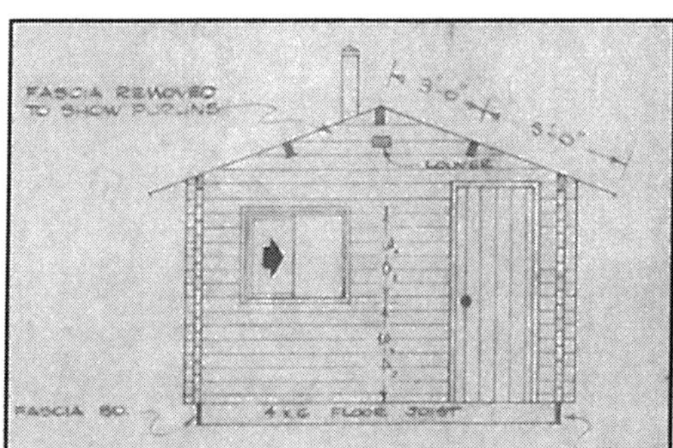

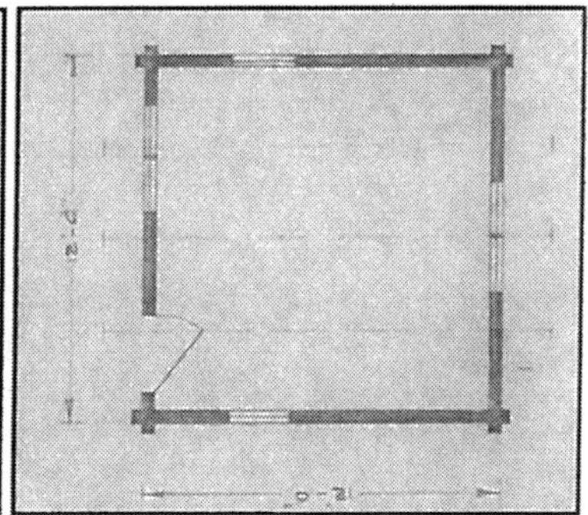

Middle: Outlying Cabin Plate 29B1 1964: Side elevation detail 12 x 12; no porch in design. Floor plan is rectangular with no jog as in the 29B plan.

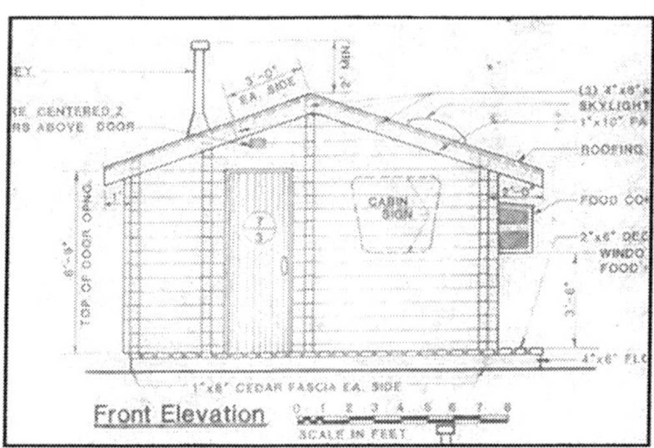

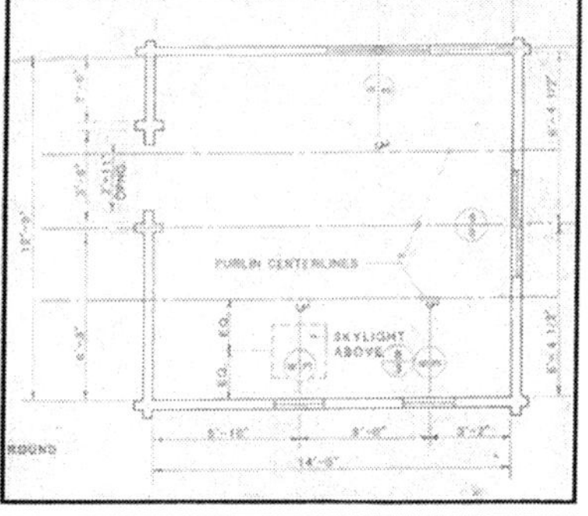

Bottom: Outlying Cabin design number 29-B 1985: Front elevation detail and floor plan 12'9" x 14' detail.

Pan Abode: Comparison of plan types, front façade and floor plan.

Lake Kathleen Cabin, Tongass National Forest, Admiralty National Monument.

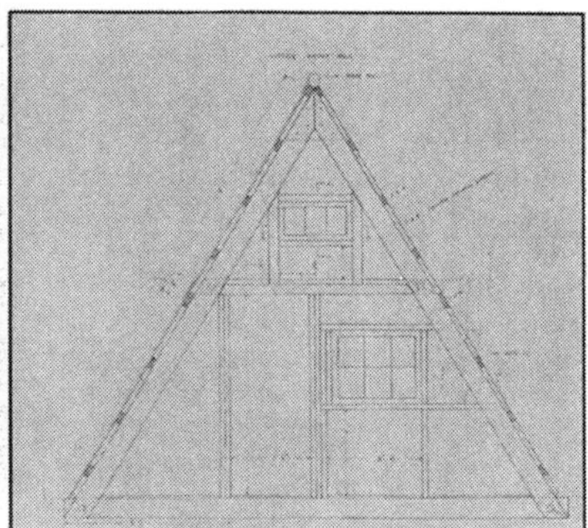

Front façade detail from cabin plan Hunter Cabin 'A' frame: ADFG: 1962.

East Florence Cabin, Tongass National Forest, Admiralty National Monument.

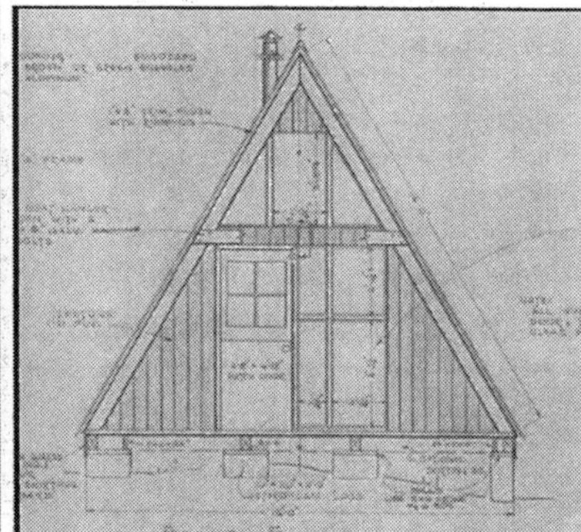

Front façade detail from Outlying Cabin Plate 29L 1963.

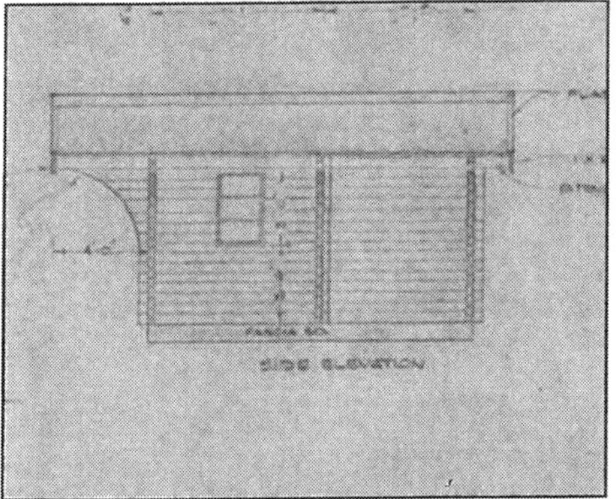

Top: Outlying Cabin Plate 29B 1963
Side elevation detail.
12' x 14' x 13' ½" not including porch.
Has a jog in the side wall where the floor cantilevers out over the foundation allowing the front half of the floor plan to be larger than the rear.
No stovepipe in drawing, however, in other details, it is in the front of the cabin by the front door.

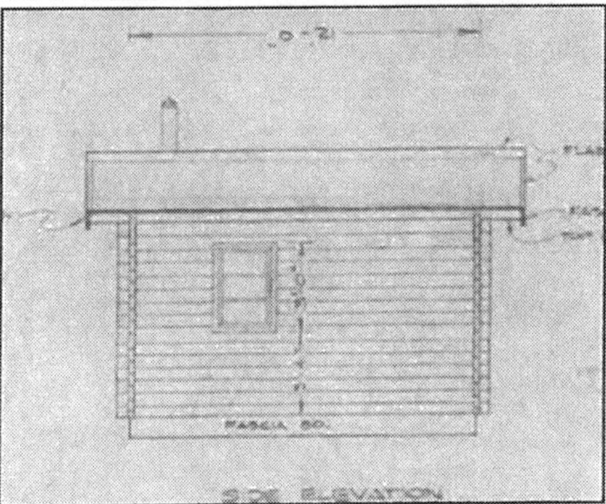

Middle: Outlying Cabin Plate 29B1 1964
Side elevation detail.
12' X 12' no porch in design.
Floor plan is rectangular with no jog as in the 29B plan.
Also stove is in the front of cabin near door.

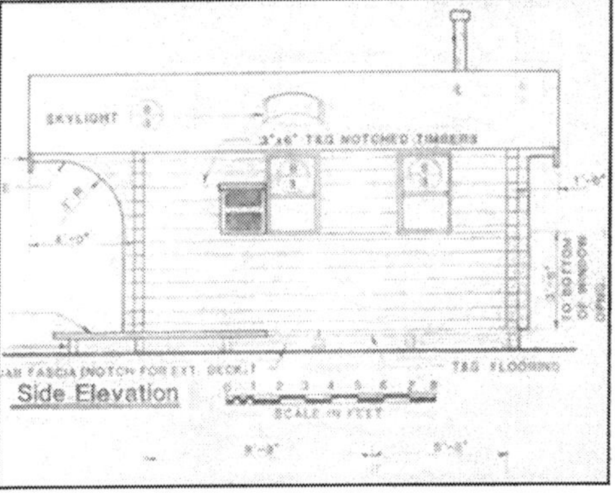

Bottom: Outlying Cabin design number 29-B 1985
Side elevation detail.
12'9" x 14' detail.

Pan Abode: Comparison of plan types, side façade.

A Case Study of the Term Occupancy Permit Act of 1915

Tahquitz Special Use Summer Home Tract

In memory of Mark M. Jones, AIA a long time tract member and leader who passed away at the age of 73 on May 15, 2016, "A Legend taken too soon..."

The following is the history of one tract. The need for an association was recognized in 1923 and officially established in 1927 as the Tahquitz Meadow Home Improvement Association. Their documents were saved and passed down throughout the decades. The earliest document is the Forest Service tract map from 1921. It is a rare thing for an organization to keep documents for ninety years, but a great opportunity and treasure for historians to use as a case study. Hence all information is presented in chronological order and verbatim as found in the collection of original minutes, memos, and correspondence on file as well as interviews. It is by no means a complete work, but serves as an example of what a tract of total strangers went through while establishing itself as a community, dealing with issues such as water, sanitation, and safety. Tahquitz tract is unique in that it participated in the exchange program into private ownership yet continues to follow the original Forest Service Tract guidelines of 1915.

Deep gratitude goes to Mark Jones and Connie Jones Pillsbury, Leigh Humphrey, the Harlowe family, and Judy Schonebaum. After contacting tract members, these five responded and provided guidance and advice that allowed the story of this historic community to be preserved.

Saunders Meadow—A Place without Fences

The story of Saunders Meadow is about perseverance and community service. The tract survived the many challenges it faced in all ten decades by the hard work and leadership of the few volunteers who responded when the need arose. Instead of walking away every time there was a major issue, they faced problems head-on with the same determination that helped develop a nation and conquer the West. As president Kennedy once said, "Why go to the moon? Not because it is easy, but because it is hard." These leaders buckled up and got it done for no other reason than "for the good of the many." This synopsis is dedicated to them. These founders resolved conflict through our democratic process, which, at the end, allowed a new generation of total strangers to enjoy the forest community they established. Hence, it is the hope of the author that these new occupants know and cherish their strong history and work toward its continuous preservation. This is Tahquitz tract.

Saunders Meadow, 1900s, after the loggers removed all the timber, you could actually see Tahquitz Rock in the background.

In the Beginning

On a hot summer day with temperatures rising above 115 degrees, a group of the Cahuilla tribe ventured up to the coolness of the San Jacinto Mountains, establishing a dirt trail that hundreds of years later would be used by logger Anton Scherman and entrepreneur George Hannahs and later still would become Saunders Meadow Road. The Cahuilla created mortar holes on the large stone near Big Cedar Spring and the California black oak trees near the meadow. The women and children dropped a few acorns for the use of future generations while gathering grass for weaving baskets while intentionally spilling water on the ground in gratitude for the bounty that it provided. From a distance, the tribe vaguely saw at the base of the mountain the strange Europeans on horseback who, for some reason, wanted nothing to do with the hot desert and the dry mountains, but preferred coastal terrain and the establishment of missions. Behind them was the view of Tahquitz rock where their god dwelled. The Cahuilla group hunted deer and other smaller animals. They gathered acorns and strawberries among the streams and the water holes. At dusk, they rested in the coolness of the valley breeze. It was just another day on this tranquil land that would become Saunders Meadow.

Days and years passed. Trees grew taller, stronger, and mightier and just as seasons change, people changed.

Loggers

The California black oak trees grew alongside the many massive pines that covered the whole range, welcoming both nature lovers and loggers. In the 1800s, homesteading pioneers roamed the area. Francisco Pico, nephew of the last governor of California under the Mexican flag, grazed cattle in the area and visited the meadow followed by Angelo Domenigoni, who pastured his herd in the same vicinity. Colonel M. S. Hall took advantage of the bounty of trees and, with a lucrative contract with Southern Pacific Railroad, started logging and supplying the much-needed timber for the nation's expansion. Loggers Anton Scherman, Amasa Saunders, and George Hannahs later joined him. Scherman worked a large mill on Saunders Meadow while Saunders bought a mill on Strawberry Creek. He built the first steam mill in order to increase productivity. Hannahs later decided to focus on recreation and opened Camp Idyllwild.

In 1884, Amasa Saunders tried to get the title to the meadow and the little remaining timber left from Scherman's endeavors, but all he got was the name: Saunders Meadow. After a few years of hard work and the realization that logging would soon end, Saunders decided to move his family to San Jacinto in 1886. As they descended the hill, they crossed paths with a little girl named Mildred and her family who were climbing the mountain to visit Strawberry Valley, an act that marked the end of logging and the welcoming of recreation. It took Mildred two whole days in a carriage to reach the valley. The road was so steep and rugged that the family had to help the horses by pushing the carriage up the mountain. They camped across from the current Idyllwild Elementary School at the corner of Saunders Meadow Road and Highway 243. The mode of communication between parties was through mirrors. The group farther up the mountain reflected the sunlight to the party below, indicating a safe ascent. Mildred would eventually marry Sam Minnich in 1910 and honeymoon in the area. They would even lease a lot at Tahquitz Summer Home Tract on Saunders Meadow in 1929.

Amasa Saunders

Anton Scherman

Saunders Meadow, 1800s

Recreation

In1889, John Keen and his wife, Mary, opened Keen House adjacent to Saunders Meadow using Saunders' home as a camp dorm. A few years later, Hannahs, a competitor, used their camp as a bathroom stop for his guests, giving his Wagon and Stage Line horses a short rest before heading to his camp. He used the old Cahuilla dirt trail by the current trash collection site and around the meadow, helping establishing the future Saunders Meadow Road. The Keens eventually moved Keen House a few miles down the hill where it was used by Cecil B. DeMille and his Hollywood actors to film *The Squaw Man* and *The Girl Of The Golden West* in 1914.

As more people visited the reserves, the need for water increased, so, in 1897, Congress passed the Organic Act that would allow the future Forest Service Tahquitz tract to drill for water (in the 1920s). As the numbers of visitors continued to increase, the Forest Reserves started to reclaim railroad and timberland that had not been sold in order to use them for the greater good of the people. As part of the greater good, many reserves were created that eventually lead Congress to approve the Term Occupancy Permit Act in 1915, which led to the creation of the Tahquitz summer home tract on Saunders Meadow. This act allowed people to lease national forest land and build private cabins for summer use and resorts for the enjoyment of the public.

One of the new visitors to the area was Elwood Jones, a young man who moved from Pasadena to a ranch in Hemet. Beginning in 1916, he and his grandparents would visit the mountaintop valley. In the words of his granddaughter, Connie Jones Pillsbury,

> This introduced Elwood, an avid fly fisherman, to Idyllwild, where he enjoyed fishing Strawberry Creek in Domenigoni Flats (now Idyllwild Arts Academy site), where the daily

limit was fifty fish! As an adult, Elwood took two Pasadena neighbors fishing with him when the season opened on the first of May, and the following year he invited friends from work to join them. By 1921, several other friends in the oil and pipe industry expanded the group, which became officially known as The Sons of May First, headed by the gregarious Elwood, with the title of the "Bahoo." They camped out at Domingoni's Flats until 1924, when the ranger told Elwood about a new tract and lots for $15 per year for a ninety-nine-year lease on Saunders Meadow.

Tahquitz Tract 1920–1925

A few years after the passing of the act, in 1920, the Forest Service started to conceptualize many special use summer home tracts in the area. This was the beginning of the Tahquitz summer home tract currently known as Saunders Meadow, Inc., which is one of the oldest associations in the nation and the only one that still follows the original Forest Service guidelines, even after going through a five-year exchange program into private ownership from the late 1960s to early 1970s. This community will celebrate one hundred years in 2020. In 1921 with Tahquitz tract approved, the Forest Service decided to build a lean-to on current 27160 Saunders Meadow Road (then lot 19, current lot 33) for their own use during fire prevention training and as a daily place of rest for working rangers. The location was selected for the view of the meadow and the shade provided by the oak tree. There, rangers continued surveying other tracts to be located in the vicinity with lots designed around the forest's natural features.

That same year, Ranger Joe and his faithful horse approached Elwood Jones and his family who regularly camped in the area from

1921 to 1922. He informed them of the 1915 act and the tracts being surveyed and developed in the vicinity. Joe told Elwood that, "The first lot, number 5 on Tahquitz tract, has been leased." *Excitement builds!* At the end of 1920 and the beginning of 1921, the Forest Service finished surveying the tract on Saunders Meadow with fifty-nine lots. The tract design used by the Forest Service on Tahquitz is both linear (because it follows the contour of the meadow) and ridgeline (because it follows the terrain and trails). It also contains a small grid pattern that almost looks like a neighborhood block with two lanes at a certain section. Mr. Durham was the first to build a cabin on lot 5, which he leased a year before in 1922. Rangers encouraged him to start what they called a special use summer home improvement association in order to address the tract's future safety needs. He thanked them politely and proceeded to dig the first outhouse. His cabin and the Forest Service shacks were the only ones standing. No need for an association!

In 1924, Ranger Joe, now a good family friend, reminded Elwood Jones about the tracts and recommended visiting Tahquitz. Elwood and his family did so and selected lot 6, located near a flowing spring adjacent to the massive granite bolder. Lot 6 was the second lot selected on Granite Spring trail/dirt road. A total of fifty-seven lots remained available. He had to share his elation of having a fishing cabin in a national forest with his compadres.

From 1924 to 1926, friends of Elwood Jones leased lots and built cabins. Archie MacDonald, from the pipe industry, leased lot 9, and in 1925, Ray H. Tecklenborg, another oil business associate, leased lot 8. All three of their cabins were located at the end of what is now Granite Springs Road. The cabins were collectively named Macteckelwood, by using a part of the men's three names: (Mac) Donald, (Teck)lenborg, El(wood), and were used for The Sons of May First's annual fishing trips, which continued on for over fifty years on the first of every May. This band of brothers brought water from Granite Springs above Ray Tecklenborg's cabin to the other cabins and became the leaders in setting up the water system for the rest of the Tahquitz tract. Eventually, in 1979, a safer trail would be created and named Macteckelwood.

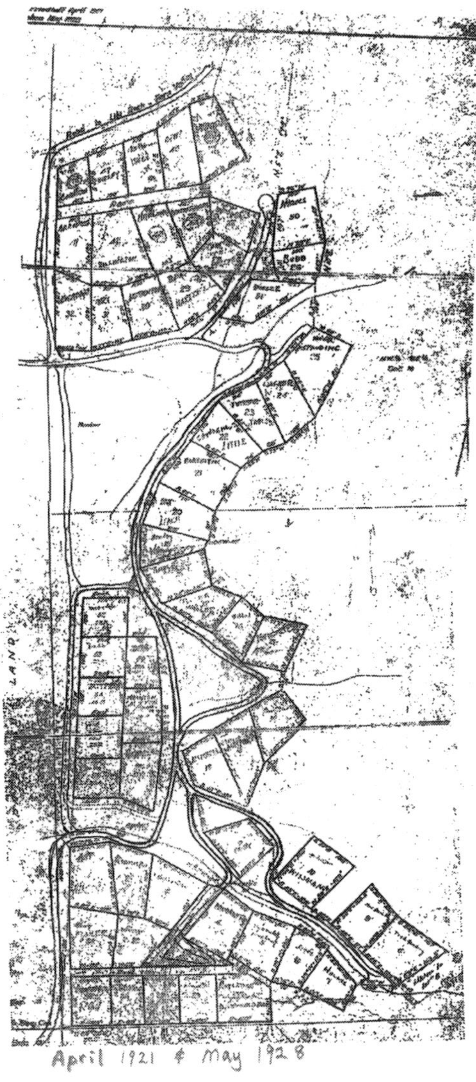

1921–1928 Tahquitz Tract Map

1942

SONS OF MAY FIRST

Bill Ackerman
Bobby Burns
Bill Beck
Jim Barr
Walter Duhig
Hugh Glen
Holly Hdyter
Elmer Jones
Martin Newell
Charlie Napier
Arch MacDonald
Jim MacDonald
Jack Schmid
Jim Simpson
Lew Smith
Charlie Schneider

Hiram Spradling
Roy Stewart
Teck
Lew Wiggins

Dear Brother:

Do you feel poorly these days? Do you get a strange tingling feeling in your feet and a nervous twitching in your legs? Are you depressed yet strangly exhiliarated as though subconsciously you sense some impending pleasurable event? Do you approach your days work with a feeling of distaste and a lack of interest? Have priorities got you down? Does the war news disturb and dissillusion you? Nervous, irritable, tired, run down at the heels, ravelled up the back? Brother, you've got it bad.

BUT I CAN CURE YOU.

Come with me my friend, to the peace? and quiet? of that matchless mountain glen known as Macteckelwood. High on the slopes of Majestic Tahquitz Peak where the babbling brook babbles and babbles and the sun shines all the day sometimes. There we shall quaff the pure nectar of Mother Natures greatest boon to Mankind, Properly diluted of course, and shall indulge our hearts desires in games and levity, friendly communion, peace and rest and never a thought of tin cans permiscously thrown or ice water poured down upon us. The raucous squak of the phonograph shall ne'er disturb us and quartets of voices shall but croon a sweetest lullaby. Hot dog! What's holding you up? So lets get going.

BAHOO

1942 Invitation to Sons of May First by the "Bahoo,"
Elwood M. Jones

1950, Sons of May First gathering at Tecklenborg cabin: Front Row (L-R): Martin Newell, Zeb Terry (Leasing Contractor, ex-big league shortstop), "Tut" Tuttle, unknown. Back Row (L-R): Holly Hayter (Tide Water Associates), Jim Simpson (Kramer & Kramer), Arch MacDonald (owner of MacDonald & Burns, Oil Producers), Jim Barr (District Manager, Pressed Steel Tank Co.), Elwood M. Jones, "Bahoo" (District Manager Stockham Pipe & Fitting Company), Oliver Spradling (Central Tube Company), Jim MacDonald (District manager, Chain Belt company), Ray "Teck" Tecklenborg (The Ray Tecklenborg Tank company), Bobbie Burns (Owner MacDonald & Burns Oil Producers).

Note the portable record player and albums.

Elwood M. Jones is holding and wearing the Golden Elephant. Each year one of the members was awarded the Golden Elephant for notable deeds or misdeeds. There was a great deal of fraternal humor and conviviality in the group.

Cabins

In the words of Connie Jones Pillsbury, "Elwood used lumber from an oil camp at Taft to build a basic 20x40 cabin with an outdoor kitchen porch during the summer of 1925. There was no foundation but only rocks at the corners to hold posts. Stringers ran from each corner of the posts, and then 1x12s were nailed on them, which made up both the outside and inside siding." Due to the Forest Service not having a set improvement amount for construction of summer homes at this time, cabins were usually shacks made of 2x4s and plywood used as temporary shelter for hunting and fishing. Others started leasing the other lots from the Forest Service and building fancier, permanent cabins that were of a rectangular plan with gable or hip roofs. Some had small loft areas used for storage or sleeping. This design style was common in the early years and was the one used for the Forest Service shack on lot 19 (current lot 33), which was leased to Richard G. Haas in 1924. He improved on the original Forest Service structure by using a Coert Dubois side gable cabin plan. Dubois was a ranger and architect who provided summer home plans he had designed for ranger cabins to permittees. The "Rustic Man" Hal Holcomb also worked on the interior of Haas's cabin. Holcomb was a pioneer of rustic American furniture and interiors made out of the local Manzanita tree. Many of the original summer homes still have his built-ins, such as dressers, mirrors, cabinets, doors, loft rafters, and banisters. All cabins at this time had outdoor cooking areas and only used oil or candles for light.

Ray H. Tecklenborg's cabin on lot 8 was referred to as Teck's Tavern. It was a simple structure of 2x4s and plywood that would collapse in the future under the weight of snow. Teck's grandfather was from Germany and worked on a ship at a young age. He hopped off at San Francisco and stayed. Many years later, Teck was given a 50-cent tip by General Patton for delivering a dress to his spinster sister.

In 1925, it was the job of the children to get pails of water from the granite springs for use in the rustic cabins as part of their summer chores. Now with more permittees on the tract, the need for an association was recognized and discussed in order to address the tract's future. Elwood Jones recognized the need for a reliable water source and spearheaded the original water project for the community. He built the "Water Spring Box" to be used by cabin owners during their summer visits. During this time, developers Strong and Dickinson started to build the Idyllwild Golf Club adjacent to the tract under the advice of their hired manager Walter Wood. Power lines reached the new golf club and the meadow, and the community continued to grow.

Great excitement hit the tract and town of Idyllwild with the return of Hollywood to the area. Over seventy films were created on location with big stars roaming the meadow and the Idyllwild Inn.

John B. and Marston Jones with their grandmother Hattie Jones during cabin construction (in the background) in 1925. Grandmother Hattie played Aunt Ri for sixteen years in the Ramona Pageant. Her husband, Horace B. Jones, was a rancher active in the Farm Bureau.

Loraine, Hattie, Marston, Elwood, John, and H.B. Jones (L-R) working on their cabin in 1925.

The Jones Family cabin. The original cabin outdoor cooking porch was changed into a bedroom, and the bedroom was converted to a kitchen. In 1957, the cabin was doubled in size by the addition of a bedroom and deck along the front. Cedar bark lined the windows.

Tecklenborg's cabin during construction. The cabin collapsed under the weight of snow during a harsh winter in the late 1930s or early 40s.

The Creation of Tahquitz Meadow Improvement Association and Further Tract and Water Development, 1926–1930

In 1926, with electricity available, some of the fancier cabins got hooked up. The rest of the permittees continued using candles and kerosene lanterns for light. The tract was busting with excitement, as the new golf clubhouse and pool were set to open in 1927. This helped build the camaraderie between summer home permittees, a bond that was strengthened by the need for water and the unselfish acts of the Jones, MacDonald, and Tecklenborg families. With so many new families at hand, the decision was made to take the advice of the Forest Service rangers and create the Tahquitz Meadow Home Improvement Association in order to work for the betterment, sanitation, and safety of the summer home community. The first Tahquitz Meadow Improvement Association meeting was held on September 21, 1927. The bylaws were written and agreed upon and signed by all. Included with the signing of the bylaws was the yearly fee of one dollar. Most members enthusiastically contributed two dollars to get things going. With this amount set, the first bank account was opened for the Tahquitz Meadow Improvement Association at Farmers & Merchants Bank. (Original checks are at the Idyllwild Area Historical Society.)

In 1927, forty-one of the tract's lots were leased with only eighteen available to the public. Jones, MacDonald, and Tecklenborg led the association to vote in order to request permission from the Forest Service to drill for and/or acquire water rights: the association applied with the United States Forest Service for a special use water permit in order to build a 200-gallon concrete reservoir to be located a few hundred feet southeast of the Tecklenborg cabin (lot 8) with 4,000 feet of pipe to serve the nineteen existing cabins and thirteen future cabins still in the planning stage of building. The first special assessment of $50 was collected per lot in order to work on the new water system. It was a blessing that Jones, MacDonald, and Tecklenborg had backgrounds in oil, drilling, and pipelines! The Forest Service granted the first special use water permit on September 22, 1928, giving them permission to use the springs. With this permit in hand, the first check for the association was written on October 17 for the amount of $40 to Fred Patton for water tunnel contract work. On November 22, the association contacted Steven A. Nash-Boulden of the Forest Service to help collect the remaining outstanding $50 from the few lot permittees who were taking too long to pay. He wrote to the permittees saying, "Please pay the $50 at once . . . your permit will come under consideration as being eligible for cancellation." In a rustic community like this, everyone had to contribute.

At the same time, the Forest Service started requiring $200 in "improvements" to be invested on the construction of cabins in order to prevent further shacks and tents from being used on lots. All original lean-to structures started to be replaced with permanent homes. Ada M. Hogue of San Jacinto leased a lot (lot 11), and her best friend Ruth Pico, granddaughter of Pio Pico—the last California governor under the Mexican flag, leased another lot. Both came to their lots by horseback from San Jacinto and tethered their horses by their future summer homes. Howard O. Hogue, Ada's brother, built their fireplaces as well as eleven of the original cabin fireplaces on the west side of the tract. Howard, a gold miner, inserted unusual rocks and petrified wood into the mortar and around the stones. Ada and Ruth would eventually cook Thanksgiving dinners on old woodstoves and invite the other permittees, helping to create a strong sense of community.

Lem Poats, a local stonemason, worked on the east side of the tract building stone fireplaces. Lem, a relative of Holcomb, built the fireplace and chimney at 27160 Saunders Meadow (lot 19/33) out of local stone. Holcomb built the mantel. Lem also supervised the construction of the future Idyllwild Town Hall. Hal Holcomb was hired at this time to work on the interior of the highly anticipated golf club. He and his crew would walk across Saunders Meadow from the golf course during their lunch break and work on the loft, the railing, and the built-in dresser and mirror at 27160 Saunders Meadow, referred to as the old Forest Service cabin. Fireplaces were very popular but not necessary due to summer use, but they proved valuable during WWII when permittees were allowed to live in their cabins year-round in order to protect the forest while rangers fought in the war.

With more people, the need for more water became a reality. On March 31, 1928, the Forest Service granted another special use permit to Tahquitz for the development of a water system. With this set, Granite Springs was developed above Tecklenborg cabin (lot 8) as a small concrete reservoir. Water flow was found to be marginal and the elevation difference too small to provide adequate pressure. (Evidence of the work can still be seen, along with a surface seep that persists to this day.) During this time, the Forest Service increased its "improvement" amount for cabin construction to $2,000—new permittees were required to spend $2,000 building their new cabins, due the program's popularity. Rangers focused on safety of the construction rather than the actual monetary amount. Many additions and improvements to cabins were noticed such as indoor facilities, kitchens, and eating areas. Porches were screened in and used for summer sleeping, and rooms were added as well.

Ada M. Hogue submitted her hand-drawn cabin plans to the Forest Service for approval before construction was allowed. The first supervisor of the San Bernardino National Forest, Steven A. Nash-Boulden, helped by ranger and architect Dubois, approved and signed off on her plans. At this time, all original shacks were being rebuilt as permanent, solid cabins in the simple, utilitarian American campground style, partly established by Dubois.The Forest Service handed out his blueprints for one- to two-room ranger structures that could easily be modified into a residence, creating the campground look. Dubois started sharing his plans in Tahquitz back in 1920, causing the community to be a place without fences, open, natural, and beautiful.

BY-LAWS

ARTICLE 1. NAME.
The name of this Association shall be the Tahquitz Meadows Improvement Association.

ARTICLE 2, OBJECTS.
The objects and purposes of this Association shall be the mutual protection of the property of members of the Association; the enforcement of all regulations of the Department of Agriculture relating to the National Forests in regard to sanitation, fires, public health and recreation and social life of its members.

ARTICLES 3, MEMBERSHIP.
Sec;1 The regular members of this Association shall be those who occupy and lease land from the U.S. under permits issued by the Government, and who construct thereon summer homes or other structures under the Act of March 4, 1925.
Sec; 2. Associate members shall include all members of the families of regular members, but associate members shall not be entitled to vote unless they hold a proxy and represent a regular member.

ARTICLE 4. OFFICERS.
The officers of the Association shall be a President, Vice President, Secretary-Treasurer and Executive Committee. and they shall hold office for one year or until their successors are elected.

ARTICLE 5, DUTIES OF OFFICERS.
The duties of the officers of this Association shall be those that usually pertain to their respective offices.

ARTICLE 6. EXECUTIVE COMMITTEE.
The Executive Committee shall be composed of the officers of the Association and two other persons elected annually by the Association. The President and any two members of the Executive Committee shall constitute a quorum to do business.

ARTICLE 7, MANAGEMENT.
The general management and business of the Association shall be carried on by the Executive Committee.

ARTICLE 8, DUES.
The regular members of this Association shall pay an initiation fee of one dollar, and said members shall also pay such assessments as the Executive Committee shall deem necessary and advise able to levy from time to time for the purpose of paying the routine expenses of the Association, provided however, that not more than Fifty Dollars may be levied at one time without the vote of the Association.

ARTICLE 9, POWERS OF EXECUTIVE COMMITTEE.
The Executive Committee shall have the power to employ a caretaker to protect and take care of the buildings and property of the members at a reasonable compensation; also to employ such other persons or agents as may be necessary, provided however, that not more than Fifty Dollars may be expended for this purpose without a vote of the Association.

ARTICLE 10, MEETINGS.
The regular annual meeting of the Association shall be held at the home of the President or such other place as he may direct on the first Tuesday in April of each year.
Special meetings may be called by the President when he deems it necessary, and special meetings may be called at any time upon the request of three regular members presented in writing to the President.

ARTICLE 11. AMENDENTS.
These by-laws may be amended at any meeting of the Association by a two-thirds vote of all the members, and that seven members constitute a quorum to do business, provided however, that any matter involving an expenditure of over One Hundred Dollars shall be passed upon by two-thirds of all the members.

ARTICLE 12, PROCEDURE.
Roberts Rulles of order shall be used as guidance in parliamentary procedure.

Original Tahquitz Meadow Improvement Association signed bylaws, articles 1–13

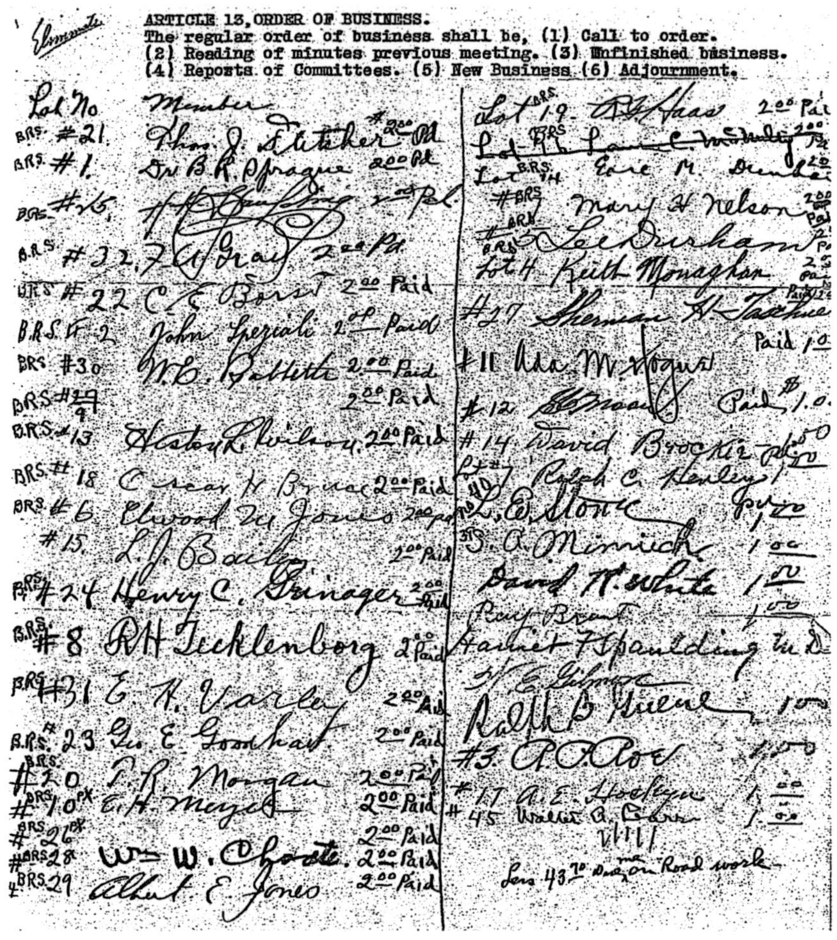

ARTICLE 13, ORDER OF BUSINESS.
The regular order of business shall be, (1) Call to order.
(2) Reading of minutes previous meeting. (3) Unfinished business.
(4) Reports of Committees. (5) New Business (6) Adjournment.

Lot No Member

1920s Tahquitz Meadow Improvement Association
member signatures

Form 603.

UNITED STATES DEPARTMENT OF AGRICULTURE
FOREST SERVICE

SPECIAL USE APPLICATION

HAVE YOU APPLIED FOR, OR BEEN ISSUED, ANY OTHER FOREST SERVICE PERMIT? No

(Case Designation.)

Application is hereby made for permit to use the following described lands: Two springs in S 1/2, SW 1/4, SE 1/4, Sec. 18, T 5 S, R 3 E, S.B.M.

for the purpose of: Domestic use for Tahquitz Group of Special Use residences

Construction of intended improvements will begin within One months and be completed within Six months; the premises will be used at least 365 days each year; the contemplated improvements will cost approximately Fifteen Hundred dollars, and will consist of the following: Describe approximately the improvements will consist of Reservoir, size of pipe and number of homes supplied → concrete cement reservoir of approximately 2000 gallon capacity 500 feet 3 inch black or galv pipe. 350 ft of 1½ inch pipe with 3/4 inch openings for connection to 19 cabins already constructed and 13 cabins to be constructed on balance of lots in the group.

Sept 22-27
(Date of application.)

Sept. 22-1927.

[illegible]
(Signature of applicant.)

By [illegible]
(Address.)

(See reverse side for general conditions under which permits are granted.)

Association Special Use Application for water use, September 22, 1927

Mar. 31, 1928

Form 832
(Revised Feb., 1921)

L
Uses-San Bernardino
Tahquitz Meadows
Improvement Assoc.,
Conduit and reservoir
1/19/28

(Case designation)

SPECIAL USE PERMIT

Permission is hereby granted to Tahquitz Meadows Improvement Association

of Hemet, California

to use the following-described lands: A right of way three feet wide starting from springs near the south line of the Southeast quarter of Sec. 18 T. 5 S., R. 3 E., S. B. M. and running in a northerly direction 4000 f to residence sites in Tahquitz Tract - 500 ft. of 3" pipe and 3500 ft. of 1-1/2" pipe is to be used in construction of line. Cement reservoi with a capacity of 2000 gallons is to be constructed also.

for the purpose of constructing and maintaining thereon a conduit line
(Briefly but clearly describe the use, giving area of inclosures, length and width of right of way, etc.)

subject to the following conditions:

1. The permittee shall pay to the NO CHARGE REG. L-2 (h)------------ Bank of -- (United States Depository), to be placed to the credit of the Treasurer of the United States, in consideration for this use, the sum of -- dollars ($--------) for the period from ------------------------, 19---, to December 31, 19---, and thereafter annually, on January 1, -- dollars ($--------).

2. The permittee shall comply with the regulations of the Department of Agriculture governing the National Forest, shall observe all sanitary laws and regulations applicable to the premises, and shall keep the premises in a neat and orderly condition and dispose of all refuse and locate outhouses and cesspools as required by the Forest officers.

3. This permit is subject to all valid claims.

4. The permittee shall take all reasonable precaution to prevent and suppress forest fires.

Association Special Use Permit, January/March 1928

May 28, 1928.

S.A.Nash-Boulden, Forest Supervisor,
San Bernardino, California.
Dear Sir:-

Re Lot 11 Tahquitz Tract.

In accordance with your regulations I am enclosing you herewith plans in duplicate of the small dwelling I expect to erect on the above numbered lot, together with description of material to be used in the erection of same, for your approval.

A few days ago I went over the lot with your Mr. Cranston and showed him where I had staked the location which I wished the house erected and he approved of the site. He also approved of the work in clearing up the lot for this year.

Kindly let me hear from you as early as possible as I am all ready to place the lumber on the ground and want to get it started.

Thanking you for your usual prompt attention, I am,

Yours very truly,

Residence application letter from Ada M. Hogue

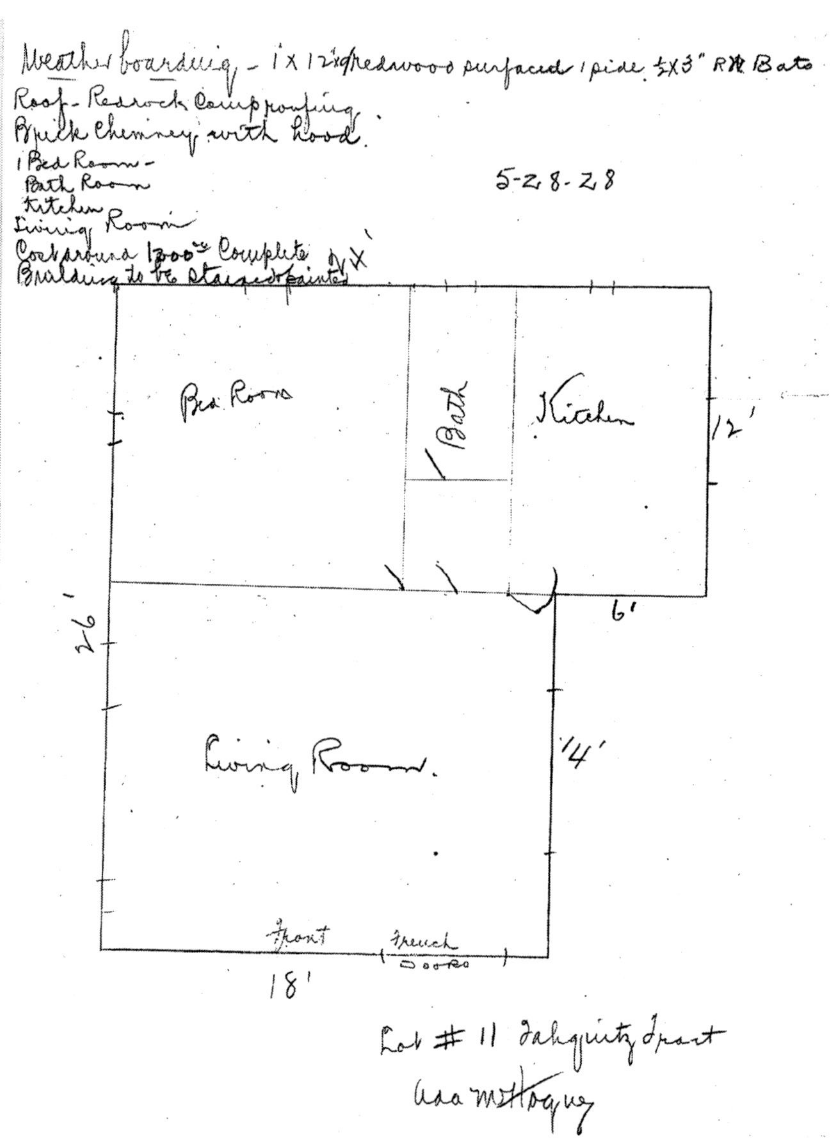

Plans for Hogue cabin

UNITED STATES DEPARTMENT OF AGRICULTURE
FOREST SERVICE
SAN BERNARDINO NATIONAL FOREST

ADDRESS REPLY TO
FOREST SUPERVISOR
AND REFER TO

SAN BERNARDINO, CALIFORNIA

L
Uses-San Bernardino
Hogue, Ada M.
Residence 10/15/27

May 29, 1928

Ada M. Hogue,
326 E. Florida Ave.,
Hemet, Calif.

Dear Madam:

Your letter of May 28 is received.

We have approved the rough sketch of cabin you propose to erect on Lot 11 Tahquitz tract and have kept one for our files.

Very truly yours,
S. A. NASH-BOULDEN, Forest Supervisor,
By ____________, Acting

Encl.

Forest Service letter to Ms. Hogue

Form 8—D-5
(Revised April, 1926)

Uses-San Bernardino
Hogue, Ada M.,
Residence 10/15/27
(Case designation)

UNITED STATES DEPARTMENT OF AGRICULTURE
FOREST SERVICE

SPECIAL USE PERMIT

RESIDENCE

Permit is hereby granted to

Ada M. Hogue,

Hemet, California

to use as a residence site the following-described National Forest lands:
Lot 11 Tahquitz tract

The permittee shall pay to the Treasurer of the United States through a designated Depository Federal Reserve Bank of San Francisco the sum of Fifteen------------dollars ($ 15.00) annually.

Improvements under this permit shall be completed by Oct. 31, 1928 and shall be used by permittee at least 15 days each year, unless the time is extended or shortened by the Forest Supervisor.

The charges for this use may be readjusted whenever necessary to place this permit on a basis consistent with the charge to other permittees for like privileges. A general readjustment may be made at the end of Dec. 31, 1930 (Date) and at the end of each five-year period thereafter.

~~Latrines shall be constructed according to the attached plan, which is made a part of this permit, and shall be located as directed by the forest officer.~~

Plans of proposed residence must be submitted in duplicate to Forest Supervisor for his approval before building is constructed.

22. The waste water from sinks or baths must be piped to a fly-proof cesspool which shall be located as far from a stream or water supply as possible.
23. Except where a regular collection system is in effect, all garbage, tin cans and other refuse must be burned or buried in a spark-proof incinerator and must not be allowed to accumulate. Incinerators must not be left burning unattended.
24. A chemical toilet with tank connected with cesspool satisfactory to the State Board of Health shall be installed and located as directed by a Forest Officer.

Oct. 27, 1927 (Date)

E. E. Nash Boulder — Forest Supervisor.

EEW

This permit is accepted subject to the conditions set out on *both front and back of this space.*

CC SAN JACINTO DIST.

Ada M. Hogue — Permittee.

GOVERNMENT PRINTING OFFICE

SUPERVISOR'S COPY

Special Use Residence Permit for Ms. Hogue

1. The permittee shall comply with the regulations of the Forest Service, Department of Agriculture, and all State laws and regulations applicable to the occupancy and use of the premises.

2. This permit is subject to all prior valid claims.

3. The permittee shall take all reasonable precaution to prevent and suppress forest fires.

4. Under this permit the permittee shall not rent or otherwise commercialize this site. If he wishes to do so, he must obtain a commercial permit from the Forest Supervisor.

5. The permittee shall pay the United States for any damage to its property resulting from this use.

6. No National Forest timber may be cut, mutilated, or destroyed without first obtaining a permit from a forest officer.

7. Upon the abandonment, termination, or revocation of this permit, and in the absence of an agreement to the contrary, the permittee, if all the rental charges due the Government have been paid, may, within a reasonable period to be determined by the issuing officer, remove all structures which have been placed on the premises by him; but upon failure to remove the structures within that period they shall become the property of the United States.

8. This permit may be transferred with the approval of the officer by whom it was given or his successor, subject to such conditions as may be imposed at the time of transfer. It shall terminate upon breach of any of the conditions herein or at the discretion of the District Forester or Forester.

9. The permittee shall provide, whenever requested by the forest officers, a right of way across the land covered by this permit for the Forest Service and for users of National Forest land and purchasers of National Forest products.

10. All buildings must present a neat appearance and be of a permanent nature and be so constructed as not to interfere with the use and enjoyment of adjoining lots. Their proposed location must be approved by a forest officer. Building to be painted or stained

11. To prevent congested conditions, but one residence building shall be constructed upon the tract involved.

12. The permittee shall take all possible precautions to prevent pollution of the waters of all streams in the vicinity of this tract. All cans and other refuse must be burned or buried.

13. Speculation on site or privileges granted by this permit will not be permitted, and approval of transfer will be withheld if it is evident that excessive prices are asked on that account.

14. All flues from ceiling through roof must be of terra-cotta pipe or other fireproof material with stovepipe completely through terra cotta, or of terra-cotta pipe encased in galvanized-iron pipe. ~~Hoods shall be placed over all outlets.~~

15. Should there now exist, or subsequently be organized, a cooperative public-service organization or association composed of a majority of the Special Use permittees located in this tract, the holder of this permit agrees to be subject to all rules and regulations of such association or organization.

16. Disorderly or otherwise objectionable conduct by the permittee or others occupying the premises with his permission, shall, upon proof thereof, be cause for revocation of the permit.

17. The permittee shall clear and keep clear the premises of all inflammable brush, undergrowth, and other débris, but shall burn no débris without consent of a forest officer. This must be done [illegible]

18. In case of change of address, permittee shall immediately notify the Forest Supervisor.

19. In case of violation of the fish and game laws of the State, while in residence on this summer home site, this permit may be revoked.

20. Barbed wire may be used in inclosing the lands occupied under this permit only by special arrangement with the officer issuing the permit.

Residence Permit Regulations

CLUB-LIKE ACTIVITIES—Beautiful scenery, in some, engenders strenuous inclinations—perhaps a moonlight trip to Tahquitz Peak to view at an early hour the refulgence of a desert sunrise on the Palm Springs side, or a quiet jaunt on horseback along one of the many mountain trails in the vicinity. Saddle horses are available, also a swimming pool, golf course, and tennis courts. Indoor amusements include bridge, ping pong, dancing and restful sociability.

RATES AND RESERVATIONS—Reservations must be made at least twenty-four hours in advance since we cater to a limited number of persons. Rates start at $5.00 per day, American plan; rooms only, from $1.50. Special discount is made for weekly and monthly accommodations. Reservations may be made for dinner parties, bridge luncheons, and Peak Trip breakfasts and lunches.

For Reservations and Further Information, Phone

Saunders Meadow Lodge

or write
C. M. SMITH, Box 39
Idyllwild, Riverside County, California

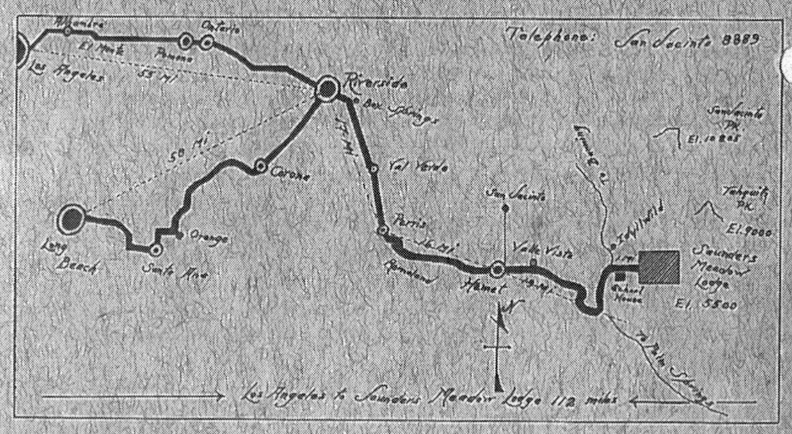

Saunders Meadow Lodge

SOMEWHAT SECLUDED, a bit off the Hemet to Idyllwild highway—this is the locale for a restful interlude at Saunders Meadow Lodge.

Here is a terrane beautiful. The Lodge, elevation 5500 feet, is flanked by a green meadow which is encircled by tall pines and oaks. Across the meadow rises the crags of 9000-foot Tahquitz Peak. Those from abroad have said, "This compares with the mountain scenery in the Old Country".

ACCOMMODATIONS—This is a Lodge, not a Hotel. On inspection, one is impressed by an air of informality and quiet dignity—yet it has been the scene of many gay parties and informal gatherings. These are held in the high gabled lobby and assembly room, which has a maple dance floor large enough for 100 couples. **Upstairs Sleeping Rooms**, with modern conveniences, are sunny, well ventilated, and electrically heated.

MEALS—Prepared for mountain appetites by one with years of ranch and resort cooking experience. But this need not alarm those limited to a regime in respect to diet. Our chef is acquainted with such requirements, also being experienced in the field of practical nursing.

1920s Saunders Meadow Lodge brochure

The Great Depression

Everyone on the tract was excited by the opening of the renamed clubhouse and golf course on Saunders Meadow. Clubhouse furniture and finishes were done by Hal Halcomb and were a big hit. Cabins with his finishes were proud to have the same touch as the golf club! In 1929, all new cabins were assessed $51. One dollar went toward association membership dues and $50 went toward pipes to connect to the water system. The Great Depression hit the nation and slowed development down. *The Idyllwild Town Crier* stated in 1960 that, "the Golf Club went out of business 20 minutes after the 1929 depression." The golf club went into foreclosure in 1930. The same year, Tahquitz Meadow Improvement Association tapped into multiple springs, enlarged tunnels, drilled, and installed a water tank.

At this time, the community was blessed with Sam and Mildred Minnich moving in and building their cabin. They became active and knowledgeable participants in the water system into the late 1960s and early 1970s, when Sam, in his late nineties, finally moved off the hill. He had worked on the recovery team after the great San Francisco earthquake and fire in 1906 and understood the value of a good water system and obtaining the greatest good for the greatest number, as past chief of the Forest Service Gifford had also believed. Tahquitz tract was blessed with many fine men and women.

The cabins built during this era were gable-ell or L plan with cross gable roofs. A few assumed the T shape common through the 1940s. At the end of this period, the Mount San Jacinto Golf Club on Saunders Meadow saw its end. It foreclosed and was sold, then was turned into a military academy summer camp. In 1940, the Desert Sun School moved to the golf course on Saunders Meadow, leasing forty acres for a summer camp. They eventually bought the property in 1944.

Water Repairs, Development, and CCC, 1931–1940s

In 1931, the Forest Service renewed the original water permit, extending it into Section 19 of adjacent forest land. The tract was also granted a second permit for further development and a holding tunnel. All tract members were asked to conserve water and required to invest in a globe cut-off valve to prevent pipes from freezing. Tahquitz also developed a lot map with the Forest Service showing the pipeline from upper tunnel, water spring, and water main to each lot in order to be able to shut off water flow in case of an emergency. Two years later, the association repaired pipes and worked on the water system. (This became a common pattern for many decades to come.)

A year later, in 1932, Forest Service Supervisor J.D. Elliot recommended placing standard family name signs on the forest residence tracts with the names of families on each trail's entrance, which are still in place to this day. The Civilian Conservation Corps entered the scene in 1933; they worked on Saunders Meadow firebreak and dirt trails as well as on Saunders Meadow Road. The CCC boys had lunch under the California oak tree next to the old Forest Service cabin at 27160 Saunders Meadow Road (lot 19/33). During this time, Pinecraft furniture maker C. Selden Belden moved his store to the corner of Saunders Meadow Road and Highway 243. (Currently, his kitchen table and four chairs command $4,000.)

Three years later, in 1938, the Great Winter Storm hit the town of Idyllwild. The snowfall was 360 percent more than normal. Many cabins in the tract were destroyed after their walls were blown out. Ray Tecklenborg's cabin collapsed under the weight of the snow. Other cabin owners added interior beams for support. Due to the storm, the Forest Service district ranger announced a tract inspection for June of 1939. The Forest Service also combined both the 1928 and 1931 water permits into one for sections 18 and 19 of adjacent forest land. This permit was for the purpose of development of springs and piping water to Tahquitz tract reservoirs. With a greater supply of water, on April 16 of 1940, the tract association contacted the Riverside County Department of Public Health in regard to the possibility of replacing outhouses with flushing toilets. In May, the health commissioner responded after inspecting cabins and lots with Forest Service rangers. Their report was titled "Survey of Toilet situation on Tahquitz Tract, San Jacinto Mountain" and contained the following information:

A. Septic tanks with cesspools allowable for lots: 33, 34, 35, 36, 39, 40, 45, 46, 47, 48, 49

B. One septic tank with leaching tile drain allowable (no cesspool), lots 1, 2 (if above house), 3, 4, 5, 6, 7, 8, 9, 10, 11 (if above house), 12, 13, 14, 15, 16, 17, 18, 19 (if above house), 22, 23, 24, 25, 26, 27, 28, 29, 30, 31, 32, 41, 42, 43, 44, 45, 50, 51. Tile must not be less than fifty feet from streambed in all cases, and at any point.

C. Chemical toilet required: lots 20, 21, 52, 53, 54, 55, 56, 57, 58, 59. (They are so low, and so near the meadow, that septic tanks would not provide satisfactory sanitation.)

The county saw this time as an opportunity to regulate building on tracts. They focused on sanitation and required fees for all improvements. Original 1920s cabins were registered for the first time on county records.

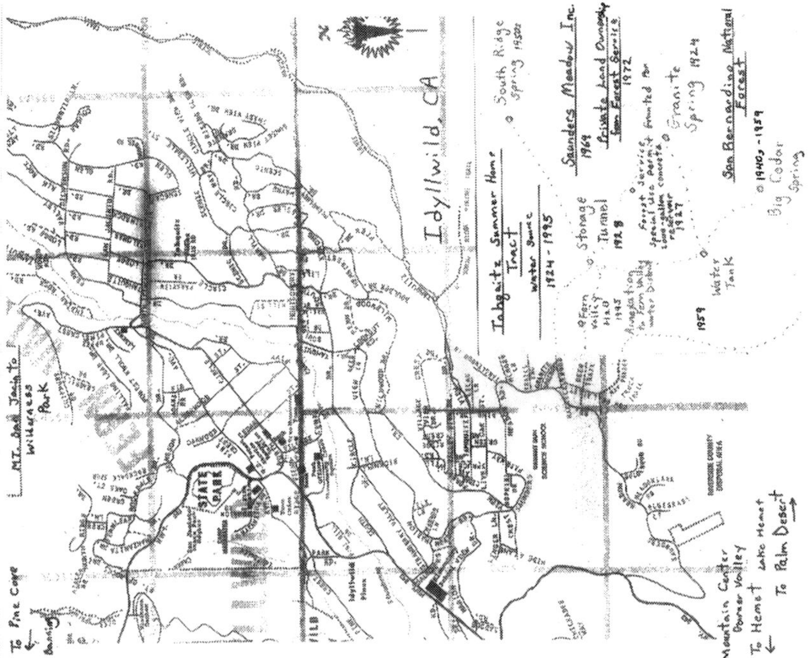

Tahquitz Tract Water History Map, 1924–1995

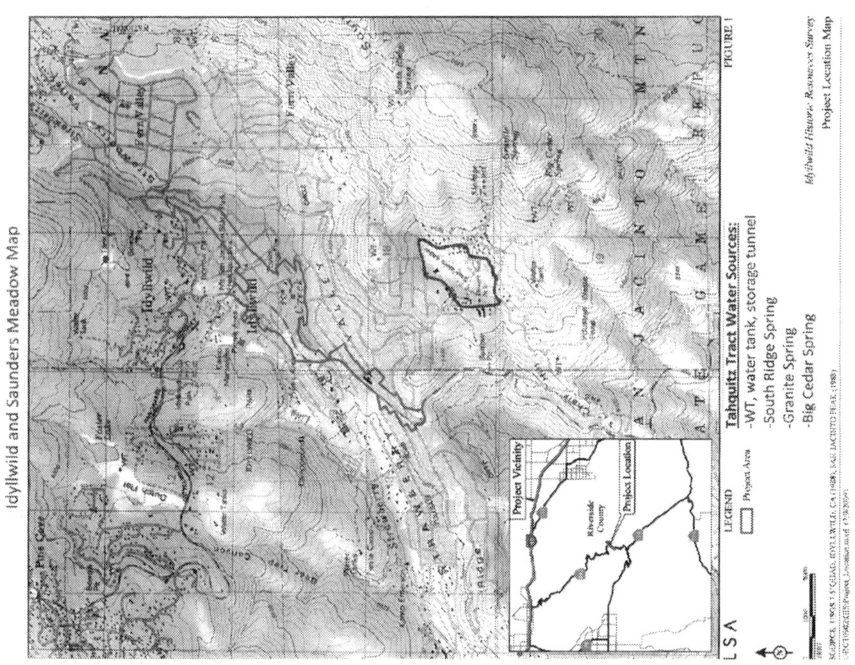

Tahquitz Tract Water Sources

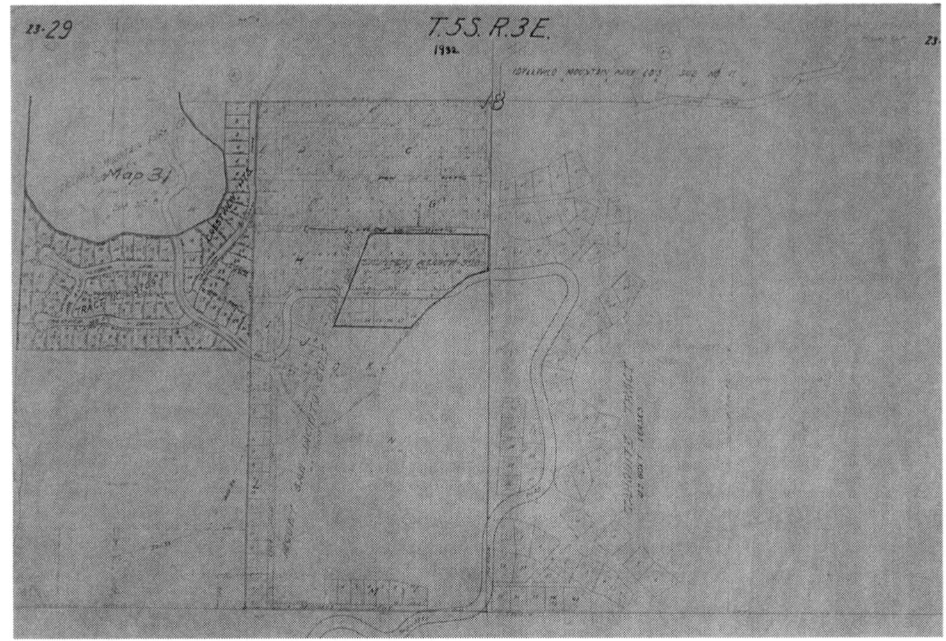

Tahquitz Tract Map, 1932

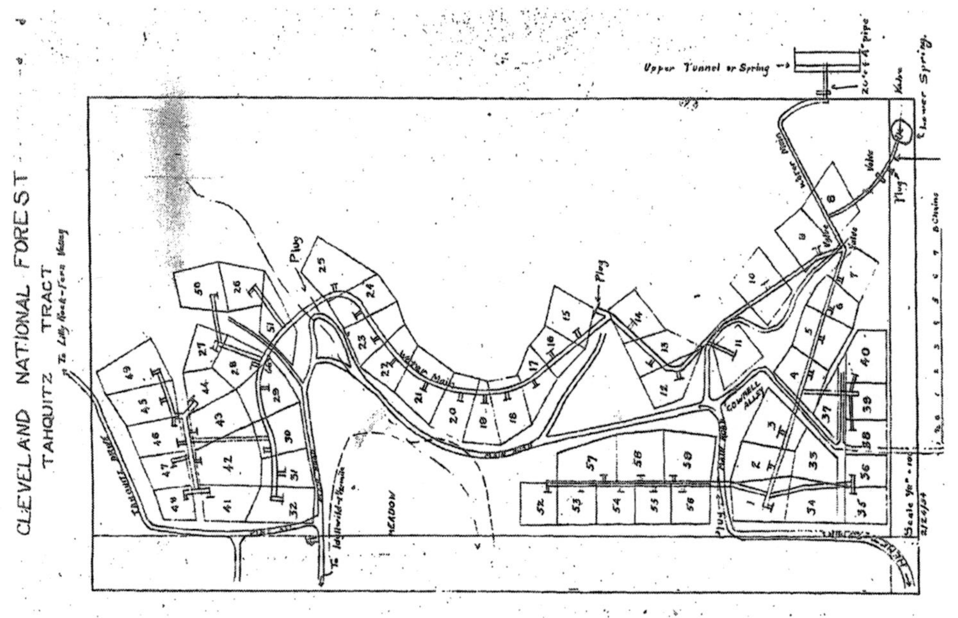

Tract Water System Map, 1934

WWII

WWII slowed recreation development down in national forests but not tracts. Permittees continued to lease and build cabins. Summer home owners were allowed to live full time in the Tahquitz tract. The town of Idyllwild benefited from the money permittees spent on goods year round, and the Forest Service also benefited from their watchful eyes in caring for the forests since most rangers had gone to war. With money being tight during this era, on July 6, permittees questioned being taxed for leasing government-owned lots. Riverside County presented five cases: State vs. Moore, People vs. Shearer, People vs. Frisbie, Bakersfield vs. Kern County, and San Pedro vs. Los Angeles County. The county stated, "These cases all refer and maintain that same principle, namely, that while the property of the government is not subject to taxation, the usufruct right to the property is subject to taxation and this applies not only to government lots and mining claims, but to the possessory interest in other government projects."

On April 2, 1942, after a cabin fire was reported on a tract in the San Bernardino National Forest, the Forest Service shared that, "it was necessary to file a criminal action against permittee who started the fire by throwing hot ashes into tinder dry pine needles. His excuse was, 'I didn't stop to think' . . . The court remarked that 'in this time of emergency it is a vital and patriotic duty of all persons to take every caution to prevent the occurrence of fire . . . we know that we can depend upon everyone's fullest cooperation in this worthwhile cause.'" District Ranger H.D. Jones inspected Tahquitz Tract and set fire safety standards for exteriors of cabins and lots and presented his report: "The most terrifying fire that will ever strike towards the tract will come from the west. Fortunately Saunders Meadow is on this side giving you time which will be precious.

Of 48 cabins inspected only one (#39) is in a safe condition to withstand the threat of fire. All others need a yard cleanup."

Water Conservation, 1942–1964

From 1942 to 1964, the focus was on the development of more springs and dealing with three years of excessively dry heat and the conservation of water. Elwood Jones stressed the importance of developing new water sources: "We must hurry, in order to protect our filing right and prevent additional tracts and campsites behind us being developed and obtaining the use of the water . . ." In response to his plea, a special assessment of $100 was applied to all members for the development of Upper Middle Spring, Big Rock Spring, and two unnamed springs in what is known as the Brimhall area. John Jones, Elwood's son, took over his father's leadership role in the water project, followed by *his* son, Mark Jones, in the future. These men proved to be steady as the river flows, working for the greater good of the community with the loving support of their wives, daughters, and sisters.

With John Jones at the helm, Big Cedar Spring and the surface spring about 2,200 feet above the northeast corner of the tract along the South Ridge trail were tapped and the 84,000-gallon tank was installed. Tecklenborg offered the community board a great deal on the tank. It only cost each member $75 per a special assessment.

With many consecutive years of high heat and dryness, the board was forced to request everyone's participation in the conservation of water. They asked that these four rules be followed:

1. Always turn off intake valve when leaving.
2. Always be sure your drain valve is closed when opening intake valve.
3. Repair all leaks.

4. No watering ferns, trees, and lawns.

On a later date, notices were mailed off once again to all members, "Tract is now entering the third excessively dry year . . . one person can completely empty the tank in days using an ordinary hose for outdoor use . . . Please take the time to return 'Ballot' and select your vote:

1. I accept/pledge to abstain from all outside-of-cabin use of water and prevent all leaks. (OR)
2. I instruct the board to install meters (installation of meters will not yield water which does not exist)."

Member R.O. Durham responded in writing, "What an asinine notice."

During this time, the Harlowes and Brocklehursts joined the tract. Ray Brocklehurst acquired lot 44 and started to build his summer home. (The Jones family first introduced the Brocklehursts to Tahquitz tract on Saunders Meadow many years before.) He built the basement first so that he and his family could live there while the home was being finished. He was a purchasing agent for Standard Oil (Chevron) and an active member and leader of the Tahquitz association. He eventually became president of the association and helped in the land exchange. (His daughter, attorney Leigh B. Humphrey, is still a resident of the tract—in fact, Leigh's children took their first steps in the Jones' cabin. Without her help, and the storage of fifteen large boxes of original documents in her father's honey house, the history of Tahquitz Saunders Meadow Tract would have been lost forever. All original documents are now safely stored in the archive center of the Idyllwild Area Historic Society Museum.)

With such extreme heat, the potential of fire and shortage of water Idyllwild Fire Protection District expressed their concern, "You have a maximum capacity of 60,000-plus gallons; but if one of our pumpers were operating at full capacity, it would pump 30,000 gallons per hour . . . I am therefore requesting that you notify your water users of this critical period now existing . . . I cannot help feeling concerned over the possibility of fires in the area during the critical months of September and October." At this time, the Forest Service required that the Tahquitz association work with the Idyllwild Fire Protection District and Fern Valley Water in the installation of one water hydrant, establishing a good relationship with them that would prove valuable in the future. The Forest Service also strongly recommended that the tract seriously consider the land exchange due to their policies changing as reflected on the new lease permit of twenty years as opposed to the original thirty years and the added "higher use" clause, which gave the Forest Service power to end tracts and use land if deemed necessary for the public's greater benefit. Cabins built during this era were of the irregular plan with shed roofs.

Eminent faculty of the local art school, such as Meredith Wilson and Ansel Adams, were seen hiking the tract behind Lot 19/33. Meredith wrote the great American musical *The Music Man* in Idyllwild, perhaps getting inspiration from the beauty of Saunders Meadow.

UNITED STATES DEPARTMENT OF AGRICULTURE
FOREST SERVICE

U
COOPERATION
Tahquitz Tract

Idyllwild, California
March 13, 1953

Mr. C. A. Borst
Route 3, Box 128
Hemet, California

Dear Mr. Borst:

In reviewing our file on the Tahquitz Tract Association I find that our list of officers is out dated. In order to keep your association apprized of the situation involving all permittees it is necessary that we keep an up to date list.

I would appreciate it very much if you would forward me an up to date list of the mames of the officers and the executive council, and in the future please notify us of any changes in the personnel of the officers. Incidently this conforms with Article V Section 1. of your By - Laws.

Very truly yours,

John C Gilman

John C. Gilman, District Ranger

Remember — Only you can
PREVENT FOREST FIRES!

1953 USDA Forest Service letter

Land Exchange, 1965–1972

During this time, Doris Day built a home adjacent to Saunders Meadow and was seen taking daily walks. Frank Sinatra Jr. was also a local celebrity—he attended Desert School on Saunders Meadow—and Elvis Presley filmed *Kid Galahad* in the area.

In the early 1960s, the Forest Service experienced changes in leadership and policy. San Bernardino National Forest rangers informed permittees about the possibility of land ownership and encouraged tracts to unite and incorporate in order to be able to purchase land desirable to the Forest Service and exchange it for the tract. The only legal method of execution was through a corporation. Karl L. Tameler, district ranger for the Forest Service, stated, "there cannot be an exchange of money, it can only be an exchange of title by law." On October 1, 1965, the tract's land exchange committee created "the resolution." This document was the plan of action the association would take for the acquisition. Member Ralph M. Rutledge who had worked on the resolution with the help of the Forest Service and association attorneys, presented four concepts fundamental to the exchange with five steps in meeting these concepts:

Concepts

1. That the majority of members desire stabilization of their property rights by acquisition of the land.
2. That a few will oppose this step.
3. That if any plan which may be proposed depends upon 100 percent participation, these few can and will prevent any action at all.

4. That these few have legal rights to continue with their present status as permittees for the balance of their twenty-year lease.

Five Steps

1. That we purchase only that portion of the eighty acres actually embraced by our present holdings.
2. That we incorporate with fifty-eight shares of common stock at "no par value" . . . with a minimum purchase of $1,500 of bonds, with voting rights in the new corporation. The "no par," common stock is designed to permit continuance of the corporation as an area-supervisory body to enforce occupancy restrictions, administer the water system, etc., even though at some later date the area is sub-divided into individual ownership.
3. The sale of $87,000 of bonds (fifty-eight lease holders at $1,500 each) will provide the estimated $80,000 of purchase cost for forty acres at $2,000 per acre will leave working capital of $7,000 for improvements, water meters, surveying costs, lawyers' fees, etc.
4. Possible changes on operating costs under this proposal could be: rental income from each leaseholder increased to $100 per year, increase the water charge to $25 per year.
5. Under these proposed changes in operating costs, this would be our annual balance sheet: $7,250.

The above proposal and suggestions were submitted to several permittees who made the following suggested changes:

1. That the full eighty acres be purchased at the start, both to create a "green belt" around our tract and to permit control of type of construction if at some future time it is decided to re-sell. Also, the profits on this might go a long way to

paying for county requirements for possible sub-division to individual ownership.

2. That the letter specify the steps the board must make to meet the requirements of the annual meeting resolution requiring a definite plan for land acquisition. They are:
   a. Secure a statement from lawyer of costs for incorporation and the paper work in making the "exchange" with the Forest Service, filing, etc.
   b. Secure from the Forest Service a definite appraisal of our tract (the full eighty acres or the lesser, possibly forty acres).
   c. Secure from the Forest Service suggestions for possible "exchange."
   d. Secure from a surveyor a statement of costs of surveying either the full eighty acres or the possibly smaller area now occupied.

This resolution was presented at the annual association meeting that was held on Labor Day weekend and voted on. It was accepted by a vote of forty-seven to one.

In 1967, District Ranger Verne Smith met with John Jones and the directors of Tahquitz Meadow Improvement Association to discuss the Forest Service exchange policy. Ranger Smith provided a detailed eleven-page guide on the long and rigorous exchange process. He explained to the members that, "this move is necessary due to the Forest Service wanting to cancel summer home tract permits in the near future and focus on public recreation through the acquisition of more land. Due to the old land grants and homesteading acts, the Forest Service found itself as a patchwork of private and public land interwoven. Now the Service is acquiring private land in order to better define boundaries across the nation as well . . ." He also presented a list of desirable properties in rank of priority. On June 24 and July 18, 1968, Brocklehurst, president of Tahquitz Meadow Improvement Association, communicated with District Ranger Tameler, attorney D. Richard Swan, and a representative from San Bernardino District Forest Service Headquarters who had responsibility in all negotiations: "We need to ascertain the exact provisions necessary to be included in our proposed articles of incorporation to ensure a legal entity qualified to negotiate a land exchange . . . as well as a 'jack-survey' of metes and bounds of the area in the Tahquitz Summer Home Tract which will be considered by you in this exchange . . ."

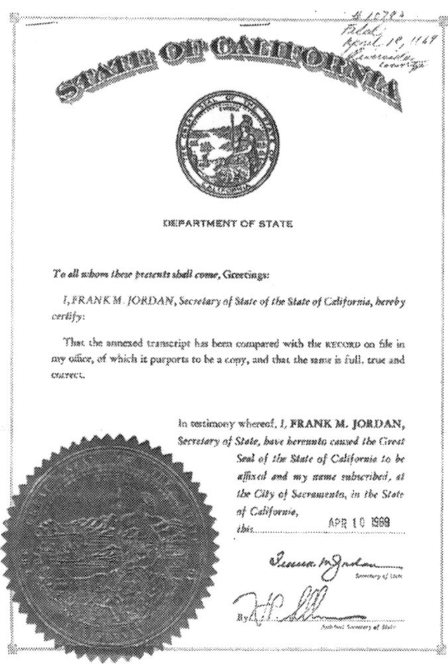

STATE OF CALIFORNIA

DEPARTMENT OF STATE

To all whom these presents shall come, Greetings:

I, FRANK M. JORDAN, Secretary of State of the State of California, hereby certify:

That the annexed transcript has been compared with the RECORD on file in my office, of which it purports to be a copy, and that the same is full, true and correct.

In testimony whereof, I, **FRANK M. JORDAN**, *Secretary of State, have hereunto caused the Great Seal of the State of California to be affixed and my name subscribed, at the City of Sacramento, in the State of California, this* APR 10 1969

Secretary of State

By *Assistant Secretary of State*

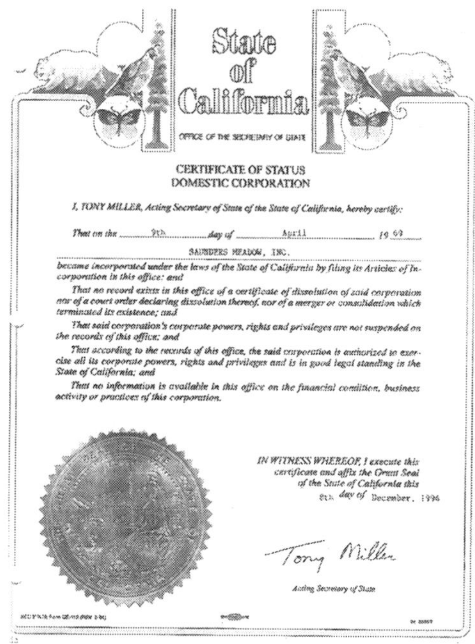

State of California

OFFICE OF THE SECRETARY OF STATE

CERTIFICATE OF STATUS
DOMESTIC CORPORATION

I, TONY MILLER, Acting Secretary of State of the State of California, hereby certify:

That on the 9th *day of* April 19 69

SAUNDERS MEADOW, INC.

became incorporated under the laws of the State of California by filing its Articles of Incorporation in this office; and

That no record exists in this office of a certificate of dissolution of said corporation nor of a court order declaring dissolution thereof, nor of a merger or consolidation which terminated its existence; and

That said corporation's corporate powers, rights and privileges are not suspended on the records of this office; and

That according to the records of this office, the said corporation is authorized to exercise all its corporate powers, rights and privileges and is in good legal standing in the State of California; and

That no information is available in this office on the financial condition, business activity or practices of this corporation.

IN WITNESS WHEREOF, I execute this certificate and affix the Great Seal of the State of California this 9th *day of* December, 1996

Tony Miller

Acting Secretary of State

Certificates of Corporation, 1969

Tract Water Tank, 1969

Around the same time, Brian Minter, lands officer for the Forest Service, stated, "the Service has not completed an exchange where there was not 100% participation of the group . . ." The association assured him that all were on board and things were moving along, "we have hired civil engineers Neste, Brudin, and Steve to work with attorneys Cox, Pendleton, and Swan on the proposal for the subdivision of US Government lease site in Saunders Meadow area as discussed and required with Riverside County Planning Department." On April 9, 1969, articles of incorporation for Saunders Meadow were endorsed and filed in the office of the secretary of state of California, where Secretary Frank M. Jordan "hereunto caused the Great Seal of California to be affixed . . . and

Filed in Riverside County #10780." On April 18, Saunders Meadow, Inc. was officially recognized. The summer home owners could now become shareholders in the corporation for $1,500. Funds would be used to purchase land for the exchange. On June 3, 1969, the new Saunders Meadow, Inc. submitted articles of incorporation and bylaws to the Forest Service for their review. The Forest Service stated that, "pursuant to a land exchange, the articles are satisfactory . . . a land exchange must be made with a legal entity which is authorized to hold and convey real property and this corporation now has these powers . . . with that said, the articles and bylaws are quite unusual and are on a different basis than any we have ever previously encountered. Under these bylaws, title to all the land is to remain in the corporation . . . if the above is the intent of the parties, we have no right to object . . ." With this said, Tahquitz Meadow Improvement Association contacted thirty-seven property owners from the Forest Service list of desirable properties. Two landowners responded with promising deals: John D. Dougherty (manufacturing jeweler) and Theodosius Arvanitis.

Dr. Ralph M. Rutledge had contacted Dougherty a month prior to see if he was willing to sell his land to the association. Eventually, the committee met with Dougherty to explain the exchange program and discuss the value of his land. Talks were going well, so the men ordered a preliminary report of Dougherty's property from Security Title Insurance Company. A month later, after Ranger Tameler deemed the acres prime land, a verbal agreement for $193,500 was made. Attorneys for both parties met at Security Pacific National Bank in Riverside to discuss a number of obstacles. At the meeting, attorney Edwin L. Talmage for Dougherty raised a number of points. Saunders Meadow, Inc. board of directors worked on the concerns and mailed the results to Talmage. Not happy with the changes, Dougherty stated, "Your new proposal cancels out our original understanding and makes an entirely new proposal . . . we will not be proceeding."

At the September 1, 1969, annual association meeting, John Jones reported that, "Daugherty's land was priced too high and the terms that he demanded were unreasonable." Mr. Jones also shared that association attorney Swan had sent Theodosius Arvanitis a form letter in regards to his property (Sections 11 and 13, T6S, RIE, S.B.B&M.), which looked like a much better deal. On November 5, Swan received a letter from realtor Mary G. Lambrou in regards to the Arvanitis property, "the assessed value of the property on tax notice is $40 per acre which is $51,080. Mr. Arvanitis is open to any reasonable offer . . ." On January 3, 1970, the board of directors authorized Brocklehurst to proceed with the possible purchase of Theodosius Arvanitis's land if the land was acceptable to the Forest Service. Mr. Patterson and John Jones worked closely with the Forest Service in the purchase of the two sections of Arvanitis's land. On March 30, Saunders Meadow, Inc. was in escrow, and on April 12 the president of Saunders Meadow, Inc. sent out a letter to all members, "You are aware, of course, that pursuant to the resolution passed by the membership in September, 1968, for two years we have made every effort to purchase privately owned land, acceptable to the Forest Service, to exchange for the parcel we are now leasing. We are pleased to report that we have recently completed an agreement to purchase two sections of land. This property is within the forest area and is listed by the Forest Service as 'desirable with a medium priority.' Mr. Swan, our attorney, has advised us that our corporation, SM, Inc. should make the purchase of this land. To finance transaction, we are hereby assessing each member $1,500, payable no later than June 1."

Escrow was opened and things moved smoothly. On July 10, members were informed that the terms of escrow involving the two sections of land in Bautista Canyon had been met and that the special assessment of $1,500 would be more than sufficient. With the recording of the grant deed of the Arvanitis Bautista Canyon land to Saunders Meadow, Inc. on July 13, the Forest Service added to the good news by informing the members that because the tract had 100 percent participation (out of fifty-seven members, fifty-four participated with the other three selling their cabins) they could proceed with the exchange. On March 16, 1971, after appraising properties, the Forest Service arrived at what they called a fair exchange, in which they recommended trading the summer home tract for the Bautista Canyon land, but that, "such transactions must be reviewed and approved in several offices between here and Washington DC." On September 10, 1971, USDA Forest Service Assistant Forest Lands Officer Robert M. Scharf wrote to Saunders Meadow, Inc. President Ray Brocklehurst, "We have received formal approval of your land exchange offer from our Washington DC office, but two items need to be addressed:

1. Riverside County newspaper must publish a public 'Notice of Land Exchange' for four weeks. After the final publication, a regular Affidavit of Publication must be received in our office.
2. Signed Amendments to the Special Use Permits from all members showing that they will no longer be permittees with the Forest Service, but shareholders/members of Saunders Meadow, Inc."

At this time, the Harlowes and Everharts hired an attorney. They informed the board and the Forest Service that they would not sign the required amendment if the bylaws were not revised in order to keep a clubhouse from being built on the meadow and limiting the board's power. President Brocklehurst, frustrated and concerned, wrote to all members with an update: "the refusal of the

Harlowes, to sign and return the Amendment to Special Use Permit (lease) either to us or the Forest Service has completely blocked all progress towards consummation of the Land Exchange . . . it may jeopardize our entire project . . . and can cost us an additional $422.91 in taxes and $160 per lot for Permit Fees to Forest Service if not signed by March 1, 1972."

All parties met on December 16, 1971, and, in order to accomplish the exchange and not lose out on this once-in-a-lifetime opportunity, the board accepted thirty-five changes to the bylaws. On December 28, Brocklehurst wrote to members: "With considerable relief I report that, as of December 16, the last remaining Amendment to Lease was submitted to the Forest Service. Our Land Exchange is now proceeding normally and should be completed within four to six months . . ." He continued, "On December 21, our secretary Mrs. Wiley, our attorney Mr. Swan, Mr. Johnson and Mr. Scharf of the Forest Service and I met to 'deed' to the Government the Corporation's two sections of land in Bautista Canyon. This is a required step that has a built-in safeguard that assures everyone of return of the land if for any reason the Government chose not to consummate the exchange."

After reading the revised bylaws, the Everharts wrote a letter to all the members of Saunders Meadow stating that, "the Board had changed the bylaws back to give themselves more power . . . be advised that if a certain Board Member had any idea that what he had heard, read, and voted upon would be changed after the note, He Never Would Have Signed the USFS Release Amendment . . . be alerted that SM, Inc. will be a ¼ to ½ million dollar corporation . . ."

The association responded with, "it is obvious that when fifty-eight entities are involved in a complex project such as ours there will be differences of opinion and objectives. Ownership of the property will bring an unending series of problems that we have not had in the past. We are entering a training period when we learn how to get along with each other and develop dependable leaders. Everyone is penalized, we will find, if we can't work together in harmony." Hill, Farrer, and Burrill Law Firm wrote to attorney Swan, "We received the bylaws and have reviewed them with the Everharts. It appears that the revised do not accurately reflect the understanding reached at the December 16th meeting." The Law Office of Cox, Swan, and Carpenter responded, "I am satisfied that the Board of Directors has been entirely fair with your clients and that at no time deceived or intentionally misled any prospective shareholder. The bylaws are without question fair and workable. I appreciate your efforts in aiding to streamline the bylaws and I hope that we have been able to accommodate a sufficient number of your suggestions to satisfy your clients in order that further controversy can be avoided."

On May 5, 1972, the Forest Service granted the deed for the eighty acres of the Tahquitz Summer Home Tract to Saunders Meadow, Inc. It had taken five years for the Tahquitz Meadow Home Improvement Association to incorporate and find affordable land acceptable to the Forest Service. After many rejections, the Forest Service finally agreed upon the 1,277 acres of Bautista Canyon land near Hemet for the exchange. On the 28th of May, the Saunders Meadow, Inc. members and stockholders celebrated with a great outdoor picnic in the glade at the upper end of Tanglewood Lane. All members received a copy of the fair and appropriate bylaws.

Lawsuit, Appointed Receiver, and Subdivision, 1972–1980

The Mitchell family wrote to President Brocklehurst:

> Pleasant memories of our recent barbeque celebrating our ownership of land will remain for a long time. The Mitchells are grateful for the efforts of all who made it possible. Our

family . . . looks forward to many years of use of our cabin. It is most important to them. It is disquieting to have a certain amount of controversy appear early in our history. We earnestly and sincerely hope that it can be minimized in the future. We all have a complex job ahead of us that demands fairness, tolerance, and cooperation from each and everyone. It will not be possible to make everyone completely satisfied. Compromises are necessary and unavoidable. I earnestly hope that every effort will be made to keep all members posted, as many troubles are the results of misinformation or lack of information. The proposed bylaws that were sent out contained some features that I believe could be changed to the advantage of all. We do not want our Board of Directors to become all-powerful, nor do I think that they want too great a responsibility. Checks and balances are a part of our heritage. On the other hand, I have no sympathy for any small group that battles over unimportant features and does not make every reasonable effort to achieve friendly teamwork in all of our undertakings. Leland Yost and I were concerned enough about the quality of our proposed bylaws that we got some legal advice designed to spotlight the places where some improvements could be made, we hope!

6-2-72

It's all theirs now!

Celebrating the successful culmination of five years of effort to acquire private ownership of the land on which most of them have owned cabins for decades, members of Saunders Meadow, Inc., with their families and guests, gathered on Sunday, May 26, for a gala barbecue dinner. Festively decorated tables for 150 were set up in the shady glen at the upper end of Tanglewood Lane. The outdoor party was planned and organized by Mrs. Paul Woosley, Mrs. Harry Bubb and Mrs. Jack Cody.

At the entrance of the glen, guests walked under a huge overhead banner on which was painted "This Land Is Our Land!" Hanging conspicuously, from an old cedar beside the heavily laden serving table was the proudly framed original of the deed, granted by the National Forest Service on May 5, 1972. Greeting the assemblage were the Directors who were mainly responsible for the success of the land exchange: president Ray Brockiehurst, secretary-treasurer Cosette Wiley, Wayne Ricker, Leonard Harlowe and O. W. Miller.

Many of the cabins, all in the former Tahquitz Summer Home Tract, were built in the 1920's. Some still belong to the original owners or their descendants. Among the "oldtimers" present were Mr. Sam Minnich, Mr. and Mrs. Eberhard, Mrs. Hollis, Mrs. Helen Bell, Mr. and Mrs. Leland Yost, Mr. "Tech" Techlenborg and Mr. Jack Cody, who inherited his cabin from his aunt, Mrs. Ada Hogue, with Mrs. Cody.

Computers in the arts

Cabin owners acquire land

As a result of five years of negotiation, 80 acres of Section 18 in the San Bernardino National Forest were deeded by the U.S. Forest Service to Saunders Meadow, Inc., on May 5, for two sections of land in Bautista Canyon near Hemet. The 80 acres have been known for decades as the Tahquitz Summer Home Tract.

During the 1920's, this tract was made available for lease to individuals for construction of cabins for summer-home use. Over the years, a total of 57 cabins have been built. Prior to 1930, the cabin owners formed the Tahquitz Meadow Improvement Association, members of which annually elect five directors who assess and allocate funds for improvement and maintenance of the area.

In 1967 Verne Smith, then District Ranger, met with the directors to explain the U.S. Forest Service policy which encourages summer home tract cabin owners to acquire ownership of the tracts through exchange of equivalent land. Early in 1968, the directors began a search for land acceptable to the Forest Service. After nearly five years, the Bautista Canyon land was purchased and a mutually acceptable land exchange was worked out.

Association members responsible for the project's success were W. Ray Brockiehurst, president; Cosette Wiley, secretary-treasurer; directors Leonard Harlowe, Willis Leach, William Miller, M. W. Patterson and Wayne Ricker, assisted by John Jones and Ralph Rutledge. Forest Service personnel involved were Karl Tamsler, Bill Johnson and Murry Taylor, all of Idyllwild, and Bob Scharf of San Bernardino.

Saunders Meadow, Inc., is a stock cooperative in which each cabin owner is entitled to own one share of stock and to continue in the use of that portion of the tract which he originally leased from the Forest Service and on which his cabin is located. The cooperative plans to continue operating under the same policies and rules as were established by the Forest Service. The number of building sites is restricted to the 57 now existing.

Anticipating growth, the Fern Valley Water District currently is erecting this 750,000-gallon water storage tank alongside two other storage tanks at the entrance to Humber Park. Sixty-five feet in diameter, it is the largest tank that could be accommodated at the location.

Town Crier article, Tract acquires land

As a county requirement, civil engineers Neste, Brudin, and

Stone met with Riverside County officials to review the matter of converting the Saunders Meadow government leases into a subdivision of fifty-seven parcels or a planned unit development or a non-statutory condominium. They reported, "Your association is not in a position to proceed with the preliminary engineering and planning work necessary to allow you to subdivide the property. The following steps are required:

A. Topographic map and aerial photos $1,000

B. Tentative Subdivision Map $1,600

C. Conditional Use Permit Application $400

D. Variance Application $150

E. Permit to serve water to the project."

The boards of directors of Saunders Meadow, Inc. and Tahquitz Meadow Improvement Association met on June 12, 1972, for the purpose of considering the outline of engineering work and estimated costs as set forth by Neste, Brudin, and Stone. After a short review, the boards directed Neste to proceed with the work. The association provided assistance during the surveying and helped in locating property stakes, springs, and tank. Water was also tested for presentation to the department of health. Now that the community was on private land, they had to abide by many county, state, and federal regulations. It was a time of much learning and many challenges. Due to the fact that the community was rustic in nature and wanted to remain so, Neste, Brudin, and Stone had to work with the Riverside County Planning Commission in providing supplemental information on the standard application forms for Variance and Conditional Use on Tract 5418. The following supplemented the standard application:

1. The existing use of the total seventy-six acres is mountain-resort, single family, residential. There is absolutely NO change in this use proposal, nor will additional use be made.

2. The present owners, who are the users, of the property wish only to preserve the area AS IS and to assure that their property rights are clearly defined on a recorded map . . . A recorded lot line will avoid future neighborhood disputes and give definite property rights which may be passed to heirs or others.
3. All of the individual owners and users are in agreement today to the proposed lot lines shown on the plot. This total agreement may not last forever, so now is an appropriate time to record such lines.
4. We are asking for a variance from the minimum building set back from interior drives of the required ten feet in the following cases: lot 33, six feet; lot 34, three feet. In both cases, the existing drive has been there for years and is not used by the general public, and serves only three parcels. All users are in agreement that no problems exists, but to relocate the driveway would necessitate removal of trees—Which Is Not Acceptable
5. In regards to Section 18.5 (4), it is specifically desired that the existing dirt roads be left AS IS and that no realignment or improvement be made. This is a rustic-residential mountain area . . . the rustic atmosphere is EXACTLY what attracted the owners many years ago to this area.
6. In regards to Section 18.5 (10), there is no recreational area today, nor is one contemplated. Therefore, there is no need for five-foot wide paved pedestrian walkways.
7. In regards to Section 18.5 (12) Parking, all automobiles have been adequately parked in the area for years. There are, however, no marked-out spaces with numbers . . . when the ground is frozen, parking is done wherever it is safe. When the ground is wet, parking is done where no damage

> will occur to soft ground . . . In any manner, parking is an individual thing in the area, with more than two and a half places available for each residential unit.

Another issue that Saunders Meadow, Inc. had to deal with was the escrow process in the sale of its cabins since the corporation was the sole owner of all the land. On July 25, 1972, attorney Swan wrote to Saunders Meadow, Inc.,

> I met with Security Title Insurance Company to discuss their role, if any, as an escrow and/or title company in assisting with the present and future of the rights of each individual owner of stock . . . the following conclusions were reached:
>
> A. The only map, which should be recorded, is a perimeter map . . .
>
> B. No title insurance will issue with respect to these transactions. SM, Inc. will have to advise prospective buyers of the status of the corporate assets.
>
> C. The escrow, if any, would be handled in the manner of a bulk sale escrow and not as a real property escrow. Very few banks and/or trust companies now handle bulk sales . . .
>
> D. We will not obtain a separate assessment for each individual house . . . County Tax Assessor and Collector will issue one tax bill . . .
>
> I suspect that in the ultimate analysis, we are going to have difficulty finding an escrow willing to handle these transactions, and will probably have to handle them ourselves here in this office for some sort of predetermined fee arrangement . . .

For cabins that were already in or about to start escrow with Hemet Escrow Company, attorney Swan stated that,

> . . . in order to assist in the processing of escrows for the sale and purchase of the various interest in Saunders's Meadow,

Inc. we have prepared a form of the following:

A. Agreement and Escrow Instructions for Purchase and Sale of Stock, Purchase and Sale of Real Property.
B. Security Agreement
C. Statement of Warranty with bylaws attached
D. Assignment and Bill of Sale

It is the present plan and policy of SM, Inc. that no share certificates shall be issued though the right thereto exists at this time until such time as the tract map has received its final approval by Riverside County and is ready for filing in the office of the County Recorder . . ."

158

SAUNDERS MEADOW, INC.

CAPITAL STOCK 57 SHARES

This Certifies that .... is the record holder of .... Shares of the Capital Stock of

SAUNDERS MEADOW, INC.

transferable only on the books of the Corporation by the holder hereof in person or by Attorney upon surrender of this Certificate properly endorsed or assigned.

This corporation is organized pursuant to the general non-profit law of the State of California.

In Witness Whereof the said Corporation has caused this Certificate to be signed by its duly authorized officers and its Corporate Seal to be hereunto affixed this .... day of .... A.D. 19....

ASSESSABLE

No. A 66

Certificate of Membership

(A NON-PROFIT CORPORATION)
INCORPORATED UNDER THE LAWS OF THE STATE OF CALIFORNIA

SAUNDERS MEADOW, INC.

This Certifies That .... is the record holder of a Membership Certificate in SAUNDERS MEADOW, INC.

with all the rights and privileges and subject to all the conditions and limitations set forth in the Articles of Incorporation, By-Laws and said Declaration.

Witness the Seal of the Corporation and the signatures of its duly authorized officers.

Dated: ....

Stock Certificates of Membership for Saunders Meadow, Inc

In order to create a sense of community and focus, Saunders Meadow, Inc. sent out a statement of objectives:

> In order to preserve a near fifty-year heritage of association with this mountain area, the cabin holders have formed a stock-co-operative, SM, Inc., a private residential community, in which the property is jointly owned by the stockholders, with the buildings and improvements individually owned by the members. The objectives of the corporation are to preserve the eighty acres in their natural state for the mutual and co-operative use of the members, to avoid and resist all efforts to urbanize them, and to strive at all times to upgrade the personally owned improvements to the end that this beautiful and invaluable forest oasis may remain intact for the enjoyment of present and future generations. Feeling strongly the need for co-operation, understanding, and mutual trust, and bearing these objectives in mind at all times, while striving throughout to guarantee the rights, privileges, and responsibilities of all members stockholders, the following set of bylaws has been drawn.

Also drafted was a set of rules and regulations for guidance of the fifty-seven members of Saunders Meadow, Inc.: "In general the community expects to follow the original and longstanding Forest Service rules and regulations with only such additions and modifications as seen appropriate by the private ownership of the property." On August 4, 1973, the boards of directors held a joint meeting. They looked over the engineering map and discussed the placement of boundary stakes. Mr. Everhart, disgruntled once again, disliked the subdivision work and recommended that the civil engineers correct the map, reverting to metes and bounds as shown on the US Forest Service map of 1928. Attorney Swan and engineer

Hawk explained that the Forest Service map was based on a survey dated 1928 and left a gap of approximately 100 feet in the perimeter line and that some of the presently existing buildings were not actually on the lots as set forth in said map. In fact, a Mr. Kowalchuk stated, "upon examination of maps of 1921 and 1928 surveys, it appeared that twelve to fifteen structures in the tract have lot lines running through them." But, you cannot reason with crazy. At this time, the boards of directors received a letter from the law firm of Young, Henry, McCarthy, and Mason stating that they had been retained by certain members and shareholders, among whom were the Harlowes, the Hedricks, the Stocktons, and Mrs. Arrance. They asked to examine the books and business affairs of the corporation and association. There were no selfish intents for any monetary gain among the volunteers who had to constantly justify their every move. These directors were scrupulously honest family men and women who had full-time careers, yet took it upon themselves to serve their summer home community by trying to get a difficult process accomplished for the benefit of all cabin owners. Certain shareholders were fearful that with all the new changes, fees would increase and those on a fixed income would no longer be able to afford to live in their homes. They also wanted fee property status.

The Riverside County Planning Commission met with shareholders and stated the following:

1. Unless you have 100 percent agreement on lot lines and boundaries, without one person dissenting, we can't take it in to the planning commission.
2. We can have fee title to our own individual lots and 1/57th ownership of all the common ground.
3. The board of directors, as functioning now, would in reality be the management company and would only govern the common ground.

4. The lots will be under Riverside County, so we have to set up "Rights and Covenants" compatible to rules such as: no fences are allowed, livestock control, style of home, clean yards . . .

In regards to the co-operative, a study was conducted to show pros and cons of two types of ownership:

1. Corporate Ownership

   Advantages:

   a. Unified control of entire property
   b. Single voice through board of directors in working with governmental agencies
   c. Democratic action through the rules established
   d. Properties are worth less, hence lower taxes

   Disadvantages:

   a. Difficulty in transferring title
   b. Problems in dealing with government entities
   c. Lower value as stock ownership and problems of securing financing
   d. Continual problems dealing with individuals who refuse to pay their taxes and assessments
   e. The number of problems would be increased because the corporation would own all the property

2. Fee Ownership

   Advantages:

   a. Higher values on individual parcels
   b. Transfer of title would be easier
   c. Individual owners would have complete control of their fee property subject only to covenants and restrictions of record

   Disadvantages:

   a. Increase in value means higher taxes

b. No control of the group over individuals except through covenants and restrictions of record

c. There would be a need to maintain and control the common areas. It would be necessary through fees

On June 11, 1974, the board of directors received a letter from attorneys Young, Henry, McCarthy, and Mason who represented shareholders Dr. Stockton, Mr. Kowalchuk, Mr. Yost, and Ms. Arrance regarding the handling of the administration of the corporation including the parcel map submitted: "Demand is hereby made upon the Board of Directors, we will proceed with litigation . . . this will include Temporary Restraining Order and Preliminary Injunction forestalling further actions by the current Board of Directors and possible appointment of a Receiver . . ." Saunders Meadow, Inc. responded, "We now have a continuance with the Riverside Planning Department until August 28 . . . no legal action can be taken by us on any map until after the meeting. We will have two board meetings prior to the planning department meeting, and on our next scheduled board meeting of July 13, we will have your letter on the agenda, and full discussion and action will be taken at the time. We hope this is satisfactory to you, because we would like to circumvent all unnecessary legal action and costs, etc."

Yet, on June 12, 1974, Mrs. C.J. Hedrick wrote a letter of complaint to the attorney general of California in regards to a "concerned group of shareholders," and on August 7, Saunders Meadow, Inc. received Notice of Complaint Code Section 2240 from the State of California, office of the Attorney General Department of Justice: "Enclosed is a shareholder's complaint alleging that the above named corporation has failed to comply with those Corporations Code sections marked:

#3000 Failure to maintain records of shareholders and director's meetings

#3001 Failure to maintain adequate and correct accounts of business transactions

#3003 Failure to permit inspection of records by shareholders

#3306–3010 Failure to permit to send annual report to shareholders."

Unfortunately, things got worse. On August 30, Young, Henry, McCarthy, and Mason, now acting as attorneys for Albert and Arlene Stockton, Aurelia Harlowe, Cloa and Frank Hedrick, Raymond and Marlene H. Kowalchuk, Helen Arrance, and Leland J. Yost, "file a civil complaint-lawsuit, against Defendant(s): Saunders Meadow, Inc., Tahquitz Meadow Improvement Association, Ray Brocklehurst, Wayne C. Ricker, Cosetter C. Wiley, O.E. Miller, Willis R. Leach, Harry G. Bubb, and Does I through XX, inclusive. Case Number 109929. Complaint for Preliminary and Permanent Injunction, Appointment of Receiver, and Accounting, Damages For Fraud, Removal Of Directors. COURT SUMMONS – August 31, 1974."

On January 25, 1975, a letter was sent to all shareholders from Dr. Yandell informing them that, "there will be a court hearing on February 3 in the Riverside Superior Court in the action of Stockton, et al, vs, Saunders Meadow, Inc., et al. One of the issues to be decided at the hearing will be the appointment of a receiver for SM, Inc. and Tahquitz Meadow Improvement Association." On January 25, another letter went out: "this letter will inform you that there will be a court hearing on February 3 . . . the attorneys now report that they have been unable to effect a settlement and the matter must be submitted to the court . . . your Boards of Directors reluctantly acknowledge the inevitability of the appointment of a receiver . . ."

On February 1, 1975, the board of directors for SM, Inc. met at Dr. Yandell's cabin,

> Attention was called to Mrs. Harlowe's input in regards to the reason for separation of the Corporation and Association . . . Dr. Yandell reported on his telephone conversation with Mr. Ward . . . It was also reported that plaintiffs agreed to drop individual lawsuits. Mrs. Hedrick discharged her attorney . . . in discharging, she instructed him to withdraw the lawsuit . . . the bad news is that the dismissal is without prejudice, which leaves her the right to proceed again with the lawsuit if she wishes. Also, receiver has been selected and will be so designated by the court on Thursday February 6, according to present plans . . . he will recommend whether we should have individual titles to the lots our cabins are on or if we should retain title to the land in the corporate name . . . he will also investigate the division of land in to two parcels and advisability of returning one parcel . . .

On the same day, the boards of directors of The Tahquitz Meadow Improvement Association met right after the SM, Inc. meeting. There was no input and no further business, just the approval of December 14, 1974, minutes. After working so hard on behalf of the community to have to justify unfounded accusations must have been very frustrating.

On February 10, Case No. 109929, "Plaintiffs and Defendants request for appointment of Receiver, by Stipulation, also request that Ray O. Womack be appointed as such Receiver." On February 26, Womack took his oath of receiver and on March 20, he filed his Inventory of Assets In Possession of Receiver with the courts. John B. Jones wrote the history of SM, Inc. in order to assist the receiver as per his request. On May 28, Ray Womack, called for a SM, Inc. board of directors meeting. Womack expressed his appreciation to the board for their cooperation and the board stated, "this has our enthusiastic endorsement as a necessary and desirable means of resolving the controversy." On August 20, Ray Womack from Law Corporation presented his Receiver's Preliminary Report:

1. It is my recommendation that application be refiled with Riverside County Planning Commission for qualification as a planned residential development (PRD).
2. It is my recommendation that all owners receive fee title to their respective lots along with an undivided ownership in the common parcel.
3. As a result of the lawsuit, it is my opinion that the Riverside Superior Court has jurisdiction to settle all lot lines disputes and to approve a final map.
4. I will recommend to the court that the road alignment in front of the Hedrick property be returned to its former alignment.
5. Having two separate entities creates undue confusion and causes needless duplication in administration and accounting. Accordingly, one of the entities should be dissolved after completion of the subdivision.
6. The additional costs of the subdivision, map, Riverside County Planning Commission should be borne from the $1,500 paid in by each property owner and after the completion of the subdivision and the deeding of the property to the individual owners any excess funds should be returned to the property owner on a prorate basis.
7. I have found no improprieties from the Land Exchange with the U.S. Forest Service.
8. I do not believe that it is necessary to incur the cost of an audit by an accounting firm.

On August 27, a Harry Bubb wrote to Mr. Womack, "I welcome and appreciate your preliminary report, we will update and change the Covenants, Conditions, and Restrictions to reflect fee title lots." On August 31, John B. Jones was elected president of SM, Inc.

On November 21, 1975, Mr. Jones and the board hired attorney James Ward to deal forcefully with the office of attorney general and work with receiver Womack to wrap things up.

1976

The recently hired attorney James Ward of Thompson and Colegate wrote to John M. Jones, "I am confident that things will work out well . . . most assuredly, there will be some difficulties involving Mrs. Hedrick . . . but eventually the court will rule on all of these matters, and the problems will be put to bed." Receiver Womack worked with the court and shareholders in the final draft of the covenants, conditions, and restrictions, which had to be submitted to Riverside County along with a map of the subdivision under preparation by Neste, Brudin, and Stone. The covenants, conditions, and restrictions addressed the granting of fee simple and the preservation of the community, "it is our stated objective that this tract shall be preserved in its natural condition so far as possible and that there will be no more than fifty-seven residence lots in said tract. Water rights are leased to us by the US Forest Service and the storage tanks belong to us." Everyone involved worked hard to tie all the loose ends. Mrs. Hedrick continued to circulate highly inaccurate and untrue information to all members and have it printed in the *Town Crier* and, of all places, an Arizona newspaper. The Forest Service attempted to address her inaccurate statements as did the receiver who had to spend more time with her and her attorney than with any other shareholder, but to no avail. She was then informed of the restraining order accompanying the order appointing a receiver. Eventually the judge had to inform her that if she continued with such frivolous lawsuits, he would throw "her bony ass into jail." On October 15, 1976, President John B. Jones wrote to attorney J. Ward, "On Thursday, October 14, the SM, Inc. board met with Mr. Womack . . . he and the board established the following calendar to deal with all issues and wrap things up:

A. Line dispute between Brocklehurst and Harlowe . . . Womack will take necessary action to finalize a line by October 31.
B. Hedrick road issue will be solved no later than October 31.
C. Mapping and staking by Neste, Brudin, and Stone will be done by November 30.
D. Womack will write covenants, conditions, and restrictions while surveying is being done November 30."

1977

The board worked to solve the last three remaining boundary issues. Ray Womack wrote to John Brudin in regard to a lot line problem between Brocklehurst and Harlowe, "Since the parties are unable to resolve their dispute between them, I propose the following result . . . between the two lots there is a loss of .037 acres. You are hereby instructed to apportion that loss between the two lots whereby each lot holder has the same percentage of reduction from the Forest Service map to the present map. My rough calculations indicate that this would entail moving the present boundary between the properties approximately two and one third feet toward the Brocklehurst property." In regards to the Hedrick's issue, Ray Womack wrote to attorney Hugh. M. Gallaher, "My position on the road in front of Mrs. Hedrick's property, that she wants moved, should not be moved . . . she acquired the property with the road in its present location." On May 24, James C. Montgomery wrote to Ray Womack requesting that his main water valve be in Montgomery's lot by moving the lot line a few inches. Ray Womack wrote to the attorney general's office, "It is my opinion that SM, Inc. is maintaining adequate records which correctly reflect all of its business transactions . . . I have also recommended to the Riverside

Superior Court that SM, Inc. be dissolved after we are in a position to transfer fee title to each of the individual lot holders . . . Moreover, all of the attorneys involved in this matter believe that SM, Inc. should not be hastily dissolved as there may be some water rights or other legal rights held in the name of the corporation."

On September 4, after decades of service, John Jones decided not to continue as president. Elwood Wissman was elected to take his place. On October 17, receiver Ray Womack presented the Second Account and Report to the superior court and submitted Petition for Instructions to Court.

1978

On February 16, the court responded, "It is Hereby Ordered That:

1. The Declaration of Protection Covenants, Conditions, and Restrictions of SM, Inc., is hereby approved and said C, C, & Rs shall be binding upon Lot 1 & 2 of Tract No. 5103 and Lot 1 through 57, inclusive, of Tract No.11049, including common areas . . .
2. The Court hereby approves the tentative Tract Map No. 11049 subject only to Court's right to make changes pursuant to objections filed by Fred Hedrick and Jewel Hedrick, owners of Lot 57, Judge of the Superior Court R.T. Deissler, and Received for Record April 13."

On June 27, Ray Womack wrote to shareholders of SM, Inc. and shared the county report and conditions for subdivision: "The condition with which we are most concerned at present is No. 5, which sets forth a requirement of five fire hydrants with six-inch water mains. My concern is that the present water pressure is not adequate to maintain the hydrants and it would be necessary to obtain the water from Fern Valley Water District."

On August 14, Neste, Budin, and Stone, civil engineers for the tract, reported on their meeting with all involved: "Discussions at the Planning Commission hearings indicate that the Idyllwild Fire Protection District wanted easements along the private driveways and that there be a practical and useful clear drive with a turn-around at the ends of said driveways . . . Please note again that the request is for a fire protection system, and that there will be no domestic water service taken from this water system." The Fern Valley Water District responded, "It is the board's opinion that the people in Saunders Meadow Tract No. 11049 would benefit by annexation to the Fern Valley Water District. This will solve present and future problems."

On December 6, the Department of Public Health wrote to SM, Inc., "It is necessary to place the water supply and distribution system operated by you under a Riverside County Water Permit . . . after your application is received, a sanitary appraisal of your system will be made by our representative before a permit is issued."

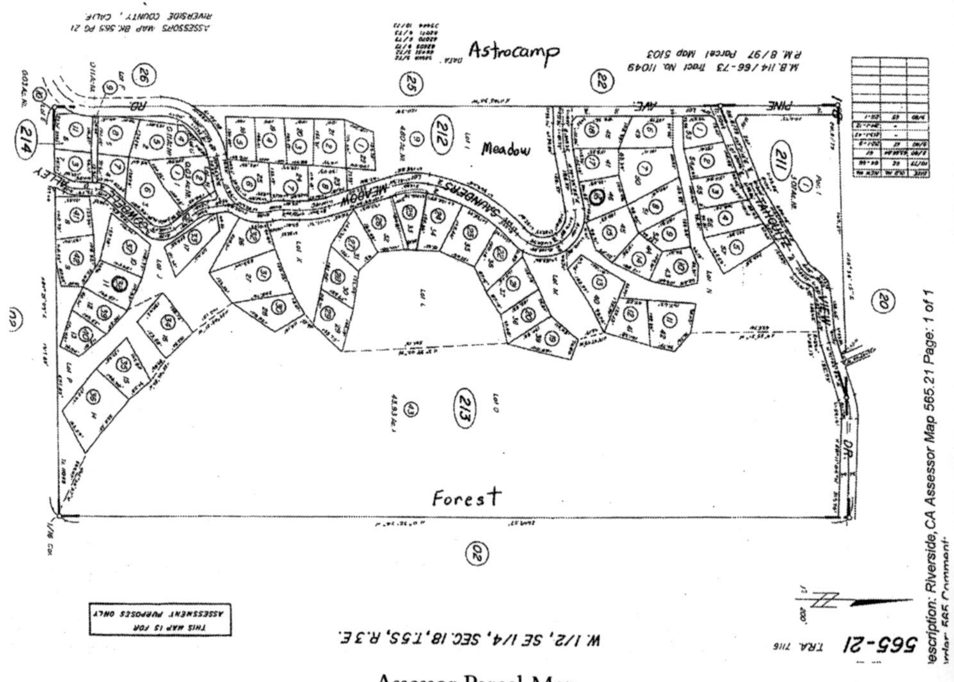

Assessor Parcel Map

1979

SM, Inc. continued to deal with water issues and worked with both Fern Valley Water District and Idyllwild Fire Protection in meeting the county's requirements. They also started to deal with future taxes as private fee lots.

1980

The subdivision map couldn't be recorded until the Idyllwild Fire Protection signed off on the condition of the trails. On March 6, Idyllwild Fire Protection District Chief David E. Hunt replied to Neste, Brudin, and Stone:

"Dear Sirs:

> At this time we cannot give the approval for the road conditions in this tract. Neither of the two that were improved is very negotiable. It would seem a more lasting improvement could be provided for this area. Should there be a mishap on either of these roads due to fire or medical aid we could have a serious problem in gaining access."

The board of directors met with the Idyllwild Fire Protection District directors and presented their case, "The purpose of the residents . . . of Saunders Meadow has been in the past, throughout this process just described and for the future of our eighty acres to maintain the ecological environment as much as possible as it has existed for over fifty years in this tract; and to provide a restful and comfortable environment for our residents to either live full time or occasionally in the Idyllwild area . . ."The goal is to maintain a rustic natural forest setting just as it was in 1920.

On April 17, David E. Hunt, the fire chief of Idyllwild Fire Protection District, wrote to Riverside County, "The owners of

Tract 11049, represented by their board of directors, have met the conditions of approval that we felt were necessary; however, due to the extreme weather conditions occurring this winter we have asked for and received a letter of intent for additional work to be accomplished on Macteckelwood within ninety days. We hereby acknowledge the developers' compliance and give you our concurrence that the owners have complied with our requirements."

On August 1, a letter with new lot numbers went out to SM, Inc. shareholders, "The filing of the subdivision map will necessitate a different lot numbering system by the County of Riverside. However, for our internal Saunders Meadow, Inc. purposes, we will continue to use the familiar lot number system," which was established by the Forest Service back in 1920. On September 5, Saunders Meadow Subdivision Map was recorded. Shareholders received deeds to their lots after ten years of dealing with issues. On September 8, Neste, Brudin, and Stone informed President Wissman that Tract No. 11049 was recorded on September 5 in Book 114, pages 66–73 in the records of Riverside County.

Annexation into Fern Valley Water District, 1981–1995

On August 26, 1981, the Forest Service amended the water special use permit, extending the expiration date to December 31, 1988. Saunders Meadow, Inc. started thinking about a permanent solution to their water need.

1982

The chairman of the water committee wrote to the SM, Inc. board, saying, "The shareholders at the last annual meeting issued a mandate that a committee be formed to conduct a study of all aspects of water supply for Saunders Meadow Tract. Our approach was to secure the proposal of Bub Smith and Son of Crestline, the leading horizontal well drillers of California. They confidently recommended horizontal drilling of both our tunnel sites to produce a completely sealed well system so that further deterioration of our old tunnel system would be of no concern at a cost of $10,000. Ranger Douglas Pumphrey and the Forest Service have approved such work since tunnels are on Forest Service land."

In October, Bub Smith and Son drilled a horizontal well adjacent to Big Cedar Springs Tunnel. He went in 200 feet and got a good well that ran twelve gallons per minute on initial testing. He drilled another well near the original tunnel at Granite Springs . . . with the new Big Cedar SM, Inc. felt the need of professional advice as to how to valve it for control so as to preserve the water in place, in the mountain, rather than allowing it to overflow and deplete the source. To this end, John engaged a well-known water engineering firm, Webb Associates, to help. Albert A. Webb contacted SM, Inc., "Per your request, we field-checked portions of subject domestic water system facilities on 11/1/82, and we listed our comments and recommendations in regards to: Cedar Spring upper tunnel, lower tunnel, Pipeline between Cedar and the 84,000-gallon tank and existing new horizontal well adjacent to Cedar Spring upper tunnel. Total amount due, $1,271." Webb Associates also recommended a new storage water tank.

John B. Jones presented a few options to shareholders ranging from $9,000 to $47,000 for a tank. On June 25, Thomas D. Horne, the general manager of Fern Valley Water District wrote to John Jones and SM, Inc. saying, "I have learned from District Ranger Douglas Pumphrey that you have applied to use the USFS for permission to install a new tank in the Saunders Meadow, Inc. water system. Mr. Pumphrey was inquiring about the possibility of Fern Valley Water District annexing the Saunders Meadow tract . . . The board of directors of the FVWD feels that any move would have to be initialed by the property owners of your tract."

On July 1, 1984, the Forest Service approved the replacing of the deteriorated tank with a new 84,000-gallon tank, but warned that the basic permit would expire December 31, 1995, and would not be renewed. Furthermore, "Forest Service policy and guidelines state that national forestland will not be used to support private land development when and if there are reasonable and acceptable alternatives . . . annexation to Fern Valley Water District appears to be a viable alternative . . . we hope that SM, Inc. will pursue annexation with FVWD at this time. With this notice of termination of the water and supply system on national forestland by the year 1995, the investment of a replacement tank at this time should be considered in your decision-making process."

John Jones working on the new water tank in 1984

The Old Water System was dug by grinding holes in rock

1991

In November, plans and drawings were made showing Saunders Meadow Subdivision Water System and Fern Valley Water District Fire Hydrants. Plans showed tract lots, service valves, and main line valve in box, Granite Spring Tunnel/Storage 64,000-gallons, 84,000-gallon steel storage tank and Big Cedar Spring Tunnel.

1992

Mark Jones, Elwood Jones' grandson and John Jones' son, took over as the leader on the water Issue. In November he wrote the history of the water development for the board: "The files reveal that the same issues have come up over and over again through the years: The water permit, conservation, catastrophic water loss, additional water development, storage, piping valve issues, and the question of annexation . . . " He recommended the use of low flow heads and 1.5 gallon-flush toilets and the possibility of water meters. On December 3, the California Department of Public Health, Drinking Water Program office contacted all public water systems in regards to implementation of the phase II and phase V federal regulations, "The purpose of this letter is to inform you that the US Environmental Protection Agency (USEPA) has adopted several sets of new drinking water quality regulations for monitoring and maximum contaminant levels for both inorganic and organic chemicals." Saunders Meadow, Inc. worked with E.S. Babcock and Sons, Inc. in testing the water. That same month, shareholders got the 1992 "Water Watch: Conserve Our Water" flyer adapted from the 1989 flyer. "Each one of us has a responsibility to safeguard our most valuable resource—our water supply . . . Please remember, the cost and availabilities of water has a direct and major impact on the value of each of our cabins . . . Do not leave faucets on to drip in cold weather to prevent freezing . . ."

1993

The Forest Service encouraged Mark Jones and the Saunders Meadow association to seek annexation with a water district due to, "Riverside County now requiring a quarterly water quality test that asks for the collection and delivery of samples." On March 11, Mark Jones contacted Webb Associates regarding the water system: "The current board believes there are a number of issues that need to be reevaluated now that ten years have passed since your report to us in 1982." Webb responded with an estimate of $2,500 for the study and report. On March 25, Webb suggested that according to Mr. Babcock's coliform tests, Saunders Meadow, Inc. "must dose the

Granite Spring Tunnel Storage and the Bolted Storage Tank with chlorine ASAP . . . We suggest that you continue to coordinate closely with John Watkins of Riverside County Environment Health Department until this matter is fully resolved." The board informed all shareholders:

> This is done with great reluctance, for the first time in the system's sixty-seven-year history, but in recognition that we have an obligation to our members to try to meet current regulatory requirements . . . we hope . . . that we will return to the much-valued untreated spring water we have enjoyed for these many years . . . also, we retained Webb Associates in March to come back after eleven years and once again help us with the our water issues and to provide pros and cons of annexation . . . One change is very clear: We are now confronted by a vastly different, much tougher regulatory environment, with all water systems required to meet strict new state and federal standards, not only for bacteria and turbidity, but for all sorts of chemicals and heavy metals. Accompanying this are extensive and expensive testing requirements, as well as the possibility of future required water treatment.

Webb Associates presented their recommendations and options, "Alternate I: Remain a water purveyor, Alternate II: Annexation to Fern Valley Water District. The board decided to precede with Alternate I and remain a water purveyor." They hired Best Best & Krieger, a partnership including professional corporations, to represent SM, Inc. in the acquisition of water rights from the Forest Service. On April 28, Best Best & Krieger told SM, Inc., "Do not take on the Forest Service. They have the staff, size, and money to fight forever. Also, you already have permit from them. They, however, could deny access to the water. You can look into land swap so that you get the land, the springs, and acreage leading to them . . ." At this time, Webb Associates presented work estimates, "under Alternate I, it will cost $60,000 to repair Big Cedar Spring Tunnel. Alternate II will be $40,000, or simply abandon tunnel and replace source of water supply by drilling of a horizontal well at a cost of $35,000."

With such high expenses on the way, Mark Jones contacted Farmers Home Administration, "We anticipate a significant investment of $200 to $400,000 in order to remain a viable water provider and are looking for financing and possible grant assistance . . ." Jeff Hays, assistant district director for Farmers Home Administration (FMHA), informed Jones that he thought SM, Inc. would qualify. Jones reported to the board, "We now need to prove that we cannot get conventional financing. Then we fill out pre-application with Fred's rough cost estimate of all work required to determine eligibility . . . then we have an on-site visit to look at our current system and assist in planning the next steps . . . Formal application process will need detailed engineering plans and estimates, and satisfying any environmental requirement . . . this usually takes six months."

1994

On February 16, SM, Inc. informed Webb Associates, that, "we are pursuing the issue of permit renewal with the Forest Service as a first step in making the decision whether to stop being a water company or annexation so no further investments in the system will be made until decision is made." After talking to the Forest Service about permit extensions in order to be compatible with the long terms of FMHA financing and getting their approval, the pre-application package was sent to Mr. Hays at Farmers Home Administration for loans and grants consideration. On May 16, the Forest Service contacted SM, Inc.:

In a letter dated July 1, 1984, we indicated that your permit would expire at the end of 1995 and you would then have to seek annexation to the Fern Valley Water District. The permit was instead reissued and now terminates in 1998. With your latest inquiry as to water system modification, we again raise the issue of annexation by the water district and ceasing to use water sources on national forestlands. Besides the increasing regulation by state and federal agencies as to water quality: there is also an increasing interest and concern over the export of water from the national forest without an environmental analysis of the effects. It is our job to manage water resources to assure adequate supplies are secured and maintained to meet the national forest system resource needs before making excess water available to private parties for their uses.

On June 13, SM, Inc. wrote to California State Clearinghouse in regards to application for federal assistance based on the Webb Associates water system options cost chart. If the community upgraded its current water system, the cost would be $489,500, if the community went with annexation, the cost would be $325,000. The board and shareholders met with Fern Valley Water District. After many meetings and debates, Fern Valley Water District accepted Saunders Meadow's request. Fern Valley Water District found the increased potential in revenue as an advantage in the form of one-time hook-up fees totaling $142,500 and annual water rates estimated to be around $17,000. On May 12, Fred Hanson of Webb Engineering joined SM, Inc. and had the FMHA final application for signatures transmittal to Fern Valley Water District. FVWD then submitted the LAFCO filing. "Fern Valley Board will meet on the 20th where they will formalize a resolution to initiate annexation." At the same time, attorneys received a call from Jeff Hays at Farmers Home Administration stating that the USDA approved SM, Inc.'s letter of May 1.

On June 12, SM, Inc. called for a special meeting of members for Sunday, July 9, at 1:00 p.m. in order to act on the FMHA loan for construction of a new water system to be operated by the Fern Valley Water District. The board stated, "A great deal of water has gone over the dam or should we say through the pipes since your prior and present board began their work on a long-term resolution of our water problems. As a result of this multi-year effort, we now present, recommend, and endorse the described course of action. Your affirmative vote is solicited and will be appreciated." Seventy percent of the members voted in person or by proxy in favor to continue with the loan and annexation. Each meter would cost $3,500 per cabin, and the entire cost for the construction of the new water system would total $640,000. The tract association was able to get a government grant of $275,000 toward water development; the remaining $365,000 would have to be borrowed. Saunders Meadow got loan approval from Farmers Home Administration. It would be paid over forty years with an interest rate of 5.5 percent. A yearly special assessment district and county tax of approximately $424 was to be charged as part of the property tax bill. With the loan approved, the future of the historic community was secured. The loan would be paid in full in 2035.

Saunders Meadow agreement in the pipelin

By Holly Vicente
Staff Reporter

At a special meeting last Sunday, home owners from Saunders Meadow unanimously agreed to proceed with complete annexation by the Fern Valley Water District, said Harry Bubb, president of Saunders Meadow Inc.

The 57 home owners in the Saunders Meadow area are waiting for the approval of a Farmers Home Administration loan which will pay for a new pipeline system to connect to the Fern Valley Water District. Mr. Bubb said there have been informal indications that the loan would be approved. Saunders Meadow also had to get approval from the U.S. Forest Service, which has provided water to the area.

"The forest service was most cooperative in assisting us to develop a program," Mr. Bubb said.

AT THE SAME time, an application requesting that Saunders Meadow Inc., the homeowner's group, be annexed by the Fern Valley Water District has been sent to the Local Agency Formation Commission (LAFCO). Prepared by a Saunders Meadow engineer, the request will be presented at a LAFCO hearing.

Once LAFCO approves the request and the new pipelines are laid, the FVWD will open the valves and begin service to the Saunders Meadow home owners.

FVWD General Manager Tom Horne said annexation would not drain resources from the district's current customers.

"Since it's a new [pipeline] system, there won't be so many maintenance problems," said Tom Horne, FVWD General Manager.

ADDITIONALLY, EACH HOME owner of Saunders Meadow Inc. is paying the FVWD a "buy-in" of $2,500 for a total of $142,500 from the group. The district will utilize the money for new wells and for locating new water sources.

"We're gaining a cash infusion for capital improvements that will benefit everybody," Mr. said.

Because Saunders Meadow Inc. is having put in with the new pipelines, it will not have the district the $500 per person meter instı charge.

Mr. Horne said that he does not believe percent increase in the customer base caused annexation would decrease the amount of wate able to the district's current consumers. He that Saunders Meadow has a low demand or as the area already has restrictions on lands and on other water usage.

ALTHOUGH FERN VALLEY has not rienced a drought in the last couple of yea Horne said that if a drought occurs, FVWD wi the same stance it took before the annexatic

"The [FVWD Board of Director's] policy in a drought everyone shares equally in wha is," Mr. Horne said.

The Saunders Meadow area has been s for possible well or water source sites by Mr. and a hydrologist. Mr. Horne said that althou hydrologist did not give any "absolute positive ı there is at least one accessible area which n studied as a potential water source.

"[FVWD] did not put any water source re ment into the [Saunders Meadow] agreement Horne said.

Saunders Meadow Inc. has been receivi water from U.S. Forest Service-owned spring property owners' group sought the annexatic September in an effort to update its antiquated system.

"For roughly 50 years, you could say w didn't have a problem," Mr. Bubb said.

For many years, volunteers from Sau Meadow had cleaned out tunnels and taken samples to be tested. With water standards tightened, it became difficult to maintain the system, Mr. Bubb said. About two and a half ago, the board of directors of Saunders Meado initiated a study to look into other options.

UNITED STATES DEPARTMENT OF AGRICULTURE FOREST SERVICE | San Bernardino National Forest | San Jacinto Ranger District, P.O. Box 518, Idyllwild, CA 92549, (909)659-2117 (909)659-5748 TDD

File Code: 2720 Special Uses Admin
Route To: Saunders Meadow 3068

Date: January 9, 1995

Fern Valley Water District
Board of Directors
Attn: Clyde Mitchell
PO BOX 387
IDYLLWILD CA 92549

Dear Clyde:

After reading the Town Crier article of December 22, 1994 concerning the board meeting and Saunders Meadow association request for annexation, I felt I should clarify the Forest Service position in the situation.

In a 1984 letter to Saunders Meadow tract (copy attached), I reiterated a Forest Service request that the tract pursue annexation to Fern Valley. The tract was now out of national forest land ownership due to a land exchange but we allowed continued use of the water system until they could make other arrangements. The water rights are in the name of the United States and we felt that, at some future date, we needed the water for other resource uses on the National Forest.

In the fall of 1993, Saunders Meadow, Inc. approached us as they needed to do work on one of the primary springs as well as upgrading lines to the tract. I again asked that they pursue annexation. I am writing to the board to say I feel that the actions of Saunders Meadow are an intelligent and pro-active way to deal with an inevitable situation. The Saunders Meadow board has done extensive research into both upgrading the existing system as well as annexation and has diligently pursued logical answers to the problem. They have been wonderful to work with; keeping us well-informed and using professional consultants to get scientific data.

Just as I encouraged Saunders Meadow to seek the annexation, I am asking the Board to consider the request very seriously. Should you have any other questions, feel free to call me or Resources Officer, Kathy Valenzuela at this office. Thank-you for your time.

Sincerely,

C. DOUGLAS PUMPHREY
District Ranger

Saunders Meadow & Fern Valley Water District

6 - IDYLLWILD TOWN CRIER, Dec. 22, 1994

'own Hall head s Donna John

Philip Michaels
ff Reporter

The Town Hall Recreation program received an ly Christmas present last week — a new perma- t director.

The Idyllwild Chamber of Commerce Board of ectors voted unanimously on Monday, Dec. 19, hire Hill resident Donna John as Town Hall di- tor. Ms. John had been serving as interim director e July when former director Theresa Gray re- ed.

Ms. John's hiring ends a six-month search in ich the chamber sorted through 52 applications interviewed over a dozen candidates.

CHAMBER MEMBERS HAD originally ed to fill the position in August, but delays had e members fearful that a new director would not hired until mid-January unless the board agreed a candidate this month.

"I'm just really pleased we were able to get it lved [Monday] night," said Fran Ballard, presi- t of the Chamber of Commerce.

Ms. John, who did not initially apply for the said she was "still in shock" but happy that the

Continued on page 27

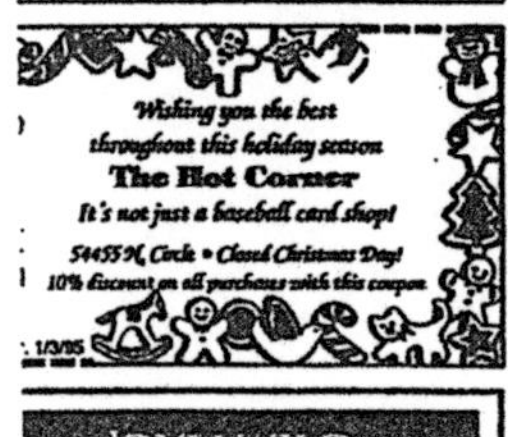

IDYLLWILD

FVWD interest in annexation diluting

By Philip Michaels
Staff Reporter

Some members of the Fern Valley Water District Board of Directors are cooling toward the idea of annexing Saunders Meadows Inc. into the district and may vote to nix any annexation discussions with the property owners group at the next FVWD board meeting in January.

In September, the Board of Directors for Saunders Meadows Inc., an association of 57 home owners, was given the green light by its home owners to pursue discussions on the costs of upgrading its antiquated water system. Saunders Meadows had previously approached FVWD about annexing into the water district.

At the October FVWD board meeting, the Board of Directors voted to authorize Tom Horne, FVWD general manager, to continue talks with Harry Bubb, president of Saunders Meadows Inc., about annexing the 57 home owners into the water district.

BUT LAST WEEK, some FVWD board members questioned whether annexation was in the best interest of the current FVWD ratepayers.

Merritt Van Sant, a FVWD director who was not present during the board's vote in October, said he was concerned that the annexation would not provide the water district with any new wells or sources of water. Without new water coming into the district, Mr. Van Sant said he would not be inclined to support annexation.

"If there's nine good reasons for doing it and only two reasons not to do it, then we have to take a hard look at those two because maybe one's important," Mr. Van Sant said.

Currently, Saunders Meadows provides its own water service from springs owned by the U.S. Forest Service. Those springs would not become the property of FVWD if the annexation is approved.

THE CONCERNS RAISED by the Board of Directors echo those raised last month by Fern Valley property owners Charles and Diana Johnson, who fear annexation could deplete the district's water supply and put FVWD in jeopardy should a drought occur.

"Our concern is there's a finite source of water," Mr. Johnson said. "In an extended drought, the water levels would drop and the district cannot serve its current customers."

Both Al Gillette, FVWD board member, and Clyd Mitchell, president of the FVWD Board of Director said the concerns raised by the Johnsons were valid.

"They have brought up a really legitimate questio that we need to consider," Mr. Mitchell said.

THE BOARD WILL re-examine the propose annexation at its January meeting. The water district ha also informed Mr. Bubb and Saunders Meadows Inc. tha the annexation discussions may fall through.

"We owe it to these people to be honest," Mr. Va Sant said. "If the whole idea is to be good neighbor then maybe we should tell them up front [that annex ation] may not happen."

Mr. Bubb said he could not fully comment on las week's turn of events as he did not attend the Saturday Dec. 17 meeting of the FVWD board. However, he re mained hopeful that the annexation discussions woul proceed.

"I would hope that with an objective and frank dis cussion, I would be able to resolve the doubts of thos who are dubious," Mr. Bubb said.

IN AN OCTOBER letter to the FVWD, Mr. Bubl outlined the possible advantages of annexation, whic included better water service for Saunders Meadow residents.

"We've talked a lot about the advantages to them," Mr. Van Sant said. "What we haven't talked about is th advantages to us."

Mr. Bubb said in his letter that advantages for Fer Valley included extra revenue generated by the additional rate payers, a fixed number of customers and 80 acre of land that could potentially be used as a well site.

According to Mike Winslow, FVWD director, an- nexing Saunders Meadows would net the water distric approximately $142,500 in initial hook-up fees and $17,000 a year in perpetuity for water rates.

"THAT'S A [GOOD] amount of money if it doesn' impact our cost-structure," Mr. Winslow said.

At the January meeting, FVWD board members intend to closely examine the pros and cons of annex- ation.

"The downside is 57 more thirsty people and no new source of water," Mr. Gillette said. "The upside is 57 people times the $2,500 hook-up fee."

The next meeting of the FVWD Board of Directors is scheduled for Saturday, Jan. 14, at 9 a.m.

IDYLLWILD TOWN CRIER, Sept. 8, 1994 - Page 23

Saunders Meadow is looking at a FVWD future

By Philip Michaels
Staff Reporter

Saunders Meadows Inc., an association of 57 home owners, has given the green light to its board of directors to explore the possibility of annexing into the Fern Valley Water District.

"We're starting down a long road which requires extensive and sensitive discussions," said Harry Bubb, president of Saunders Meadows Inc.

At a meeting on Sunday, Sept. 4, the home owners orized the board to move ahead with discussions on the costs of upgrading its antiquated water system.

CURRENTLY, SAUNDERS MEADOWS provides its own water service from springs owned by the U.S. Forest Service, Mr. Bubb said.

"Our thought has been to come to grips with an aging system," said Mr. Bubb, adding that Saunders Meadows first began discussing the issue two years ago.

While Saunders Meadows has not decided which Hill water district they might annex into, Fern Valley Water District is thought to be the likely choice. Fern Valley currently provides Saunders Meadows with water for its fire hydrants, and all discussions to date have been with Fern Valley.

According to Tom Horne, FVWD general manager, the next step in the process is for Saunders Meadows representatives to meet with FVWD's Board of Directors. Mr. Bubb has already presented FVWD with a letter containing a rough schedule of the annexation process, Mr. Horne said.

"To take a formal action, we need a refinement of the letter they sent and the legal steps involved," Mr. Horne said.

The future of Saunders Meadows' water system was also discussed briefly at last month's meeting of the Idyllwild Water District. According to Tom Lovejoy, IWD general manager, Mr. Bubb had said that Saunders Meadows was looking into annexation with either FVWD or IWD.

Town Crier Articles on Water Annexation, 1994

While the storms of the past week and a half m[illegible] have been a nuisance to some Idyllwild residen[ts] the sound of falling rain and the crunch of snow was music to the ears of the general managers of the Hill's three water districts.

As a result of the steady downpour of rain and snow, local water district general managers say water levels are right on target for where they should be this time of year.

"I would say we're on track," said Tom Lovejoy, general manager of the Idyllwild Water District. "The picture is normal for the year. We're not ahead, but we're certainly not behind."

MR. LOVEJOY'S COMMENTS echoed those of his counterparts, Jerry Holdber at the Pine Cove Water District and Tom Horne at the Fern Valley Water District, who both reported that water levels are where they should be for this time of year on the Hill.

Continued on page 27

No end for snow, rain

By Philip Michaels
Staff Reporter

After two days of heavy rains, Hill residents were met by an unfamiliar visitor on the afternoon of Thursday, Jan. 12 — the sun, which made a brief appearance in Southern California following a week of storms.

But the sun's visit to the Hill was a short one, giving way

Continued on page 31

Parts of Idyllwild were not exempt from flooding last week during the storms that washed over and flooded parts of California. On Jan. 11, Tim Gustafson and others from the Idyllwild Fire Department were busy shoveling mud and pine needles on Toll Gat[e] in an effort to sand bag water gushing d[own] drainage toward homes on Idyllbrook Drive. (Photo by Andrea[...]

FVWD will annex Saunders Meadow

Board members agree pluses outweigh risks

By Philip Michaels
Staff Reporter

For the past few weeks, the outlook for residents of Saunders Meadow Inc., an association of 57 property owners hoping to annex into the Fern Valley Water District, was as overcast as the recent weather.

Annexation talks between the property owners association and the FVWD Board of Directors stalled last month after board members expressed concern the move would pose no advantages to the water district while depleting its water supply.

However, the outlook for Saunders Meadow brightened considerably over the weekend after the FVWD board voted unanimously to continue with the annexation discussions following a presentation by Harry Bubb, president of Saunders Meadow Inc., which allayed the directors' concerns.

"I'M GRATIFIED THAT after careful and thoughtful discussion, they acted unanimously and decisively in moving ahead with the annexation," Mr. Bubb said.

Members of the FVWD board said they were persuaded to continue with the annexation after Mr. Bubb discussed some of the advantages and the minimal risks annexation would pose to the water district.

"The advantages to them are so great and the risks to us are so minor," said FVWD Director Merritt Van Sant, who said the board reached its decision after considering the matter carefully over the past three weeks.

Among the advantages outlined by Mr. Bubb was increased revenue to the FVWD in the form of one-time hook up fees totalling $142,500 and annual water rates estimated to be around $17,000.

"IT DOESN'T TAKE too many years until that adds up to real money," Mr. Bubb said.

In addition, the proposed annexation is not expected to increase the operating costs of the water district in the near term, according to Tom Horne, FVWD general manager.

With the annexation of the 57 Saunders Meadow properties, the district would also increase its water storage capacity. The capital facility fees could be used to buy additional tanks and wells, a factor that Clyde Mitchell, president of the FVWD Board of Directors, said reduced the threat a drought would pose to the expanded water district.

The FVWD board also received assurances

Continued on page 27

The Town C[rier] introduces its Financial Planning Sect[ion]. See pages 15 for ways t[o] improve yo[ur] monetary manageme[nt]

"Almost all the News — Part of the Time"

Idyllwild Town Crier Jan. 19, 1995

[...]r supply would benefit over the long-

[...] be beneficial in the long run," Mr. [...]ere's lots of snow in the higher com[...] springs in the spring."

[...] importance to local water districts is [h]igher elevations. With a high amount [...] mountains, the Hill's water districts [...] source of water.

[...]LLEY, for example, as the snowpack [...]s melts, it flows into the streams which [...]r supply.

DIFFERENT WEATHER PATTERNS can affect the water districts in different ways. For example, FVWD benefits largely from snowfall in higher elevations, while the IWD benefits from rainfall that raises the water levels in Foster Lake. That water can be used by the district right away, according to Mr. Lovejoy.

"I suspect that a lot of water melting at lower elevations would help Idyllwild," said Mr. Horne, adding that the major supply of Fern Valley's water comes from streams at higher elevations.

Heavy rains can also negatively affect the water supply in the short term. Last week, the FVWD was

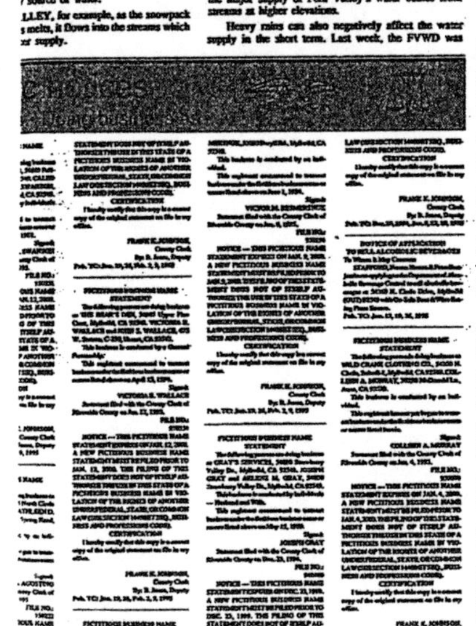

Fern Valley

Continued from page 1

from Mr. Bubb that the number of Saunders Meadow properties would remain at 57. The current property owners agreement prohibits lot-splitting at Saunders Meadow; however, a vote of 85 percent of the property owners could override that agreement.

AT THE REQUEST of FVWD Director Al Gillette and the agreement of Mr. Bubb, FVWD and Saunders Meadow will include in any annexation agreement a provision giving the water district veto power over a proposed lot-splitting at Saunders Meadow. Mr. Gillette said he felt the provision was necessary even though both the water district and the property owners currently oppose lot-splitting.

"When I'm gone and you're gone, the sentiments of the boards could change," Mr. Gillette told Mr. Bubb. "I don't want it to happen, and I'm trying to ensure that it doesn't."

Speaking in opposition to the proposed annexation at last week's meeting were Charles and Diana Johnson, two Fern Valley ratepayers who have criticized adding more customers into the district. The Johnsons have contended at past FVWD board meetings that annexation would reduce property values within the district in the event of a drought and water shortages.

"When you talk about a drought, I don't see how adding 57 more homes is beneficial at all," Mr. Johnson said.

THE JOHNSONS WERE not pleased with the decision of the board. "What you did is give other people's property values away," Mrs. Johnson told the FVWD directors after the vote was taken.

However, Marsha Davis-Serizawa, FVWD director, disagreed, saying property values would not be affected and that the issue was irrelevant from the water district's point of view.

"We are here for one reason — to serve people with water. Property values are not our concern," Ms. Davis-Serizawa said. "I see no reason why we shouldn't annex [Saunders Meadow] into the district."

Mr. Bubb said the discussion last week was productive because it formally addressed the concerns of FVWD board members, who were also pleased with the results of the meeting.

"WE WERE ABLE to see some pluses for the district in addition to the benefits for [Saunders Meadow]," Mr. Van Sant said.

Saunders Meadow had approached FVWD about annexing into the district in September. The property owners group, which currently provides its own water service from U.S. Forest Service-owned springs, sought the annexation in order to improve its antiquated water system.

The property owners group is currently awaiting the approval of a loan from Farmer's Home Administration to finance the annexation.

1995 *Town Crier* Article

Termination of the Special Use Water Permit, 2013–2014

The annual membership meeting was held at AstroCamp on Saunders Meadow, as had been the tradition for the last eighty-six years. Discussion was made about the Granite Springs pipeline that runs to a spigot on Mactacklewood, "The well is non-potable water that has in recent years been used by some shareholders during drought conditions for irrigation (i.e., by driving a truck up to the spigot and filling barrels then taking them to water the lot pine trees). We have had a ten-year permit to use pipeline at a cost of $58 a year." Pat Maloney, member-at-large, met with Ranger Heidi Hogan who indicated that the price would go up to $292 that year with 1.9 percent per year annual increases. In addition, the well had to be maintained, including installation of a water meter, annual maintenance cost, and environmental impact report ($1,100). There was a recommendation to allow the well to revert back to the national forest. At this time, Bob Wissmann discussed history aspects of the well and transition to Fern Valley Water. Ms. Judy Schonebaum, a member of SM, Inc., made a motion to research with a knowledgeable lawyer to see if there was any compelling reason not to abandon the well.

2014

February 19, Saunders Meadow, Inc. called the Forest Service in regards to a water bill dated November 12, 2013, for the use of Granite Springs Pipeline.

On February 25, Ranger Heidi Hogan responded,

> I received a letter from you addressed to the Recreation Officer John Ladley in regards to the bill for the spring and pipeline under US Forest Service Special Use Permit . . . I have not heard from you since September 2013—I am glad you were able to come to a decision. In regards to the annual bill,

bills are sent out automatically to remind permittees to pay rent which is due prior to the use period . . . Since I had not heard of your decision to close, the permit is still considered issued . . . There are a few steps that need to occur in order to officially close your permit, and cease billing for annual rent:

1. You must restore the site . . . cut off the spring at the pipeline so that the water returns to the land at the spring site. The pipe can be left in place to avoid ground disturbance.
2. You must inform me that site has been restored so that I can inspect. I recommend that you take photos of your work; this is in your best interest.
3. I can then cancel the current bill and issue a final bill.
4. Once the corrected bill has been paid, I will close the permit and annual billing will cease.

At the annual membership meeting, everyone present voted to allow the well to revert back to the Forest Service after ninety-two years of having a special use water permit . . . ending a satisfying relationship of ninety-five years with the Forest Service, which started back in 1920.

Present Day

Saunders Meadow, Inc. is the only original association still in existence that went through the exchange program, with covenants, conditions, and restrictions focusing on maintaining the original principals of design from 1917 through the 1920s as originally conceived by landscape architects Waugh, Carhart, and Dubois. The community continues to strive to have lots blend into the forest that surrounds the area, as well as protect the common grounds that have been kept just as they were when they were a part of the San Bernardino National Forest.

Currently there are fifty-seven cabins out of the original fifty-nine. Two lots were used to expand trails and needed roads. Out of the fifty-seven summer homes, only two have been rebuilt in the same original design; these cabins are on lot 34 and lot 17, the rest have been modernized and upgraded. Out of the fifty-seven only one remains authentic to its 1921–24 design and construction: the cabin located on lot 33, which qualifies to be registered as a State and National Historical Place after ninety-four years of existence while still maintaining its original integrity. Saunders Meadow truly is a beautiful place without fences maintaining the national forest spirit.

It has been one hundred years since the Term Occupancy Permit Act passed Congress, and in celebration, Dr. Robert Reyes and Patrick Kennedy published *Saunders Meadow—A Place without Fences: A History of The Term Occupancy Permit Act of 1915, Celebrating 100 years* to preserve the history of our grand community.

All information comes from original minutes, secretary reports, letters, and memos dating back to 1921. All mentioned Tahquitz association or Saunders Meadow, Inc. files are located at the Idyllwild Area Historical Society archives. Members of the IAHS and serious inquirers are welcome to review documents at a scheduled time hosted by a historian.

Closure

The 1970s and 1980s were very challenging years that revealed many emotions in the acquisition of land, the subdivision, and lawsuit. Once it becomes your land, feelings get involved and rules change. Patience played a very important part in muddling through this new territory; leaders had to "keep on keeping on" while dealing with many issues and different personalities. But, at the end, the majority prevailed in accomplishing the impossible.

Throughout the research process, I had the privilege and honor of meeting (online) Mark Jones and his sister, Connie Jones

Pillsbury, whose grandfather Elwood and father John founded the community. I asked them what names stood out in regards to serving the tract and this is the list they provided:

1. Sam Minnich—Sam is the only person I knew who actually worked on the recovery from the San Francisco earthquake and fire in 1906. He became a successful walnut rancher in Chino. Sam was an excellent craftsman, as one could tell by all the custom features of their home. He was also a famous penny pincher and salvager scrounger, even though he had plenty of money. Mrs. Minnich cooked on a wood stove until the 1970s. Sam was instrumental in the water system throughout many years and worked closely with my dad. The last time I saw Sam at age ninety-four he was at the dump loading a discarded Forest Service picnic table weighing about 250 pounds into his trailer, by himself. He said it was for firewood. He already had about a ten-year supply stacked in sheds. He told me he would keep cutting for a couple more years, then coast on in.
2. Clark Hapeman—Clark was a high-level construction manager who oversaw many projects, including the reconstruction of the Burbank Airport, a huge challenge he successfully completed. He and my dad were contemporaries, and Clark was a major player in the water system in the ten to fifteen years or so before we joined Fern Valley Water District. He was a smart, savvy guy with a good heart, and very helpful on many issues in Saunders Meadow, Inc. Clark died of esophageal cancer I think maybe mid-1990s, shortly before our dad died. I will never forget their last meeting, two old co-campaigners, sick and aged, saying good-bye to each other. Clark was a very active member of the Idyllwild Area Historical Society (IAHS).

3. Ray Brocklehurst—Ray was a lifelong friend, along with his wife, Marge, of my grandparents, Elwood Marston Jones and Naomi Cory Jones. Ray was with Standard Oil for his entire career, I think maybe fifty years. A quiet, hardworking, and trustworthy man, he was also a craftsman. He and Marge were regular visitors at our cabin, and did much good upgrade work there before they built their own cabin across the meadow (later owned by Leigh Humphrey, their daughter). She was on the board for years and very helpful to me during my service and a friend for many years. Ray was on the board and helped my dad a great deal with the land exchange. No finer man could you ever have expected to meet.
4. Mr. Wissmann—I don't know much about Wissmann's career, but I believe it was in business. He was solid, reliable, and a community-minded contributor. He was the other main player with my dad in the land exchange. They were both smart, educated, and successful, but quiet guys—with a focus on getting things done for the good and not making a big bluster about it and that is what they did.
5. Martin Aguirre—Martin was a quiet distinguished older man when I knew him as a kid. I think he was a successful rancher from Hemet and may have had deep California roots. He was seen as a wise man and was very instrumental on the board.
6. Ed Calderon—Ed was a technical consultant of some kind, very smart and educated, and very detail oriented. He was a loner and extremely dedicated to Saunders Meadow. He was the unofficial major-domo (boss) of the water system, checking it daily for maybe the last ten years or so before conversion. He would leave these incredibly detailed notes

for my dad in the door of the cabin. Ed was a gracious and honorable man. He did a great deal for SMI.

7. Harry Bubb—He was the SMI president and board chair at the time I served in the 1990s. Harry was the retired CEO of Pacific Life, a very heavy hitter. I saw Harry as very supportive of the initiative to convert the water system to FVWD, and he was very much the CEO, happy to delegate and let me do the work and get the project done. It was a good working relationship and I really enjoyed working with Harry. His wife, Berdie, was a hoot! Harry is a strong financial supporter of the IAHS.
8. John B. Jones—My dad was the finest man I have ever known, honest to a fault, true to his family and friends, smart, purposeful, and steady, steady, steady. John suffered severe asthma as a child in Culver City and went to live with his grandparents on their apricot farm in Hemet. He graduated from Hemet High and went on to the University of Redlands where he met my mother. He had a successful business career, was highly trusted and respected by all who knew him. But he was quiet and modest, incredibly organized, not at all a swashbuckler or a hail-and-well-met guy. He served on the Saunders Meadow board for forty years, and we have a plaque of appreciation for that. His leadership was the main driver in transforming Saunders Meadow from a Forest Service lease deal about to expire, to full fee ownership. I have spent my whole life trying to live up to his example.
9. Elwood M. Jones—Elwood graduated from Pasadena High School and went on to a very successful business career in the oilfield supply industry. For years he worked the oil fields in the Central Valley as a traveling salesman, and ended up

as west coast vice president for Stockham Valve and Fitting Corp. He was an avid fly fisherman. He was very driven, highly respected by all. He essentially started the SM water system.

10. Mark Jones—I am rooted in Idyllwild, my first visit there was in a basket at about six weeks. Our regular visits to the cabin were very formative during my childhood, even up to my first working years as a teenager in construction at Idyllwild. Then I became a homebuilder there at age nineteen. But I am very different from my father and grandfather in that I am equally or perhaps more driven but not place-anchored. I have pursued remarkable career opportunities all over the Southwest. I don't want to bore you with my resume, but I offer it as my testimony to those who went before. When I returned to LA in 1990 to take over as university architect at USC, I was asked to join the SMI board as secretary and then when we realized that with tightening EPA regulations our days as an independent water supplier were numbered. The rest is history, of which I am very proud. If my grandfather could start the water system, and my dad could expand and improve it over the decades, then the least I could do was to secure its future. I would have stayed with the SMI board, but in 1994, I was asked to become director to the $250 million-a-year capital construction program at Stanford University, reporting to Provost Condi Rice.
11. Connie Jones Pillsbury—She grew up seeing the history unfold. She is the family historian and is writing a book on the history of the family cabin and their contribution to the community.

Many years have passed since the 1970s and 1980s, and all is water under the bridge. Those still alive are living as civil neighbors and those long gone have been forgotten. The tract is still there, just as peaceful and tranquil as before. The old California black oak tree in front of the old historic Forest Service cabin of 1921 on 27160 Saunders Meadow Road (lot 33) still stands in all its majesty as the protector of the community as it has for the last 300 years. The stories it must have. On a cool starry evening while the breeze blows, if you try hard enough, you can hear it whispering how the Cahuilla tribe gave it birth and gently watered it making sure that there would be a future in this lovely place called Saunders Meadow.

Saunders Meadow Road

Saunders Meadow, looking toward historic cabin on the far left

Idyllwild, California, a Mountain Community Surrounded by the San Bernardino National Forest

The history of the Forest Service is in part connected to its relationship with small mountaintop communities such as Idyllwild. The recreational, social, and economic links between both is unquestionable and sealed in their dependence on each other. These small towns relied on the protection provided by the rangers and recreation visitors to the national forests. In turn, these communities provided the guests what the Forest Service could not: places to stay, dine, and shop. To understand the development of both is to appreciate the wonderful heritage and historic value that these mountain communities share.

Riding toward the Rock

Area History

San Bernardino National Forest was nothing more than a prehistoric shallow swamp during the late Paleozoic and early Mesozoic eras. As a result of volcanic activity and fault movement, the mountain range was formed and pushed to its present location.

Many primitive tribes roamed the region. In the 1500s the Cahuilla tribe occupied the land. The Cahuilla "Iviatim" tribe was first drawn to the area in the 1400s by a body of water, later referred to as Lake Cahuilla, that had been created by the Colorado River. The true lake is long gone, but the tribe remains. Iviatim is believed to mean "masters," for they truly understood their land. In fact, the Apapatcem clan had superior knowledge of the medicinal uses of native plants. (It is rumored that these medicine people used Trichostema Parishii, or Mountain Wooly Blue Curls, for male erectile dysfunction. The females would sneak a little into the men's drinks in order to protect their egos.)

These peaceful people were the first to venture up the San Jacinto Mountains, establishing trails that were later used by adventure seekers and loggers. The men would hunt while the women collected pine needles and deer grass used to weave baskets while finding relief from the 120-degree weather below. High in the cool springs of Strawberry Valley, the children collected acorns for the women to grind into flour while dropping a few in the ground for future generations. Their mortar holes are still present and always found by springs of water and California oak trees. The acorns were very important to their diet.

These early Native Americans viewed the sharp rocky mountain peaks of the San Jacinto Mountains as a step down from heaven where gods dwelled and spoke among the thunder. Lily Rock, a famous climbers' destination, better know as Tahquitz, was one of these steps and used by early climbers such as Royal Robbins, who developed the first safety and scale techniques, later applying them in Yosemite, which are still being used worldwide. Tahquitz Peak was named after a greatly feared deity who brought unspeakable harm to all who dared to approach and explore his domain. Many fair maidens vanished who did not heed the warnings. These spiritual, peace-loving, and brave people eventually became *vaqueros* at the Rancho San Bernardino where they were given the name Cahuilla.

From the 1500s to 1800s, explorers from Spain came to California to spread the Roman Catholic religion, save the innocent, and claim the land. Juan Rodriguez Cabrillo sailed from Mexico to what is now San Diego Bay. Sebastian Viscaino explored and named Monterey Bay in 1602.

From 1697 to 1821, the San Jacinto Mountains were admired but ignored by the European explores who found no value in the desert. The focus of the Spanish was colonization by the establishment of missions and ranchos. In 1804, Father Antonio Cruzado from Spain planted what became California's first orange grove. The early 1820s saw the end of the Spanish rule when Mexico fought for and won its independence from Spain. In 1821, the Mexicans switched focus from the missions to land grants, ranching, and trade, none of which affected the San Jacinto range. Pio Pico became the last Mexican governor of California. In the 1860s, his nephew grazed his cattle in the vicinity. Coincidentally, his granddaughter, Ruth Pico, lived in the special use summer home tract of Tahquitz on Saunders Meadow, Idyllwild, in the 1920s.

In 1846, the United States declared war with Mexico. Concurrently, American settlers in California revolted and declared their independence from Mexico forming the California Republic, which lasted only twenty-six days. When the leaders of the republic finally heard of the Mexican-American War, they disbanded and welcomed the United States forces. In 1848, California was acquired by the United States under the terms of the Treaty of Guadalupe Hidalgo. With the discovery of gold in 1849 and the American westward expansion, California joined the Union in 1850 as a free state, to the delight of President Abraham Lincoln. In 1853, Mr. Levi Strauss moved to California after the initial gold rush. He and a friend noticed that miners needed stronger pants. They started selling heavy denim blue jeans in 1873.

During this time, the lack of gold in the San Jacinto Mountains kept it in a deep slumber, but events to come were brewing just below the surface, the winds of change were near. The sleepy, tranquil mountaintop valley would finally see more movement than ever before.

Homesteading

After the devastation of the Civil War in 1865, the United States government encouraged national growth and expansion through the many homesteading acts passed by Congress. Many easterners moved west to escape and forget the horrors of the past. Horace Greeley, in the nineteenth century, penned the nation's sentiments well, "Go West, young man, go West and grow up with the country." This American author and politician viewed the West as a guaranteed success for those willing to work hard. Covered wagons, farmers, herds, and pioneers soon spread across the Great Plains and into the West. Throughout this century, the San Jacinto area and mountains attracted these westward-bound pioneers. From 1855 to the late 1800s, homesteaders, miners, and settlers arrived at the foot of the mountain range. Using the ancient Cahuilla footpaths, Francisco Pico, nephew of the last governor of Mexican California, and Swiss immigrant Angelo Domenigoni and their herds of sheep and cattle ascended the steep terrain to find themselves among the wild strawberry-filled valley later known as Idyllwild.

With the Homestead Act of 1862, which encouraged settlement in timberland to provide the needed ties and fuel for the expanding railroads, and with the Pacific Railroad Land Grant Acts that Congress so liberally approved in 1862, 1864, and 1867, many loggers moved west and up the range into the higher elevations. Colonel Milton Hall was one who secured a contract with the Southern Pacific Railroad. He helped establish the beginning of forestry commerce within this virgin valley. Not only did the colonel have a sawmill, he also set up a town with a store, boarding house, blacksmith, saloon, and a laundry run by Chinese workers. With the high demand for timber being abundantly supplied, the first transcontinental railroad opened in 1869. With the connection of the East to the West, many new towns and cities rose over night. The nation grew and the West was won, at the expense of our natural resources.

The nation eventually became aware and concerned with the effects of clear cutting and deforestation, which led to the birth of America's forestry movement. As a result, in 1891 the president was given power to establish forest reserves from public lands with the passing of the Forest Reserve Act.

Pioneer Homestead Cabin, 1910

Idyllwild History

From 1875 to 1906 lumber was the main source of income in Strawberry Valley. Loggers no longer used the Cahuilla trails, but had a choice between one of two new toll roads. The first was by logger Colonel Milton Sanders Hall. After acquiring a contract from the Southern Pacific Railroad for track ties, Hall hired E.Y. Bucharan to build a wagon road he could use to bring down his timber. Bucharan managed to do a great job in hewing a horrid and deathly steep, zigzagging, rocky road. Businessman Joseph Crawford, who noticed the need for a better road and the opportunity for a profit, hired the Cahuilla to help build the second toll road that would cater to both loggers and horseback parties. Yet both Hall and Crawford's roads proved to be very challenging. Teams of oxen would carefully descend the steep mountain carrying full loads of the local native pines. These grand trees of sugar, Jeffrey, and ponderosa species were known to grow between 100 to 250 feet high with bark seven to ten inches wide. With such heavy loads and steep trails, many lost their lives. If the brakes gave out, the animals would lose their grip and all would be destroyed. Those who survived would crawl only to find the remains of both man and beast. These early rugged and fearless entrepreneurs established the first need for commerce up on the hill.

Horseback-riding adventuresome visionaries impressed with such natural beauty recognized the opportunity for commerce in both providing supplies to loggers as well as the many possible recreational ventures that this area had to offer. Such was the case with logger and entrepreneur George Hannahs, who, with his wife, Sarah, built the Strawberry Valley Hotel in 1889; they added Camp Idyllwild in 1890 to accommodate the growing number of guests. John and Mary Keen also opened Keen House that same year and Keen Camp in 1905. Recreation quickly grew around all the logging activities, each interacting with the other. As the number of visitors to the forest increased, their cry against the destruction of the forest was heard by Congress. On February 22, 1897, President Grover Cleveland established the San Jacinto Forest Reserve. The forest was finally protected and the end of lumbering was at hand. With the switch from logging to recreation, Idyllwild grew. A post office and health sanatorium joined the village between 1899 and 1901, established by George Hannahs and Dr. Walter Lindley, respectively.

As a publicity stunt, the first car visited the town in 1900 driven by Dr. Lindley who opened the Idyllwild Sanatorium in 1901. Regular round trips from Los Angeles to the sanatorium followed, offered by Dr. Lindley's San Jacinto–Idyllwild Transportation Company in 1901. Nine years later, in 1910, with the completion of the high gear and safer Banning Idyllwild Road in 1910, the "Banning-Idyllwild Stage Line" provided better and safer travel, bringing guests to the San Jacinto forest reserve and the blooming village of Idyllwild in 1911. President Theodore Roosevelt, as an act of respect, proclaimed the area as part of the new Cleveland National Forest in honor of the former president. After much protest and outcry, on September 30, 1925, the San Jacinto mountain range became the San Bernardino National Forest.

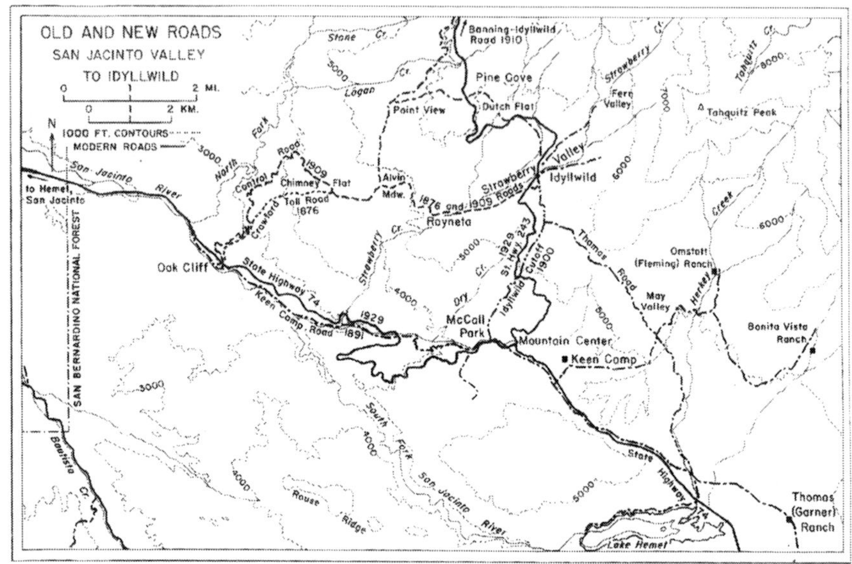

Roads to Idyllwild

Local Ranger Station, 1903

Our San Jacinto-Idyllwild Forest Rangers

In the newly created reserve surrounding the growing town of Idyllwild, the San Jacinto rangers had their work cut out for them. They had to organize and create a plan of action that would meet the growing recreational needs of the public as well as provide forest fire prevention and protection for both reserve and town. Rangers were hired on a part-time basis and only during the fire season. They were required to supply their own equipment, which included a saddled horse, bags, axe, shovels, cooking supplies, and provisions, all on only a monthly salary of $55 or less.

Due to the harsh local terrain, forest fires were a major threat and these brave men came to be recognized for their hard work in fire control techniques that were emulated across the country. These early innovators began studying effects and methods of fire control as early as 1910. They pioneered new fire management methods such as fixed-point observations, fire trails, breaks, crew tactics, and field communication and, in 1919, the first detection aerial plane patrols. In the 1920s, Coert Dubois, both architect and ranger, not only provided cabin construction plans to special use summer home permittees at Tahquitz tract on Saunders Meadow and across California, he also worked with Ranger Steven Augustus Nash-Boulden in developing fire-prevention and fire-fighting tactics. In 1926, Nash-Boulden was appointed the first forest supervisor of the newly named San Bernardino National Forest. He implemented the Fire Control Plan, which included lookout towers and the first fire permit system. Shortly thereafter, Region 5 published the "Fire Manual" which contained all of these cutting-edge policies and techniques that would eventually be improved upon and used across the regions.

While fighting fires, our rangers walked over fifteen miles to surround mountainside flames. After a full day, they slept under the stars, or in a Forest Service lean-to like the one built on Tahquitz tract on Saunders Meadow in 1921, only to start all over again until the forest was safe. This disproved the belief of many critics that rangers only lounged at the Idyllwild Inn gallivanting among the ladies in their pressed and smart uniforms topped with a stiff-brimmed army campaign hat and sharp high leather boots. Nothing could be further from the truth. Rangers were heroes, the new cowboys admired by all and desired by the opposite sex.

One of these heroes was Miss Rita Morris, the first female ranger in San Bernardino National Forest to work the lookout towers. She became an instant celebrity, a hero to the local women. In appreciation, the townsfolk would occasionally bring her meals. Morris was as sweet as the cookies her admirers provided. She gave herself a Roaring Twenties flapper bob hairstyle to keep the hair off her face while watching for fires, this safety change made her all the rage. Miss Rita had many would-be suitors as well, but her faithful tower companion pooch would only let them get so far. Morris was the first of the future Rosie the Riveters, strong and intelligent women who would keep the country moving while the boys were overseas during WWII.

Another perhaps notorious ranger was Chad. Whether truth or legend, one thing was certain: after a day's work, this redhead continued his nocturnal activities with the ladies. Some even claimed he tasted like a cherry pop. Needless to say, he thought he was the cat's meow and a bag of chips. Humor aside, our young foresters were smart and brave. No tenderfoot ever lasted but a day.

Some of our rangers were Yale educated at the university's School of Forestry, which had been funded by Gifford Pinchot's father. These interns had to overcome their East Coast lily-livered backgrounds once they were assigned to the West. Many of our first rangers from the late 1800s and early 1900s were tough pioneering homesteaders accustomed to the local terrain and lifestyle. They knew how to work hard and survive, but were too rough and, at times, one egg short of a dozen. Pinchot needed rangers who were not only capable of protecting the wilderness, but capable of becoming inspectors and forester assistants. These young eastern interns quickly earned their hats and boots, becoming full-fledged Californians through good-natured kidding. The old rangers placed any available varmint in the college boys' tents at night causing them to yell and scream like "pretty little girls," which would haunt them for months. The boys got over the teasing and in no time became true rangers and the pride of Idyllwild.

In the early 1920s, with the end of WWI and an increase in both the reliability and affordability of the automobile along with the public's interest in recreational outings, camping became a major focus and the San Bernardino National Forest became a desired destination. The government responded by providing funding for the turning of old trails into public roads and building of highways to and within national forests. At this time, Forest Service supervisors started using the Ford Model T automobile to tour and inspect terrain. Their young whippersnapper drivers terrorized them by driving at the deathly speed of ten miles per hour over trails covered with large debris and holes created by erosion, causing the youthful rangers to lose control and their bosses to literally bounce up and out of the car. This only encouraged the Forest Service to rush the improvement of all roads and trails and consider the possibilities of letting the youngsters drive motorcycles instead. Their justification was that more forest ground would be covered in a shorter amount of time.

Forest Rangers, 1920s

Forest Service/Army Air Corps Fire Patrol, 1919

Automobiles in the Forest Service

Ranger Rita Morris

Idyllwild Continues to Grow

The new San Jacinto Forest Reserve helped to establish Idyllwild as a recreation destination. Referred to by regional newspapers as the Garden of Eden, Alps of Southern California, and Yosemite of the Southland, investors bought land, sold lots, and established neighborhoods. Many secular and religious camps were founded as well. In 1912 and 1913, Los Angeles real estate investors Frank Strong and George Dickenson purchased thousands of acres and competed with George Hannahs in subdividing and selling individual lots. That same year the "Touring Car" company provided round-trip transportation to the wealthier who had the resources required for a summer-long vacation. If they were going to make the long trip up, they were going to stay three months. The local Idyllwild Inn opened in 1906, replacing the 1905 bungalow resort that had replaced the burned down Idyllwild Sanatorium of 1901, which had served as both a tuberculosis hospital and recreation luxury resort, providing the latest in modern comforts to both patients and vacationers.

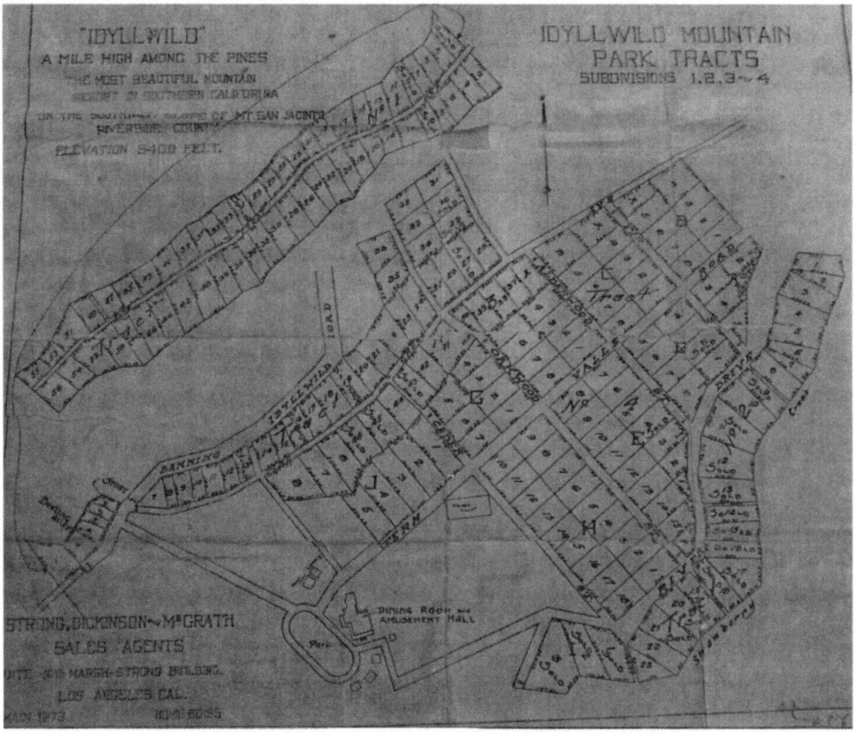

Strong & Dickinson, 1913 Idyllwild Mountain
Park Tracts, Subdivision 1, 2, 3, and 4

Idyllwild Inn Cottages, 1900s

The new Idyllwild Inn provided activities required for fun and social gossip. Local and regional newspapers filled their society pages with the latest comings and goings of the upper class, calling others up the hill to join in the fun and frolic. Seeing the opportunity presented by these long-term and annual visiting elite, investor Claudius Lee Emerson bought a portion of Strong and Dickinson's subdivisions in 1917 that included the Idyllwild Inn and 1,000 acres. He and his wife, Zelma, made the inn the social center of the area, offering many activities and events such golf, horseback riding, religious retreats, camping ventures, and lots for sale. In a savvy move, Emerson gave a portion of his land for Boy Scout camps and church retreats in 1919, which only attracted more guests. A year later, with the increase of new visitors, vacationers, and investors, Emerson's lot sales boomed. He also started the first local newspaper, the *Idyllwild Breeze*, that served as a sales brochure for his properties while reporting the latest social events.

In 1923, the growing community of Idyllwild saw the replacement of their old faithful 1800s sawmill steam boiler generator with modern lines from Southern Sierras Power Company. To the delight of all residents and visitors, electricity was now available twenty-four hours a day. Between 1920 and 1924, as a result of the Term Occupancy Permit Act of 1915, the Forest Service surveyed and opened a few local special use summer home tracts: Fern Valley, Lily Creek, and the Tahquitz Saunders Meadow tracts, all offering a total of 112 lots that private citizens could lease for $25 a year on a thirty-year permit and build summer homes, with many more on the drawing board. Summer homes in Forest Service tracts continued to be very popular and successful during the Great Depression. In 1928, Emerson donated land to the Southern California Religious Education Council that opened Idyllwild Pines Camp. In his honor, Emerson Hall was built. A year later, a Christian group from Los

Angeles acquired Tahquitz Pines from Strong and Dickinson and, in 1931, ran a conference center. (It later became the Wycliffe Bible Translators training center. The center, is currently under the ownership of California Baptist University.)

During the 1920s and 1930s, Hollywood discovered Idyllwild: seventy-plus films were made in the area. It all started back in 1914 with Cecil B. DeMille filming *The Squaw Man* and *The Girl of The Golden West* in the Keen Camp vicinity. Big stars like Mary Pickford, Katharine Hepburn, and Paulette Goddard, all friends of Idyllwild, stayed at the Idyllwild Inn.

The growth of the Roaring Twenties ended with a crash in 1929. Idyllwild inched ahead during the Great Depression and WWII. It survived off Emerson's summer camps and all their patrons and the special use summer home tracts and permittees who needed goods and building materials. Idyllwild also benefited from the Desert Sun School on Saunders Meadow as well as Hollywood filming movies in the area, Army officers visiting, the CCC, and regular summer home owners who built quite a few new cabins during the 1930s.

Bungalow Hotel, 1905

Idyllwild Inn, 1906

Idyllwild Pines Camp

Emerson Hall

Claudius Lee Emerson's vision for Idyllwild, 1928

Idyllwild under snow

Civilian Conservation Corps

On March 4, 1933, President Franklin D. Roosevelt stated, "Our greatest task is to put people to work. This is no unsolvable problem if we face it wisely and courageously. It can be accomplished in part by direct recruiting by the government itself, treating the task as we would treat the emergency of war, but at the same time, through this employment, accomplishing greatly needed projects to stimulate and recognize the use of our national resources." Congress responded by passing the Emergency Conservation Work Act (ECWA) on March 31, 1933. A few days later, one of President Roosevelt's New Deal programs, the Civilian Conservation Corps, was created to provide jobs in conservation and development of natural resources in rural and forest lands owned by the government. Surrounded by national forests, mountaintop communities such as Idyllwild benefited from the hundreds of young men recruited by this relief program.

The young men enrolled for six months. After a physical examination and vaccinations, the boys took the CCC oath in Camp Idyllwild on Alvin Meadow. The new recruits received shoes, socks, underwear, blue denim work clothes, and surplus Army uniforms to wear into town and during formal inspections. Their days started with the sound of the bugle at exactly 6:00 am. Breakfast was after the morning exercise session. After roll call, the "Cs" were on their way to work by 7:45. Their hour-long lunch was in the field under the local pines and oaks. The boys returned to the Idyllwild Camp by 4:00 pm with dinner ready at 5:30. Instructional classes were provided after dinner. Many of the men learned to read and write for the first time. Some were awarded both intermediate and high school diplomas. Others received vocational training as truck drivers, welders, builders, and mechanics. During their term, the boys earned $30 a month. The lads had five dollars to spend in town, the other twenty-five were sent home to help their large families in accordance with the Great Depression relief plan stipulations. With their shelter and meals provided, the town benefited from the boys' extra money. Camp Idyllwild averaged 213 recruits. Each had $5 to spend for a grand total of $1,065 per month and this did not include the needed supplies that the camp required for both meals and construction materials.

The Army and the United States Forest Service got the inexperienced and uneducated juniors in shape and disciplined. The Forest Service trained them in fire prevention and construction. In fact, with the help of the boys, our rangers in San Bernardino National Forest took first place for the highest number of ready-cut buildings completed before winter in 1933. The military also provided self-improvement skills and practical life training. No longer bewildered, lost, unskilled, and untrained, these eighteen-to-twenty-five-year-old men were ready to meet the demands and needs of both life and the Forest Service.

"The Copeland Report—A Nation Plan for American Forestry"— which had just been released by Congress, contained hundreds of projects that needed completion. The timing was perfect, the Forest Service was in great need of funding and manpower while the nation was desperate and willing to work. These young men, alongside and under the direction of our rangers, built trails, campgrounds, cabins, roads, stations, lookouts, firebreaks, and ran telephone lines. They even added swings to campgrounds for the local children and visitors. They also built concrete picnic benches, replacing the wooden ones that had been used as firewood by enthusiastic guests. The CCC boys also worked side by side with specially appointed and trained rangers in landscape design and construction. Their focus was on recreational areas such as camping facilities, ranger stations, and summer home tract trails and firebreaks.

They worked tirelessly on Saunders Meadow Road and the dirt trails in the Tahquitz tract. They also surveyed for future recreation summer home tracts adjacent to Saunders Meadow and Tahquitz along the old Thomas Road to May Valley.

The boys worked very hard, but also had time to rest. After their thirty- to forty-hour weekly schedule, the town would provide dancing and fun social activities where the "Juniors" would meet the locals and tourists. If the boys were lucky, there would be many a peck and good old-fashioned kissing with the local young ladies. The Rustic Tavern, built by Manzanita furniture maker Hal Holcomb, was one of the boys' favorite hangouts. "Ma" Poates's Sunday Fried Chicken Dinner Special was a hit with the lads and their lady friends. One of the last projects the boys worked on was inspecting the Tahquitz tract on Saunders Meadow in order to prevent forest fires and raking all pine needles. After the attack on Pearl Harbor in 1941 and the beginning of WWII, the CCC ended, abolished by a Congressional Joint Committee on July 1, 1942.

Through the war, military personnel from the many local bases visited Idyllwild, helping the local economy. In 1943, Keen Camp (also known as Tahquitz Lodge) burned down and was followed by the Idyllwild Inn in 1945. Ernie and Betty Maxwell became full-time Idyllwild residents and started a new local newspaper, the *Idyllwild Town Crier*, creating a strong sense of community and perseverance in 1946. The young chamber of commerce worked hard through these tough times on establishing Idyllwild as a weekend resort thanks to the infrastructure prepared by the CCC.

The CCC boys, 1930s

The CCC boys working on a campground

Post-WWII Era, 1945

The end of the war brought prosperity and growth to Idyllwild. People were ready to forget the pain. Soldiers returned with benefits. They were ready to work, buy homes, and vacation. The San Bernardino National Forest was ready for them, thanks to all the facilities built by the CCC and the soon-to-be approved 1950s Operation Outdoors, a congressional recreation program that would provide funding for more recreation facilities. The number of visitors to the national forests jumped from 8.5 million to 81 million during this era. Emerson's camps were full. Tourists and visitors took interest in Idyllwild as an ideal place for a second home.

Two schools were established, the arts school, Idyllwild School of Music and The Arts (or ISOMATA), which became one of the finest in the nation, and the Desert Sun School, which later became the renowned science camp AstroCamp, both attracting students from across the nation and abroad. Eminent ISOMATA faculty included Meredith Wilson, who wrote the *The Music Man* in Idyllwild, Alfred Eisenstadt, a *Life* magazine photojournalist, Harvey Sternberg, a prominent New York printmaker, Bella Lewitsky, a renowned dancer, and Ansel Adams, the great photographer. Hollywood also returned to Idyllwild with Elvis Presley filming *Kid Galahad* and Doris Day building a home adjacent to Saunders Meadow. Frank Sinatra Jr. also attended school on Saunders Meadow. Thanks to the visionary foresight of Emerson and the CCC's work, both the San Bernardino National Forest and Idyllwild were set and established as summer and weekend destinations for the next millennium.

As presented by Dr. Robert B. Smith in the Idyllwild Historic Resource Survey, "In 1947, the local postmaster estimated that about 300 families lived in town, several new businesses opened. The Fern Valley Bakery, the Hillbilly Variety Store, a new post office next to the

Log Cabin Realty building, and the Rustic Theater all made Idyllwild more appealing as a resort town to the weekend visitor. By 1956, the area boasted 800 residents. In 1957, the permanent population topped 1,000 residents and the *Town Crier* reported that over one million visitors came to Idyllwild. In the 1960s, Idyllwild continued to grow with the addition of the Red Kettle, Village Market, and the Fern Valley Market. The Security First National Bank completed in 1964 as an A-frame building solidified the center of town." During this time, Idyllwild attracted many barefooted "high"-ly creative hippies, adding to the town's developing artistic sector.

Currently 2016

"Over the subsequent years," Smith wrote, "Idyllwild continued to grow. Hundreds of thousands of tourists continue to visit Idyllwild, enjoying the same stunning natural beauty and quiet, reflective activities that have come to characterize the area for more than a century. This natural beauty we call our home is the single factor that has caused the residents with varying backgrounds and lifestyles to unite and live in harmony, protecting the quiet that only Idyllwild can offer."

Many thanks go to the Idyllwild Area Historical Society and historian Dr. Robert Smith for their support and contribution to this section. All credit goes to them and their prior research, www.idyllwildhistory.org.

Appendices

1. National Register of Historic Places: Historic Cabin original Forest Service Lot 19, currently Lot 33—27160 Saunders Meadow Rd. Idyllwild, California—San Bernardino National Forest
2. Forest Service Timeline
3. Idyllwild Timeline
4. Saunders Meadow Timeline
5. References
6. Author's Biography

NOTE: National Register listing is an honor that signifies that your property is an important part of America's cultural heritage and worthy of preservation.

The National Register of Historic Places is the official list of the nation's historic places worthy of preservation. Authorized by the National Historic Preservation Act of 1966, the National Park Service's National Register of Historic Places is part of a national program to coordinate and support public and private efforts to identify, evaluate, and protect America's historic and archeological resources.

The National Register nomination process usually starts with your local State Historic Preservation Office (SHPO). Contact your SHPO or check their webpage for information, research materials, and the necessary forms to begin the nomination process. They also have examples to help you with the process as well. To be considered eligible, a property must meet the National Register Criteria for Evaluation. This involves examining the property's age, integrity, and significance.

Age and Integrity: Is the property old enough to be considered historic (generally at least fifty years old, but not necessarily), and does it still look much the way it did in the past?

Significance: Is the property associated with events, activities, or developments that were important in the past, or with the lives of people who were important in the past? With significant architectural history, landscape history, or engineering achievements? Does it have the potential to yield information through archeological investigation about our past?

Nominations can be submitted to your SHPO. Your state's historic preservation office and the state's National Register Review Board review proposed nominations. The length of the state process varies but will take a minimum of ninety days. Complete nominations, with certifying recommendations, are submitted by the state to the National Park Service in Washington, DC, for final review and listing by the keeper of the National Register of Historic Places. The National Park Service makes a listing decision within forty-five days.

The following is an example of the main required written sections (7&8) on the application form using the subject Historic Cabin, Lot 19/33.

National Register of Historic Places—Historic Cabin, 27160 Saunders Meadow Rd.

The cabin used as an example can represent many of the cabins built as a result of The Term Occupancy Permit Act of 1915. Hence, this book can be used as your justification for your cabin's historic significance.

Section 7 of the registration form is the narrative description: "Describe the historic and current physical appearance and condition of the property. Describe contributing and noncontributing resources if applicable. Begin with a summary paragraph that briefly describes the general characteristics of the property, such as its location, type, style, and method of construction, setting, size, and significant features. Indicate whether the property has historic integrity." It goes without saying that you will have to modify this section to match the details of your own cabin, but the main ideas are presented in order for you to put in your specific details.

Summary Paragraph:

The 773-square-foot "Old Forest Service Cabin" is found at 27160 Saunders Meadow Road (Lot 19/33) and is located one half mile northeast of the mountain community of Idyllwild, California, in the San Bernardino National Forest mountain range of San Jacinto. It is one of fifty-seven cabins originally known as the Forest Service Tahquitz Summer Home Tract of 1920, based on the Term Occupancy Permit Act of 1915. The property consists of approximately .30 acres of forested ridge adjacent to a meadow and surrounded by pines and a 300-year-old California black oak tree. Other Forest Service summer homes are in close proximity. The cabin's north side is facing Saunders Meadow Road and the meadow. The low-profile, single-story cabin with a tiny loft was built in 1921 by the Forest Service as a 2x4 and plywood structure and upgraded in 1924 using Coert Dubois's "Side Gable" Forest Service plans, with further modernizations and improvements in the 1940s. The cabin has not changed much since its construction. A few improvements after all these years were necessary, such as a new roof and plumbing, but all improvements have been made to maintain the cabin's historic integrity.

The cabin's setting is rural former national forest land. Landscape is natural vegetation consisting largely of native pines, oaks, and Manzanita bushes. The property has two dirt trail driveways, both located off Saunders Meadow Road. One leads to the original wood pier foundation that accommodated the minor slope. The other driveway leads to the porch by the 300-year-old California black oak tree, welcoming guests into the kitchen entrance added in 1949.

The cabin has the original paired casement windows, retaining their original casings, glass, and hardware with built-in screens on the exterior. The outer finish is shiplap siding with the exception of the southern side, which is still the original 2x4s and plywood construction. The roof is composite and retains the original Forest Service color to blend with nature. This lovely rustic Forest Service cabin is a prime example of a period cabin and its improvement stages that were so common at the time. For example, when water and electricity were available, these rustic cabins would add bathrooms, kitchens, and power while maintaining the Forest Service required rustic standards of construction.

Included is a timeline of significant events:

1921—With Tahquitz Special Use Summer Home Tract approved, the Forest Service built a lean-to structure on current 27160 Saunders Meadow Road (then lot 19, currently lot 33) for their own use during fire prevention training and as a daily place of rest for working rangers. The location was selected due to the view of the meadow and shade provided by the oak tree planted perhaps by the Cahuilla tribe. Rangers surveyed and planned many more tracts in the vicinity of this lean-to. Its foundation was only piles of stones that held up the corner posts.

1924—The Forest Service leased lot 19 with its 2x4s and plywood lean-to to Mr. Richard Hass. Ranger and architect Coert

Dubois offered Hass his plans for a ranger structure. Hass accepted and enhanced the old shack into a Dubois "Side Gable Cabin" on a wood pier foundation. Hass kept the original plywood siding on the south side; the rest of the cabin was shiplap. All cooking was done outdoors, so the cabin only had a food storage and prep area with an icebox.

1927–1930s—Hal Holcomb, a pioneer of rustic American furniture and interiors, worked on the cabin. He built the loft hand railings, fireplace mantel, kitchen cabinets, and bedroom built-in mirror and dresser.

1933—CCC worked on Tahquitz tract's firebreak, dirt trails, and Saunders Meadow Road. The CCC boys had lunch and rested under the oak tree on subject cabin lot 19.

1938—A great winter storm hit the tract. Many cabins collapsed, Mr. Hass has rustic log beams added for support.

1940—Tahquitz tract hit a new water source and decided to contact the county for the possibility of replacing outhouses with flushing toilets. County of Riverside Office of Health stated that a septic tank with leaching tile drain was allowable on lot 19.

1943—Mr. Hass sold the cabin to Ralph C. Henly who became tract association president for a term. He also added a flushing toilet. Riverside County added the cabin to their building records for the first time due to the toilet permit.

1945—Mr. Henly built a shower area next to toilet and, in 1949, added a propane tank and a Magic Chef stove. (The company claimed that 50 percent of American homes had a Magic Chef stove!)

1953—Ralph Henly turned porch into a screened-in summer sleeping area, and in 1955 he turned it into a bedroom using the original 1924 windows and moving the entrance to the west side. This increased the cabin from 504 square feet to 773.

1962–1972—Henly sold the cabin to Richard Spaulding. The

Forest Service told the tract association to participate in the exchange program. In order to do so, the association had to incorporate.

1970—Tahquitz had its first meeting as the new Saunders Meadow, Inc. As part of the exchange program, the county required lots to become a recorded subdivision, so the long process is begun.

1972—The land exchange was completed with the Forest Service after five years of hard work. Mr. Spaulding sold the cabin to Jim Montgomery who became tract secretary.

1980—After ten years of work, the tract was finally recorded as a subdivision with lots privately owned by cabin owners.

1982—Taxes increased due to fee ownership title status.

1995—Saunders Meadow, Inc. joins Fern Valley Water District. After many years of struggling with the water issue they annex securing the future of the cabins. The Montgomery family inherit the cabin from Jim. The original "Forest Service Cabin of 1921" is now a teardown in need of a new roof, foundational work, septic tank, plumbing, electrical, and exterior painting.

1995–2010—The Montgomery family had everything fixed and repaired while maintaining all historic integrity.

2010–2012—The cabin is vacant for two years then sold in 2012 to Dr. Robert Reyes and Patrick Kennedy. They work on the exterior (priming and painting) and furnish with period, vintage furniture and décor.

2016—Dr. Robert Reyes publishes book *Saunders Meadow—A Place without Fences: A History of The Term Occupancy Permit Act of 1915, Celebrating 100 years.*

Narrative Description:

Architect Frank A. Waugh, landscape engineer Arthur H. Carhart, ranger and architect Coert Dubois, and recreation specialist Frederick William Cleator, all influenced by the American Society of Landscape Architects, produced a rustic charm that characterized and helped define the special use summer home cabin's architecture as the "American campground" design. These cabins were grand and beautiful in their utilitarian simplicity so properly located in our nation's pristine forests and proud to have survived one hundred years of life.

Original cabins that are still standing continue to produce a rustic charm with their simple rectangular shapes. Painted in Manzanita reds and browns they easily blend into their natural terrain and reflect the Forest Service philosophy of being safe, useful, practical, and cost effective while using local materials. These cabins helped establish recreation as a legitimate use of our national forests.

Historic Cabin

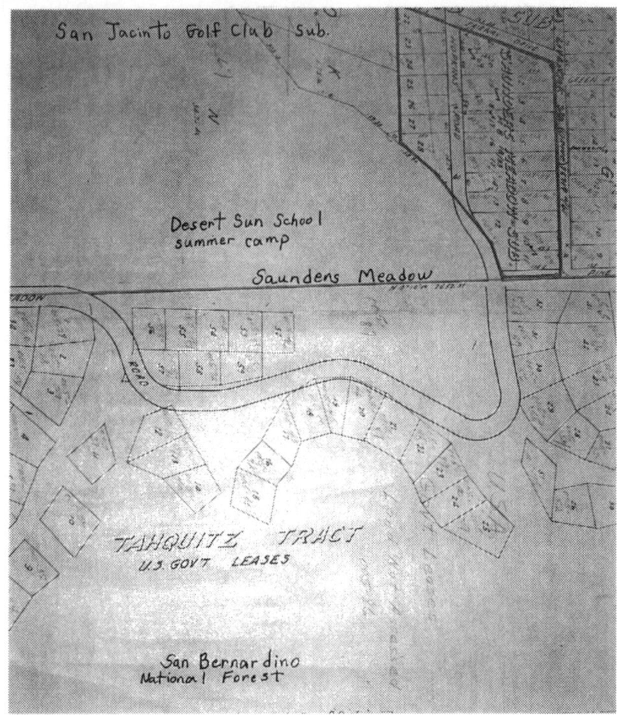

Tahquitz Tract Map, 1932

East Exterior—Back façade:

This side of the cabin has the original shiplap siding and stone chimney stack, which extends above the gable roof line, built in 1927–1930 by Lem Poats, a locally known stonemason who not only worked on other Forest Service summer home cabins, but also supervised the construction of the local town hall.

The original firewood box opening is also located on this side, located left of the chimney stack.

South Exterior—Side elevation:

This side has the original 2x4s and plywood siding with the eating area built in 1945. It faces the San Bernardino National Forest. Original casement windows and framed screens are also located on this wall.

West Exterior—Front façade:

The front gable has a high-pitched roof that is ideal for heavy snow and allows for a tiny loft. There is a deck that was added in 1949 in order to accommodate the new eating area. A 300-year-old California black oak tree wraps over the cabin as if to shield and protect it. The Forest Service required that all construction work be designed around nature as not to disturb it. Hence, a 200-year-old pine tree is located in front of the kitchen door. The siding is the original shiplap. The toilet exhaust pipe is located on the exterior of the wall since it was installed when Riverside County approved the flushing toilet in 1943. It was very common for these cabins to evolve and change to accommodate modern amenities.

The whole cabin is a campground Manzanita color with forest green window trim as allowed by the Forest Service in 1927.

North Exterior—Side elevation:

This side has the dirt driveway that leads to the original wood pier and concrete/stone foundation that accommodates the minor slope. The shiplap siding and casement windows are original and maintain the Forest Service Manzanita paint. The foundation area is covered with plywood siding to match the original construction of 1921 and is painted the same color as the rest of the cabin.

Interior Plan:

The cabin consists of two bedrooms, a tiny loft, and one small bathroom. All floors are original 1x3 fir planks; some carpet and vintage rope rugs are used in certain areas. All walls and ceilings are original tongue-and-groove knotty pine planks. Windows are original casement-style with original glass and hardware. Board-and-batten doors are also original with drop-latch hardware. Most electrical switches and outlets date from the late 1930s to 1940s.

There are two built-in wall lamps from the 1940s, one in the living room and the other in the loft. The loft lamp still has the original shade. The toilet is the original from the 1940s. The entire cabin is furnished with period pieces and décor reflecting the many decades of its existence.

Interior Details:

The kitchen has the original knotty pine cabinets and hardware. The board-and-batten doors have the rustic Manzanita branch handles. A special sized refrigerator had to be ordered for the original icebox area. A 1940s Magic Chef stove was added in 1949 when the eating area was built. All walls and ceilings are the original tongue-and-groove knotty pine planks. In the 1920s, all cooking was done outside so the inside area was used for food storage and preparation. If you look up at the ceiling, you can see where the ceiling planks end and the 1940s eating area begins since its ceiling is just drywall/plaster. The original kitchen was ten by seven feet. With the addition of the eating area, it increased to ten by fifteen feet. The kitchen also has an original 1930s Pinecraft C. Selden Belden four-drawer cabinet. He was a renowned craftsman. There are no hallways hence the kitchen leads to the living room.

The living room is a seventeen- by thirteen-foot space. The vaulted ceiling is over twenty feet high and has the original rustic log rafters supporting the high-pitched gable roof added in 1938 after the great snowstorm that hit the area. The loft is on the west side and has all of the original pine log railing and balusters. On the east side is the massive stone fireplace with huge rustic timber mantel, both locally crafted in the late 1920s to early 1930s by Lem Poats and Hal Holcomb, both well-known mountain artisans. The south sidewall has two original double casement windows at each end. The west wall has the loft stairs, the bathroom, and the small bedroom.

The bathroom and small bedroom ceilings are boxcar siding with original board-and-batten doors with drop-latch hardware. Walls are original tongue-and-groove knotty pine planks. The loft is small and was originally used for storage. It currently sleeps two on two WWII-era army cots. The loft's window is original as are the ceiling, walls, and floor. The second bedroom is ten by seven and a half feet and has an original 1930 Selden Belden Pinecraft bed and Hal Holcomb's built-in dresser and mirror. All windows, walls, and doors are original.

The bathroom is a five- by six-foot space and has the 1940s toilet with original walls, door, ceiling, and floor.

The second bedroom is a twenty by ten foot space located on the north wall. It was the original sleeping porch that extended the entire length of the cabin, covered by the roof's overhang, turned into a permanent bedroom in 1953. It has the original windows, glass, and hardware and is heated by a vintage wood-burning stove and features a panoramic view of the meadow.

Front view of historic cabin

Side view of historic cabin

Side and Back view of historic cabin

Plan 1D From DuBois Improvement Circular of 1917

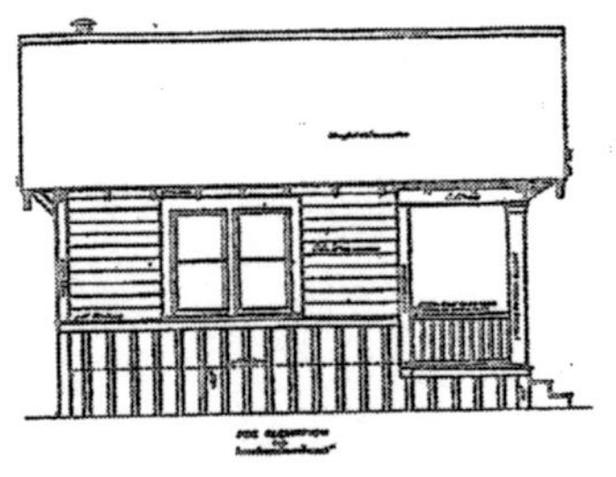

Cabin plans by Dubois

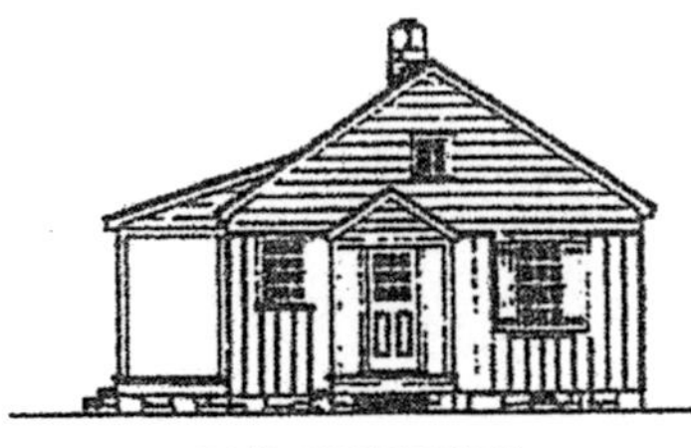

END ELEVATION

FRONT ELEVATION

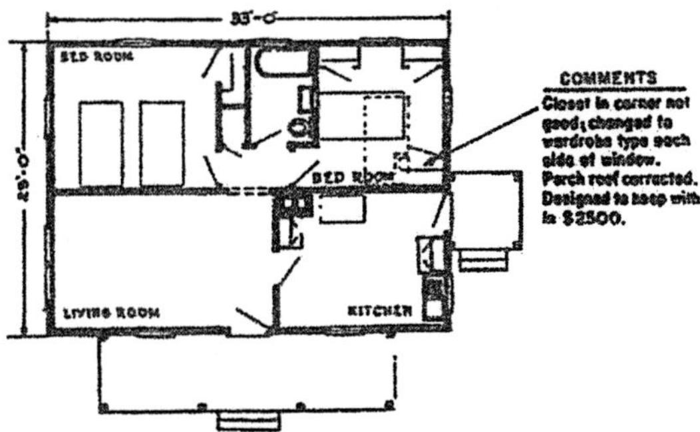

FIRST FLOOR PLAN

Dubois cabin plans with loft

Living room

Gathering place for family and friends

Vintage cabin kitchen

Cabin bedroom

Cabin loft

Stairs to loft

Original siding and windows

Original built-in dresser and mirror

Original stone fireplace

Original kitchen cabinets and handles

Original bathroom door handle

Original door hinge

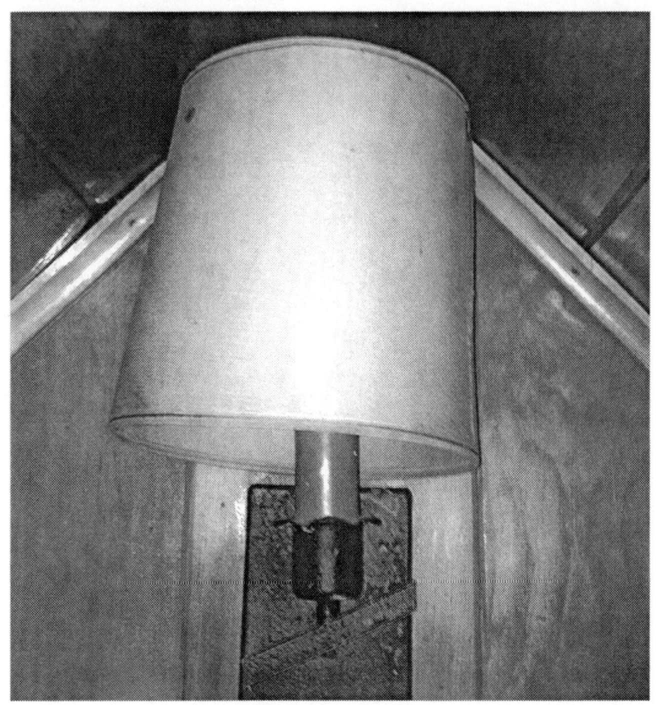

Original loft built-in lamp

Original bathroom door latch leading to bedroom

Section 8:

This section is the Statement of Significance under Criteria letter A and C, of the registry's form.

Criteria A states: "Property is associated with events that have made a significant contribution to the broad pattern of our history."

Criteria C states: "Property embodies the distinctive characteristics of a type, period, or method of construction or represents the work of a master, or possesses high artistic value, or represents a significant and distinguishable entity whose components lack individual distinction."

The application form also asks for the following information:

Area of Significance: Criteria A and C

Period of Significance:Term Occupancy Permit Act of 1915

Significant Dates: 1921, 1924, 1940s (Cabin construction and improvements)

Cultural Affiliation: National Forest Special Use Summer Home Recreation Program

Architect/Builder: Architect Frank A. Waugh, who worked for National Parks Service and Forest Service.

Landscape engineer Arthur H. Carhart, who established recreation sites on national forests.

Ranger and architect Coert Dubois, who provided cabin construction plans.

Recreation specialist Frederick William Cleator, who designed tracts and lots for cabins.

All were influenced by the American Society of Landscape Architects, which helped establish the American campground look in the national parks and forests.

The next sections of the application form ask for historic significance, hence the entire book can be quoted or presented verbatim to fulfill requirements.

Statement of Significance Summary Paragraph (Provide a summary paragraph that includes level of significance, applicable criteria, justification for the period of significance, and any applicable criteria considerations.)

Narrative Statement of Significance (Provide at least one paragraph for each of significance.)

The rest of the book can be used for both sections, under Criteria A and under Criteria C on the National Register of Historic Places Registration Form.

Ernie Atencio, as prior National Forest Homeowners Executive Director, wrote a great article that can be used for this section as well. It is transcribed below and can be found on the NFH website under Newsletter—Winter 2015. www.nationalforesthomeowners.org

The Forest for the Trees— "The First 100 Years"

—Ernie Atencio

> Summer homes—as they were known at the time—existed on forestland since at least the 1870s in the form of hunting or fishing huts, well before national forests. The U.S. Forest Service was established in 1897, absorbing lands previously set aside as federal forest reserves. In 1905, summer homes were added to the list of public activities that the agency could grant permits for. It was a successful and popular program, valued both by the public and the agency.
>
> A 1913 report from Chief Forester Henry S. Graves said, "Hundreds of canyons and lake shores are now dotted with camps and cottages built on land of which is obtained through permits of the Forest Service. This is a highly important form of use of the Forests by the public . . . In an age of voracious exploitation of natural resources, the location of cabin tracts was used as a rationale to preserve the natural beauty of the location unmarred, for the enjoyment of the public . . ." Cabins

contributed not only to the enjoyment but also to the quality of the forests.

Before 1915, however, forest cabins were under year-to-year permits, which made building on forestland a very risky proposition. The 1915 law changed everything, authorizing the Forest Service "to permit the use and occupancy of suitable areas of land within the national forests, not exceeding five acres and for periods not exceeding thirty years, for the purpose of constructing or maintaining summer homes . . ." Now it was feasible for people to make the investment of building a cabin on national forestland without fear that the agency could cancel their permit the next year.

In 1917, Chief Forester Albert Potter said, "Already it has been demonstrated that this legislation was just what was needed, and as a result of it the National Forests are performing a larger public service."

This was a heady time of new and innovative ideas about public lands and recreation. The fledgling U.S. Forest Service was still trying to create a clear identity for itself, and at the same time competing for public support with another new agency, the National Park Service, established in 1916. The Forest Service developed the cabin program in part to show that it, too, could provide meaningful recreational opportunities for the public.

The program was aggressively marketed in articles with such titles as "Vacations Made Easy," "Summer Homes for All," and "A Kingdom for a Song." A Forest Service promotional pamphlet from 1932 gushed, "If the seeker of a mountain summer home desires to be near a lake, a river, a creek, a hot spring, a mineral spring, a cold spring, or a falls, he can be satisfied within reason if he will but inquire."

In 1920, a report from Chief Forester William B. Greeley extolled the welcome revenue from the program, but also the importance of cabin owners as stewards of the forest at a time when the Forest Service was thinly staffed.

Over the years cabin associations were formed, according to the agency, as "a medium through which forest users can advise the Forest Service of their needs and by round-table discussion arrive at an amicable solution of common problems."

Cabin tracts were established and plotted and the program grew steadily throughout the country for several decades. By the 1960s, at the height of the program, almost 20,000 recreation residence cabins existed. With a growing population, more recreational pressures on public lands and evolving ethics regarding forest management, the Forest Service stopped setting aside new tracts in the 1960s and by 1978 put an end to the development of new lots within existing tracts . . .

It has been a colorful and fascinating hundred years and reaching this milestone cements the program's place in the history and heritage of the U.S. Forest Service.

National Register of Historic Places Frequently Asked Questions for Property Owners

Presented by the Registry Department

What is the National Register of Historic Places?

- The National Register of Historic Places is the official list of the nation's historic places worthy of preservation. Properties listed in the National Register include districts, sites, buildings, structures, and objects that are significant in American history, architecture, archeology, engineering, and culture.

These historic places can be significant at the national, state, or local level. The National Register was created through the National Historic Preservation Act of 1966 and is maintained by the National Park Service.

What are the criteria for listing a property on the National Register?

- Your property may be eligible for the National Register if it represents the work of a master architect or is characteristic of a significant architectural movement, like Modernism.
- Your property may also be eligible if it is associated with significant events or persons in local, regional, or national history.
- Properties must typically be more than fifty years old to be listed on the National Register, unless they are exceptionally significant.
- Modern resources are underrepresented on the National Register. Listing your historic Modern property would help preserve this important era of history and architecture in the United States.

What are the benefits of listing my historic property?

- A National Register listing is an honor that signifies that your property is an important part of America's cultural heritage and worthy preservation.
- Listed properties may qualify for grants, tax deductions for donation of protective easements, or tax credits for qualified rehabilitation activities (see below).
- Consideration of impacts to your property from federally funded or licensed undertakings, as well as a mandate to minimize, avoid, or mitigate impacts to your property per

the provisions of the National Historic Preservation Act.

- In California, owners of National Register properties enjoy additional benefits.
- Review of potential project impacts to National Register properties is required through the California Environmental Quality Act (CEQA).
- The State of California also maintains a Register of Historical Resources. Properties listed on the National Register are automatically listed on the California Register.
- Listed properties may use the State Historic Building Code instead of the Uniform Building Code.This is a more lenient code and gives homeowners more flexibility when making repairs or rehabilitation to their National Register property.
- National Register property owners may be eligible for local property tax reduction through the Mills Act.

What are the restrictions of listing my historic property?

- The National Register does not restrict a property owner's private property rights.Owners of National Register properties can remodel, renovate, sell, or even demolish their property with no restrictions. However, significant modifications may result in removal from the National Register.
- The federal government does regulate alterations to historic properties where federal funds have been invested. If you have not received federal grant funds then you are not under any federal restrictions as a homeowner.
- The same applies at the state and local level. If you have received state or local funds or tax benefits to preserve your historic home, then you may be subject to design review for any alterations.
- Your city government may regulate National Register

properties through a local historic preservation ordinance or zoning. Please consult your local government for potential restrictions.

Can I apply for grant money or tax credits?

- Income-producing properties (including rentals) may be eligible for a 20 percent federal income investment tax credit through the Federal Historic Preservation Tax Incentives program. To qualify, properties must undergo rehabilitation according to set preservation standards.
- In California, National Register property owners may be eligible for local property tax reductions through the Mills Act.
- Owners of listed properties may apply for federal, state, and local historic preservation grants, when available.

How will listing on the National Register affect my property value?

- Listing on the National Register generally does not decrease property value and, in some cases, may actually increase the value or marketability of a property.

Can I still modify, remodel, or renovate my historic property after listing?

- Yes. Unless your home is subject to the above restrictions (receiving federal tax credit, protected under a local historic preservation ordinance, etc.), listing on the National Register does not restrict your right to modify your home. Severe alternations may, however, result in removal from the National Register.
- Sustainability and historic preservation can work hand

in hand. You may still upgrade your home's energy efficiency or incorporate other green design ideas.

- Even if your property is subject to a local design review process, solutions can generally be reached to allow you to meet your needs within historic design guidelines.
- Design review processes generally do not regulate paint color or aspects of a historic property not visible from a public way.

Where can I go for additional information?

- National Register of Historic Places: http://www.nps.gov/nr/
- Historic Preservation Tax Incentives: http://www.nps.gov/history/hps/tps/tax/
- California Office of Historic Preservation: http://ohp.parks.ca.gov/
- National Trust for Historic Preservation: http://www.preservationnation.org/
- California Preservation Foundation: http://www.californiapreservation.org/

A listing on the National Register of Historic Places is an honor. A source of pride for you and your family, this special recognition from the federal government can only give your only house the prestige it deserves as an important part of our American past.

The most relevant links to the National Register listing program can be found here:

http://www.nps.gov/nr/publications/index.htm

Particular items including an overview of the program and what it means to be listed can be seen here:

https://www.nps.gov/nr/faq.htm

http://www.nps.gov/nr/publications/bulletins/pdfs/MyProp.pdf

http://www.nps.gov/nr/publications/bulletins/NR_Brochure_Poster/NR_Brochure_Poster.pdf

http://www.nps.gov/nr/publications/bulletins/brochure/

http://www.nps.gov/nr/publications/bulletins/brochure/#results

With regard to maintaining historic properties:

http://www.nps.gov/tps/standards.htm

http://www.nps.gov/tps/standards/four-treatments/treatment-guidelines.pdf

http://www.nps.gov/tps/standards/rehabilitation/rehab/index.htm

http://www.nps.gov/tps/standards/four-treatments/standguide/index.htm

Some federal agencies, and/or Forest Service tracts have produced additional guidelines or rules by virtue of their unique status in association with federal lands. These are separate from any National Register listing provisions. The best of the list is the recently (2014) produced:

http://www.fs.fed.us/eng/pubs/pdfpubs/pdf14232815/pdf14232815Pdpi100.pdf

Other sources included:

http://www.fs.usda.gov/Internet/FSE_DOCUMENTS/stelprdb5356821.pdf

http://www.fs.usda.gov/main/mthood/passes-permits/other

Forest Service Timeline

1812	Congress creates the General Land Office (GLO) to manage land and protect farmers, ranchers and homesteaders. The GLO could not give the nations land fast enough.
1861	Civil War began
1862	Department of Agriculture is established
1862	The Homestead Act of May 20th granted westward bound pioneers timberland in order to provide the government and railroads the needed lumber for the expansion of the nation.
1864	Abraham Lincoln signs the Yosemite Grant. Congress makes CA's Yosemite Valley the first State Park "for public use, resort, and recreation." Later it becomes Yosemite National Park...This can be seen as the beginning of conservation and recreational thought for "the benefit and enjoyment of the people."
1872	Yellowstone National Park is established.
1873	The American Association for the Advancement of Science appointed Franklin B. Hough as Chair of the Federal Forestry Association to conduct a study. The result was, "The duty of Governments in the Preservation of Forests" which was presented to Congress. In 1876, he is appointed the first Federal Forestry Agent. This begins the American Forestry Service. Hough is referred to as The Father of American Forestry.
1876	Congress allocates $2,000.00 to the 1st Federal Forest Agent Franklin B. Hough for the study of timber and preservation. Ulysses S. Grant is President.
1881	A Division of Forestry is established temporarily in the Department of Agriculture to study and report on forestry matters. Franklin B. Hough is the Chief.
1891	Congress gives the President power to create Forest Reserves on the 3rd of March. General Land Office establishes Yellowstone Park Timber Land Reserve on March 30. It becomes the Yellowstone Forest Reserve in 1902.
1892	Sierra Club is established on June 4th. John Muir is the founder and first president. The SC starts ski trips in CA.
1897	On February 22, President Grover Cleveland creates the San Jacinto Forest Reserve and in doing so protects the majority of forests in the San Jacinto Mountains.
1897	Sundry Civil Appropriations Act, also known as the Organic Act and the Forest Management Act specified the purpose for the reserves as well as providing some direction in management of natural resources such as timber, water, mining, grazing and implied recreation. This Act will allow many future Summer Home Tracks to have a water source from local natural water springs. Act also established the practice of "Permit Regulated Occupancy".
1898	Gifford Pinchot becomes Chief of the Division of Forestry. The title of "Chief" is changed to "Forester" from 1898 to 1935, then back to Chief again from1935 to date. William McKinley is President.
1899	The Mineral Springs Leasing Act also known as "The Terminable Permits Act" allowed the building of tents and shacks for the recreational enjoyment of the public.
1901	A separate Division of Forestry is created in the General Land Office on November 15. On March 2, Division of Forestry becomes the Bureau of Forestry. Theodore Roosevelt is President.
1902	Congress authorizes the GLO to lease land for private health sanatoriums.
1905	Power over the Forest Reserves is transferred from the Department of Interior to the Department of Agriculture. On March 3, the Bureau of Forestry-forest agency becomes the U.S. Forest Service. "Summer Homes" are added to the list of permitted uses to the 1902 Congressional authorization for health sanatoriums.

Forest Service Timeline

1906	The Forest Homestead Act of June 11 allowed individuals on forest reserves that were no longer suitable for timber. These private citizens were allowed to move in and built cabins. Homesteading lead to many land frauds. Congress passed Act on June 30 that allowed 10% of receipts from Forest Reserves to be returned to state or local territories for benefit of public roads and schools. Later an additional 25% would be applied.
1907	March 4, Forest Reserves renamed National Forests. As per Gifford Pinchot, forests belong to the people; they are not "reserved".
1908	Forest "Districts" established by Gifford Pinchot on December 1. Changed to "Regions" in1930. On July 1, President Theodore Roosevelt proclaimed San Jacinto Reserve the "Cleveland National Forest" in honor of ex-president Grover Cleveland.
1910	On Jan.7th, President William H. Taft fires Gifford Pinchot. Henry S. Graves becomes the new Forester on Jan. 12. William H. Taft is President.
1911	On May 1, Congress takes the right to create national forests from the President.
1913	President Woodrow Wilson and congress grant permission to San Francisco for the building of the Hetch Hetchy Valley Dam in Yosemite causing national outcry. In response, the Forest Service presents the Term Occupancy Act.
1914	WWI begins
1915	Congress approves the Term Occupancy Permit Act, which allows individuals to lease lots on National Forests, and built summer homes. Western states embrace the program and establish the "American Campground" look in tract and cabin layout and design.
1916	National Park Service is established in the Department of the Interior.
1920	Henry S. Graves resigns. William B. Greeley becomes the new Forester.
1922	On March 20, a Congressional Act allows the exchange of land in national forests for private land of equal value within national forest boundaries. This will allow Summer Home Tracks to purchase private land and exchange it for the land their cabins are built on, resulting in private ownership.
1924	President Calvin Coolidge speaks at the National Conference of Outdoor Recreation, as a result, congress funds recreation. Forest Service Special Use Summer Homes are to be built based on the new "improvement" investment amount of $100 – $250.00 dollars. All permittees are required to spend this amount on construction.
1925	On September 30, the Cleveland National Forest becomes the "San Bernardino National Forest"
1929	The Great Depression (1928)
1930	Forest "Districts" are changed to forest "Regions".
1933	The Forest Service submits The National Plan for American Forestry also known as The Copeland Report to congress on March 27. It states many needed projects, and sets standards in operating and managing the forest. The presented projects help recreational and mountain top communities located within the forest reserves boundaries survive the Great Depression. The CCC will work on the mentioned projects and met the needs of the Forest Service and towns such as Idyllwild. Ferdinand A. Silcox replaces Robert Y. Stuart as Chief of the Forest Service. Franklin D. Roosevelt is President.
1934	There are 6,959 permits-summer home cabins in Region 5 over 50% are located in Southern California. $150,000.00 dollars are collected from permit fees. Summer Home permits were the only national forest resource that did not show a decline during the Great Depression, but actually grew. This same year, 150 lots were added and permits granted.
1935	The title of "Forester" is changed back to "Chief" of the Forest Service.

Forest Service Timeline

1942	WWII (1941). Peal Harbor is attacked. We enter the war. Acting Chief of the Forest Service is Earle H. Clapp.
1945	Harry S. Truman is President Possible development of High Sierra Mineral King Valley, CA as a year-round ski resort. The Forest Service issues a prospectus inviting proposals from private developers. In 1965 the Forest Service will try again and issues a second prospectus. Forest Service will select Walt Disney Enterprise's proposal in the 1960s. WW II ends.
1952	15,520 permits for Summer Home Cabins in Region 5.
1957	Operation Outdoors Act is approved. It provides funding for recreation, money will be used to repair CCC's work and for the construction of new facilities.
1959	Last Special Use Summer Home tract is surveyed and developed in Region 5. Dwight D. Eisenhower is President during this era. Richard E. McArdle is Chief of the Forest Service. Peak of Summer Home program reports approximately 20,000 permits-cabins. 75% are located in Region 5.
1960	The Multiple Use Sustained Yield Act passed congress on June 12. Gives clear and specific guidance to the Forest Service on management of the National Forests. It clearly states that all natural resources such as outdoor recreation, timber, water, minerals, fishing, and grazing will be given equal consideration and decisions will not be based on monetary gain.
1961	John F. Kennedy is President.
1968	Last original Special Use Summer Home tract lot leased in California. Lyndon B. Johnson is President. Edward P. Cliff is Chief of the Forest Service. The Forest Service encourages Special Use Summer Home Tracks to participate in the "Exchange Policy" program.
1969	On Jan., the Forest Service approves Walt Disney's Master Plan for a 300-acre resort in Northern California to accommodate 8,000 people a day. Resort would have restaurants, gondolas, ski lifts, conference center and stores. Sierra Club files a lawsuit to stop construction. Case goes to the Supreme Court. The project was eventually dropped.
1979	Forest Service announced that no new Special Use Summer Home Tracts would be developed nationwide.
1985	There are 15,782 Special Use Summer Home permits across the nation.
1987	There are an estimated 7,063 Summer Home permits in Region 5 at this time.
1998	The Forest Service in California collects $4,209,000.00 million dollars in recreation residence summer home cabins.
1999	There are 6,314 permits for summer home cabins in 269 tracts all located in the 18 California forests in Region 5.
2002	There are 14,600 permits nationwide
2006	There are 14,500 permits nationwide
2010	There are 786 permits in the San Bernardino National Forests in CA
2011	There are 14,300 permits nationwide. Region 5 has approximately 6,300 permits at this time.
2014	There are approximately 13,252 permits nationwide. Region 5 has approximately 5870 permits at this time.
2015	There are approximately 13,660 permits nationwide. Region 5 has approximately 5857. Numbers vary due to permit renewal dates.

Idyllwild Timeline

1400s-1700s	The Cahuilla tribe migrated up the San Jacinto Mountains. Tribe establishes many trails up the mountain and many grinding mortar holes by water spring next to the California Black Oaks. Some are near the future sight of Tahquitz Summer Home Tract on Saunders Meadow.
1812	Congress creates General Land Office (GLO) – to help manage public land as the nation expands to the west. Private primitive tent camps begin to be established in the area. The governor of California while under the Mexican flag, Pio Pico, pastures his cattle in the base of the San Jacinto Mountains.
1846	Ruth Pico granddaughter of Pio Pico will move into the Forest Service Tahquitz Summer Home Tract on Saunders Meadow in 1927.
1848	Lack of roads kept most prospectors away from the San Jacinto Mountains during the Gold Rush.
1860s	Gold is not found in the San Jacinto Mountains. Homesteaders and settlers begin arriving in Strawberry Valley in the late 1860s.
1861	Civil War begins
1862	The Homestead Act of May 20th granted those westward bound pioneers timberland.
1865	Civil War ends
1868	Francisco Pico, nephew of the last Governor of California under the Mexican flag Pio Pico, pastures his cattle in the Strawberry Valley and Saunders Meadow area.
1872	Loggers Anton Scherman and John Metcalf open Prairie Flats Sawmill. Anton also opens his own mill on Strawberry Flat, it closes in 1879
1875	Lumbering begins in a large scale thanks to Colonel Milton Sanders Hall and the Southern Pacific Railroad. Colonel Milton Hall's Grade, a lumber toll road between present-day Cabazon and Hall's Camp Mill in the San Jacinto Mountains, opens. Milton charges .50 cents per wagon and .10 cents per horseback rider. Adventure seekers continue to arrive on horseback.
1876	Congress allocates $2,000.00 for the 1st Federal Forest Agent Franklin B. Hough to study timber and preservation, which will lead to future forest reserves. Sacramento investors Bartholomew, Gilbert and Moore install new steam sawmill after taking over Colonel Milton Hall's lumber business.
1876	Joseph Crawford, a local businessman, opens toll road from the San Jacinto Valley to Strawberry Valley in May competing with Hall's Grade.
1878	Mr. Fuller uses Hall's abandoned water powered sawmill and opens "The Fuller Mill" (1879).
1879	San Diego County declares the Hall's Grade road a "free public road." Anton Scherman dismantles his sawmill and starts moving it little by little to Strawberry Valley. It takes him many months.
1880	San Jacinto pioneers acquire many acres of present-day Idyllwild from the federal government and the Southern Pacific Railroad. Logger Amasa Saunders arrives in Strawberry Valley and builds home at the corner of current Highway 243 and Saunders Meadow Road were the Idyllwild Elementary School sits. Angelo Domenigoni grazes sheep up in Strawberry Valley. Angelo homesteaded Domenigoni Flat, current site of Idyllwild School of Music and The Arts.
1884	Logger Amasa Saunders is granted 120 acres for timber.
1888	Crawford's toll road declared a "free public road" by San Diego County.
1889	Anton Scherman and George Hannahs open "The Strawberry Valley Lumber Company" in March. George Hannahs and wife spend summers in Strawberry Valley.

Idyllwild Timeline

1889	The Strawberry Valley Hotel resort is built, with proprietors George and Sarah Hannahs. They provide horse stalls for their growing guests. Later changes to "Mitchell House" to reflect the other owner – Mrs. M. Mitchell.
1890	John and Mary Keen open "Keen House" hotel – camp. Located at the corner of Highway 243 and Saunders Meadow where the Idyllwild Elementary School is located. Amasa Saunders home was part of the hotel campsite. George and Sarah Hannahs open Camp Idylwilde. Logger Amasa Saunders is granted Pine Cove timber acres with the exception of his meadow. Camping grows with 500 campers in area Mr. G.D. Allen opens a general store to cater to both loggers and campers.
1891	Mayberry Road is made to Hemet, later becomes the Keen Camp Road Hemet Dam construction begins. Congress gives the President power to create Forest Reserves. General Land Office establishes Yellowstone Park Timber Land Reserve on March 30. It becomes the Yellowstone Forest Reserve in 1902.
1893	San Jacinto Mountains are no longer a part of San Diego County due to the creation of Riverside County. George Hannahs opens 1st post office in Strawberry Valley located in his general store. He becomes Postmaster of the new Community of Rayneta named after his son Raymond.
1895	Hemet Dam construction completed. Hannahs, Fred Hards, and Homer Daggett start the "Native Lumber Company". Area is established as a resort destination.
1897	President Grover Cleveland creates the San Jacinto Forest Reserve and in doing so protects the majority of forests from loggers in the San Jacinto Mountains.
1897	Sundry Civil Appropriations Act, also known as the Organic Act and the Forest Management Act specified the purpose for the reserves as well as provided some direction in management of the natural resources such as timber, water, mining, grazing and implied recreation. This Act also would allow the future Forest Service Tahquitz Summer Home Track on Saunders Meadow to have a water source from the local natural water springs. Special Use Permit Act of June 4 will give future Tahquitz Summer Home Tract permission to draw water by drilling on forest reserve land.
1899	Construction begins on a three-story sanatorium by a group of Los Angeles doctors. It will eventually become the Idyllwild Inn. Post Office officially accepts the name "Idyllwild."
1900	First recorded trip to Idyllwild by automobile driven by Dr. Lindley of the future Sanatorium.
1901	George Hannah's successful Native Lumber Company is destroyed by fire. Post Office is moved from the earlier location in Rayneta to present location in Idyllwild. The San Jacinto-Idyllwild Transportation Company is incorporated, providing round-trip travel between Los Angeles and Idyllwild. Half was funded by Dr. Lindley to draw patients to his Sanatorium. The Keens move to town and open "Keen Camp" in 1905. Dr. Walter Lindley opens "The Idyllwild Sanatorium". He built it on George Hannah's old "Idylwilde Camp" site. Sanatorium fails. Trips up the mountain were too difficult for the ill. Vacationers wanted nothing to do with the sickly. The Idyllwild Store opens.
1903	The Idyllwild Sanatorium closes its doors and reopens as the Strawberry Valley Hotel - Lodge.
1904	The Idyllwild Sanatorium/Strawberry Valley Hotel building is destroyed by fire on April 20.

Idyllwild Timeline

1905	Chief Gifford Pinchot is moved from under the GLO in the Department of the Interior to the Department of Agriculture. The Bureau becomes the Forest Service. Dr. Lindley replaces the burned Strawberry Valley Hotel with the new "Bungalow" hotel. It was sold to Frank Strong and George Dickinson in 1906, later to become the Idyllwild Inn. Strong and Dickinson buy "keen House" land. The Keens open "Keen Camp" near Mountain Center.
1906	The "Bungalow" is sold to Los Angeles real estate investors Frank R. Strong and George W. Dickenson.
1906	Scherman Lumber Mill is destroyed by fire. "White Special" makes daily trips to the "Bungalow" from Hemet. It takes the 4 white horses and white stagecoach just 4.5 hours. Provided by the Hemet-Idyllwild Stage Line.
1907	Autos start to replace horses
1909	New Control Road is created to control auto traffic.
1910	On September 1, the 32-mile Banning to Idyllwild Road is completed with funding by Riverside County.
1911	The Banning-Idyllwild Stage Line opens and provides round trip passages from the Santa Fe Station in Banning to the Idyllwild Inn. The Strong and Dickinson Realty Company of Los Angeles purchase 4,200 acres of land including parts of Idyllwild, Pine Cove, and Saunders Meadow and subdivide for cabin lots. They buyout Dr. Lindley and reincorporate as the "Idyllwild Mountain Park Co.
1913	"Touring Car" automobiles begin providing round-trip transportation between San Jacinto and Idyllwild replacing the horse stage lines. George Hannahs subdivides his land and sells individual lots know as Wildwood. President Woodrow Wilson and congress grant permission to San Francisco for the building of the Hetch Hetchy Valley Dam in Yosemite causing national outcry. In response, the Forest Service presents the Term Occupancy Permit Act to show their commitment to conservation, preservation and recreation in 1915. This will lead to the creation of many Forest Service Special Use Summer Home tracts within the area.
1914	WWI begins Horses are replaced with cars. Hollywood discovers Idyllwild and starts to film. Over 70 movies will be created throughout the decades. Congress works on the Permit Act
1915	Congress approves the Term Occupancy Permit Act, which allows individuals to lease lots on National Forests, and built Special Use Summer Homes. Saunders Meadow was a government track with 59 lots - known then as The Tahquitz Summer Home Track.
1916	National Park Service is established.
1917	Strong and Dickinson sell the Idyllwild Inn and 1,000 adjacent acres to Claudius Lee Emerson and three other investors, forming the company, "Idyllwild Incorporated." Claudius and wife Zelma, make the Inn the social center of town and area. The "Idyllwild Pines Pool" is built below Emerson Hall among the pines.
1919	Claudius Emerson donates land for public and institutional religious use. He also starts the Idyllwild "Breeze" a weekly summer newspaper. WWI ends "Keen Camp" is renamed "Tahquitz Lodge" a pool and tennis courts are added.

Idyllwild Timeline

1920	The Boy Scout camp and Camp Emerson, open on land donated by Emerson. The Forest Service starts to conceptualize the area's future Special Use Summer Home tracts, one being Tahquitz on Saunders Meadow. This can be mark as the beginning of the "Tahquitz Special Use Summer Home Tract on Saunders Meadow" Which will become Saunders Meadow, Inc. in the 1970s. Rangers start to tell campers about the coming lots on these tracts by showing them maps and locations. Emerson's "Idyllwild Incorporated" offers ½-acre home site lots.
1920-1930s	Hollywood Movie Filming in Idyllwild is common: Mary Pickford, Katherine Hepburn, and Paulette Goddard all big stars are friends of Idyllwild. Future stars to film in Idyllwild: Doris Day and Elvis Presley. Doris Day had a home in town, adjacent to Saunders Meadow, until it burned down. 70 plus films are made in area. Stars and directors like Cecil B. DeMille stay in the Idyllwild Inn. Frank Sinatra Jr. will attend school on Saunders Meadow in the future. Forest Service Special Use Summer Home Tracts are created in area, Tahquitz being the largest with 59 lots.
1921	The Riverside County Idyllwild Public campground opens on land donated by Claudius Emerson. Due to auto traffic, Riverside County mandates "Control Roads". The Forest Service designs the Special Use Summer Home tract layouts. Rangers continue to inform campers of tract development of their lots.
1922	Congressional act is passed that will allow the exchange of land in national forests for private land of equal value within national forest boundaries. This will allow the future Saunders Meadow/Tahquitz summer Home Track to exchange the forestry land their cabins were built on. Resulting in private ownership of the leased land. The Forest Service places lots on the many Special Use Summer Home tracts with emphasis on Tahauitz on Saunders Meadow. The first lot is leased that had been selected in 1920 from the conceptual plans.
1923	Electricity arrives in Idyllwild via a 32,000-volt power line from the San Jacinto Valley. Service is provided to over 400 cabins. The first Special Use Summer Home lots are leased to the public located on National Forest land. Tahquitz Summer Home Tract has its first cabin built.
1923	Strong and Dickinson begin developing residential subdivision in Fern Valley area. They hire Walter Wood to manage their "Idyllwild Mountain Park Company". Wood convinces them to built Clubhouse and golf course on Saunders Meadow.
1923	The Peak and Pine Summer Camp for Girls is established on South Circle Drive in Idyllwild. "The Rustic" man Hal Holcomb builds and opens "The Rustic Shop" where he sells his Manzanita handmade furniture while his wife and mother in law Anna Poates serves delicious homemade food in Ma Poates's "Rustic Tavern" a side-by-side shop that Hal added on. Hal Holcomb works on many built in furniture for local cabins including Forest Service Tahquitz Summer Home Tract cabins and the future Golf Club Hall on Saunders Meadow. Anna's son Lem Poates becomes a well know stonemason and builder. He works on many local stone foundations, chimneys, fireplaces and eventually the local Town Hall. He also works on the Forest Service Tahquitz Summer Home Tract cabins on Saunders Meadow.
1924	Long Beach investors purchase 800 acres from George Hannahs and begin subdividing the area now known as Pine Cove. Idyllwild Pines Camp, an inter-denominational religious training school, is founded on land donated by Claudius Emerson, will open in 1925.

Idyllwild Timeline

1924	Forest Service establishes other tracts and continues leasing the 59 lots on Saunders Meadow as part of the Tahquitz Tract. The second cabin is built. Rangers encourage the few permittees to organize into a neighborhood association in order to deal with sanitation and water needs. These new permittees as called by the Forest Service, begin to organize into the "Tahquitz Improvement Association" - Summer Home Track. This original association still existence after 95 years making it one of the oldest in the nation. It is also, the only one in the country that went through the Forest Service "exchange program" into private ownership in 1972 that still follows the original Forest Service guidelines in order to keep the community looking like a forest with the "least disturbance to nature", truly making it a unique place.
1925	Construction begins for the Idyllwild Golf Club on Saunders Meadow by Strong & Dickerson. The area forest is no longer a part of the Cleveland National Forest; it becomes the San Bernardino National Forest. Idyllwild Pines camp opens for business and grows through the 20s.
1927	Last Governor of Mexico California Pio Pico's granddaughter moves into the Forest Service Tahquitz Summer Home Tract on Saunders Meadow. The Clubhouse for Idyllwild Golf Club opens on Saunders Meadow. "The Idyllwild Inn's" pool, the "Plunge" opens. It is located where the current sit of the "Fort" quaint shops will be, in the middle of town.
1928	Strong and Dickinson rename Golf course to Mt. San Jacinto Golf Club on Saunders Meadow to compete with Emerson's golf course.
1929	A new 23 ½-mile "high gear" road is opened between the Hemet Valley and Idyllwild. Tahquitz Pines is founded by Christian Endeavor organization. Wycliffe Bible Translators will eventually operate it. The Great Depression (1928) Idyllwild survives on Emerson's camps, the CCC and the Forest Service Tahquitz Summer Home Tract as well as the other Special Use Summer Home Tracts in the area.
1931	Tahquitz Pines begins operating as a Christian conference center. California Baptist University is the current owner (2013) of which they purchased from Wycliffe Bible Translators.
1932	The Desert Sun School opens a summer camp in Saunders Meadow.
1932	The 36-mile Palms to Pines highway is completed between the Coachella Valley and Idyllwild on July 23.
1933	The Forest Service submits The National Plan for American Forestry also known as The Copeland Report to congress on March 27. It states many needed projects, sets standards in operating and managing the forest. The presented projects help recreational and resort mountain top communities located within the forest reserves boundaries survive the Great Depression. The CCC will work on the report's projects and met the needs of the Forest Service and towns such as Idyllwild.
1933	The Civilian Conservation Corps (CCC) works on firebreaks, trails, and campgrounds, Ranger Station and cabins both around Idyllwild and Saunders Meadow Tahquitz government Summer Home Track.
1933	First place goes to San Bernardino National Forest for the highest number of ready-cut buildings completed before winter with the help of the CCC.
1934	John and Clara Postle open "Fern Valley Café". They receive the first liquor license in town.
1935	C. Selden Belden establishes his Pine craft Furniture Studio in Pine Cove before relocating to the corner of Saunders Meadow Road and Highway 243 a few years later.
1935	Desert Sun School leases 40 acres of the old golf course on Saunders Meadow. Will buy property in the future.
1936	Sierra Club begins using Tahquitz Rock for organized climbs. Emerson's Idyllwild, Inc. goes bankrupt.
1938	The Emerson family moves off the mountain.
1939	Gray's Photo Shop moves from Ridgeview Drive and reopens at new location.

Idyllwild Timeline

1940	Flushing toilets reach the government Tahquitz Summer Home Track on Saunders Meadow, replacing outhouses.
1941	The Idyllwild Store is destroyed by fire. Pear Harbor is attacked
1941	The Village Market opens.
1942	The Azalea Trails Girl Scout Camp is established in Dark Canyon, north of Pine Cove.
1942	WWII (1941), we enter the war Keen Camp – Tahquitz Lodge ends to foreclosure then burns down Idyllwild serves General Patton's officers and soldiers who trained in the dessert. Military troops on R&R visit. Their families find housing here. Skiing comes to Idyllwild, but never takes off.
1943	The Tahquitz Lodge is destroyed by fire.
1945	40-year old Idyllwild Inn destroyed by fire. WWII ends 400 to 450 residents live in Idyllwild after the war.
1946	USC professors, Dr. Max Krone and Dr. Robert Kingsley purchased 340 acres of land on Domenigoni Flats for the construction of an art school.
1946	Ernest and Betty Maxwell start the Idyllwild Town Crier newspaper in October.
1946	Dr. Paul Foster, owner of the Idyllwild All-Year Resorts, sells company to real estate broker Jerry Johnson and two partners. Sale includes numerous downtown village businesses, 1,500 subdivided lots, and an additional 320 acres.
1946	Developers Jerry Johnson and Clifton Russell build the recreational facility, "Sport land." (1947)
1947	The Idyllwild Town Hall is dedicated on July 10. Construction supervised by Lem Poates.
1947	Idyllwild Fire Protection District organized.
1948	The "Sport land" recreational facility is destroyed by fire.
1950	Official opening of Idyllwild School of Music and The Arts, (ISOMATA). Eminent Faculty include: Meredith Wilson - wrote The Music Man in Idyllwild. Alfred Eisenstadt – Life magazine photojournalist Harvey Sternberg – prominent New York printmaker Bella Lewitsky – renowned dancer Ansel Adams - photographer
1950	Banning-Idyllwild paved "high gear" road completed on October 14 and renamed Highway 243 three years later. Idyllwild is seen as an artist and outdoor enthusiast's destination.
1960	Pine craft Furniture closes its doors.
1962	Elvis Presley films *Kid Galahad* in Idyllwild.
1963	The Palm Springs Aerial Tramway opens on September. Tramway goes up to 8,516ft of MT. San Jacinto that has an elevation of 10,831 feet.
1972	Saunders Meadow Forests Service Summer Home Track incorporates and through a land exchange with the government becomes independent from the National Forest lease land program. All cabin owners now own their land.
1972	Owners Ernest and Betty Maxwell sell the Idyllwild Town Crier newspaper.
1983	The Idyllwild Arts Foundation acquires ownership of Idyllwild School of Music and the Arts from USC.
1983	The Desert Sun School name is changed to the Elliott-Pope Preparatory School located on Saunders Meadow

Idyllwild Timeline

1990	On December 31 the Elliott-Pope Preparatory School closes and the Desert Sun Science Center (Astro camp) opens at the same Saunders Meadow location.
1992	Fort Idyllwild retail complex is complete in November. It is renamed "The Center of Idyllwild".
1993	John W. Robinson and Bruce D. Risher publish "The San Jacintos".
1995-1996	Annexation to Fern Valley Water District is announced for Saunders Meadow Tahquitz Summer Home Track – securing the future of the community. Saunders Meadow is no longer dependant on the original natural spring used by the Cahuilla tribe.
2000	Palm Springs Aerial Tram redesigned and reopened with the world's largest rotating tramcars.
2001	A few tough and bright woman establish Idyllwild Area Historical Society (IAHS).
2009	Dr. Bob Smith and IAHS publish book on Idyllwild – "Idyllwild and The High San Jacintos".
2010	The California Society of Archivists recognize the Idyllwild Area Historic Society with the "Archive Appreciation Award"
2011	The Idyllwild Area Historic Society (IAHS) receives the "Dave Byrd Award of Meritorious Performance" from the California Council for the Promotion of History
2013	San Bernardino National Forest - "San Jacinto Mountain Fire" hits the area from July 15-24. 3,500 people fight the fires day and night. 27,265 acres burn at a cost of $21.6 million dollars. It is ten days of terror and suspense. The town of Idyllwild and cabins on Saunders Meadow were almost destroyed. But our Rangers and volunteers saved the day once again.
2015	Dr. Robert Reyes and Patrick Kennedy publish "Saunders Meadow A Place without Fences", a historic synopsis of The Term Occupancy Permit Act of 1915 – a case study of the National Forest Special Use - Summer Home Recreation Program. Recapturing a forgotten part of both Forest Service and Idyllwild history.

Saunders Meadow Timeline

1400-1800	Cahuilla tribe roams up the San Jacinto mountains establishing dirt trails. One of which will become the future Saunders Meadow Road. Tribe creates grinding mortar holes on the large stone near Big Cedar springs and below the California oak trees. Cahuilla women and children drop oak acorns in fertile ground by the future Forest Service Summer Home cabin site on future Saunders Meadow. They intentionally spill water on the ground in gratitude for the bounty that it provides.
1850	Homesteading occurs as well as primitive camping opportunities in the vicinity of Strawberry Valley.
1868	Francisco Pico, nephew of the last Governor of CA when under the Mexican flag grazes cattle in area.
1870	The Southern Pacific Railroad through Congressional Land Grants owns most local land. Logging begins in area. Colonel Milton Sanders Hall gains contract with Southern Pacific Railroad to provide company with 300,000 ties and fuel for their trains. He also provided construction wood for the southern part of CA. Anton Scherman also logs future Saunders Meadow in 1879, establishing Scherman Mill in 1882. George Hannahs joins the lumber community around 1879.
1880	Logger Amasa Saunders arrives and builds home below meadow that will bear his name. Begins logging in Strawberry Valley. Angelo Domenigoni homesteads and pastures cattle in area.
1882	Amasa Saunders buys mill on Strawberry Creek Anton Scherman works mill on Saunders Meadow. Then moves to Dutch Flat in 1889.
1884	Amasa Saunders tries to get the title to the meadow and all its timber, but all he gets is the name – "Saunders Meadow". He did acquire 120 acres within the Pine Cove area.
1885	Amasa Saunders builds the first steam mill in order to increase productivity. Moves family to San Jacinto in 1886 and dies in 1902.
1886	A little girl named Mildred visits Strawberry Valley with her family. It takes them 2 whole days on carriage to reach the top. The road is so steep and rugged that the family has to help the horses by getting off and pushing the carriage up the mountain. They camp across the current Idyllwild Elementary School at the corner of Saunders Meadow Road and Hwy 243. Their mode of communication between parties was through mirrors. The party further up the mountain would reflect the sunlight to the party below indicating a safe ascent. Mildred will eventually marry Sam Minnich in1910 and honeymoon in the area and lease a lot at Tahquitz Summer Home Tract on Saunders Meadow in 1929. They will use the same mode of communication while building their cabin and hauling materials up the mountain.
1889	Logger John and wife Mary Keen open "Keen House" Hotel/Camp adjacent to Saunders Meadow using Saunders old home as a camp dorm. Their next venture Keen Camp located a few miles down the hill, will be used by Cecil B. DeMille and his Hollywood actors to film "The Squaw Man" and The Girl of The Golden West in 1914. Anton Scherman and 2 others join Hannahs to open the Strawberry Valley Lumber Company.
1897	Congress passes the Organic Act that will allow the future Forest Service "Tahquitz Summer Home Tract" on Saunders Meadow to drill for water. US government reclaims unused Railroad land. Reclaimed land becomes Reserves and than National Forests.

Saunders Meadow Timeline

1900	Hannahs follows the Cahuilla dirt trail by current refuged collection site and around the meadow establishing Saunders Meadow Road. He has wagons and Stage Line stop at Keen House located on current SM Road and Hwy 243 as a potty break before heading to his Mountain Resort – Camp Idylwilde.
1905	The Forest Reserves gains railroad land that had not been sold or used surrounding Saunders Meadow.
1906	Strong and Dickinson Realty Company from LA buy a private portion of Saunders Meadow.
1915	Congress approves the Term Occupancy Permit Act that will lead to the "Tahquitz Summer Home Tract" on Saunders Meadow. Act allows private citizen to lease National Forest land and build private cabins for summer use; after all it is the publics land. The Forest Service does not require any expenditure for "improvement" investment on permittee's cabin construction. Hence many cabins built on tracts during this time were lean to shacks or temporary tents.
1916	Elwood Jones camps and fishes in the bend of Strawberry Creek in Idyllwild, where the daily limit is 50 fish.
1918	Elwood starts to invite his Pasadena neighbors fishing with him. Every year, more friends join them. This group will become some of the first permittees of The Forest Service Tahquitz Summer Home Tract".
1920	Forest Service starts to conceptualize many Special Use Summer Home Tracts in the area. This is the beginning of the Tahquitz Summer Home Tract now know as Saunders Meadow, Inc. one of the oldest associations in the nation and the only one that still follows the original Forest Service guidelines even thought it went through a 5 year "exchange" program into private ownership in the 1960s. This community will be celebrating 100 years in 2020. Currently it is 95 years old. Rangers start to announce tract plans to regular campers in the area. They also pitch the idea of having "improvement associations" for the tracts future sanitation and water needs.
1921	With Tahquitz Special Use Summer Home Tract on the go, the Forest Service builds a lean-to-shack on current 27160 Saunders Meadow Road (then Lot 19, current lot 33) for their own use during fire prevention training and as a daily place of rest for working rangers. Location is selected due to the view of the meadow and the shade provided by the CA Oak tree planted by the Cahuilla, there, rangers continue surveying tracts and designing lots around the forest's natural features. The lean-to is now a historic 94 year old cabin.
1922	Ranger Joe and his horse approach Elwood Jones and his family who regularly camped Domenigoni Flats – Isomata at the big bend of Strawberry Creek – Idyllwild, CA in the San Bernardino National Forest. He informs them of the Term Occupancy Permit Act of 1915 and the new tracks being surveyed and developed in the area. The first Lot (#5) on Tahquitz Tract is leased. A Congressional Act is approved that will allow the Tahquitz Summer Home Tract to go through the Forest Service "Exchange Program" into private ownership in the far future, (1972).
1923	The Forest Service finishes surveying Tahquitz Summer Home Tract on Saunders Meadow with 59 lots. The Tract design used by Forest Service on Tahquitz is both "Linear" because it follows the contour of the meadow and "Ridgeline" because it follows the terrain and trails. It also contains a small grid pattern that almost looks like a "block" neighborhood with two lanes at a certain section. Mr. Durham is the first to build a cabin on (Lot 5) of which he leased in 1922 after looking at it in 1921. Ranger encourages him to start what they call a Summer Home Improvement Association in order to address the tracts future safety needs. Durham digs the first outhouse.

Saunders Meadow Timeline

1924	Horseback riding Ranger Joe, now a good family friend reminds Elwood Jones about the tracks and recommends Tahquitz. Elwood and his family do so and select lot 6, located near a flowing spring adjacent to a huge granite boulder. The trail is currently known as Granite Springs Road. This was the second lot to be selected. A total of 57 lots remain available. 25% of permit fees from summer homes will go towards local roads and public schools. From 1924 – 1926, friends of Elwood Jones known as "The Sons of May First" lease lots and build cabins. Archie MacDonald leased lot #9 and in 1925, Ray H. Tecklenborg leased lot #8. All 3 of their cabins are located at the end of current Granite Springs Road. Cabins were collectively named "Macteckelwood" and used for The Sons of May First's annual fishing trip that went on for over 50 years on the first of May. This band of brothers brought water from Granite Spring above Tecklenborg's cabin to the other cabins and became the leaders in setting up the water system for the rest of Tahquitz Special Use Summer Home Tract and future Saunders Meadow, Inc. Eventually a safer trail will be created and named "Macteckelwood", by using a part of the men's (3) names: (Mac)Donald, (Teck)lenborg, El(wood). Due to the Forest Service not having a set "improvement" amount for construction of summer homes, cabins are 2x4, plywood shacks used for hunting and fishing. Soon all shacks will be required to become permanent structures by the Forest Service. Most of the fancy cabins at this time are of a "Rectangular Plan" with gable or hip roofs. Some have small loft areas for storage or sleeping. This design style was common through 1927. The Forest Service Lean-to-shack, lot 19, currently 33, is leased to Richard G. Haas. He improves on the Forest Service shack by using a Coert Dubois "Front Gable" cabin design. Dubois was a ranger and architect who provided summer home plans to permittees. Now with more permittees on the tract, the need for an association is recognized and discussed in order to address the needs of the tract's future. The "Rustic Man" Hal Holcomb works on the interior of some of the Summer Home Cabins, one being lot 19 currently 27160 Saunders Meadow cabin lot 33. This cabin qualifies to be a State and National Historic Place after 94 years of existence (2015). Holcomb was a pioneer on rustic American furniture and interiors made out of the locale Manzanita tree. Many of the original Summer Homes still have his built-ins.
1925	Summer Home Families have their children get pails of water from the Granite springs located above Ray Tecklenborg's cabin as part of their daily summer chores. Elwood Jones spearheads the original water project for this rustic new community. He built the "spring Box" used by the few cabin owners, during their summer visits. He recognizes the need for a reliable water source. He becomes the primary mover in setting up the water system for the rest of the Tahquitz Summer Home Tract. The Tahquitz community continues to grow. Strong and Dickinson start to build Idyllwild Golf Club under the advice of their hired manager Walter Wood. They will rename it The Mount San Jacinto Golf Club on Saunders Meadow in 1928. Power lines reach the new golf club.
1925	Ray H. Tecklenborg builts his cabin on lot #8. It is know as "Teck's Tavern".

Saunders Meadow Timeline

1926	Electricity is made available to the Tahquitz Summer Home Tract community due to power lines reaching the new golf club. Some permittees continue to use candles for light. The Brubaker family of Hemet joins the Tahquitz community building a cabin on Lot #4. Excitement increases, as the new golf club and a pool get ready to open in the meadow and the area in 1927.
1927	Camaraderie between Tahquitz Summer Home Tract permittees is strengthened by the need for water and the unselfish acts of the Jones, MacDonald and Tecklenborg families. The decision is made and advice taken from Forest Service Rangers to create the Tahquitz Meadow Home Improvement Association in order to work for the betterment, sanitation and safety of the Summer Home community. The first Tahquitz Meadow Improvement Association meeting is held on September 21. By-Laws are written and agreed upon and signed by all. Included is their $1.00 yearly fee. Most permittees enthusiastically contribute $2.00 dollars. The first bank account is opened for the Tahquitz Meadow Home Improvement Association at Farmers and Merchants Bank. 41 of the tract lots are leased with only 18 lots available to the public. Mr. Jones, MacDonald and Tecklenborg become the leaders of the official water development program and lead the Tahquitz Meadow Improvement Association to vote in requesting permission from the Forest Service to drill for and/or acquire water rights. Hence, the Association applies with the United States Forest Service for a Special Use Water Permit in order to build a 200-gallon concrete reservoir to be located a few hundred feet of the Tecklenborg Cabin (lot #8) with 4000' of pipe to serve the 19 existing cabins and 13 future cabins still in the planning stage of building. The first special assessment of $50.00 dollars is collected per lot in order to work on the water system on top of the now yearly $1.00 association membership fee. On September 30th, association considers contacting Forest Service S.A. Nash Boulden to help collect the $50.00 dollars from the few lot permittees that were taking too long to pay. United States Department of Agriculture USDA – Forest Service grants first water permit on September 22, 1927. On October 17th, the first check for the association is written for the amount of $40.00 to Fred Patton for water tunnel contract work. On November 22, S.A. Nash Boulden is contacted and a letter goes out stating, "Please pay ($50.00) at once…your permit will come under consideration as being eligible for cancellation." Forest Service is now requiring $200.00 to be invested on "improvements" construction of cabins in order to prevent further shacks and tents from being used on lots. All original shacks start to be replaced with permanent structures.

Saunders Meadow Timeline

1927	Ms. Ada M. Hogue of San Jacinto leases lot 11 as does her best friend Ms. Ruth Pico, granddaughter of Pio Pico the last California Governor under the Mexican flag. Both of them come to their summer cabins by horseback from San Jacinto and tether the horses by their future homes. Howard O. Hogue, Ada's brother will build their fireplaces as well as 11 of the original cabin fireplaces on the west side of the tract. Howard was a miner and inserted unusual rocks and petrified wood into the mortar and around the stones. Ada and Ruth cook thanksgiving dinner on the old woodstove and invite the other permittees helping create a stronger sense of community. Lem Poats, a locale stonemason, works on the east side cabins building their stone fireplaces. Hal Holcomb is hired to work on the interior of the Golf Club. He and his crew walk across Saunders Meadow to work on the loft hand railing and the built in dresser and mirror in current 27160 Saunders Meadow Cabin then Lot #19, currently Lot #33. He also works on a few other cabins. Lem Poates, a relative of Holcomb, builds cabin 27160 Saunders Meadow fireplace and chimney out of local stones. Holcomb builds the mantel. Lem also works on other of the cabins and will supervise the construction of the future Idyllwild Town Hall. Fireplaces were not necessary due to Summer Homes limited use, but will prove valuable during WWII due to permittees being allowed to live in summer homes year round in order to protect the forest while rangers fought in the war.
1928	On March 31, the United States Forest Service Special Use Permit covering Section 18 was granted to Tahquitz Summer Home tract to develop water source. Granite Spring was developed above Tecklenborg cabin Lot 8 with a small concrete reservoir. Evidently flow was marginal and elevation difference too small to provide adequate pressure. Evidence of the work can still be seen, along with a surface seep that persists to this day. Ada M. Hogue submits her cabin drawing to Forest Service for approval before construction. The first Forest Supervisor of the San Bernardino National Forest, S. A. Nash-Boulden with help from ranger-architect Dubois, approves her plans. The Forest Service increases its "improvement" amount for cabin construction to $2000.00. New permittees are required to spend 2k in building their new cabins. Rangers focuse on safety of the construction rather then the actual spending of the $2000.00. Many additions and improvements to cabins are noticed such as indoor facilities, kitchens and eating areas. Porches are screened in and used for sleeping, rooms are added as well. Strong and Dickinson open renamed clubhouse and golf course on Saunders Meadow. Clubhouse furniture and finishes are by Hal Holcomb and are a big hit. All original shacks are being rebuilt as permanent solid cabins in the simple utilitarian "American Campground Plan" partly established by Ranger and Architect Dubois. The forest service shared his building plans that were for a one to two room ranger offices that could easily be modified into a residence, creating the campground look. Dubois started sharing his plans in Tahquitz in 1920.

Saunders Meadow Timeline

1929	A second Tahquitz Tract Special Assessment of $51.00 for all new cabins is approved. One dollar goes towards association membership fees and $50.00 towards pipes to connect to the water system. The $50.00 is a one time special assessment. Sam and Mildred Minnich lease lot #39, now #8. Mildred visited Idyllwild in 1886 as a child. It took her family 2 days to reach the top on carriage. They build their cabin in 1930. The Great Depression hits the nation and slows development down. The Town Crier newspaper will state in 1960 that the Golf Club "went out of business 20 minutes after the 29 depression."
1930	Tahquitz Meadow Improvement Association will deal with water challenges through 1995. Association taps into multiple springs, enlarges tunnels, drills and installs water tank. Sam and Mildred Minnich move into community. They become active knowledgeable participants on the water system up into the late 1960s early 70s when Sam is in his late 90s. Sam had worked on the "Recovery Team" from the great San Francisco quake and fire in 1906 and understood the value of a good water system. Cabins built at this era are "Gable-ell or L-plan" with cross gable roof. A few assume the "T" shape. This was common through the 1940s. The M. San Jacinto Golf Club on Saunders Meadow closes. It foreclosed and sold then turned into a military academy summer camp.
1931	USFS renews original Permit, extending it into Section 19, toward, what is today, Granite Spring and is granted a second permit for further development and a holding tunnel. All tract members are asked to conserve water and required to invest in a globe cut-off valve to prevent pipes from freezing.
1932	Desert Sun School opens a summer camp at High Castle and rents part of Saunders Meadow. Forest Service Supervisor J.D. Elliot recommends placing standard signs on the forest residence tracts on forests. They will contain names of families on each trails entrance, which still stand today. Tahquitz Association develops lot map with Forest Service showing pipeline from Upper Tunnel or Spring and water main to each lot.
1933	CCCs work on Saunders Meadow firebreak and dirt trails as well as on Saunders Meadow Road. The C's (boys) have lunch under the California Oak tree that grew from the acorn dropped by the Cahuilla women on their way to Big Cedar and Granite Springs in the 1800s next to cabin 27160 Saunders Meadow Lot 19/33.
1935	Mid 30s was a period of development of Granite Spring and holding tunnel. There were always repairs and maintenance to be done on the water system. Pine Craft Furniture maker C. Selden Belden moves his store to the corner of Saunders Meadow Road and Highway 243. Currently, his kitchen table and four chairs command 4K. Desert Sun School moves to the Golf Course on Saunders Meadow leasing 40acres for a summer camp. They will eventually buy property in 1944.

Saunders Meadow Timeline

1938	Great winter storm hits town, the snowfall is 360% of normal. Many cabin walls bowed out, "Teck" Ray Tecklenborg's cabin collapsed under the weight of the snow. Other cabin owners added interior beams for support. Cabin on lot 19 (current lot 33) has the original beams.
1939	January 6, the Forest Service recommends combining both 1928 and 1931 water permits into one for Tahquitz water use. March 16, District Ranger informs Tract of yearly lot/tract inspection set for June. On June 21, the United States Forest Service renews the combined Permits again for Section 18 and 19. This permit is for the purpose of development springs and piping water to reservoirs for use on Tahquitz Special Use Tract.
1940	April 16, Tract Association contacts County of Riverside Office of Health in regards to the possibility of replacing outhouses with flushing toilets. May 1, Health Commissioner responds after inspecting cabins and lots with Forest Service. Their report is titled, "Survey of Toilet situation on Tahquitz Tract, San Jacinto Mountain" and contains: a. Septic Tanks with cesspools allowable for Lots, 33,34,35,36,39,40,45,46,47,48,49. b. 1 Septic Tank with leaching tile drain allowable (no cesspool), Lots 1,2 (if above house), 3,4,5,6,7,8,9,10,11 (if above house) 12,13,14,15,16,17,118,19 (if above house), 22,23,24,25,26,27,28,29,30,31,32,41,42,43,44,50,51. Tile must not be less than 50 feet from streambed in all cases, and at any point. c. Chemical toilets required: Lots 20,21,52,53,54,55,56,57,58,59. (They are so low, and so near the meadow, that septic tanks would not provide satisfactory sanitation. County sees this as an opportunity to regulate permits on Tracts. Now that roads up the mountain are less treacherous, the County focuses on sanitation and requires fees for any improvements. WWII slows development down and Summer Home owners are allowed to live fulltime in their summer homes. The town of Idyllwild benefits from the money they spend on goods year round. The Forest Service also benefits from their watchful eyes in caring for the forests since most rangers have gone to war. July 6th, permittees question being taxed for leasing Government owned lots. The County of Riverside presents 5 cases: State vs. Moore, People vs. Shearer, People vs. Frisbie, Bakersfield vs. kern County and San Pedro vs. Los Angeles County. County stated, "These cases all refer and maintain that same principle, namely, that while the property of the Government is not subject to taxation, the usufructuary right to the property is subject to taxation and this applies not only to Government lots and mining claims, but to the possessory interest in other governmental projects."
1941	August 3rd, fire occurs in a cabin on a Special Use Tract in the San Bernardino Mountains. The Forest Service sends out a letter to all permittees, "Investigation disclosed that this fire resulted from the throwing of hot ashes from a stove of a special use cabin into the yard, into tinder dry pine needles. It was necessary to file a criminal action against this person…his only excuse for his act was that 'he didn't stop to think'…The court remarked that 'in this time of emergency it is a vital and patriotic duty of all persons to take every caution to prevent the occurrence of fire'…We know we can depend upon your fullest cooperation in this worthwhile cause."…Signed Dewitt Nelson, Forest Supervisor.

Saunders Meadow Timeline

1942	Granite Springs tunnel is enlarged to contain 52,000 gallons; it averages 3.5 gallons per minute. April 2nd, District Ranger, H.D. Jones, inspects tract and sets fire safety standards for exterior of cabins and lots and presents report to Tract after his inspection. "The most terrifying fire that will ever strike towards the tract will come from the West. Fortunately Saunders Meadow is on this side giving you time which will be precious. Of 48 cabins inspected only one #39 is in a safe condition to withstand the threat of fire. All others need a yard cleanup." On July 16 and September 10, Elwood M. Jones stresses the importance of developing a new water spring, "The assessment of $50.00 dollars per lot was levied for the prompt development of this other spring. We must hurry, in order to protect our filing rights and prevent additional Tracts behind us being developed and obtaining the use of the water…I very much fear that we have put it off too long…I also know that pipe will be higher in price 10 to 20%...since all steel products are under priority restrictions or reserved for defense work."
1945	The Forest Service requires all new cabins to spend or invest $1,000.00 on "improvements" as oppose to the old amount of $2,000.00 towards cabin construction. After WWII, 16 more lots on the Tahquitz Summer Home Tract are leased. Cabins built at this time are of a "Rectangular Plan" with modified gable roofs, typically 1.5 stories consisting of only a sleeping loft. This plan was common through the 1950s.
1946	Desert Sun School moves permanently to Saunders Meadow.
1947	On Oct.28, 47-members of the Tahquitz Association unanimously assess themselves $100 each for further development of spring filed on earlier (believed to be upper middle spring, above granite spring). Could have been Big Rock Spring records and dates are vague. $50.00 due on Dec. 1 and $50.00 on Feb. 1. This was used seasonally, and later discontinued because of maintenance problems. Big Rock Spring averages only 2 gallons of water per minute. Forest Service informs permittees that their lease fees are now due between Feb. and March 1 instead of Dec. This change is due in order to help the postal service during the holiday season. County collects property taxes on cabins and charges improvement fees. Counties and States start to take a greater interest in Tracts around the nation and fee permits for any construction increase.
1948	Big Cedar Springs averages 5 gallons per minute. Lower Spring water main is removed; focus is now on upper spring. May 12th, State of CA-Department of Public Works grants Tract license for Diversion and Use of Water from two unnamed springs for the purpose of domestic use based on the priority of the right herein confirmed dates from November 15, 1927…Application #5758…Permit#2952…License#3127…
1951	For sanitation reasons, the State of CA is required to issue permits as well so on January 15, State of California issues License # 3127 for Diversion and Use of Water, for up to 10,300 gallons per day, recognizing precedence and continuous use of water since 1927 from the Forest Service. Evidently the State reassigns the permit rights to the USFS. There were always questions as to the States having power over the National Forests located within their boundaries. July 12, S.A. Minnich continues working on pipeline from Big Rock and states that "This is Snake Year" He killed 3, Mr. Stevenson 2 more to be reported!
1952	March 1st, United States Department of Agriculture Forest Service San Bernardino National Forest Supervisor Rep. Walter J.P. addresses major concerns in regards to the increase in Special Use Fees that were placed in effect in 1950 on all new permits, "and which we have now announced will go in effect on all permits in 1953."

Saunders Meadow Timeline

1953	The Forest Service requests an updated list of officers from Tahquitz Tract Association in order to better keep association informed and up to date. August 26th, Idyllwild Fire Protection District expresses concern. "You have a maximum capacity of 60,000 plus gallons; but if one of our fire pumpers were operating at full capacity, it would pump 30,000 gallons per hour...I am therefore requesting that you notify your water users of this critical period now existing...I cannot help feeling concerned over the possibility of fires in that area during the critical months of September and October."
1955	USDA Forest Service informs Tracts that, "in August, after a decision by the U.S. Solicitor, Regulations A-9 and U-17 were amended...associations across the nation such as yours are effective only insofar as membership is voluntary and comply with the Constitution and By-Laws. In the event present members do not care to participate in the services rendered by the Association they may withdraw and the Association may withdraw the services sundered." April 12th, only Lots 48 and 44 are available for lease. The entire cost of participating in the water system of the Tahquitz Tract on SM is $238.00 as of now, which includes $237.00 for participation in the "water" company and $1.00 for the "initiation fee". There is also a $12.00 dollar per year assessment which was made effective September of 1954. On May 31st, Tahquitz Meadow Improvement Association advises Mr. Cross, who did most of the work on the water tunnel to make a complete examination of the facility prior to the summer season. "We may be facing the necessity of increasing the capacity of the upper line since at least 3 of the vacant lots on this line have been taken up and one house is already started..." June 22nd, letter from the Board of Directors to the permittees goes out, "It has been a dry year. We still have about 8 to 10 gallons per minute continuous flow from our 3 springs. But there will probably be a large usage of cabins in our beautiful summer home tract. And this means we'll all have to be careful of water especially during weekend peak load...Please follow the following 4 Rules: a. Always turn off intake valve when leaving b. Always be sure your drain valve is closed when opening intake valve c. Repair all leaks d. No watering ferns, trees and lawns August 11th, Board works on New By-Laws updating the original from 1927. Leland J. Yost writes to Roger Brubaker Secretary-Treasured of the Board, "I briefed up a set of by-laws last Fall but will have to have a copy of the old ones before I can put them into final form for submission to the Board of Directors...also, it was my understanding that the Association did not wish to incorporate. If it is desired to incorporate, and I believe incorporation is necessary, the work should be done by an attorney who is familiar with Mutual Water Company Law as I think we really are in that classification...also, we can't really arrange an insurance program until our legal status is decided on..." August 31st, the Association fee to join and connect to the water system is increased to $249.00 to any new permittee. September 1st, member R.H. Tecklenborg writes to G. Roger Brubaker offering to help in providing new government surplus tanks if Board decides to put in more water storage. "If more storage is needed I can furnish tanks on time payment, rental basis or on any reasonable deal except 'for free'...." June 3rd, Brubake, Yost and Minnich all working on the water system agree that, "in the matter of the water supply, the proposed work should be done as soon as possible..."

Saunders Meadow Timeline

1956	August 14th, Ralph C. Henley President of the Tahquitz Meadow Improvement Association contacts the United States Forest Service in regards to using unnamed spring in what is known as the Brimhall area. "I wish to make formal application for the necessary permit to develop said spring...the retention of the spring for a POSSIBLE camp site SOMETIME in the future at a HIGHER ELEVATION than the spring does not seem particle to us. We need the water in the tract and are ready to do development work." September 15, USFS letter approves concept of spring development on South Ridge. "It was talked over with District Ranger Gilman who in turn discussed it with Forest Supervisor Jarvi. It was agreed upon that your requests were completely justified..." Cabins built during this time were of an "Irregular Plan" with shed roofs. A bit modern in look and style.
1957	September 12 USFS issues a new Special Use Permit covering Sections 17, 18, and 19, including South Ridge area – spring. South Ridge Spring is averaging ½ gallon per minute. **John Jones,** Elwood's son takes over his father's leadership in the water project for the Tahquitz Saunders Meadow community and continues the effort for the summer home tract that his father Elwood Jones began in 1924. These men prove to be steady as the river flows, always working for the greater good of the community with the loving support of their wives, and families. John Jones' daughter, Connie Jones Pillsbury, and husband Norman are 3rd generation owners of the Jones cabin. Work on both the water system and By-Laws continues...
1957-1959	Believed to be the period of development of Big Cedar Spring and the installation of the first 80,000-gallon tank. Water from both storages would overflow 9 to 10 months per year. The tank and Granite Spring were at identical elevations to equalize stored water between them. Also, believed to be the time of development of a surface spring about 2200' above the NE corner of the tract, along the South Ridge trail. Later abandoned due to concerns about surface water quality. Mr. L.O. Harlowe and wife Aurelia Harlowe purchase lot # 43 from Miss Jane Westenberger. January 20th, New By-Laws of the Tahquitz Meadow Improvement Association are accepted and approved and signed by directors and President – Ralph J. Henley. Board members meet on November 14th at Minnich cabin to discuss water storage tank and other problems related to the water system.

Saunders Meadow Timeline

1960s	In 1960, Ray Brocklehurst, friends of Elwood Jones, acquires lot #44 and starts to build his summer home. He builds a finished basement first where his family lives until the home is ready. He was purchasing agent for Standard Oil (Chevron) and an active member and leader of the Tahquitz community. His daughter attorney Leigh B. Humphrey is still a resident of the community in the cabin her father built. She too is a leader and pillar of the Saunders Meadow community. Without her help and the storage of original association documents, the history of Tahquitz Summer Home Tract would have been lost forever. She safe guarded 18 boxes of original documents now safely stored in the archive center of the Idyllwild Area Historic Society February 4th, Tecklenborg offers Board 84,000 gallon reconditioned, bolted steel storage tank, delivered and erected on prepared foundation for $3,785.00. "Tank will be cleaned and given protective coating inside for domestic water use." New tank will be $4,717 plus $390.00 for inside coating. February 18th, Board of Directors meet for the purpose of discussing the purchase of water storage tank. March 23rd, USDA Forest Service approves pipe and tank application. August 9th, one of the last lots is leased and new permittee is asked by association to pay $296.00 for water system and an additional $75.00 assessment for 1959. "This last amount is the assessment which will help pay for the new storage tank now being installed." In September, the new 84,000-gallon storage tank is delivered and notices go out to members who have not paid their special assessment of $75.00 dollars in order to pay for work. The few cabins built or rebuilt during this time reflected modern trends such as the "A" frame design.

Saunders Meadow Timeline

1961	Tract enters third excessively dry year. "One person can completely empty the tank in...days using an ordinary hose for out doors use...Cedar Spring, South Ridge Spring and Big Rock Spring have filled tunnel and tank, once emptied with this year's holiday and increased summertime use, we will have no possibility of refilling them until the winter season of 1961-62...and this, in a year when the fire hazard is greater than it has ever been before and our best insurance is a full tunnel and a full tank of water." The Board of Directors are forced to present "Ballot" to permittees to vote for one of two actions to take: 1. Accept (your) pledge to abstain from all outside-of-cabin use of water and prevention of all leaks within cabins and pray for the best; or 2. I instruct the Board of Directors to present a motion at the next member meeting on Labor Day, to install meters and increase membership charges to cover meter reading and water-use costs. Note: installation of meters will not yield water, which does not exist. April 20th, member John Vevers writes to member Ralph Henley, "All but 14 have singed the assent to the new by-laws. Enclosed is the opinion of the attorney...it is the opinion of attorney and leadership to incorporate." April 22nd, Special meeting of the Tahquitz Meadow Improvement Association was called. The following water regulations were adopted based on the "Ballot" results. "During the period beginning April 22, 1961 and ending at midnight, September 4, (the date of the annual meeting) all users of such water shall restrict usage to inside dwelling domestic purposes and shall not use water for outside of dwelling irrigation, car wash, yard sprinkling, or running of water for wildlife. The Board of Directors shall at its discretion suspend any membership for such a misuse of the water facilities upon action taken in any legal meeting of the directors by a vote of the majority in attendance." Some members like R.O. Durham responded in writing, "What an asinine notice." June 2nd letter from members reads, "As you know, we are doing everything we can to assure an adequate supply of water for our summer homes this exceptionally dry year. Apparently everyone, with possibly one exception (Ms. Hendrick) is showing a strong willingness to cooperate. June 11th, Board of Directions meet and discuss, Safeguards to the water system, termination of membership for violation of the Regulations and Rules adopted by the Board concerning the usage and maintenance of Tract signs. June 13th, with a spirit of continued cooperation rather than termination, Mr. Brubaker sends letter to Mr. and Mrs. Frank E. Hendrick, "I reported to the meeting that you had assured me that you too would use water sparingly when the necessity arose. And I know you will do just that." July 5th, Brubaker writes to Mr. Minnich, "Shirlee and I dropped by the Hendrick place. Sampled their home brew and they voluntarily handed me a signed 'Assent Form'..." August 15th, notice is given that the annual meeting of the members of Tahquitz Meadow Improvement Association will be held at the S.A. Minnich residence on Labor Day, September 4th at 9:30 A.M. Included is Notice of Assessment, "the annual assessment has been increased to $18.00 and is due and payable on September 1. September 4th, officers are elected. September 17th, Board of Directors send letter to Riverside County Road Superintended requesting Road maintenance, "due to our contribution in County taxes and our contribution to the Forest Service, one quarter of which goes to the County..."

Saunders Meadow Timeline

1962	September 3rd, R.H. Tecklenborg tenders his resignation as a member of the Board based on how they including President W. Ricker have treated and viewed Ed. Calderon unfairly after many years of unselfish and unpaid service. Ed C. monitored and reported on the water system for many years. He was a character that would write all his notes/reports in rhyme. This Board was finally removed for their lack of historic understanding of the tract and a true commitment to its future. September 17th, County responds to the Board asking them to work on the roads, "Surely you are not suggesting that road improvements in this great county are made on a political bases?" On September 21st, Board responds, "As a long time admirer of your ability and integrity I hope that I would be the last to insult you by trying to pull politics." Work was done!
1963	USDA Forest Service would like to attend next Directors Board meeting to discuss term permit for the conduit right of way for Tahquitz Tract.
1964	June 16th, Special assessment collected $10.00 dollars for grading of the dirt roads in Tract from cabins located on such dirt roads. March 5th, First Water Service Agreement reached with Fern Valley Water District for the first fire hydrant to be installed in the meadow and fed the by Fern Valley Water District. "Fern Valley Water District and Idyllwild Fire Protection District arrange for the installation ...cost will be $2,000.00 or $15.00 per lot. Ada Hogue leaves mountain and Mr. "Teck" laments, "she was such a splendid character and this world needs more of her type..." April 9th, USDA Forest Service adds Amendment to Tract's Water Terminable Special Use Permit of February 7, 1937 in regards to liability. Association informs Forest Service that, "we do not carry liability insurance for our operation of the water permit." June 24th, Water Service Agreement is signed for the installation of water hydrant between Fern Valley Water District, Idyllwild Fire Protection District and Tahquitz Meadow Improvement Association. August 26th County of Riverside addresses delay of roadwork on Saunders Meadow; "due to weather, work has been delayed...the material has been prepared and will be placed on the road within the next few days and should be fully completed by the Labor Day weekend." August 28th, USDA Forest Service addresses Tracts desire to transfer current conduit permit (reservoirs, tanks, water lines) to a 20-year term permit that would be consistent with the residential permits within the tract. "Our San Bernardino FS office is quite hesitant...due to...exchange...In fact it may be well if you could allow sufficient funds in your treasury for you to prepare the necessary easement deeds that the association may need for your water system in the exchange land." September 7th, Annual Tahquitz Meadow Improvement Association meeting is called to order, topics covered: Fire Hydrant and water line (have been installed), Roads graded by contract (have been paid for), County road work (also completed), Water report – it was suggested to install another water tank (67,200-gallons). "Teck" made a great offer at $1,730.00.

Saunders Meadow Timeline

1965	On September 6th, the Board of Directors meet and: a. Nominate new officers b. Discuss water lines c. Discuss proposal to obtain concrete information as to the cost of getting title to the property d. It was agreed that a reasonable amount of land to request from the Forest Service around the water tank would be one acre. On October 1st, Ralph M. Rutledge presents to President Wayne Ricker, "The Resolution" for the next meeting, which is a definite program for acquisition of property from the Forest Service. He presents 4-concepts fundamental to proposal with 5 steps in meeting concepts, one being to incorporate. December 1st, Ranger Vern E. Smith writes to Mr. and Mrs. J.J. Dosser stating that they have to stop renting their lot #51 or it will be "returning…to higher public use." Which means, their permit will be terminated.
1966	February 21st, Association sends letter to Dosser informing him that unless he pays dues and fixes pipes due to former occupants leaving water on, his membership will be canceled as his association water service. July 12th, Association sends letter to F.E. Hedrick in regards to complaints regarding his use of water. Stop, the use of sprinklers outside or a water meter will be used on your premises and bill you for all water furnished you. August 5th, Notice of Annual Sept. 5th (Labor Day) Meeting is sent to members. September 4th, Board of Directors meets. They agree to raise membership to $25.00 dollars per year in order to pay expected expenses. September 5th, Annual Meeting of Tahquitz Meadow Improvement Association is held. President Ricker reports that water level in tank was down 69 inches and membership is urged to conserve water and only use for domestic purposes. Director Brocklehurst reports on the condition of the South Ridge overflowing spring. Annual rate is raised to $25.00 and Transfer (sale) fee was also raised to $50.00 dollars. There was a discussion regarding efforts to obtain concrete proposal as to exchange of land. Motion was carried to install another tank at the far end of the tract to catch the overflow from the spring. September 29th, J.B. Jones writes to Riverside County Road Commissioner, Mr. A.C. Keith in regards to badly needed repairs to the road from Idyllwild Schoolhouse to Saunders Meadow. "This road has deteriorated rapidly in the past year, in fact it now approaches a hazardous condition…this road serves fifty odd cabins, Desert Sun School and many other private residences." November 6th, Board of Directors of Tahquitz Meadow Improvement Association meet. Bill Snellbaker presents 2 properties surrounded by forestland for sale that could be used for exchange. Board also meets on November 14, "Ranger Smith reported on the land exchange for the association, stating that a request had been taken to the San Bernardino office and forwarded to the Regional office of the Forest Service. He also instructed the directors not to proceed with a survey of the tract as yet." December 22nd District Ranger Karl L. Tameler requests a list of Board of Directors and present officers from the association. On December 27th, the list is provided: a. President – Wayne C. Ricker b. Vice President – Ray Brocklehurst c. Treasurer - L.O. Harlowe d. Secretary – Cosette C. Wiley e. Director – John B. Jones

Saunders Meadow Timeline

1967	District Ranger Verne Smith meets with directors of Tahquitz Meadow Improvement Association to discus the U.S. Forest Service exchange policy that encourages Summer Home Tract cabin owners to acquire private ownership over their tract through a land exchange. Tahquitz Meadow Improvement Association starts process to become Saunders Meadow Inc. after seeking legal advice from attorney. The Board believes that this move will facilitate the land purchase and exchange. This move is necessary due to the Forest Service wanting to cancel summer home tract permits in the near future. Forest Service presents, "Guidelines For Negotiation of Summer Home Tract Exchange". This is a detailed 11-page guide on the long and rigorous exchange process. April 12th, association secretary Cosette writes to Boy Scouts of America, "we are interested in purchasing your dismantled water tank at your Camp Emerson site near Idyllwild, California." September 1st, association passes out "Rules and Regulations" both from association and Forest Service to all members of tract as a reminder of appropriate conduct and protection of natural resources. September 4th, Annual association meeting is held. Ray Brocklehurst reports on the water situation, "the Forest Service prefers that we work out some agreement with the Fern Valley Water District to provide water in case of necessity." Ray also reported on a conversation he had with Ranger Tameler, "Tameler would like to have the association obtain a contour map of the tract." Wayne Ricker reports on the efforts to find land to exchange and describes properties that have been considered. Board of Directors meets immediately following the regular annual meeting of the association. New officers are elected. President-Brocklehurst, Vice President-Jones, Treasure-Harlowe, Secretary-Wiley 1. Mrs. Wiley was instructed to find out the cost of incorporation of the association 2. Directors agree to tack "Rules and Regulations" on the houses of members not present at the annual meeting 3. John Jones is appointed Chairman of roads committee 4. Ray Brocklehurst is appointed Chairman of water committee On September 14th, President of Association writes to Fern Valley Water District. "The Forest Service is reluctant to permit us a new water tank and suggests we procure additional supplies of water from your company...a few years ago, we financed and you constructed a pipeline into the center of our area for fire fighting purposes...is it possible for us to connect our line to this one?" December 10th, Ranger Tameler requests an accurate map of the tract showing all improvements such as water lines, springs, tanks, etc. The Forest Service will provide surveyor if the association provides volunteers to carry chain. Association appoints Ralph Rutledge to chair committee to find out ways and means of trading property and to find properties available for trade, He uses the "Guidelines For Negotiation of Summer Home Tract Exchange" guide. The Forest Service provides specific guidelines and a list of desirable properties they are interested in. These properties are ranked as to the desirability by the forest service. Due to the old land grants and homesteading acts, the National Forests found themselves as a patch works of private and public lands. The Forest Services was working hard at acquiring private land in order to expand and better define their boundaries across the nation. At this time, the association also moved and seconded that the question of incorporation of the association be postponed for at least three months, pending further investigations.

Saunders Meadow Timeline

1968	Through the leadership of John Jones and the Board of Directors, the Association continues searching for land acceptable to the Forest Service. On June 12th, Association Secretary Mrs. Wiley contacts President of National Forest Recreation Association and states that, "we have received a letter from Ken Chandler from Snowcrest Heights Improvement Association, MT. Baldy, CA inviting us to join. Thank you for the included February 15 newsletter. June 24th, President Brocklehurst of Tahquitz Meadow Improvement Assn. writes to Karl L. Tameler, District Ranger USFS. "This is to confirm the appointment you have made with our attorney, D. Richard Swan, at your office on Thursday, July 18th...included at the meeting will be a representative from San Bernardino Forest Service District headquarters who has responsibility in all negotiations for the exchange of forest land...we need to ascertain from your representation the exact provisions necessary to be included in our proposed Articles of Incorporation to insure a legal entity qualified to negotiate a land exchange...This letter will also confirm an arrangement made with you on June 5th with respect to a jack-survey of the metes and bounds of the area in the Tahquitz Summer Home Tract which will be considered by you in this exchange...survey to be completed by August, together with the completion of our incorporation, should put us well on our way towards early consummation of the proposed land exchange..." June 30th, Board of Directors meet to discuss information received from the National Forest Recreation Association, an organization of owners of residences and businesses on national forest lands throughout the western states. The NFRA states "Join us in our efforts to protect the homeowners on National Forest Lands." Joining was postponed due to possible land exchange. July 24th, Tahquitz Meadow Improvement Association contacts District Ranger Karl Tameler, "It is unfortunate that our appointment did not mature, although it had been made three weeks earlier and had been confirmed by our letter of July 14th...We are pleased however, that you have arranged with Mr. Minter for another date now set for Friday, August 2 at 1 p.m....we are also pleased that you plan to attend our annual meeting on September 1, which will afford our members an opportunity to become acquainted with you and understand the problems involved in negotiating for the acreage we are leasing. August 14th, USDA Forest Service provides Tahquitz Meadow another list of desirable land that it is willing to exchange for. Tahquitz Meadow Improvement Association starts to contact owners with form letter to see if they are interested in selling their land. August 16th, Lawyer Jack E. Grisham writes back to Dr. Ralph M. Rutledge of Tahquitz, "I received your recent letter making inquiry regarding the possible sale or exchange of my ranch property near the Vista Grande Ranger Station...it is listed with a broker at $2,500.00 per acre..." August 17th, Dr. Ralph M. Rutledge writes letter to land owner John D. Dougherty, "This is a summary of our conference...relative to possible exchange of land with the US Forest Service which might involve your property..." August 18th, Notice of Annual Meeting is mailed off. Meeting is for, "the purpose of electing new officers, for consideration and discussion of the steps taken and progress made toward acquisition of title to the real property upon which our cabins are located..." August 27th, "Dear Sirs: I am sorry to be so late getting a reply to you concerning the Lynwood Sportsman Inc. property at Anza...I read your letter to the membership at their last meeting and as usual their instruction was to reply in the negative."

Saunders Meadow Timeline

1968	August 29th, Civil Engineers Neste, Brudin & Steve report to Attorneys at Law Cox, Pendleton & Swan. "Please refer to the proposal for the subdivision of US Government lease sites in the Saunders Meadow area which we discussed with Riverside County Planning Department staff and the US Forestry Service officials on August 12th. The discussion of the conversion of these lease sites into subdivided lots referred to above is partially based on approval of a satisfactory subdivision map by Riverside County Planning Commission, US Forestry, the property owners and the acquisition of other lands by the property owners for trading with the Forest Service for the lands on which the lease sites are located. We would estimate the cost of this work to be between $5,200 to $5,700 in addition to those costs for preparing the tentative work outlined at the beginning of the letter of $2,105." Summer Home owners see the value of their cabins drop due to the uncertainty of the future lease terms.
1968	September 2nd, Board of Directors meets and elects officers: President-Brocklehurst, Vice-President-Miller, and Treasurer-Harlowe, Secretary-Wiley. Also on September 2nd, the Annual association meeting was held at the lecture Hall of Desert Sun School. Ranger Tameler stated that the Forest Service would like to go along with the concurrence of the majority of the membership in the matter of the exchange of land. He also stated that he hoped that the association would plan ultimately to join a water district. September 3rd, The "Resolution" was adopted at the regular annual meeting by a vote of 47 to 1. The Resolution is the association's plan of action and commitment to go through the land exchange. There will be a meeting of the Board of Directors on September 22nd, for the purpose of discussing the enclosed Resolution and the proposed land exchange with members of the association who were not personally present. Both the Forest Service and the Planning Commission of the County of Riverside require a survey showing the metes and bounds of our cabin sites. Every member should put in corner stakes at his desired boundaries. If owners do not place stakes at corners mutually agreed upon with their neighbors, the Forest Service will place stakes at the corners as originally located. September 4th, It is reported that, "in early August 1968, Assn. wrote to Mr. John Dougherty-Manufacturing Jeweler in regards to the sale of his land. He met with Assn. and Forest Service August 16th, discussions continue and look promising…" September 15th, Association writes to members, "There will be a meeting of the Board of Directors for the purpose of discussing the enclosed resolution and the proposed land exchange…you are invited to attend…remember the needed survey and your placing of stakes...

Saunders Meadow Timeline

1968	The Forest Service would like 100% participation and approval for the land exchange. Brian Minter, Lands Officer for the Forest Service stated, "the Service has not completed an exchange where there was not 100% participation of the group. Ranger Tameler also noted that, "there cannot be an exchange of money, it can only be an exchange of title by law." September 22nd, special meeting of the Board of Directors is held, the "Resolution" passed and the association voted to proceed with the land exchange. They also voted not to join the National Forest Recreation Association due to exchange. On September 30th, a conference was held at the office of the Division of Real Estate in Los Angeles. Present: Mr. William Wall – Chief of the Subdivision Section Mr. Passman – Counsel for the Division of Real Estate Mr. Patterson and Mr. Brocklehursts of the Tahquitz Meadow Improvement Association. D. Richard Swan – Attorney for the Association Conclusion of Conference: 1. The vehicle of a stock cooperative appears ideal 2. The Division of Real Estate will make every effort to facilitate the establishment of the stock cooperative. 3. A survey showing each of the respective cabin sites as well as the exterior boundaries of the association property will have to be prepared and submitted in conjunction with the application for approval.
1968	John Jones, Brocklehurst and Patterson discuss talk with John Dougherty, "Dougherty indicated that he has had other offers for the land...we need to meet with our lawyer and Dougherty whereas we would actually make the deal and escrow, also, a formal letter should be written to the Forest Service outlining our requests for the land transfer and outlining the arrangements we have made with Dougherty." October 14th, President Brocklehurst writes to Lake Hemet Municipal Water District about purchasing some of their property, "We appreciate your willingness to entertain a proposal and will take such action when and if this proves feasible." October 31st, Security Title Insurance Company Provides Preliminary Report on John D. Dougherty's property. November 4th, Albert L. Johnson Real Estate Appraiser writes to Tahquitz Meadow Improvement Assn., "Our fee for rendering a short form letter report of the current cash market value and the current market value (under prevailing terms) will be $250.00 November 7th, Tahquitz Meadow Improvement Assn. approves Appraisal by Johnson Albert L. November 18th, Albert L. Johnson presents Appraisal report, "...Current market value under cash equivalent concept i.e., all cash to seller, $162,000, approximately $250 per acre...Under currently prevailing terms, $193, 500.00 or $300 per acre, adjusted... November 29th, M.W. Patterson of Tahquitz Meadow Improvement Assn. writes to John J. Dougherty, "John Jones and myself certainly enjoyed meeting and talking with you on Wednesday, November 27th. We would like to confirm the verbal agreement made at that time...of $193,500.00 for your property...We will place $5,000.00 in escrow which will apply toward the purchase price..." December 19th, The Law offices of Cox, Pendleton and Swan write to Edwin Talmadge, "This letter will confirm our phone conversation with you yesterday wherein you and your client, Mr. John Dougherty, were extended an invitation to attend the scheduled meeting at 9:00 a.m. January 7th with us and certain bank officers of Security Pacific National Bank in Riverside, CA. There are, of course, a number of obstacles which must be met and overcome..."

Saunders Meadow Timeline

1969	February 19th, Attorney At Law Edwin L. Talmage writes to Tahquitz Meadow Improvement Assn. attorney Swan, "your letter of February 10th, enclosing rough drafts of the option agreement and escrow instructions, was duly received. Mr. Dougherty and I have studied the draft and I have been instructed to raise a number of points..." February 28th, Board of Directors meet to discuss the results of negotiations regarding the acquisition of the "Daugherty Property". Ranger Tameler stated, "Daugherty property is prime land and will continue to be so." March 13th Attorney Edwin Talmage writes to Attorney Swan, "Your letter of march 5th was received by me and passed along to Mr. Dougherty...our letter cancels out the original understanding and makes an entirely new proposal...M. Dougherty has decided not to proceed..." April 9th, Articles of Incorporation of Saunders Meadow are Endorsed and Filed in the office of the Secretary of State of the State of California. April 10th, Secretary of State Frank M. Jordan, has hereunto caused the Great Seal of the State of California to be affixed...Filed in Riverside County #10780 on April 18, 1969 – Saunders Meadow, Inc. Saunders Meadow, Inc. is formed in order for community to be able to purchase and then exchange land with the Forest Service. The Summer Home owners become shareholders in the corporation for $1,500.00 dollars each. Funds will be used to purchase land for exchange. June 3rd, Forest Service District Regional Acting Attorney William L. Anderson responds to Saunders Meadow, Inc. request of May 7th, "we have reviewed the Articles of Incorporation and By-Laws of SM, Inc. If your inquiry is directed solely to whether SM, Inc. may convey land to the US and take land pursuant to a land exchange agreement, the Articles are satisfactory. As you know, a land exchange must be made with a legal entity which is authorized to hold and convey real property, and this corporation has these powers... The Articles and By-Laws are quite unusual and are on a different basis than any we have ever previously encountered. Under these By-Laws title to all the land is to remain in the corporation...if the above is the intent of the parties, we would have no right to object..." June 17th, Saunders Meadow, Inc. Attorney Richard Swan receives letter from Charles R. Tutor Re: Property in Snow Creek Canyon Area, "In answer to yours of May 21st, we would have, in the Snow Creek Canyon Area, the entire of Section 5, Township 4 South, Range 3 East, San Bernardino Base and Meridian, available for sale...selling price would be $96, 000.00...This property is surrounded by the San Bernardino National Forest in the San Jacinto Wild Area..." July 1st, Richard Swan, Esq. receives letter from Attorney Schlesinger Re: Estate of Joseph M. Shapiro, deceased Section 7, T 7S, R5E-636.64 acres...estate will sell property for $325,000.00 July 21st to October 29th, Big Shot Tony Burke Real Estate Broker in Palm Springs since 1929 would like to sell 640 acres to SM, Inc. for $320.000 that handsome devil! August 17th, letter goes out to new tract members from President Ray Brocklehurst explaining Tract history, association fees and current land exchange. "When an acceptable tract is available and its cost is known, each member will decide on what basis he wishes to participate in the corporate purchase, in accordance with the choices outlined in the 1968 'Resolution'. It is hoped that each cabin owner will be able to fund his share of the investment and become a shareholder in the corporation being formed to negotiate this transaction."

Saunders Meadow Timeline

1969	September 1st, Annual Association meeting is held. John Jones reports, "Daugherty land is priced too high and demanded terms too unreasonable." At the same meeting, Brocklehurst reports, "due to work done on the upper middle spring and the tunnel cleaned out, the flow is better than ever, but more work is required on the South - Big Cedar Spring" September 29th, Esq. Swan sends, "Form Letter" to Theodosius Arvanitis in regards to his property Sections 11 and 13, T6S, RIE, SBB & M. November 5th, Esq. Swan receives letter from Realtor Mary G. Lambrou in regards to Theodosius Arvanitis real property, "The assessed value of the property on tax notice is $40.00 per acre which is $51,080.00. Mr, Arvanitis is open to any reasonable offer..." John Jones reports on property owned by Arvanitis and of other properties available for purchase.
1970	January 3rd, Board of Directors authorize President Brocklehurst to proceed with the possible purchase of Theodosios Arvanitis property if the said is accepted by the Forest Service in trade for the Association land. M.W. Patterson and John Jones work with Forest Service and Arvanitis's agent in the purchase of two sections of his property. January 9th, Board of Directors of "Saunders Meadow, Inc." a California corporation meet for their first meeting at the office of Cox, Swam and Carpenter, Attorneys in Hemet, CA January 20th, Esq. Swan writes to Commissioner of Corporations State of California in regards to SM, Inc., Swan inquires about 2 questions: 1. Must Saunders Meadow, Inc., obtain a permit from the Commissioner to borrow $57,000 in one or two increments from Tahquitz Meadow Improvement Association? 2. Will Saunders Meadow, Inc., be required to obtain a permit from the Commissioner prior to the issuance of any of the 57 proposed shares of stock in conjunction with the establishment of the stock co-operative-condominium? January 28th, Department of Corporations writes back to Esq. Swan, "The request for interpretive opinion contained in your letter is under consideration by this office... We need a copy of the articles of incorporation, by-laws, and other documents of Saunders Meadow, Inc..." March 30th, SM, Inc. is in Escrow (#301-10-658), Security Pacific National Bank sends a copy of preliminary Title report dated 3/25/70...The land referred to in this report is...Section 11 & 13, Township 6 South, Range 1 East, San Bernardino Base and Meridian, according to US Government Survey, approved April 27,1905...Taxes for 1970 - $786.38... April 12th, letters are sent out to members from President Brocklehurst informing them about land exchange. "You are aware, of course, that pursuant to the Resolution passed by the membership in September, 1968, for two years we have made every effort to purchase privately owned land, acceptable to the Forest Service, to exchange for the parcel we are now leasing. We are pleased to report that we have recently completed an agreement to purchase two sections of land. This property is within the forest area and is listed by the Forest Service as 'desirable with a medium priority'. Mr. Swan, our attorney, has advised us that our corporation, Saunders Meadow, Inc., should make the purchase of this land. To finance transaction, we are hereby assessing each member $1,500.00, payable no latter thank June 1.

Saunders Meadow Timeline

1970	April 12th, Attorney Swan writes to association members, "...transactions of this kind must be reviewed and approved in several offices between here and Washington D.C.... stock certificates will be issued to all participating members as soon as the Forest Service approves the transfer and all expenses have been funded..." May 8th, letter goes out explaining why the stock co-operative was chosen rather than the condominium and why the $1,500.00 amount will not go up by much if any. SM, Inc. President W.R. Brocklehurst writes to Karl Tameler, District Ranger in Idyllwild, California, "This is a preliminary offer by our corporation, Saunders Meadow, Inc., successor to Tahquitz Meadow Improvement Association, to exchange Sections 11 and 13 T6S R1E SBBM (1277 acres) for the W1/2 SE ¼ Section 18 T5S R3E SBBM (80acres) and NE1/4 Section 19 T5S R3E SBBM (Approximately 160acres). This action is taken in accordance with your letter of November 19· 1968, indicating no serious objection to an exchange by the permittees of the Tahquitz Summer Home Tract..." June 3rd, President Brocklehurst and Secretary Wiley met at the office of attorney Cox, Swan and Carpenter, with representatives Tameler, Johnson and Scharf of the Forest Service...to discuss the exchange, water tanks and two springs... June 29th, SM, Inc. continues to rely on Tahquitz Meadow Improvement Association financially, "On demand, after date, for value received, the undersigned, Saunders Meadow, Inc., a California corporation, promises to pay to Tahquitz Meadow Improvement Association, $34,454.00...The sum shall be credited to this note upon the issuance of each share of the stock of SM, Inc. to a member of Tahquitz Meadow Improvement Association." June 27th, certain members are reminded to pay land exchange assessment. Options were made available as per the "Resolution". July 10th, Tahquitz Meadow Improvement Association writes to members, "We are happy to inform you that the terms of our escrow involving the purchase of two sections of land in Bautista Canyon have been met and we expect to receive a deed to that property soon...the $1,500.00 per lot will be sufficient...Forest Service has offered the 80 acres we are leasing...now we have to work in determining lot boundaries and setting new stakes... July 13th, SM, Inc. receives Grant Deed for Arvanitis land to be used in Forest Service exchange from Security Title Insurance Co. July 31st, 49 members have paid in full. 6 selected a payment plan with 10% interest and 2 will not be participating. They plan to sell and or remain on the FS permit that the cooperative will now own and carry. Cabin owner Ed. Calderon walks up and checks the water tank everyday while at his summer home which is 99% of the time. He leaves notes reporting water status under John B. Jones family cabin door. This was one of his many volunteer contributions to the community. On a certain occasion, he miscalculated the chemical balance in the water tank and had to inform all residence not to wash their clothing or drink the water. Many did not get the message! There were reports that people were walking around town with holes on their clothes mooning the tourists. Cabins rebuilt and upgraded at this time were contemporary two-story homes. By now, many of the original 1920s cabins had been remodeled or replaced. August 14th, Tahquitz Meadow Improvement Association President Brocklehurst writes to Karl L. Tameler, District Ranger of the US Forest Service in Idyllwild, CA, "The Forest Service requires that the majority of permittees desire the exchange. For your information and guidance we can report that out of our 57 members, 54 are participating. The other 3 are selling their cabins."

Saunders Meadow Timeline

<table>
<tr><td>1971</td><td>February 1st, Southern California Edison Electric Company – Chief of Federal Permits Harry A. Wells writes to Mr. Murry A. Taylor – Recreation and Land Officer San Jacinto Ranger District San Bernardino National Forest in regards to land exchange with SM, Inc., "Enclosed is...a Grant of Easement for execution by the proponents to the subject land exchange. Please note that the easement includes General Telephone Company of California because the pole line is jointly used between both companies..."

February 25th, A special meeting of the Board of Directors of this corporation is held for the purpose of considering an amendment to the Articles of Incorporation of this corporation correcting an error in the legal description contained in the present Articles, adopting By-Laws, and considering the desirability of submitting a firm proposal for land exchange to the United States Department of Agriculture.

February 26th, Official Land Exchange Documents are sent from Law Offices of Cox, Pendleton and Swan to Karl Tameler, District Ranger US Forest Service:
1. Original firm land exchange offer of Saunders Meadow, Inc.
2. Minutes of Saunders M., Inc. directors' meeting with resolution authorizing the execution and submission of the enclosed Land Exchange Offer.
3. Copy of proposed Certificate of Amendment of Articles of Incorporation
4. By-Laws of SM, Inc.
March 8th, Lots: 34, 46, 54, 59 go on sale.
March 12th, Land Exchange Offer is filed.
March 13th, "The Forest Service requires a change in By-Laws in respect to existing permittees who do not become shareholders of the corporation, protecting their rights until the expiration of their term permits..."
SM, Inc. adopts Article III, Section 2 to its By-Laws; " it is by and through its provision that an orderly and just transition will be made from the current status to that of the stock co-operative. Special provisions are been made with respect to existing permittees who fail to join the stock co-operative..."

March 16th, Brocklehurst writes to members, "Early in February the Forest Service informed us that they had completed their appraisal of the properties involved in our proposed land exchange and that after meeting with our attorney Mr. Swan and board members of our corporation as well as our association, they would recommend trading the Summer Home Tract for the Bautista Canyon land.

August 24th, letter goes out to new owners of sold lots explaining history of tract, association and land exchange resolution. "In 1970 we finally acquired 2 sections of land which the Forest Service offices in San Bernardino and San Francisco have agreed to accept in exchange...currently, we are waiting for approval form Washington D.C. and Department of Agriculture...a special assessment was also levied against each permittee in the amount of $1,500.00, payable no later than July 31, 1970...this assessment is for the purchase of one share of our corporation SM, Inc. at such time as title to the land is transferred to the corporation."

September 6th, Board of Directors of Tahquitz Meadow Improvement Association meet following the regular annual meeting held to day. It was moved, second and carried that the same officers serve for the coming year, namely: President, Brocklehurst, Vice President, Miller, Secretary-Treasurer, Cosette C. Wiley, Directors, Willis Leach and Wayne Ricker.
There was also discussion regarding differences among the members as to the position of stakes on the proposed lot lines.</td></tr>
</table>

Saunders Meadow Timeline

<table>
<tr><td>1971</td><td>
September 10th, Out of the blue, issues arise from a small group in regards to the By-Laws. They contact and hire their own attorney rather than talking to the leadership.
USDA Forest Service Assistant Forest Lands Officer Robert M. Scharf writes to SM, Inc. President Ray Brocklehurst, “We have received formal approval of your land exchange offer from our Washington D.C. Office. Two items are needed from you to further process this exchange.
1. Letter to the Riverside County newspaper and
2. Signed amendments to the Special Use Permits.
Letter to newspaper will appear each week for four consecutive weeks…with a cost of around $40.00…
September 11th, The Riverside Enterprise Newspaper receives letter to publish a public Notice of Land Exchange for four weeks. The Forest Service requests that, “After the final publication, you should send us the regular Affidavit of Publication…”
October 5th, A new stipulation is added by the Forest Service and numbered 30-Land Exchange Amendment #2 for Special Use Permit, “It is understood that this permit will automatically terminate when the land described as the Tahquitz Tract in conveyed to any permittee goup organized for the purpose of acquiring this tract through exchange…”
October 9th, Letter from President Brocklehurst is sent to members, “The refusal of Mr. & Mrs. Leonard Harlowe to sign and return the Amendment to lease either to us or to the Forest Service has completely blocked all progress towards consummation of the Land Exchange…Mr. and Mrs. Leonard Harlowe and Mr. and Mrs. William Everhart demands changes in the Corporation By-Laws…
October 13th, Press-Enterprise Company sends out Affidavit of Publication in regards to Land Exchange…public notice reads… “Persons claiming such properties or having valid objections to this proposed exchange must file their claims or objections with the Regional Forest, US Forest Service…within 30 days after date of first publication of this notice…”
December 6th, around 35 proposed changes in the By-Laws are presented and agreed to, subject to the approval of members and attorneys for the Everhart’s and Harlowes’, Esq. Hill, Farrar and Burrill.
Edith Elliot dies – Founder of Desert Sun School on Saunders Meadow.
December 9th, Tahquitz Meadow Improvement Association writes to members in regards to progress or lack there of, “In regards to the Land Exchange, the refusal of the Harlowes to sign and return the Amendment To Special Use Permit (lease) either to us or the Forest Service has completely blocked all progress toward consummation of the Land Exchange…it may jeopardize our entire project…cost us an additional $422.91 in taxes and $160.00 per lot for Permit Fees to Forest Service if not signed by March 1, 1972…
December 10th, Association Law Offices of Cox, Swan and Carpenter communicate with Law offices of Hill, Farrer and Burrill over Saunders Meadow, Inc. By-Laws
December 14th, Law Offices of Hill, Farrer and Burrill respond, “We have received the By-Laws of the above corporation as revised December 8th and have reviewed them in light of the meeting which the Everharts and Harlowes had with the directors of the corporation. We feel that the revised By-Laws are greatly improved and generally reflect the wishes of our clients. However, there are several areas which still give us concern…”
</td></tr>
</table>

Saunders Meadow Timeline

1971	December 16th, a special meeting was held where the revised By-Laws were adopted as approved by Hill, Farrer & Burrill and, Cox Swan & Carpenter Law firms. December 17th, W.D. Everhart, Mary Everhart and Robert Everhart write one of their crazy letters to members of Tract stating how the final "Amendment to Lease" was delivered to Forest Ranger Bill Johnson in Idyllwild, "This long delay is chargeable to Saunders Meadow, Inc. Board of Directors and, possibly, to their lawyer..." December 21st, Neste, Brudin & Stone – Civil Engineers send letter to Mr. Brocklehurst, President of Saunders Meadow, Inc., "Enclosed is our standard work order form authorizing us to check deeds for dedication of Saunders Meadow Road, Tahquitz Drive, Pine Avenue, Crest Drive and Cowbell Alley…" December 24th, the Everharts and Harlowes are still upset. December 25th, an information notice is sent out, "On December 21, Brocklehurst and Cosette C. Wiley met with Robert Sharf of the San Bernardino office of the Forest Service, and William Johnson of the Idyllwild Office of the Forest Service, at the office of Cox, Swan and Carpenter in Hemet. At said meeting Brocklehurst as President and Cosette C. Wiley, as Secretary of Saunders Meadow, Inc., executed the following documents: Grant Deed in favor of the US Government to the two sections of land in Bautista Canyon known as the Arvanitis Property and Easement in favor of the Southern California Edison Company for utility lines in the Tahquitz Tract. Mrs, Wiley was instructed to order a Preliminary Title Report covering the Tahquitz Tract." December 28th, SM, Inc. President Brocklehurst writes to members, "With considerable relief I report that, as of December 16th, the last remaining Amendment to Lease was submitted to the Forest Service. Our Land Exchange is now proceeding normally and should be completed within four to six months, as estimated based on previous experiences of the Land Officer of the Forest Service in San Bernardino…On December 21st, Mrs. Wiley, Mr. Swan, Mr. Johnson and Mr. Scharf of the Forest Service, and I met to deed to the Government the Corporation's two sections of land in Bautista Canyon. This transaction, a required step has a built-in safeguard which assures us of return of the land if for any reason the Government chooses not to consummate the exchange. The Forest Service will record the deed on Dec. 29th. Everharts and Harlowes are not happy and state that, "the Board changed By-Laws back to give them more power…be advised that if Board Member Harlowe had any idea that what he had heard, read and voted upon would be changed after the note, He Never Would Have Signed The USFS Release…and be alerted that SM, Inc. will be a ¼ to ½ million dollar corporation…" The Association responds, "It is obvious that when 58 entities are involved in a complex project such as ours there will be differences of opinion and objectives. Ownership of the property will bring an unending series of problems that we have not had in the past. We are entering a training period when we learn how to get along with each other and develop dependable leaders. Everyone is penalized, we will find, if we cant work together in harmony." December 29th, Attorney for Association D. Richard Swan receives letter from Hill, Farrer & Burrill Law Firm, "We have received the By-Laws…and have reviewed them with the Everharts. It appears that the revised By-Laws do not accurately reflect the understanding which the Harlowes and Everharts reached with the Board of Directors at the December 16th meeting."

Saunders Meadow Timeline

1972	January 5th, Law Office of Cox, Swan & Carpenter write to Law Office of Hill, Farrer & Burrill, "I am satisfied that the Board of Directors has been entirely fair with your clients and that at no time deceived or intentionally mislead any prospective shareholder. The By-Laws as not drafted are with out question fair and workable. I appreciate your efforts in aiding to streamline the By-Laws and I hope that we have been able to accommodate a sufficient number of your suggestions to satisfy your clients in order that further controversy can be avoided." January 19th, Everhart writes to Tract Association members giving them the family's life history and qualifications and how they support the Harlowes, "finally…now back to bare facts, Do Not Sign A Proxy. A Proxy can be used against your best interest even in the hands of a dear friend…" January 30th, Board of Directors of Saunders Meadow, Inc. meet. Failing a quorum, the meeting could not be held, but for the sack of those members present, certain provisions of the revised By-Laws were discussed. President Brocklehurst also appointed Wayn C. Ricker to fill the vacancy on the Board created by the resignation of Patterson, such appointment subject to the legality of the same. February 1st, Everhart once again writes to all, " Dear share-holder-to-be of Saunders Meadow, Inc.…don't give up your power…take it away from the Board…Do not sign a proxy…" February 3rd, Hill, Farrer & Burrill write to Cox, Swan & Carpenter…Everhart and Harlowes are upset that Ricker was appointed and not voted on. February 10th, Cox, Swan & Carpenter respond to Hill, Farrer & Burrill, "Apparently, Mr. Harlowe, your client, was available to attend the meeting; it was anticipated that he would attend, but at the last minute he declined to attend. Perhaps, his absence is completely explainable and justifiable, however, his absence coupled with your letter leads me to believe that Mr. Harlowe is trying to play some sort of game which essentially acts to his inconvenience and expense of the remaining Directors…rest assured and may so advise your client that the remaining Directors are aware of the facts that a quorum will have to be present at a meeting in order to validate the appointment of Mr. Ricker." February 18th, Board of Directors of Saunders Meadow, Inc. meet to select a director to fill vacancy created by Patton. Wayne C. Ricker and Mary Everhart are nominated. Vote was called: Ricker – 3, Everhart – 1. April 7th, Letter is written to all members, "Although there have been several very encouraging hints and signs, we have as yet not received definite notice from Washington, D.C. that the deal has been formally consummated…We have every reason to continue to expect ultimate success…also, while, as of this writing, we have sufficient water to satisfy immediate needs, we anticipate a serious shortage unless we have adequate amount of rain or snow in the near future or every member of our group fully and consistently co-operates in conserving water…" May 2nd, "We have been notified that Washington, D.C. has O.K.'d the Land Exchange…by the end of May, all legal details will have been completed…this calls for a celebration on May 28th…" May 5th, Deed granted by the National Forest Service to the Tract – Saunders Meadow, Inc. It takes 5 years for association to find land acceptable to the Forest Service. After many rejections, the Forest Service agrees upon the "Bautista Canyon" land near Hemet. On May 5th, the 80 acres of the Tahquitz Summer Home Tract is deeded to Saunders Meadow, Inc.

Saunders Meadow Timeline

1972	May 6th, Association submits article on the history of Tahquitz Tract to the Town Crier newspaper. May 8th, Civil Engineers Neste, Brudin & Stone write to Saunders Meadow, Inc., "We have reviewed with Riverside County officials the matter of converting the Saunders Meadow U.S. Government leases to a subdivision of 57 parcels…" May 28th, Saunders Meadow, Inc. members-stock holders celebrate with a great outdoor picnic in the glade at the upper end of Tanglewood Lane. All members get a copy of the By-Laws. June 2nd, Idyllwild's Town Crier features story, "Its all theirs now!" A large banner is placed over the picnic tables, "This Land is Our Land". June 7th, Neste, Brudin & Stone – Civil Engineers hired by SM, Inc., report back in regards to subdivision development. "We have reviewed the requirements for the conversion of your 57 leased sites to a planned unit development or a non-statutory condominium…your association is not in a position to proceed with the preliminary engineering and planning work necessary to allow you to subdivide the property. The following steps are required: a. Topographic map and aerial photos $1000.00 b. Tentative Subdivision Map $1,600.00 c. Conditional Use Permit Application $400.00 d. Variance Application $150.00 We discussed with you the need to obtain a permit to serve water to the project as well…" June 9th, The Mitchells write to Brocklehurst. "Pleasant memories of our recent barbeque celebrating our ownership of the land will remain for a long time. The Mitchells are grateful for the efforts of all who made it possible. Our family…looks forward to many years of use of our cabin. It is most important to them. It is disquieting to have a certain amount of controversy appear early in our history. We earnestly and sincerely hope that it can be minimized in the future. We all have a complex job ahead of us that demands fairness, tolerance and cooperation from each and every one. It will not be possible to make everyone completely satisfied. Compromises are necessary and unavoidable. I earnestly hope that every effort will be made to keep all members posted, as many troubles are the results of misinformation or lack of information. The proposed By-Laws that were sent out contained some features that I believe could be changed to the advantage of all. We do not want our Board of Directors to become all-powerful, nor do I thing that they want too great a responsibility. Checks and balances are a part of our heritage. On the other hand, I have no sympathy for any minority group that battles over unimportant features and does not make every reasonable effort to achieve friendly team work in all of our undertakings. Leland Yost and I were concerned enough about the quality of our proposed By-Laws that we got some legal advice designed to spotlight the places where some improvements could be made, we hope! Please look over the enclosed sheet and see if you agree…" June 12th, There is a joint meeting of Boards of Directors of Saunders Meadow, Inc., and Tahquitz Meadow Improvement Association for the purpose of considering the outline of engineering work and estimated costs as set forth from the firm Neste, Brudin & Stone, Civil Engineers. "The secretary was directed to point out…that one of our members should be present at the time the survey was commenced in order to assist in locating stakes; and to ask that the location of our springs and tank be shown on maps…we will also have samples of our water tested for presentation to the Department of Health. SM, Inc., directs Neste, Brudin & Stone, Inc., to proceed with work. June 15th, Everhart write another Looney letter to Mitchell and Yoset. "Sirs: It is most heartening after 12 months of almost fruitless efforts to find a small group willing to initiate a further effort to head off what the Deputy Attorney General in Los Angeles termed 'a most vicious set of By-Laws'. I beg to differ with you on your inference that the small minority was battling over small issues…

Saunders Meadow Timeline

1972	June 20th, Neste, Brudin & Stone incorporated Civil Engineers write to Riverside County Planning Commission. "Variance and Conditional Use on Tract 5418. This letter supplements the standard application forms in order to make the application clearer. 1. The existing use of the total 76 acres is mountain-resort, single family, residential. There is absolutely NO change in this use proposal, nor will any additional use be made. 2. The present owners, who are the users, of the property wish only to preserve the area AS IS and to assure that their property rights are clearly defined on a recorded map…A recorded lot line will avoid future neighborhood disputes and give definite property rights which may be passed to heir or others. 3. All of the individual owners and users are in agreement today to the proposed lot lines shown on the plot. This total agreement may not last forever, so now is an appropriate time to record such lines. 4. We are asking for a variance from the minimum building set back from interior drives of the required 10 feet in the following cases: Lot 33, 6 feet, Lot 34, 3 feet. In both cases, the existing drive has been there for years, is not used by the general public, and serves only 3 parcels. All users are in agreement that no problem exists, but to relocate the driveway would necessitate removal of trees – Which Is Not Acceptable. 5. In regards to Section 18.5 (4), it is specifically desired that the existing dirt roads be left AS IS and that no realignment or improvement be made. This is a rustic-residential mountain area…the rustic atmosphere is EXACTLY what attracted the owners many years ago to this area… 6. In regards to Section 18.5 (10), there is no recreational area today, nor is one contemplated. Therefore, there is no need for five-foot wide paved pedestrian walkways. 7. In regards to Section 18.5 (12) Parking, all automobiles have been adequately parked in the area for years. There are, however, no marked-out spaces with numbers…when the ground is frozen, parking is done wherever it is safe. When the ground is wet, parking is done where no damage will occur to soft ground…In any manner, parking is an individual thing in this area, with more than 2 ½ places available for each residential unit… July 25th, Attorney Swan writes to Saunders Meadow, Inc., "I met with Security Title Insurance Company to discuss their role, if any, as an escrow and/or title company in assisting with present and future transfer of the rights of each individual owner of stock…the following conclusions were reached: 1. The only map, which should be recorded, is a perimeter map… 2. No title insurance will issue with respect to these transactions. SM, Inc. will have to advise prospective buyers of the status of the corporate assets. 3. The escrow, if any, would be handled in the manner of a bulk sale escrow and not as a real property escrow. Very few banks and/or trust companies now handle bulk sales… 4. We will not obtain a separate assessment for each individual house…County Tax Assessor and Collector will issue one tax bill… I suspect that in the ultimate analysis, we are going to have difficulty finding an escrow willing to handle these transactions, and will probably have to handle them ourselves here in this office for some sort of pre-determined fee arrangement… September 6th, Esq. Swan writes to Hemet Escrow Company, "In order to assist in the processing of escrows for the sale and purchase of the various interest in Saunders's Meadow, Inc. we have prepared a form of the following: 1. Agreement and Escrow Instructions for Purchase and Sale of Stock, Purchase and Sale of Real Property 2. Security Agreement 3. Statement of Warranty with By-Laws attached 4. Assignment and Bill of Sale …It is the present plan and policy of SM, Inc. that no share certificates shall be issued though the right thereto exists at this time until such time as the tract map has received its final approval by the County of Riverside and is ready for filing in the office of the County Recorder…

Saunders Meadow Timeline

1972	On September, Saunders Meadow, Inc., sends out "A STATEMENT OF OBJECTIVES" "In order to preserve a near 50 year heritage of association with this Mountain area, the cabin holders have formed a stock-co-operative, Saunders Meadow, Inc., a private residential community, in which the property is jointly owned by the stockholders, with the buildings and improvements individually owned by the members. The objective of the Corporation is to preserve these 80 acres in their natural state for the mutual and co-operative use of the members, to avoid and resist all efforts to urbanize them, and to strive at all times to upgrade the personally owned improvements to the end that this beautiful and invaluable forest oasis may remain intact for the enjoyment of present and future generations. Feeling strongly the need for co-operation, understanding and mutual trust, and bearing these objectives in mind at all times, while striving throughout to guarantee the rights, privileges and responsibilities of all member stockholders, the following set of By-Laws has been drawn. December 6th, Neste, Brudin & Stone – Civil Engineers, write to SM, Inc., regarding the Subdivision development. "The meeting held on Oct. 21 resulted in several assignments: 1. The 80 acre parcel is traversed in the northwesterly corner by an existing dirt road which physically serves about 2 ½ acres from the remainder of the property…we understand that you wish to legally separate for possible sale, and that the new owners would not be involved in the Saunders Meadow Corporation at all. If this is to be accomplished, it will be necessary to file a parcel map showing this division BEFORE we file our tentative map for non-statutory condominium. 2. We have reviewed letter from attorney Swan. We are aware of only one procedure available to you that will NOT result in recording a map showing and defining all of the lots is a Statutory Condominium, where each of your 57 owners would own only airspace within their building, but the building and lot would belong to the corporation and the C.C. & R's would require corporation maintenance of each. In such a case, NO individual lot line could be established. The only other way to NOTE file a map with lot lines shown is to do nothing and continue as you are today…Mr. Swan's concept of a "stock co-operative" that would record only a 'perimeter map' seems contradictory with your stated purpose of being able to sell parcels that have recorded boundaries. You should resolve this matter before proceeding. 3. We understand that the 57 parcels as shown on our latest plot plan (file No. 4-7423) have been agreed to by your people…We will label the area between lots 12 & 17 as 'site of future recreational and assembly building'. 4. Our recent contact with Riverside County Health Department indicates that they will consider your existing water supply in regards to submitted of a tentative map. They are now assuming certain responsibilities of the State in these regards and will soon have new application forms for requesting a water permit. They will require a bacteriological report and a full chemical analysis. 5. It will be necessary to obtain some written statement from your company regarding the existing use of septic tanks or cesspools by all dwellings and facts that you can relate to their adequacy. For example, you might say that such and such septic tank was installed in (year) and has never failed since then, being maintained by a service truck every (6 months, 1 year, whatever is factual). 6. It will be necessary for the conditional use permit application and the variance application to 'locate existing and proposed structures'. 7. We will be asked to submit to County requirements for an Environmental Statement due to a recent court decision.

Saunders Meadow Timeline

1973	January 9th, Board of Directors of Tahquitz Meadow Improvement Association was held. Attorney Richard Swan gave resume in the matter of acquiring title to the Tahquitz Tract, including incorporation, and preparation of By-Laws, etc. Neste, Brudin & Stone, Civil Engineers gave a resume of meeting with the Riverside County Planning Commission in regards to parcel map, file application for conditional use permit and tentative subdivision map. January 19th, Neste, Brudin & Stone write to President Brocklehurst. "We have studied the work involved in order to legally divide the 2 ½ acres from the remainder of the 80 acres. A tentative map for a parcel map must be prepared and processed. New regulations require an environmental impact statement to be made regarding the proposal...If the conditions of approval (by Riverside County Planning Commission) are acceptable to your board, we can include most of our further work within the scope necessary for the larger Planned Residential Development work (non-statutory condominium), thereby saving money and time. We propose to do all the work outlined above...for the lump sum price of $450. This amount does not include Riverside County Fees; Tentative Map Number ($2.00), Tentative Map Filing Fee ($130.). We will proceed with the work upon receipt of your written authority to do so. February 20th, Riverside County Planning Commission writes to Health Officer, "Attached hereto is a tentative land division map. Please examine it and return to this office in time for the Subdivision Committee meeting on 3-5-73 together with such recommendations as you deem appropriated. Non-receipt of a recommendation or request for additional time must be considered approval of said map as presented. Parcel Map No. 5103" February 27th, Saunders Meadow, Inc., writes a progress report to members. 1. Fire Protection District and County Planning Commission recommend needed upgrades to meet county standards. Four additional hydrants will be needed. 2. County Planning Commission will request improvements on all private roads and trails including Saunders Meadow Road. 3. The land survey has been completed and submitted to the Riverside County Planning Commission. Response is scheduled for March 20th. February 28th, Riverside County Food Control and Water Conservation District writes to Riverside County Planning Commission in regards to Parcel Map No. 5103, "Our review indicates the topography of the area consists of well defined ridges and natural watercourses which travers the area...some flood control and drainage facilities may be required in order to fully develop the area under the existing R-1 A zoning. Following are the District's recommended conditions of approval: 1. The natural watercourse, which traverses the southerly portion of parcel 2, should be delineated on the final map. 2. A note should be placed on the final map stating that all natural watercourses are kept free of buildings, obstructions and encroachment by landfills. 3. A copy of the final map should be submitted to the District for review and approval prior to recordation... March 2nd, Health Officer responds to Riverside County Planning Commission in regards to Parcel Map No. 5103 and request of 2/20/73, "Returned herewith is the tentative map together with our recommendations as follows: This Department has no recommendations to make at this time relative to the above parcel map, however, the Riverside County Building Department should be notified that prior to the issuance of a building permit it will be necessary to detailed soils information be presented to this Department to assist us in determining effluent disposal requirements. March 14th, Riverside County Planning Commission sends notice in regards to Parcel Map No. 5103, "the tentative parcel map shall be approved subject to the following 7 conditions..."

Saunders Meadow Timeline

1973	March 16th, The Riverside County Planning Commission sends information to Saunders Meadow, Inc., "The above listed parcel map, subject to the attached conditions was approved by the Planning Commission at its regular meeting of March 14. Enclosed is the tentative map, the conditions and copies of the Health Department and Flood Control District letters on the subject matter…" April 15th, Committee Chairman John B. Jones writes to SM, Inc. members: "The Board of Directors has appointed a committee to draft a set of Rules and Regulations for the guidance of the 57 members of Saunders Meadow, Inc. In general we expect to follow the longstanding Forest Service Rules and Regulations with only such additions and modifications as seen appropriate to our private ownership of the property. The committee needs your help and direction and welcomes any suggestions…" July 28th, Board of Directors of Tahquitz Meadow Improvement Association meet and Mr. Jones submits list of Rules and Regulations agreed upon by his committee and Board of Directors of Saunders Meadow, Inc. The Rules and Regulations will be submitted to shareholders for acceptance in the near future. August 4th, Joint meeting of Boards of Directors is held, the engineering map submitted and they discuss the placement of boundary stakes. August 25th, SM, Inc. writes to Shareholders, "A public hearing for final approval of the stock co-operative proposed by SM, Inc. has been scheduled for September 14, before the Board of Supervisors of the County of Riverside. We have pending at that hearing applications for Variance and for Conditional Use Permit to allow this project to be completed without imposing upon us the customary, but in our case inappropriate conditions of construction usually associated with subdivisions…it was the pleasure of the Board that we proceed to issue stock as planned at this time…" September 3rd, The first meeting of Shareholders of Saunders Meadow, Inc. is held. President Brocklehurst calls meeting to order and Mr. Ricker reports on the survey of the property. There being no funds in the treasury, there is no financial report. Mr. Bubb presents certain proposed revisions to the By-Laws as recommended, and submitted to the shareholders for consideration in 1972. The proposed Rules and Regulations are submitted and discussed, certain changes are made such as; #7 "No fences are allowed except with the approval of the Ecology Committee". The Rules and Regulations are accepted, "The objective of the corporation is to preserve this area in its original natural condition. These Rules and Regulations are so directed. They are published for the guidance of members, and Voluntary Compliance is Expected." It was noted that the sum estimated ($2,000.00) for water system maintenance is for the purpose of bringing the tank up-to-date, making the same clean and sanitary, and painting to preserve the facility.

Saunders Meadow Timeline

1973	September 9th, Everhart writes to President expressing concern over subdivision and recommends that civil engineers correct map reverting to metes and bounds as shown on the US Forest Service map of 1928. He quotes attorneys Hill, Farrar & Burrell as they stated vehemently in 1971, "no one should give in on these land grabs before the corrected map is ready to be filed." September 20th, USFS renews water Special Use Permit October 12th, License for Diversion and Use of water is granted by State of California and Governor Ronald Reagan #3127 to SM, Inc. for the use and development of "Unnamed Spring in Riverside County", San Bernardino National Forest, securing water for tract for a few more years. October 23rd, Mr. Leland J. Yost recommends to Mr. O.W. Miller in regards to Water Resources Board; "Apparently our priority use goes back to November 15, 1927 and title is in the name of the San Bernardino National Forest...I recommend that the description of land on our agreement-permit with the Forest Service should be changed from Tahquitz to Saunders Meadow Inc. Special Use." October 14th, Board of Directors of SMI meet, present is Attorney Swan and Myron Hawk of the Firm of Neste, Brudin & Stone, engineers. Mr. Swan gives a brief history of land exchange and incorporation. Hawk explaines that the Forest Service map based on a survey dated 1928 did not close, leaving a gap of approximately 100 feet in the perimeter line and that some of the presently existing buildings were not actually on the lots as set forth in said map. Original FS maps from 1920 were no longer available. CPA, stated that firm in Hemet would give us satisfactory service in the matter of an audit for both SMI and TMIA.
1973	November 11th, letter from Sate of California Division of Water Rights is received, "a license had been issued to U.S. San Bernardino National Forest in 1951, which license states that the priority of the right there in was confirmed on November 15, 1927, and that the lands or place where such water is used is within Tahquitz Special Use Tract of San Bernardino National Forest..." December 9th, A meeting of the Boards of Directors of Saunders Meadow, Inc., and Tahquitz Meadow Improvement Association is held at the cabin of Dr. Yandell and called to order by President Yandell. "A letter from Harold Chapman, CPA setting forth his charges per hour for an audit is read and considered...also, a letter from Mr. Barry Mason, of the Firm of Young, Henry, McCarthy, attorneys, stating that said firm has been retained by certain members and shareholders, among whom are Mr. and Mrs. Harlowe, Mr. and Mrs. Hedrick, Dr. and Mrs. Stockton, and Mrs. Arrance asking to examine the books and business affairs of the corporation and the association is described by Dr. Yandell. It was determined that Mr. Mason should be informed that the books would be made available for his examination on any week day, upon 24 hours notice. It was moved and seconded that Yandell obtain a certified audit of the books of the corporation and of the association..." Bills are paid at this meeting as well. " Riverside County Taxes - $5,470.34, Minimum payment to Franchise Tax Board - $200.00, Neste, Brudin & Stone - $137.50, Cox, Swan, Carpenter & Powers $182.90." Mr. Kowalchuk states, "upon examination of the maps of 1921 and 1928 surveys, it appeared that twelve to fifteen structures in the tracts have lot lines running through them." It is moved and seconded that we ask for a continuance of the hearings set before the Planning Commission of Riverside County for January 11th. Dr. Yandell proposes that an information-gathering meeting of any shareholders desiring to attend be held at the Office of the Riverside County Planning Commission on January 8, 1974. With the Forest Service "Land Exchange" completed, the Tahquitz Meadow Improvement Associaton is succeeded by Saunders Meadow Inc.

Saunders Meadow Timeline

<table>
<tr><td>1974</td><td>January, Mr. Everhart in opposition of the elected Board sends out another letter warning everyone of the doom to come, "This is a review of letters of the 'little people' of Tahquitz Meadow Improvement Association, and a foreboding of things to come…".

March 4th, President Yandell writes to shareholders in regards to results from meeting held on February 22nd, at the Riverside Planning Commission Offices. "We received nearly all of the information necessary for us (members) to continue to a completely satisfactory solution to our property line problem. The following seven points were brought out by this meeting."
The Planning Commission stated that:
1. Unless we have 100% agreement on all lot lines and boundaries, without one person dissenting, we can't take it in to the Planning Commission."
2. We can have fee title to our own individual lots and 1/57th ownership of all the "common ground".
3. The Board of Directors as functioning now, would in reality be the Management Company and would only govern the "common ground".
4. The lots will be under Riverside County. So we have to set up "Rights and Covenants" compatible to SM, Inc., the Planning Commission, and County Board of Supervisors. "Rights and Covenants are rules such as: no fencing, style of home, use of property, livestock control, building plans and the problems that we have regarding boundaries, we must settle between ourselves. Agreement must be reached between all 57 of us or we cannot progress toward owning our own lots…"

March 27th, James D. Ward of Thompson and Colegate Attorneys at Law writes to Shareholders and Leases of SM, Inc., "I have been asked by the Board to investigate the advantages and disadvantages of a continued corporate ownership versus a fee ownership of individual lots with a joint ownership of common areas."</td></tr>
<tr><td>1974</td><td>April 2nd, Riverside County Planning Commission sends Notice Of Continued Hearing – Planned Residential Development and Reduction of Development Standards and Parking Requirements. Variance Case No. 1247-C (Tract No. 5418) and Conditional Use Case No. 1564-C (Tract No. 5418) Saunders Meadow Inc.

May 13th, James D. Ward writes to Board of Directors and shareholders, " I communicated with your Board of Directors, 10 members and two attorneys representing individual groups of owners. I had a long conversation with Dick Swan, your corporate attorney and Jim White acting Planning Director from the County Planning Department. I also spoke with Mr. Hawk, your engineer from Neste, Brudin and Stone as well as with County Assessor, Frank Seeley…"
Mr. Ward presented the following: Scope of Investigation, Areas of Agreement, Areas of Disagreement, Method of Ownership Property, Sale or Retention of Separate Parcel, Individual Boundary Line Problems, and Suggested Approach For An Over-All Solution.

May 24th, Hired CPA firm Westheimer, Fine, Berger & Co. presents their report. "Our review disclosed a high degree of informality in record keeping and a casually cavalier attitude in maintaining any acceptable level of internal control…"

June 7th, Attorneys At Law Thompson and Colegate write to The Board of Directors. "At the request of your president, Dr. Yandell, I am sending you a letter to supplement my letter to you of May 13th, regarding your real property… " I contacted…(continue)…</td></tr>
</table>

Saunders Meadow Timeline

<table>
<tr><td>1974</td><td>"I contacted a Superior Court Judge in San Bernardino who helped a group of homeowners complete an exchange with the Forest Service...They had a great many problems, but in the end the individual lots were owned in fee, and the common land was owned by a corporation, the stock of which was shared by all of the owners of the individual parcels.
Here are Pros And Cons of Two Types of Ownership:
1. Corporate Ownership if the entire parcel of ground, with areas designated as area of exclusive use for individual homeowners.
Advantages:
a. Unified control of entire property
b. Single voice through Board of Directors in working with governmental agencies
c. Democratic action through the rules established
d. Properties are worth less, hence lower taxes
Disadvantages:
a. Difficulty in transferring title
b. Problems in dealing with government entities
c. Lower values as stock ownership and problems of securing financing.
d. Continual problems dealing with individuals who refuse to pay their taxes and assessments
e. The number of problems would be increased because the corporation would own all the property.
2. Fee Ownership of individual parcels, with joint ownership of the common ground.
Advantages:
a. Higher values on individual parcels
b. Transfer of title would be easier
c. Individual owners would have complete control of their fee property subject only to covenants and restrictions of record.
d. The group is not required to concern itself with the financial problems of individual owners.
Disadvantages:
a. Increase in value means higher taxes
b. No control of the group over individuals except through covenants and restrictions of record
c. There would be a need to maintain and control the common areas. It would be necessary through fees.

June 11th, Association Secretary C. Wiley writes letter to members regarding the possible purchase of a 126,000-gallon water storage tank completely installed for $13,500.00 dollars. "This cannot be done without the consent of a majority of the members who paid $1,500.00 assessment of which account has a balance of $41,000.00 dollars left over from the Lang Exchange." Wiley includes a ballot... "Please express your desire by voting on this proposal." By original agreement, that money was to be returned to shareholders.</td></tr>
<tr><td>1974</td><td>Also on June 11th, Board of Directors of corporation who are entrusted to handle money from the Tahquitz Meadow Improvement Association receive demand from Attorneys Young, Henrie & McCarthy who represent Saunders Meadow, Inc., shareholders, Dr. Stockton, Kowalchuk and Mr. Yost and Ms. Arrance, regarding, the handling of the administration of the corporation including Parcel Map submitted, "Demand is hereby made upon the Board of Directors to withdraw the current Parcel Map No. 5718 and prepare a new map that reflects lot lines from 1921 and 1928 government maps...If we do not receive written commitment by Board of Directors, we will proceed with litigation...this will include Temporary Restraining Order and Preliminary Injunction forestalling further actions by the current Board of Directors, possible appointment of a Receiver..."

June 12th, A letter of complaint is written to The Attorney General Business Law Section State Building Los Angeles, CA by "concerned group of shareholders" – Mrs. C.J. Hedrick</td></tr>
</table>

Saunders Meadow Timeline

<table>
<tr><td>1974</td><td>June 18th, Thompson & Colegate Attorneys At Law write to Board of Directors – Saunders Meadow, Inc., and shareholders/members. “The question now posed is whether it would be possible to simply do nothing further regarding the property and leave it in its present state...after discussing matter with Mr. Struter of the Planning Department, it is his view that the matter could be dropped with no particular adverse effects. At the present time, he feels that the County Building Department would probably continue to give building permits for alterations or additions to structures. It is my opinion that if you do not resolve the matter of boundary lines, some of the individuals among your group will instruct their attorneys to file suit to establish their individual rights.”

June 20th, Westheimer, Fine, Berger & Co. CPAs write to the Stockholders of SM, Inc., “At your request we are submitting schedules which summarize and categorize deposits made for the period from September 1, 1968 to August 31, 1973...information is additional to and forms a part of the report submitted...on May 24, 1974.”

June 26th, President of SM, Inc., Dr. Yandell replies to Young, Henrie & McCarthy - attorneys. “This is in answer to your letter of June 11th, we now have a continuance with the Riverside Planning Department until August 28th...no legal action can be taken by us on any map until after the meeting. We will have two Board Meetings prior to the Planning Department meeting, and on our next scheduled Board Meeting of July 13th, we will have your letter on the agenda, and full discussion and action will be taken at the time. I hope this is satisfactory with you, because I would like to circumvent all unnecessary legal action and costs etc.”

June 28th, Mr. Brocklehurst writes letter to Board Members in regards to their June 11th letter concerning water storage. “I wish to explain why I believe we should try to develop our own source of water rather than invest in additional storage facilities due to the following:
a. Special Use Water Permit from Forest Service terminates December 31, 1978 but may be cancelled at any time.
b. It includes no provision for renewal, the permit was issued with great reluctance only after the Forest Service failed to get either of the local water districts to service our area.
c. Unless you have recent and firm assurance from the Regional Forester or Chief, that the permit will be renewed; I would not count on it.
d. Furthermore, it is highly significant that the permit was issued for only 5 years, rather than for the 20 year period previously allotted Special Use Permits of this type.
I suggest...we develop water resources on our own property...”

June 30th, County of Riverside Secured Property Tax Bill paid for July 1, 1973 to June 30, 1974 - $952.30 dollars.

July 24th, Letter from Westheimer, Fine, Berger & Co. Certified Public Accountants sent letter to Dr. M.E. Yandell, Re: SM, Inc., “Our report to you of May 24th, indicated that from information then available to us it appeared that the land exchange with the U.S. Government had not been effective. We have just today received a copy of a document from the U.S. Forest Service Government granting to SM, Inc. to have and to hold the said...with all the rights, privileges...unto the said claimant, its successors and assigns, forever...This document is dated April 6, 1972 and was recorded in Riverside County on May 5, 1972. Also enclosed was a grant deed by SM, Inc. to the U.S. Government conveying to the latter approximately 1,277 acres that property which was purchased for the purpose of effecting the land exchange offer.</td></tr>
</table>

Saunders Meadow Timeline

1974	August 7th, Saunders Meadow Corporation receives Notice of Complaint Code Section 2240 from the State of CA, office of The Attorney General Department of Justice. "Enclosed is a shareholder's complaint alleging that the above named corporation has failed to comply with those Corporations Code sections marked; # 3000 failure to maintain records of shareholders and director's meetings # 3001 failure to maintain adequate and correct accounts of business transactions. # 3003 failure to permit inspection of records by shareholder # 3306 -3010 failure to permit to send annual report to shareholders." August 11th, A letter to Shareholders is sent by their Committee To Investigate And Reconcile Auditors Report, "We went through the auditors report item by item. We attempted to match each expenditure with a bill, a receipt and an authorization. We were able to do this with all significant items over $30.00 dollars. Hence, we feel we have located and organized specific receipts, which the auditors did not have, to verify. We feel that records are now available to make possible a certified audit." August 30th, Young, Henrie & McCarthy – Attorneys for Plaintiffs: Albert and Arlene Stockton, Aurelia Harlowe, Cloa and Frank Hedrick, Raymond and Marlene H. Kowalchuk, Helen Arrance, and Leland J. Yost, file a civil complaint-lawsuit, against Defendant(s): Saunders Meadow, Inc., Tahquitz Meadow Improvement Association, Ray Brocklehurst, Wayne C. Ricker, Cosette C. Wiley, O.W. Miller, Willis R. Leach, Harry G. Bubb, and Does I through XX, inclusive. Case Number 109929. Complaint For Preliminary And Permanent Injunction, Appointment of Receiver, and Accounting, Damages For Fraud, Removal Of Directors. The lack of communication and trust with a little bit of crazy leads to lawsuit. August 31st, COURT SUMMONS
1974	December 13th, Attorney General Evelle J. Younger writes to Saunders Meadow, Inc., attorneys and sends copy to Barry Mason, Esq. Young, Henrie & McCarthy in regards to SMI Notice of Complaint. "This letter shall serve to notify you and the corporation that the response provided by your letter dated August 7, 1974, has been determined to be unsatisfactory...you have failed to maintain adequate and correct accounts of business transactions...SMI has managed to operate over a period of some five years without ever having accounted to its shareholders for its actions in the manner prescribed by the Corporations Code...It is arguable, in fact, whether it was ever really the intent of the residents in the Tahquitz tract that Saunders Meadow, Inc. be organized...In light of the foregoing fact, please note the following complaints: 1. Each $1,500 deposit paid by the shareholders to acquire Tahquitz Meadow was originally to be paid into the Tahquitz Meadow Improvement Association. Corporate documents indicate that in fact, such funds were paid to Saunders Meadow, Inc. Despite this fact, it was somehow necessary for Saunders Meadow, Inc. to borrow the funds for acquisition from the Tahquitz Meadow Improvement Association. The minutes of a January 9, 1970 meeting of the board of directors indicate the officers of Saunders Meadow, Inc. were authorized to borrow the necessary funds from Tahquitz and to execute a promissory note therefor. There is nothing to indicate in the corporation's records, however, how much funds were in fact borrowed from Tahquitz. The corporation does not have a promissory note in its files. The Saunders Meadow Summary of Cash Transactions (unaudited), for the period of September 1, 1968 to August 31, 1973, indicates total cash of $43,196.24. I understand approximately the same amount is presently on deposit with the bank holding the Tahquitz Meadow Improvement Association account. It is probable that this cash on deposit should be reflected in one account or the other, but not both. It would appear that the records of both Tahquitz and Saunders are in need of serious review on this point... 2. I understand that journal entries of Saunders Meadow, Inc. show that the two sections in Bautista Canyon were purchased by the corporation for $38,744.00. Since over fifty association members paid $1,500 to acquire the property, a substantial sum was left in the corporation's account after the acquisition. Despite the fact that the deed to the Tahquitz tract was apparently recorded May 5, 1972 in the name of Saunders Meadow, Inc., no funds have ever been returned to the shareholders as required by the resolution hereinbefore mentioned. There is, therefore, a question as to whether the corporation books and records reflecting such sum on deposit are in fact accurate...continue...

Saunders Meadow Timeline

1974	3. The board of directors for Tahquitz Meadows Improvement Association and Saunders Meadow, Inc. are apparently the same individuals. These individuals are holding the meetings of both the corporation and the Association at the same location at the same time. This is extremely confusing to the shareholders, especially in light of the fact the records seem to indicate Tahquitz Meadow has been undertaking the duties and responsibilities of Saunders Meadow. As an example, I understand that at a recent board meeting, Mr. Bubb, a director, apparently stated he thought legal fees and surveys for Saunders Meadow should be paid for by Tahquitz Meadow. In another instance it was allegedly noted at a board of directors meeting that the CPA report by Westheimer, Fine, Berger & Co., while ostensibly a report of Saunders Meadow, Inc., was in reality a report on the activities, receipts, and disbursements of Tahquitz Meadow Improvement Association, and was entered in the minutes of the meeting as such. As you know, Saunders Meadow was formed to acquire and manage the Tahquitz tract, not the Tahquitz Association. It would appear that the directors of Saunders Meadow may have delegated their authority to the Association and perhaps may have even transferred corporate assets to the Association – acts which they have no authority to do. Instances such as the two cited above and the fact that the corporation has not issued financial reports to its shareholders from 1969 through 1974 brings me to the conclusion that the practices of holding joint meetings is in violation of section 800 and 812 et seq. of the Corporations Code. It is impossible for the shareholders to determine what actions the corporation is taking (or what powers it may have delegated to Tahquitz when the directors are taking action without specific reference to the appropriate entity). 4. It has been brought to my attention that stock certificates issued to the shareholders incorrectly state the tract number of the land held by the corporation to be Tract 5418. This matter should be corrected immediately. 5. Pursuant to resolution of the Tahquitz Meadow Improvement Association, occupancy of cabin sites was to continue as prior to the acquisition by Saunders Meadow, Inc. It was provided that 'where metes and bounds of adjacent lots are affected by requested changes, there must be mutual agreement of cabin site owners subject to the approval of the Board of Directors or as recommended by an Arbitration Committee appointed by the Board of Directors.' It has been alleged that Mr. Wayne Ricker, a corporate officer at the time of the new survey, had the cabin site map redrawn to include in his cabin site a portion of the site occupied by Mrs. Cloa Jewel Hedrick. This was done without conferring with Mrs. Hedrick and without her subsequent approval. This matter has never been decided by an Arbitration Committee. This is a matter of utmost importance and should be resolved immediately. The final two points set forth in paragraphs 6 and 7 hereafter are recent developments that I wish to bring to your attention. 6. It has been alleged that minutes of the annual meeting held on Labor Day, 1973, were requested and never received. The minutes were requested because at the 1973 meeting the shareholders agreed to accept changes to proposed revisions of the by-laws of Saunders Meadow. The final revisions of the by-laws were to be voted on at a later date. It has been alleged that the minutes of the 1973 meeting have been revised to read that the revised by-laws were adopted by the shareholders. 7. In light of the allegation that the minutes of a board of directors meeting have been changed and the failure on the part of the corporation to keep adequate corporate books and records, it is suggested that future board meetings be opened to all shareholders. Better communication between shareholders and directors might help resolve the disputes that have arisen. In the interest of promoting communication and possibly preventing a future dispute concerning water rights, it is also suggested that a special meeting be called to discuss the transfer of water rights from Tahquitz Association by Saunders Meadow. It is my understanding such a transfer may have the effect of prematurely terminating the water rights in 1973. It would be advantages to discuss the effects of such a transfer and to plan accordingly.

Saunders Meadow Timeline

<table>
<tr><td>1975</td><td>Assessment is now $208.00 per share

January 5th, Saunders Meadow, Inc. Board members respond to members questions:
1. We continue to operate under both organizations because we still have two members of Tahquitz Meadow Improvement Association who have not yet purchased stock in Saunders Meadow, Inc. We also have bank accounts that are still under Tahquitz.
2. The copy of the Articles of Incorporation is kept at the Corporate Office (the secretary's cabin) at Saunders Meadow in Idyllwild. It is quite lengthy and would require a considerable amount of time to copy. Since the By-Laws dated December 1971 and the 1972 By-Laws (which are on blue paper—hence "Blue By-Laws") were mailed to all shareholders, may I suggest that you check your files to see if a member of your group have them. If you cannot find them, let me know and I will try to have them and the Articles of Incorporation copied when the Board meets in February.
3. A survey was conducted by Neste, Brudin & Stone in 1972-73, they were instructed to include a survey of each site so that exact boundaries of lots would be known by owners. In connection with this survey, one of our members was to be present in order to facilitate finding the existing stakes. The stakes were set down by a survey committee instructed to layout lines and stakes with the mutual agreement of parties involved. The new survey committee, headed by Mr. Kowalchuk, was instructed to determine lot size areas using the 1921-1928 maps, and to settle differences by mutual agreement of parties involved. They were further instructed not to move the existing stakes placed by the previous survey, but to use stakes of another color so the difference in lot size areas could be easily determined. (Sept. 14, 1974 minutes and October 12, 1974 minutes).
4. A copy of the lawsuit will be mailed to you by Mrs. Everhart.
5. The agenda will be substantially the same at each meeting. We welcome your comments on any matter, and if not on the agenda, they can be taken up as old or new business or input.

January 10th, A letter is sent to shareholders from Yandell informing them that, "there will be a court hearing on February 3rd, in the Riverside Superior Court in the action of Stocton, et al, vs. Saunders Meadow, Inc., et al. One of the issues to be decided at the hearing will be the appointment of a receiver for SM, Inc. and Tahquitz Meadow Improvement Association."

January 15th, USDA Forest Servicer issues Special Use bill for $65.00 to SM, Inc. for water use.

January 25th, another letter goes out, "This letter will inform you that there will be a court hearing on February 3rd, ...the attorneys now report that they have been unable to effect a settlement and the matter must be submitted to the court...your Boards of Directors reluctantly acknowledge the inevitability of the appointment of a receiver..."

February 1st, A meeting of the Board of Directors of SM, Inc. was held at Dr. Yandell's cabin, "attention was called to Mrs. Harlowe's input in regards to the reason for separate meetings of the Corporation and the Association...Dr. Yandell reported in his telephone conversation with Mr. Ward the previous day. Plaintiffs have agreed to drop individual suits. A receiver has been selected and will be so designated by the court on Thursday, February 6th according to present plans...he will recommend whether we should have individual titles to the lots our cabins are on or if we should retain title to the land in the corporate name...he will also investigate the division of land in two parcels and the advisability of returning to one parcel..."
On the same day, the Board of Directors of the Tahquitz Meadow Improvement Association met right after the SM, Inc. meeting. There was no input and no further business just the approval of December 14, 1974 minutes.</td></tr>
</table>

Saunders Meadow Timeline

1975	February 7th, SM, Inc. attorneys Thompson and Colegate send letter to all individual Defendants of lawsuit, "Good news is that all lawsuits against you have been dismissed by all plaintiffs. Mrs. Hedrick discharged her attorney...in discharging, she instructed him to withdraw the lawsuit...the bad news is that the dismissal is without prejudice which leaves her the right to proceed again with the lawsuit if she wishes." February 10th, Thompson & Colegate Attorneys At Law send documents to Stockholders of SM, Inc. pursuant of the order of the Riverside Superior Court in regards to: Stockton, Everhart, Harlowe, Kowalchuk, Arrance, and Yost, vs. SM, Inc., Tahquitz, Riverside Superior Court No. 109929: 1. Case No. 109929 "Stipulation" – this court shall appoint a Receiver to take over the management and operation of defendants. 2. Plaintiffs and Defendants request for appointment of Receiver, by Stipulation, request that Ray O. Womack be appointed as such Receiver. 3. Case No. 109929 "Order Appointing Receiver" Ray O. Womack, be and hereby is appointed Receiver. 4. Case No.209929 "Oath Of Receiver" (CCP567) February 26,1975. March 20th, Receiver Ray O. Womack files to the Court his "Inventory of Assets In Possession of Receiver" Case No. 109929 March 31st, The Attorney General Department of Justice contacts Mrs. Aurelia B. Harlowe in regards to "Complaint Against SM, Inc. and the appointing of Womack as the receiver." May 15th John B. Jones writes the history of SM, Inc. in order to assist Receiver Ray Womack as per his request. May 28th, Receiver R. Womack calls for SM, Inc. Board of Directors meeting. Womack expresses his appreciation to the Board for their cooperation and the board states, "this has our enthusiastic endorsement as a necessary and desirable mean of resolving the controversy."
1975	August 20th, Ray O. Womack from Law Corporation presents his Receiver's Preliminary Report 1. It is my recommendation that applications be refilled with Riverside County Planning Commission for qualification as a planned residential development (PRD). 2. It is my recommendation that all owners receive fee title to their respective lots along with an undivided ownership in the common parcel. 3. As a result of the lawsuit, it is my opinion that the Riverside Superior Court has jurisdiction to settle all lot lines disputes and to approve a final map. 4. I will recommend to the Court that the road alignment in front of the Hedrick property be returned to its former alignment. 5. Having two separate entities creates undue confusion and causes needless duplication in administration and accounting. Accordingly, one of the entities should be dissolved after completion of the subdivision. 6. The additional costs (of the subdivision, map, Riverside County Planning Commission should be borne from the $1,500.00 paid in by each property owner and after the completion of the subdivision and the deeding of the property to the individual owners any excess funds should be returned to the property owner on a prorate basis. 7. I have found no improprieties from the Land Exchange with the U.S. Forest Service. 8. I do not believe that it is necessary to incur the cost of an audit by an accounting firm.

Saunders Meadow Timeline

1975	August 27th, Harry G. Bubb writes to Mr. Womack, "I welcome and appreciate your preliminary report…" we will update and change the C,C & R's to reflect fee title lots. August 29th, Vernon L. Armstrong has been checking up on the water system on a daily basis but has to give it up due to arthritic condition. August 31st, The Board of Directors of SM, Inc. meets following the Regular Annual Meeting of Shareholders at the Desert Sun School Lecture room. The following officers were unanimously elected for the fiscal year 1975-76: President John B. Jones, Vice President Jane Harveston, Treasurer Bill Arntson, Secretary Harry Bubb and Parliamentarian Mary Everhart. Mr. Jones appoints Mrs. Brocklehurst as chairwoman to make plans regarding Recognition Ceremony to be given in honor of Mr. and Mrs. Minnich. The Directors agreed to tentatively set the Board Meetings on the second Saturday of every other month, subject to the availability and approval of Mr. Womack. September 8th, President John B. Jones thanks Ray Womack. October 15th, John B. Jones reports to R. Womack about Board meeting, "the usual complaints were voiced before and during the meeting by Stockton and Hedrick alleging that the meeting was illegal due to lack of adequate notice, failure to comply with corporate law, etc., we suggested all such complaints be directed to you…" November 21st, the First Account and Report of Receiver is filed. Womack presents specific findings and recommendations on what SM, Inc. needs to do. November 24th, New board hires Attorney James Ward to respond forcefully to the Office of the Attorney General – Department of Justice – LA and pushes to get Womack into Court and moving towards ending the Receivership. "This Board strongly represents the majority of members of SM, Inc., and Tahquitz Meadow Improvement Association…prior elected president had little knowledge of the background of land acquisitions procedure and frankly had little interest in the outcome. He in no way represented the members and tried to solve the problems by giving in to the dissident's every whim…this position has now been proven to be weak and unsuccessful in solving our problems." December 9th, Ray Brocklehurst expresses his opinions on Womac's recommendations of private ownership…he disagrees due to higher taxes and maintaining control … "speculators will move in…"
1976	January 6th, Attorney James Ward of Thompson & Colegate writes to John B. Jones, "I am confident that things will work out well…most assuredly, there will be some difficulties involving, Mrs. Hedrick and others, but eventually the court will rule on all of these matters, and the problem will be put to bed…" February 17th, "In accordance with the Court Order, the Receiver is preparing a final draft of the C.C. & R's which must be submitted to Riverside County along with a map now under preparation by Neste, Brudin & Stone, under the direct supervision of Mr. Womack." February 27th, Ray Womack informs SM, Inc. that Riverside County Public Health Department has just passed Ordinance 554 requiring an annual fee of $100.00 from small water companies supplying less than 200 service connections. March 25th, The board members consider recommendations received from shareholders regarding Covenants, Conditions and Restrictions to be an integral part of the granting of Fee Simple. "It is our stated objective that this tract shall be preserved in its natural condition so far as possible and that there will be no more than fifty-seven residence lots in said tract. Water rights are leased to us by the U.S. Forest Service and the storage tanks belong to us…"

Saunders Meadow Timeline

<table>
<tr><td>1976</td><td>September 1st, Mr. Brudin took a surveyor and an assistant to meet with Mrs. Harlowe and the Brocklehursts in an effort to establish a line between their lots. "When he arrived, he found in addition to the above people also present the following:
a. A surveyor from Big Bear engaged by Mrs. Harlowe
b. Mrs. Harlow's son, Herb
c. A lady friend of Mrs. Harlowe
d. Mrs. Hedrick
e. Mr. & Mrs. Everhart
With this audience, Mr. Brudin attempted to do his assigned work, but amidst the consequent din he spent most of his time trying to calm the participants and the grandstand. He did finally establish a line which the other surveyor agreed with...It was about as bad a day as he had ever spent..." information was sent to Attorney James Ward from Thompson & Colegate, on Oct. 25th.

October 15th, Mrs. Hedrick continues to circulate highly inaccurate and untrue information to all members, and has it printed in the Town Crier and the Arizona newspaper. The Forest Service attempts to address her inaccurate statements without success...Mrs. Hedrick was also informed of the Restraining Order accompanying the order appointing a Receiver...Mrs. Hedrick as well as a few other "ladies" are referred to as the crazy 5. The Judge finally tells them that if they don't stop the none-sense lawsuits he will place their boney asses in jail, enough is enough.

October 25th, President J.B. Jones writes to Attorney J. Ward of Thompson & Colegate. "On Thursday, Oct. 14th, the SM Board met with Mr. Womack...he and the board established the following calendar:
a. Harlowe – Brocklehurst line dispute...Womack will take necessary action to finalize a line by Oct. 31st.
b. Hedrick road problem will be solved no later than Oct. 31st.
c. Mapping and staking by Neste, Brudin and Stone will be done by November 30th.
d. C, C, & R's will be written by Womack while surveying is being done – November 30th.

December 20th, Harry Simpson Land Officer, US Forest Service informs SM, Inc. that Special Use Permit for springs and rights of way to tanks is not a "Water Rights" per se, these are held by the U.S. government, although the Sate of California also claims them."</td></tr>
<tr><td>1977</td><td>March 17th, Ray Womack writes to John Brudin in regard to lot line problem between Harlowe and Brocklehurst. Since the parties are unable to resolve their dispute between them I propose the following result...Between the two lots there is a loss of .037 acres. You are hereby instructed to apportion that loss between the two lots whereby each lot holder has the some percentage of reduction from the Forest Service map to the present map. My rough calculations indicate that this would entail moving the present boundary between the properties approximately two and one-third feet toward the Brocklehurst property.

May 4th, Ray Womack writes to Attorney Hugh M. Gallaher, "My position on the road in front of Mrs. Hedrick's property, that she wants moved, should not be moved...she acquired the property with the road in its present location..."

May 24th Lot 19 – James C. Montgomery writes to Ray O. Womack requesting that his water valve be in his lot by moving lot line.

May 31st, Ray Womack writes to Charles Delgado Attorney General Office of the Attorney General Department of Justice, "It is my opinion that SM, Inc. is maintaining adequate records which correctly reflect all of its business transactions...I have recommended to the Riverside Superior Court that SM, Inc. be dissolved, however...(continue)...</td></tr>
</table>

Saunders Meadow Timeline

1977	...I believe it necessary that the corporation not be dissolved until such time as we are in a position to transfer fee title to each of the individual lot holders. My reasoning on this point is that legal title to the subject property is not held in the name of SM, Inc. Moreover, all of the attorneys involved in this matter believe that SM, Inc. should not be hastily dissolved as there may be some water rights or other legal rights held in the name of the corporation. Mrs. Hedrick's attorney Hugh Gallaher and I have discussed Hedrick's problem with him on numerous occasions...Mrs. Hedrick openly accuses me of not listening to her position, although I have had more meetings with her attorney than any other member or shareholder of SM, Inc." September 4th, Board Meets, John Jones decides not to continue as President. The following officers are elected for 77-78 Corporate year President Elwood Wissman, Vice President William Devlin, Secretary Jim Montgomery, Treasurer Mary Everhart, Member-at-Large John Jones. The Board sets up meeting schedule with Mr. Womack on the first Tuesday of every other month at 6:30 p.m. The Board also discusses the water situation and directs John Jones to continue to pursue the various avenues of solving this problem. October 17th, Receiver Ray Womack, presents Second Account and Report to Superior Court and submits Petition For Instructions to Court. Also, Case No. 109929 Response To Petition For Instructions With Objections To Proposed Tentative Map 11049 Plaintiffs, Stockton, Everhart, Harlowe, Hedrick, Kowalchuk, Arrance and Yost vs. Defendants SM, Inc., Tahquitz Meadow Improvement Association; Brocklehurst, Ricker, Wiley, Miller, Leach, Bubb and Does 1 through XX, Inclusive. Filed by Attorneys for Plaintiffs. November 7th, Mr. Stockton contacts Washington D.C. in regards to SM, Inc. water rights. They respond, "The licensee appears to have complied with all requirements and License 3127 (that goes back to November 15, 1927) is in good standing. December 12th, Board hires Gary Mayfield to patrol water system as recommended by John B. Jones, "Gary is a young family man who lives in Idyllwild and works full time for Fern Valley Water, he has a 4-wheel drive Jeep and will do a good job."

Saunders Meadow Timeline

<table>
<tr><td>1978</td><td>February 16th, Receiver Ray Womack presents, "Order Re Petition For Instruction" Stockton, et al., vs. SM, Inc. et al. "It is Hereby Ordered That:
1. The Declaration of Protection Covenants, Conditions and Restrictions of SM, Inc., is hereby approved and said C, C & R's shall be binding upon Lot 1 & 2 of Tract No. 5103 and Lot 1 through 57, inclusive, of Tract No. 11049, including common areas...
2. The Court hereby approves the tentative Tract Map No. 11049 subject only to the Court's right to make changes pursuant to objections filed by Frank Hedrick and Jewel Hedrick, owners of Lot 57, Judge of the Superior Court R.T. Deissler, and Received for Record April 13th.

March 9th, "Town Crier" prints, "The County Planning Department intends to publish Negative Declarations regarding EA No.6852, Conditional Use 2020-W, and EA No. 6968, Tract 11049." A Negative Declaration is the Planning Department's assertion that it knows of no significant environmental impact that would result from a project. Before the above Declaration...the public may comment..."

June 27th, Ray Womack writes to Shareholders of SM, Inc. "Enclosed please find copies of the Riverside County Planning Department staff report and the proposed conditions relating to Conditional Use Case No. 2020-W which will come before the Riverside County West Area Planning Council on Monday, July 10, 1998. The condition with which we are most concerned at present is No. 5, which sets forth a requirement of five (5) fire hydrants with six-inch water mains. I have been advised that the cost to comply with this condition would be somewhere between $25,000. - $75,000. Even if we were agreeable to installing the fire hydrants the present water pressure is not adequate to maintain the hydrants and it would be necessary to obtain the water from Fern Valley Water District. Mr. Brudin and I have continually advised the Riverside County Planning Department that the purpose in the Saunders sub-division is to keep everything in its natural status and that the lot owners do not desire to have any expensive improvements made to the tract."

August 7th, Riverside County Planning Department Board of Supervisors report approval of SM, Inc. application for a planned residential development and variance planned residential development standards Case No. 1341-W...with an extra set of conditions pertinent to permit..."

August 8th, Office of The Clerk of The Board of Supervisors called the Tentative Tract 11049 matter for hearing...no one present desired to be heard on the matter and Board finds no significant impact on the environment and it is further ordered that Tentative Tract 11049, be approved subject to conditions dated July 12, 1978 as recommended by the Planning Commission.

August 14th, Neste, Brudin & Stone incorporated, Civil Engineers report to Ray Womanck, John Jones, Ray Brocklehurst and Bud Hunt. "We met at 10:00 a.m., August 9th and the conclusion of our discussion was that SM, Inc. is to install five (5) fire hydrants along Saunders Meadow Road and Cowbell Alley...Discussion at the Planning Commission hearings indicate that the Idyllwild Fire Protection District wanted easements along the private driveways and that there be a practical and useful clear drive with a turn-around at the ends of said driveways...I (Brudin) will contact the manager of Fern Valley Water District to be sure that the fire protection installation requested by Chief Hunt is agreeable and plan to construct the facilities as soon as possible...SM, Inc., will involve itself in the grading and improving of the private driveways for the fire district's use; and Neste, Brudin & Stone will not be involved in this work...Please note again that the request is for a fire protection system, and that there will be no domestic water service taken from this water system."</td></tr>
</table>

Saunders Meadow Timeline

<table>
<tr><td>1978</td><td>November 17th, Fern Valley Water District reply to Neste, Brudin & Stone. "Your letter of November 7th, was presented to the Board at our Nov. 16th meeting...Due to the large capital expenditure various, methods of financing have been considered...It is the Boards opinion that the people in Saunders Meadow Tract No. 11049 would benefit by annexation to the Fern Valley Water District. This will solve present and future problems."

December 6th, Mr. D.R. Boling and Jerrold L. Wheaton, M.D. from the Department of Public Health, County of Riverside, Division of Environmental Health write to SM, Inc. "It is necessary to place the water supply and distribution system operated by you under a Riverside county Water Permit...after your application is received, a sanitary appraisal of your system will be made by our representative before a permit is issued."</td></tr>
<tr><td>1979</td><td>USDA Forest Service writes to President Wissmann. "The Special Use Permit for the water system that supplies water to Saunders Meadow, Inc. expired on 12/31/78, a new permit has to be issued!"

January 31st, Fern Valley Water District General Manager G.G. Johnson writes to John B. Jones. "Preliminary figures of what it may cost the consumers appears to be:
1. $30.00 increases in minimum yearly water billing.
2. $25.00 annual charge for any home site.
3. No increases in the monthly consumption water rate.
We expect to benefit from a loan and grant from the Farmers Home Administration totaling some $1,500,000.00 dollars.

February 5th, John B. Jones of the water committee writes to Members of the Board of Directors of SM, Inc. "In a nutshell, Mr. Johnson said the Fern Valley Board was adamant about furnishing us water until we make an honest and sincere effort to annex to their system. He pointed out to the Board that we have been hooked up to for Fire Service to one hydrant for many years.

On February 16, USFS again renews water Special Use Permit
On June 29, Riverside County issues its own water supple permit and starts to monitor water quality.
On October 24, a contract is signed to install new fire system with 5 hydrants and new fire-only main through out the tract. Cost: $24,975.
On November 28, A New Water Service Agreement is signed with Fern Valley; the water will only serve the new fire system.

Idyllwild Fire Protection District also approves of the installation.

During the survey, Lot # 37 and #38 are lost. Lot 37 becomes "common ground" since part of it is used for access. Lot 38 becomes an extension of Cowbell Alley Road.

Since Granite Springs Road was steep and always a mess in both winter and spring due to snow and mud, making it next to impossible to drive up it, "Macteckelwood" Road was created making access easer to the water infrastructure and many of the original cabins built in 1924. The name was created to honor the 3 men who worked on the original water system, A.A. MacDonald, R.H. Tecklenborg and Elwood M. Jones.
This change was also necessary as part of the new Fire protection system what was now in place and required for the subdivision status.</td></tr>
</table>

Saunders Meadow Timeline

1979	March 31st, John B. Jones writes to Elwood Wissman President of SM, Inc. "Confirming our phone conversation, the Water Committee met on March 21 and agreed to approach Fern Valley Water Co with a request for a full proposal as to what would be involved to annex and what the cost would be...Gil Johnson at Fern Valley Water on March 23...if the Board approved, would request Webb and Associates, their water engineering firm, to give us a rough estimate of what it would cost to prepare a complete proposal including plans for water service, fire hydrants and methods of financing...Since there is going to be some delay in all the above, I would recommend that we go ahead and file our application for permit to operate existing system with Riverside County Dept. of Public Health"...as Saunders Meadow Mutual Water Company. April 30th, SM, Inc. files statement by Domestic Stock with the State of California, "Acquire, Hold and Manage Land for Benefit of Shareholders". May 10th, Riverside County Planning Department – Planning Commission, Tentative Tract No. 11049 – Minor change: 1. Convey sufficient right of way along the following streets to provide the required right of way at no cost to any government agency... 2. Access roads and cul-de-sacs required by WAPC and Idyllwild Fire Department shall be as approved by the Road Department. 3. All work done within county right of way shall have Encroachment Permit. 4. All driveways shall be cleared of brush and trees for 20 feet and shall be maintained in reasonable condition. 5. There shall be no parking in the access roads. June 22nd, Neste, Brudin & Stone ask for soils report waiver from County of Riverside, "since all sites have been built on, and all sites have existing houses on them..." June 18th, Water and Fire Prevention Committee Chair John Jones writes to Elwood Wissman, "committee has met with Ranger Danny Britt and reconfirmed the position of the Forest Service that we can continue to use our present system, but no further development will be allowed since Forest Service feels we should affiliate ourselves with a regular water company...To comply with the requirements of the County Planning Commission for approval of our map and ultimate issuance of title to each lot, we must install five hydrants that requires the installation of a 4 inch system...such a system will be quite expensive...Annexation to Fern Valley is a legal procedure with concurrent expenses. Thereafter we would all be on meters. Annual rates would be approximately $120.00 per service..." June 19th, SM, Inc. opposes Public Use Permit 384-W on 54650 Tahquitz View Drive for the Morning Sky group residence for troubled students. June 29th, County of Riverside Department of Public Health Water Supply Permit is issued to Saunders Meadow, Inc. July 3rd, Gordon Burt Senior Public Health Engineer from the Department of Health Riverside County writes to S.M, Inc. "We wish to express our appreciation for the corporation you have given this Department during the investigation and survey of this water system. We trust that the information required and reported in the permit application will be of assistance to you in providing pure, wholesome, and potable water at all times." July 20th, John B. Jones writes to Water Committee, "In accordance with instructions from the Board, I met with Bill Whitener, Manager of Idyllwild County Water District...At present they have 1250 customers and are not receptive to applications for annexation. However, they might consider a fire service only..."

Saunders Meadow Timeline

1979	August 23rd, John B. Jones member of Board of Directors writes to Mr. J.A. Jacobson, Vice President Fern Valley Water District. "Our members will be gathered the weekend of September 1 in our annual meeting and your plan will be submitted to them. There is every indication that it will be favorably received. If so, we will be in contact with you for further discussions." August 27th, the Water Committee Chairman John B. Jones, sends out a letter to the members of SM, Inc. 1. "Fern Valley Water District has recently adopted a new policy which would allow us to hook up to their system for standby water for fire protection at the following annual costs to each shareholder individually, billed directly by Fern Valley: 1 to 5 acres $28.00 per acre, over 5 acres $28.00 plus $10.00 per acre. Corporation would pay for the common ground, an estimated total of $450. to $500.00 annually. We would also not have to annex now but could at a later date. Thereafter we would be individually metered at a minimum annual rate of $90.00 each, above the $28.00. 2. A distribution system must be built with 6 and 4 inch pipelines. We have a very rough quotation for installation of such a system of $29,000. from Tom Taylor Welding of San Jacinto...If we elected later to annex, additional pipelines could run as much as $300. to $400. per home... 3. The Idyllwild Fire Dept. must approve our lateral roads...This involves widening, improvements and permanent maintenance of Lilac Lane, Tanglewood, Granite Springs and Macteckelwood. We have asked Harold Smith for an estimate on such work. September 2nd, Board Meeting is held. The board proceeded to organize with the election of the following as officers for the 1979-80 corporate year: President Elwood Wissmann, Vice President Morton Civen, Secretary Quentin Edwards, Treasure Mary Etta Everhart, Member-at-large Jim Montgomery. All of the members of the board expressed a desire to have John B. Jones continue as Chairman of the water and Fire Protection Committee. September 19th, SM, Inc. John Jones writes to Fern Valley Water District, "the membership of Saunders Meadow Inc. voted to accept your proposed policy of furnishing water for fire protection..." October 24th, Tommy Taylor Welding is hired, "proceed with the installation of a fire protection piping system with 5 hydrants at Saunders Meadow." December 6th, Fern Valley Water District and SM, Inc. sign "Water Service Agreement".
1980	January 21st, Neste, Brudin & Stone Incorporated, civil engineers, write to Riverside County Planning Department. Requesting extension of time for Tact #11049. "The above-referenced tract is scheduled for consideration by the Planning Commission on Wednesday, January 23. The recommendation from staff is for continuation of the agenda item to February 20· to allow applicant time to propose mitigation for school district impaction...we have been involved with this property and have attempted to subdivide these 57 U.S. Forest Service lease sites and one open space lot since 1970... The majority of the residents of the area are part-time residents, using the cabins as a resort-recreation vacation type use, where the few permanent residents are retired...We, therefore request that the extension of time requested on this project be granted and that the request for school fees not be applied to this site since no new impact in the schools will result from the extension, approval, and ultimate recording of this 58-lot subdivision. Summer Home values start to increase due to new private property-ownership status.

Saunders Meadow Timeline

1980	February 12th, Harold K. Smith - Excavating Contractor gives SM, Inc. estimate of cost to grade the roads in tract: Lilac Lane $120.00, Tanglewood $80.00, Granite Springs $40.00, Mactecklewood $160.00, for a total of $400.00. February 15th, President of SM, Inc. H. Elwood Wissmann writes to Idyllwild Fire Protection Board showing them the letter written to the Riverside County Planning Department. "To the Board of Commissioners. It is the intention of Saunders Meadow a California corporation to grade and maintain, annually, four private roadways within our tract so that fire protection vehicles and personnel will have available access to the residential structures in this tract...It is our intention to do this grading in the spring of the year. We presently have a quote form Harold Smith Excavating Contractor to provide this annual maintenance." February 29th, Neste, Brudin & Stone writes to Idyllwild Fire Department, Chief Bud Hunt. "In regards to the Sign-off by Idyllwild Fire Protection Agency For Compliance with Conditions Of Approval, Tract No.11049, Mr. Elwood Wissmann, President of SM, Inc. has advised that the road grading improvements in the above referenced tract and the fire protection system have both been installed as per your request to the Riverside County Planning Commission in the County's Approval of the above referenced Tract Conditions. In order for Mr. Wissmann's organization to obtain approval for their subdivision and its recording, we need your concurrence that the conditions...have been met. I would appreciate receipt of a letter from your office addressed to the Riverside County Planning Commission, indicating that the conditions of approval for this project required by you have been met." March 6th, Idyllwild Fire Protection District Chief David E. Hunt replies to Nest, Brudin & Stone. "Dear Sirs: At this time we can not give the approval for the road conditions in this tract. Neither of the two that were improved are very negotiable. It would seem a more lasting improvement could be provided for this area. Should there be a mishap on either of these roads due to fire or medical aid we could have a serious problem in gaining access." March 14th, Fire Chief David Hunt writes to Elwood Wissmann, "Please be advised that during the meeting of the Board of Fire Commissions on March 13th, it was decided that the letter of 3/6/80 would stand as written, no considerations were taken, until a more substantial road agreement can be reached...Our next meeting is Thursday, April 10th..." March 20th, Neste, Brudin & Stone have meeting with the Riverside County Planning Department, and report to Wissmann, "here is the info they provided that you will need at the April 10th meeting with Idyllwild Fire Protection District Board." March 26th, Elwood Wissmann writes to Ray Womack, Morton Civen, Quentin Edwards, Mary Everhart & Jim Montgomery, in regards to their regular Board of Directors meeting, April 2nd and material concerning their meeting with the Fire Protection requirements of the Idyllwild Fire Protection District..." April 3rd, "Dear Chief Hunt, ...our Board of Directors accepts your invitation to attend the meeting of the Board of Fire Commissions on April 10th to present our position...Our Board has authorized me, Wissmann, Edwards, and Womack, Receiver to attend...we look forward to the opportunity of discussing this matter..."
1980	April 10th, Saunders Meadow Inc. staff writes a short history of the Tract to present at the Fire Commissions Board meeting. "The purpose of the residents and the Board of Directors of Saunders Meadow has been in the past, throughout this process just described and for the future of our 80 acres to maintain the ecological environment as much as possible as it has existed for over 50 years in this tract; and to provide a restful and comfortable environment for our residents to either live full-time or occasionally in the Idyllwild area..." The goal is to maintain a rustic natural setting...

Saunders Meadow Timeline

1980	April 11th, Wissmann writes to Idyllwild Fire Protection District. "As per our discussion and the action that you took at your meeting on April 10th, this letter states our agreement to bring Macteckelwood Lane, a private road-way, into such condition that it will be accessible for fire and other emergency vehicles. This work is to be accomplished within 90 days, weather permitting. The scope of the work will be grading the roadway, filling severely eroded areas, and installation of culverts to provided better drainage. It is our understanding that the motion unanimously passed by your board on April 10th, then, states that upon your receipt of this letter, you will inform the Riverside County Planning Commission that the conditions requested by the Idyllwild Fire Protection District have been met." April 17th, Fire Chief, David E. Hunt Jr. of Idyllwild Fire Protection District writes to County of Riverside Planning Commission. "Please refer to Conditional Use Permit 2020-W and Tentative Tract 11049, Riverside County…The owners of Tract 11049, represented by their Board of Directors, have met the conditions of approval that we felt were necessary, however due to the extreme weather conditions occurring this winter we have asked for and received a letter of intent for additional work to be accomplished on Macteckelwood, within 90 days. We hereby acknowledge the developers' compliance and give you our concurrence that the owners have complied with our requirements…" April 21st, President Wissmann writes to Shareholders of SM, Inc. "we have fulfilled the conditions imposed by the County regarding fire protection…we are making significant progress toward the final filing of our subdivision map and the ending of the Receivership." Wissmann also provided the list of promised work to Harold K. Smith, Excavating Contractor on Mactechelwood Lane, Lilac Lane and the meadow area…"Harold, we will appreciate your prompt attention to the completion of these projects. As you know, we are working under a time deadline of 90 days established by the Idyllwild Fire Protection District. April 30th, SM, Inc. files statement of Domestic Stock Corporation with State, "Home Owners Association". July 6th, John B. Jones writes to Elwood Wissmann in the subject of the tract's water. "Big Cedar Spring, our main producer suffered a cave-in just inside the door, filling the tunnel nearly to the ceiling and damaging the door and locking device. Secondly, Upper Middle Spring tunnel is again clogged…road to spring has become impossible even to a jeep…with Ed Calderon's help I have secured an inspection of the work to be done by Ken Busher of Intermountain Excavating Co. Ken quotes $65.00 per hour for a crawler type tractor grader which he feels could grade both roads satisfactorily in one day: 8x65 = $520.00. In addition he would furnish 2 men for 2 to 3 days to hand dig the cave-in at Big Cedar and clear the obstruction at Upper Middle at $100.00 per day, $200.00 to $300.00 total. If shoring is needed to preserve the tunnel at Big Cedar that would have to be on a Time and Material basis…" July 21st, Law Offices, Zimmer, Singer & Womack, Inc. send Elwood Wissmann a fully executed copy of the C, C, & R's executed by Womack the Receiver on July 16th… August 1st, A list goes out to all SM, Inc. Shareholders. "The filing of the subdivision map will necessitate a different lot numbering system by the County of Riverside. However, for our internal Saunders Meadow, Inc. purposes, we will continue to use the familiar lot number system"… established by the Forest Service back in 1920. On September 5, Saunders Meadow Sub. Division Map is recorded. After receiving title to land from the Forest Service, association petitioned Riverside County for subdivision status. After meeting various requirements such as installing more fire hydrants and improving roads, the new Subdivision map was recorded and each shareholder received a deed to his/her property. The process took 10 years.

Saunders Meadow Timeline

1980	September 8th, Neste, Brudin & Stone inform Wissmann that "Tract No 11049 was recorded on September 5th in Book 114, pages 66-73, Records of Riverside County." August 10th, SM, Inc. signs Special Use Permit with the Forest Service, last issued in 2/16/79, for water use to expire in 1988.
1981	On August 26th, USFS amends water Special Use Permit extending expiration date to 12/31/88. Saunders Meadow, Inc. association starts to think about a permanent solution to their water need. August 28th, Ed Calderon continues to care for the Tract and its water source, he leaves notes to John B. Jones informing him on the work done and state of the water and needed repairs or tasks to be accomplished. He was a friendly character who wrote in rhyme, he had his own style of writing and spelling.
1982	February 6th, Saunders Meadow, Inc. sends out a letter to Shareholders in regards to changes in their Taxes, "The attached information deals with the Saunders Meadow Subdivision 'Tax Laws'. Mr. James J. Brzytwa, Supervising Appraiser from the Identification Division has laid out an informative letter on changes in the individual assessments for the 1981-82 assessment years. Any questions on your tax bill should be channeled to him, directly. February 22nd, Damon Bradley Headmaster of The Desert Sun School writes to Saunders Meadow, Inc. "At this time, I wish to acknowledge formally Desert Sun's interest in exploring mutually the possibility of securing the property contiguous to the school's soccer field, as a gift from the members of Saunders Meadow, Inc. Should your organization decide to turn the property over to Desert Sun, any potential liability for Saunders Meadow, Inc., would cease." Land was not donated. March 19th, Ed Calderon continues to care for Tract and Water System and report needs to J.B. Jones. July 12th, Chairman of Water Committee J.B. Jones writes to U.S. Forest Service District Ranger Doug Pumphrey and requests, "approval of remedial work to be done on two springs that serve as domestic water source for the 57 homes known as Saunders Meadow Inc., formerly U.S. Forest Service Tahquitz Summer Home Tract. Mr. A.W. (Bud) Smith has visited the two site and feels both are well adapted for horizontal drilling…" September 2nd, United States Department of Agriculture Forest Service responds to Mr. Jones. "Your request to improve and maintain the spring development to the water tank that supplies domestic water…is approved, District Ranger Doug Pumphrey. September 5th John B. Jones writes to SM, Inc. Board, "At your request, the following written report is submitted in behalf of the Water Committee composed of: Elwood Wissmann, Dr. Albert Stockton, Bill Miller, Edward Bonds, and John B. Jones…The shareholders at the last annual meeting issued a mandate that a committee be formed to conduct a study of all aspects of water supply for Saunders Meadow Tract. If required, and with Board approval $500.00 may be spent for engineering studies…committee has done its work…at no expense: that's zero dollars! Our approach was to secure the proposal of Mr. A.W. "Bub" Smith and Son of Crestline, the leading horizontal well drillers of CA. They confidently recommended horizontal drilling of both our tunnel sites to produce a completely sealed well system so that further deterioration of our old tunnel system would be of no concern at a cost of 10,000.00. Ranger Doug Pumphrey and Forest Service have approved such work since tunnels are on Forest Service land…" October 1st, J.B. Jones writes to Mr. Bud Smith. "If you decide to do our job, call Bill Miller, a member of our Water Committee or Ed Calderon, our water patrol man, they are available to open gates for you…"

Saunders Meadow Timeline

<table>
<tr><td>1982</td><td>
October 15th, President Rune C. Hedstrom writes letter to Raymond Johnson – Waste Disposal Division, Riverside County in regards to the Proposed Dump Site on Garner Property.
October 18th, SM, Inc. President Rune C. Hedstrom writes to District 3 Supervisor Kay Ceniceros and District Ranger Doug Pumphrey. "Dear Madam Supervisor: Attached is a copy of a letter sent by our association to Raymond Johnson regarding a proposed dump site on Garner Property. The letter expresses the homeowners' deep concern and anxiety over the choice of dumpsite. We solicit your support for an alternate disposal area that would save the fragile nature of the Garner area from excessive abuse."
From Oct. – Dec. Bud Smith drills a horizontal well to improve production at Big Cedar and Granite Springs. Successful at Big Cedar but got a dry hole in solid rock at Granite Spring.
October 28th, The Mountain Area Coordinating Council met at Town Hall in Idyllwild. Items on agenda:
<ol>
<li>The proposed swap between the county and the U.S. Forest Service for Humber Park and the dumpsite.</li>
<li>A report from...Saunders Meadow Inc., the organization of 57 property owners in the SM area voicing objection to May Valley as a possible dumpsite. "The site, off May Valley Road about 1.6 miles from Saunders Meadow Road at the edge of the Garner property, has been targeted by Ray Johnson, Riverside County Waste Disposal engineer, as one of two possible Hill dump locations when the present Idyllwild dump is closed. The Saunders Meadow group is against the site because of possible traffic impact in area. The group also contends that many people will leave their garbage in SM area rather than transporting it to May Valley..."</li>
</ol>
November 19th, Albert A. Webb Associations, Inc. Consulting Engineers write to Saunders Meadow, Inc., " Dear John B. Jones in regards to Field Inspection and Recommendations Regarding Existing Domestic Water System Facilities and Connection of New Horizontal Well, "per your request, we field-checked portions of subject domestic water system facilities on 11/1/82, and we list below our comments and recommendations:
<ol>
<li>Cedar Spring (upper tunnel)...</li>
<li>Tunnel (lower)...</li>
<li>Pipeline Between Cedar Spring and the 84,000+ Gallon Tank...</li>
<li>84,000+ Gallon Tank...</li>
<li>Existing New Horizontal Well Adjacent to Cedar Spring (upper tunnel)...</li>
</ol>
Total amount of this invoice $1,271.00."
November 29th, John B. Jones writes to members of Water Committee of Saunders Meadow, Inc., Elwood Wissman, Bill Miller, Dr. Stockton and Rune Hedstrom. "To bring you up to date on proposal: In October Bub Smith and son drilled a horizontal well adjacent to Big Cedar Springs Tunnel. He went in 200 feet and got a good well which ran 12 gallons per minute on initial testing...he will drill another well near the original tunnel at Granite Springs...with the new well at Big Cedar we felt the need of professional advice as to how to valve it for control so as to preserve the water in place, in the mountain, rather than allowing it to overflow and deplete the source. To this end, we engaged a well-know water engineering firm, Webb Associates, to help us...Ed Calderon has assisted greatly in the work to date...I'm requesting the board to add $100.00 special pay to his next check..."
December 17th, John B. Jones writes to Robert R. Wood Plumbing. "Dear Bob: This is your authority to proceed with the hook up of the new horizontal well at Big Cedar Spring as recently discussed...Upon further discussion with Webb & Associates, they have convinced us that we should use the ¾ inch fittings and valves at the well head and also install ¾ inch meter, reading in gallons being used and total gallons consumed...Ed Calderon will be present during the work...
</td></tr>
</table>

Saunders Meadow Timeline

<table>
<tr><td>1983</td><td>Desert Sun School on Saunders Meadow changes to Elliot-Pope Preparatory School.

June 8th, Assemblyman Bill Leonard writes to Agriculture, Water, Parks and Wildlife Legislative Advisory Committee. This memo is mailed to SM, Inc. the subject: California Water Policies. "One of the longest-running and most divisive battles that have ever gone on in California is how to fairly and equitably distribute own limited water resources on a statewide basis."</td></tr>
<tr><td>1984</td><td>February 9th, State Water Resources Control Board – Division Of Water Rights sends Report Of Licensee For Unnamed Spring. Owner of Record: US San Bernardino National Forest. Included was a response to SM, Inc. from 1977. "In your letter of November 7, you have inquired about water use of the subject license. The Forest Service filed application 5758 on November 15, 1927, Permit 2952 issued January 19, 1928, and after several extensions of time to complete development and use, License 3127 was issued on January 15, 1950 to the US San Bernardino National Forest. Once issued, a license remains in effect as long as the licensee makes beneficial use of the water for which a right of use has lasted and for the purpose for which it was appropriated. US San Bernardino National Forest has filed reports of licensee with this office since issuance of the license, reporting use in the Tahquitz Special Use Summer Home Tract. In recent years the reports indicate use at 57 summer homes. The licensee appears to have complied with all requirements, and License 3127 is in good standing…"

April 2nd, John B. Jones writes to Jeffrey D. Smith, Elwood Wissman and Bill Miller in regards to water tank problem. "Here are some options…for your consideration:
1. Valley Sandblast of Hemet inspected the tank, found 12 holes…they quoted verbally: inside work 6,900.00, outside work 2,300.00 for a total of $9,200.00. Webb and Associates are opposed to this procedure. They feel it is too expensive and only temporary at best.
2. BH Tank Co. has quoted on three styles of tanks…
3. Trico Superior Industries of Long Beach quoted $23,235.00 for removal of old tank, new tank and grade band and ¾ inch rock…
4. David Mitchell received informal quotation on a welded 88,000-gallon tank for $40,500.
5. San Luis Tank Co., $47,907.00, they are highly recommended by Webb and Associates.
6. I asked R.H. Techlenborg to shop for a used bolted tank. He tells me they are available at about 20,000. installed plus interior coating and exterior painting. We can get financing for five years at 8% rate. Assuming that we have 15,000. on hand and settle for a 30,000 tank, this would cost each of us $64.00 per year for five years…just a thought.

April 2nd, Hamilton Satellite System, Inc. writes to Homeowners at Saunders Meadow about Master Antenna and Satellite Television. Base price of $5,000.00 with a price of $750.00 per home if 75% or more sign up.

June 25th, Thomas D. Horne – General Manager of Fern Valley Water District writes to John Jones – SM, Inc. "I have learned from District Ranger Douglas Pumprey that you have applied to the USFS for permission to install a new tank in the Saunders Meadow, Inc. water system. Mr. Pumphrey was inquiring about the possibility of Fern Valley Water District annexing the Saunders Meadow tract…The Board of Directors of the Fern Valley Water District feels that any move to annex would have to be initiated by the property owners of your tract…"

On July 1, USFS approves the replacing of the deteriorated tank with a new 84,000-gallon tank, but warns that the basic permit will expire 12/31/95 and will not be renewed.
New 84,000-gallon tank is purchased and installed. The same tank is still in service to date, and will be used by the Forest Service when permit expires in 2014.</td></tr>
</table>

Saunders Meadow Timeline

1984	In regards to the new Tank being approved, the USDA Forest Service writes, "Dear Mr. Jones: The request by SM, Inc. to replace the existing water storage tank for your water system with a new tank of the same size and type is approved...Forest Service policy and guidelines state that National Forest Land will not be used to support private land development when and if there are reasonable and acceptable alternatives...annexation to Fern Valley Water District appeared to be a viable alternative...I would hope SM, Inc. will pursue annexation with Fern Valley District at this time. With this notice of termination of the water and supply system on National Forest land by the year 1995, the investment of a replacement tank at this time should be considered in your decision making process..."
1984	November 9th, Bill Miller for the Road Committee writes to all Saunders Meadow, Inc. members. "For your benefit and the benefit of all Saunders Meadow property owners, we are asking each of you to send a letter to Riverside County Supervisor, Kay Ceniceros, protecting the future use of the present dumpsite as a transfer station..." November 15th, John B. Jones writes to the Honorable Kay Ceniceros Riverside County Supervisor, 3rd District. "This letter is written out of concern for the proposal to convert the present dump into a transfer station, a permanent installation...with Saunders Meadow Road as a principal mode of access. Such an outlook for this winding, steep, narrow residential road is just not reasonable or logical...many reasons have already been covered in letters, meetings and petitions. If a transfer station is to be built on Forest Service Property, the 'Old' dumpsite (closed in 1960s) would be much more accessible to all users. I would vote for that over the present dumpsite. Alternatively I would favor the Keen Summit Landfill. November 26th, Kay Ceniceros writes back to Jones. "I would appreciate your attendance at the Public Hearing on December, 4th at 10:00 a.m. in the Board of Supervisors meeting room on the 14th floor of the County Administrative Center in Riverside (4080 Lemon Street). Your views are valid and I encourage you to make them known at the hearing..."
1985	May 15th, John B. Jones retires as Chairman of the Water Committee. "I've served long enough to earn my varsity letter, and I think it's time to pass the baton to a younger runner...Naturally I'll be glad to assist whoever takes over in learning the intricacies of our little system so as to make a smooth transition..."
1987	January, a list of recommended improvements to the water system in order of priority is presented to board. February 26th, USDA Forest Service sends letter to SM, Inc. "Enclosed is a copy of H.R. 2921 which was ultimately signed by the President as Public Law 99-545. This Law gives certain owners of water systems on National Forest land the right to apply for and receive a permanent easement for the qualifying water system. We are notifying all known operators of water systems on National Forest land of this opportunity in the event they qualify and would like to apply for an easement. The basic requirements for acquiring such an easement are: the water system must be used solely for agricultural irrigation or livestock watering purposes at the time of application." The San Jacinto Mountain Area Water Study Agency Environmental Impact Report Project CA 06-1374 is presented, (1977 to 1987).

Saunders Meadow Timeline

1988	January 16th, Saunders Meadow water committee chairman Clark M. Hapeman sends a list of items of concern pertaining to the water system. May 6th, The Board tasked the water committee to follow up, investigate, and report on numbered items that they presented back in January as follows: Item 1. Define individual member responsibility plus provide an overview of concerns and problems with the entire water system. Item 8. Investigate with Fern Valley Water Company the possible installation of one 2-inch water meter with connection into our system. To provide backup source of domestic water in the event of dire emergency. "Costs would be considerable and all owners would pay a monthly standby charge for the one meter..." Item 9. Review water standby agreement for fire protection with Fern Valley Water Company... "In the meeting with Tom Horne the fire protection standby cost was discussed and determined to be reasonable as based on a cost of $38.60 per year per lot..." The water committee asked Mr. Horne of Fern Valley Water and requested he authorize the Fire Department to include our fire hydrant system in their regular yearly maintenance schedule along with other hydrants in Fern Valley Water Company system. Item 10. Option to drill test well for water in the meadow... "On February 1, 1988 Lynch Well Drilling of Hemet, CA was contacted for estimated cost: drilling a 7-inch test hole will cost $14.00 per foot, soft drilling at $32.00 per foot, a 5-inch casing on well accept at 5H.P. pump and deliver 30 G.P.M, if and when is found...would analyze and if potable would provide 12 inch casing at $2.00 per foot additional and install an 8-inch 50 foot sanitary seal for $400.00, based on 100 foot minimum drilling. Item 11. Remote Tank Level Readout...is still in design and study phase. Lack of power source presents problem. Considering remote battery power packs, solar 12 volt system, etc... The Water Committee contacted Ranger Douglas Pumphrey, US Forest Service, Idyllwild, CA on May 3, 1988, regarding our Special Use Permit for our Spring Water Sources, Water Storage Tank, and access there to. Pumphrey advised he does not anticipate any problems whatsoever and that when due the Forest Service will automatically issue a new permit for a ten-year period...
1989	February 13th, USDA Forest Service sends new Special Use Permit to Saunders Meadow, Inc. "The permit for the water system that supplies water to SM, Inc. expired December 31, 1988. Enclosed are three copies of Special Use Permit for signature. The termination date for this new permit is December 31, 1998..." The Water Committee sends out a 7-page "Water Watch Conserve Our Water" notice to all in order to understand the importance of our water situation and taking every measure to prevent any unnecessary waste...it mandates low flow showerheads, 1-gallon toilet tank offsets, and prohibits car washing on all summer home lots. On April 18, USFS issues a new Special Use Permit, good until 12/31/98, apparently reversing it's thinking from 1984.

Saunders Meadow Timeline

<table>
<tr><td>1990</td><td>Elliot-Pope Preparatory School on Saunders Meadow closes and sold to Guided Discoveries for Science Center it then becomes Astro Science Camp.

Significant replacement of piping and valves is done on water system.

May 8th, Clark Hapeman, Chairman of Water Committee writes to SM, Inc. Board of Directors in regards to maintenance/improvements to water storage and distribution system.
1. Repair the road and chain lock posts leading to the Big Cedar Springs water box and old steel door tunnel…
2. Remove damaged padlock and replace. Repair bullet holes in steel door…
3. Install new lockable boxes at value outlet…

Letter from SM, Inc. to all Shareholders stating the enforcement of the C,C, & R's… "All 57 lot owners should be aware that the accumulation and storage of excess materials, equipment, sheds, vehicles, trailers, etc. is a violation to County ordinances and CCRs and will be dealt with accordingly. Signed The Board of Directors:
Ken Gerard, President
Clark Hapeman, Vice President
Scott Whisler, Secretary
Margaret McFar, Treasurer
Sharon Stein, Member at Large</td></tr>
<tr><td>1991</td><td>November 1st, Plans and drawings are done showing Saunders Meadow Subdivision Water Dist. System and Fern Valley Water District Fire Hydrants. Plans show tract lots, service valves, and main line valve in box, Granite Spring Tunnel/Storage 64,000-gallon, 84,000-gallon steel storage tank and Big Cedar Spring Tunnel.</td></tr>
<tr><td>1992</td><td>Mark Jones, Elwood Jones' grandson with the Board of Directors continues with the families' commitment to work towards improving the future of the community by securing a solid and continuous water system. He suggests that the Board require all owners to install low flow heads and 1.5 gal. Flush toilets.

The issue of water metering needs to be addressed. A break at any of the 57 cabins, or anywhere else in the system could drain the system in a matter of hours.

The tract Board considers adding meters to monitor water consumption per summer home and charging according to usage.

October 14th, Secretary Mark Jones writes to Saunders Meadow Board of Directors, Harry Bubb, Quentin Edward, Elwood Wissmann and Sharon Stein in regards to status update, corporation records and files and makes recommendations.

November 27th, Clark Hapeman resigns as Water Committee Chairman. Secretary Mark Jones writes to Board of Directors in reference to the water system. "At our September 6th meeting, President Bubb asked me to prepare some background notes and suggestions as input to the upcoming December 5th discussion on the water system. I have spent…time going through the old files and records…names like Teckleborg, Brocklehurst, Minnich, and Calderon are among many who contributed. The two living individuals who have probably done the most and know the most about the system are my dad, John B. Jones, and Clark Hapeman…The files reveal that the same issues have come up over and over again thought the years: The water permit; conservation; catastrophic water loss; additional water development; storage; piping and valve issues; and the question of annexation…" Mark Johns proceeds to present the history of the water system from 1927 to 1990…</td></tr>
</table>

Saunders Meadow Timeline

1992	December 3rd, State of California Department of Health Services-Office of Drinking Water writes to all public water systems in regards to, Implementation of the Phase II and Phase V Federal Regulations. " The purpose of this letter is to inform you that the U.S. Environmental Protection Agency (USEPA) has adopted several sets of new drinking water quality regulations for monitoring and maximum contaminant levels for both inorganic and organic chemicals. These sets are referred to as Phase II A, II B, and V…" Saunders Meadow, Inc. continues working with E.S. Babcock and Sons, Inc. testing water. December 28th, Every shareholder gets the new Water Watch'92 – Conserve Our Water flyer adapted from a report in 1989 by the Water Committee… "Each one of us has a responsibility to safeguard our most valuable resources – our water supply…Please remember, the cost and availability of water has a direct and major impact on the value of each of our cabins…Do not leave faucets on to drip in cold weather to prevent freezing…" December 29th, Artist Karin Hedstrom, shareholder and gallery-owner of Mountain Artist's Gallery writes to Saunders Meadow, Inc. regarding her concern over President Bubb's construction on 2 lots and the use of common ground as his private driveway and the addition of a chain and "Private" sign, when in reality it was not private but common ground that remains to this day. CC&R's are over looked and she is not happy as she so well expressed in her artistic caricature on file.
1993	Forest Service encourages Mark Jones and the Saunders Meadow association to seek annexation with a water district. January 30th, Board of Directors of Saunders Meadow, Inc., meets and discusses filing Federal and State taxes, Insurance coverage, legal and water issues. "Riverside County now requires a quarterly water quality test, and we are required to collect and deliver the samples. Based on a previously approved proposal by Clark Hapeman, water system upgrade and repair tasks are proceeding well…as well as the work on pipe post markers for all water system live valves, fire hydrants, and cabin service valves. The main purpose of this is to make it easier to locate valves under emergency situations, especially with snow on the ground. Each valve post will be color coded, and line valve posts will be numbered to match the numbering on the Hapeman water maps…Also discussed was road repairs: the recent rains caused serious washouts on Granite Springs Road and Macteckelwood lane, one of our required fire access routes, making both impassable for ordinary vehicles. The Board will negotiate with Clark's Bobcat Service and Harold K. Smith for immediate road repairs. February 2nd, Saunders Meadow, Inc. meets with Ray Padgett of Idyllwild Water District, "the Board of Directors of SM would like to determine the desire and ability of the Idyllwild Water District to manage our water system under a formal contract…" March 11th, SM, Inc. Secretary Mark M. Jones writes to Mr. Fred Hans Hanson – Albert A Webb Associates, Inc. Consulting Engineers regarding water system, "the current Board believes there are a number issues that need to be reevaluated now that ten years have passed since your report to us in 1982. We did replace the water tank and although we visually monitor the level of our tank, we have no way to meter either production or consumption, in bulk or by cabin. We also are completely without a failsafe system; one break anywhere could drain the system before anyone knew what had happened. We are at the same time seeing a trend towards more permanent residents and are concerned about the system's ability to support them. We need to determine what consumption rates per day are reasonable to expect with and without strict conservation, and to be able to compare this to present production, and assess the need for additional production, storage, and conservation measures."

Saunders Meadow Timeline

1993	March 19th, Webb associates agree to meet with Mark M. Jones, "I am pleased that you have agreed to meet me at Saunders Meadow, Inc. at 9 a.m., for a walking tour and inspection of the water system, to be followed by your in-office review of your 1982 recommendations and interim improvements, and to prepare an updated engineering report responding to the issues outlined above, and recommending what current and future improvements the Board should consider, including but not limited to: 1. Should we drill additional wells and where? 2. Should we attempt to clean out our collapsed Big Cedar Tunnel? 3. Should we add additional tank storage? 4. How can we provide defense against catastrophic water loss? 5. What do we need to do to respond to changing regulations? 6. Where should we add monitoring for system productions and use? 7. Should we consider required conservation measures? 8. Should we consider metering at cabins? 9. Other recommendations?" March 23rd, Albert Webb Associates writes to SM, Inc. Mark M. Jones, regarding Water System Facilities; Engagement Letter For Webb's Engineering Services. "The purpose of this letter is to confirm per your request, our recent discussions regarding our engineering services. It was very helpful to meet with you at your home in Saunders Meadow...to discuss and field check some of the main features of the domestic and fire protection water system...We estimate that our engineering services outlined herein will cost about $2,500.00...We plan to complete our engineering study and letter-report within about 2 weeks following our receipt of: Babcock's water quality tests, USFS Special Use Permit(s), Fire Service Agreement with Fern Valley Water District, Diversion License from the State Division of Water Rights and ...your current water system budget...Regarding the Cedar Spring Tunnel, due to partial collapse of earth...we suggest that this condition is a serious safety problem to hikers, and also contamination of water supply...we recommend that tunnel entrance be fenced and posted no admittance...and water supply be valved-off...pending further investigation." March 24th, State of California – Department of Health Services, Office of Drinking Water writes to SM, Inc. "This letter is regarding tunnel supply...and location which leads our department to conclude that the water quality...may be directly influenced by surface water...if confirmed, complete treatment of water produced from this source will be required in conformance with the California Surface Water Filtration and Disinfection Treatment Regulations (SWTR)...The final decision regarding the need for filtration cannot be made until additional water quality information has been obtained and evaluated...Please initiate required monitoring by April 10, 1993 and submit a copy of your monitoring schedule for the next 12 months to this office for our records. E.S. Babcock and sons, Inc. is given permission to share water test results with Albert A. Webb Associates. March 25th, Albert A. Webb Associates writes to SM, Inc. regarding Babcock's Coliform Tests. "We suggest that you dose with chlorine ASAP the Granite Springs Tunnel Storage and the Bolted Tank Storage, each containing 75,000-85,000-gallons of water...we suggest that you continue to coordinate closely with John Watkins of Riverside County Environment Health Department until this matter is fully resolved. March 30th, SM, Inc. continues working with E.S. Babcock and Sons, Inc. with water testing. Relationship goes back to 1991.

Saunders Meadow Timeline

1993	April 2nd, Webb Associates presents water system recommendations and options. Alternate I – Remain a water purveyor. Alternate II – Annexation to Fern Valley Water District. April 3rd, Board of Directors send out "Water Advisory" letter to all shareholders, "On January 1, 1993, the State of CA imposed much restrictive standards for the presence of Coliform, a common form of organic bacteria, in domestic water systems statewide...the Riverside County Health Department is now requiring us to do our own quarterly testing...The Board has solicited the advice of a qualified professional consulting water engineering firm, and as a result, has decided to do a spot chlorination of our water supply, to try to bring it within the new standards...This is done with great reluctance, for the first time in the system's 67 year history, but in recognition that we have an obligation to our members to try to meet current regulatory requirements...we hope...that we will return to the much-valued untreated spring water we have enjoyed for these many years...on April 4, both the Granite Spring tunnel and the tank will be chlorinated... SM, Inc. hires Craig Coopersmith of The Family Business to amend forms 1120-H and claim a refund of $8008.05 from the IRS. Board of Directors meet and discuss water issue, " In March we retained the consulting water engineering firm of Albert A. Webb and Associates of Riverside to do a comprehensive overview evaluation of our water system. Webb...prepared a report and recommendations on the system 11 years ago...Webb did a thorough on-site inspection, and we asked them to consider much including pros and cons of annexation...One change is very clear: We are now confronted by a vastly different, much tougher regulatory environment, with all water systems required to meet strict new state and federal standards, not only for bacteria and turbidity, but for all sorts of chemicals and heavy metals. Accompanying this are extensive and expensive testing requirements, as well as the possibility of future required water treatment. April 4th, SM, Inc. Mark Jones writes to Fred Hanson, Albert Webb Associates, "I want to thank you for your extraordinary efforts to complete your SM Water report... The Board will deal with our Coliform problem...we also want to proceed immediately with items II D, E, & F on page 1, Alternate I of your report to Remain A Water Purveyor instead of Annexation to Fern Valley Water District. Second major thrust is to proceed exploring the possibility of Saunders acquisition of the Diversion License. We understand this may need a joint effort between Webb and Water Counsel, and we are interested in exploring work with Best, Best, and Krieger. April 15th, County of Riverside Department of Environmental Health presents their "Water System Inspection Report" to SM, Inc. Mutual Water Company: Chemical Quality resulted in all constituents measured in 1979 and 1991 were within acceptable limits...Bacteriological Quality sample taken on 1/12/93 was unsatisfactory containing total coliform organisms...but, resamples yielded eight acceptable samples in 4/5/93. Best, Best, and Krieger A Partnership Including Professional Corporations will represent SM, Inc. in connection with issues relating to its water supply from Springs on National Forest Land. April 28th, B, B & K recommends that SM, Inc. not take on the Forest Service. They have the staff, size and money to fight forever. Also, you already have permit from them. They however could deny access to the water. Finally, look into land swap so SM, Inc. gets land with Springs and acreage leading to them... June 11th, SM, Inc. writes to Webb Associates, "... in regards to collapsed Big Cedar Spring Tunnel and the Existing Diversion License and USFS Special Use Permit...Board has accepted both proposals...you are also confirmed to join in a June 18 meeting at the office of Best, Best and Krieger..." July 22nd, Webb presents results of Phase 1 – Big Cedar Spring Tunnel, repair Alt 1 - $60,000. Alt 2 - $40,000.00 or Abandon Tunnel and Replace Source of water supply by drilling of a horizontal well - $35,000.00

Saunders Meadow Timeline

<table>
<tr><td>1993</td><td>August 6th, Secretary Mark Jones informs Directors in regards to Farmers Home Administration, "I telephoned Jeff Hays, Assistant District Director for FMHA, to introduce our organization and follow up on the reference provided by Fred Hanson in his 7-22-93 report. I briefly described...that the storage part of our water system is located on US Forest Service land, under permit. I went on to summarize the work Webb has done for us (he knows them well) and our conclusion that under the new regulatory climate, we anticipate having to make a significant investment ($200-400K) in order to remain a viable provider. I explained that we were interested for FMHA interest financing and the possibility of grant assistance. Mr. Hays said that it sounds like we are eligible for a loan and possible grant assistance...Loans are amortized over 30 to 40 years and range from 5 to 5 5/8 % depending on medium household income, loan amount is based on engineer's estimates and bids. It can go 100%...The 10 year extension feature of the USFS permit is not a problem for the long amortization. The Forest Service is not about to cut you off...
We now need to prove that we cannot get conventional financing then we fill out pre-application with Fred's rough cost estimates...to determine eligibility...then we have an on-site visit to look at system and assist in planning the next steps...Formal application process needs detailed engineering plans and estimates, and satisfying any environmental requirements...usually takes 6 months..."

August 7th, SM, Inc. files "Emergency Notification Plan" under the requirements of Section 4029 of the CA Water Drinking Act to Riverside County Department of Environmental Health.

August 19th, SM, Inc. writes to homeowners. "...We are today in a somewhat different world and are dealing with a new water quality regulatory climate. Whatever recommendations the Board ultimately presents to the membership for approval will require substantial increases in annual dues...
a. New Federal and State water quality requirements will impact our 57 home mutual water company...estimates of system improvement added monthly chargers of $30 to $45.00 per month per member, assuming 30 year low cost financing.
b. We could, as an alternative, decide to ask to be annexed by Fern Valley or Idyllwild Water Districts."

August 20th, SM, Inc. meets with Fern Valley Water District for informal discussion of estimated improvement requirements and costs which might accompany a possible annexation in the near future.

August 31st, Webb Associates send SM, Inc. an updated estimate for Alt 1 – remain a water purveyor and Alt 2 – Annexation.

September 5th, By-Laws of Saunders Meadow, Inc. amended. Shareholders are changed to members, shares changed to membership; stock ownership was changed to membership as well...

November 13th, the Board of Directors adopts Policy on Architectural Enclosures. "The Saunders Meadow CC&R's prohibit fences. It is believed that the original rationale for this was to preserve the rural forested character of the subdivision, to deemphasize property lines, and to allow wildlife and residents to walk freely about through the subdivision...In recent years, with more families in full time residence, there are more dogs. Keeping them on a leash all the time is impractical...Therefore; enclosures which are for pets only may be built of dark green, brown or black finish to make installation less visible in a wooded setting on the side of the house that is not facing the trail.
Board also reviews an informal Realtor's appraisal of "Parcel 1", the common area above Tahquitz View Dr...sale value range from $85,000 to $130,000.00. As all 57 Saunders Meadow lot owners hold the land in undivided ownership, it could only be sold with 100% participation. There was also discussion of the ongoing efforts to resolve the USFS water permit beyond the Dec., 1998 expiration date.
Treasurer's Report shows $17,390.49 in checking and $16,322.22 in reserves account.</td></tr>
</table>

Saunders Meadow Timeline

1994	February 16th, SM, Inc. writes to Webb Associates, "Following the presentation of water system option to our membership last September, we have been pursuing the issue of permit renewal as a first step in making the decision whether to stop in business or annex…until we make the annex-or-not decision, we are reluctant to make significant further investment in the system." April 12th, County of Riverside Department of Environmental Health presents Water System Inspection Report. In regards to Chemical Quality, all constituents measured were within acceptable limits and for Bacteriological quality; the quarterly water samples have been satisfactory containing no total coliform organisms. At the same time, SM, Inc. submits the pre-application package to Mr. Jeffrey A. Hays, Assistant District Director, Farmers Home Administration, USDA for consideration under the Water and Waste Disposal Loans and Grants Program…Our discussions with the U.S. Forest Service indicate their willingness to work with us on permit extensions to be compatible with long term FMHA financing. April 18th, Mark Jones accepts an offer from Stanford University to lead its $500 million Capital Facilities Design and Construction Program… "I am committed to complete my term as secretary…I'm convinced we are at a crucial junction on the water issue, and that it is important to have all hands on board…" May 16th, USDA Forest Service, San Jacinto Ranger District, San Bernardino National Forest contacts SM, Inc. "In a letter dated July 1, 1984, I indicated that your permit would expire at the end of 1995 and you would then have to seek annexation to the Fern Valley Water District. The permit was instead reissued and now terminates in 1998. With your latest inquiry as to water system modification, we again raise the issue of annexation by the water district and ceasing to use water sources on National Forest System lands. Besides the increasing regulation by State and Federal agencies as to water quality; there is also an increasing interest and concern over the export of water from the National Forest without an environmental analysis of the effects. It is our job to manage water resources to assure adequate supplies are secured and maintained to meet the National Forest System resource needs before making excess water available to private parties for their uses." June 13th, SM, Inc. writes to California State Clearing house in regards to application for Federal Assistance, Form 424 to FMHA: Saunders Meadow Water System Improvement Project, "Enclosed is application for Federal Assistance, submitted as a pre-application to Farmers Home Administration for long term financing support…" July 18th, A Water System Options and Cost chart is presented to SM, Inc. showing monthly estimated total cost per lot if SM, Inc. stays with own water system of $72.00 and if joining Fern Valley Water District - $60.00. Also mentioned is the initial project cost of $489,500.00 to continue with own upgraded water system or $325,000.00 if annexation with FVWD. July 18th, SM, Inc. writes to Mr. Jeffrey Hayes, Assistant Director – Farmers Home Administration, USDA to confirm meeting and tour physical facilities on August 18 at 9:00 a.m. with Fred Hanson of Webb Associates and Ranger Ms. Kathy Valenzuela of the USFS On Sept. 4th, homeowners authorize the association board to move ahead with discussions on the upgrading of the old water system and/or the possibility of annexation.

Saunders Meadow Timeline

1995	January 19th, after many meetings and debates, Fern Valley Water District accepts Saunders Meadow annexation. FVWD found the increased potential revenue as an advantage in the form of one-time hook up fees totaling $142,500 and annual water rates estimated to be around $17,000. May 12th, Fred Hanson of Webb Engineering agrees to join SM, Inc. and will have the FMHA Final Application for signatures and transmittal to Fern Valley Water District. The LAFCO filing, to be submitted by Fern Valley is also expected by that date and the attorney is moving ahead as well...Fern Valley Board meeting is on the 20th when they formalize a resolution to initiate annexation and Jeff Hays Assistant Director of Farmers Home Administration, USDA has approval of SM, Inc. letter of May 1st. June 12th, SM, Inc. calls for a special meeting of members for Sunday, July 9th at 1:00 p.m. in order to act on the FMHA loan for construction of a new water system to be operated by the Fern Valley Water District. The Board states, " A great deal of water has gone over the dame or should we say through the pipes since your prior and present Board began their work on a long-term resolution of our water problems. As a result of this multi-year effort, we now present, recommend, and endorse the described course of action. Your affirmative vote is solicited and will be appreciated. 70% of the members vote in person or by proxy in favor to continue with loan and annexation. Each meter will cost $3,500.00 dollars per cabin and the entire cost for the construction of new water system will total $640,000.00 dollars. The tract association is able to get a government grant of $275,000.00 towards water development the remaining $365,000.00 dollars will have to be borrowed. Saunders Meadow waits for loan approval from Farmer's Home Administration to finance the annexation. Loan of $365,000.00 dollars is approved and will be paid over 40 years with an interest rate of 5½ percent. A yearly Special Assessment District County Tax of approximately $425.00 dollars per cabin is to be charged as part of the property tax bill. With the loan approved, the future of the historic community is secured. The loan will be paid off in 2035. Cabin on Lot 33, (old Lot # 19) is purchased. The Jones cabin has remained in the family for over 91 years.
2002	August 29th, SM, Inc. hires Fiore, Racobs and Powers A Professional Law Corporation regarding preparation of Amended and Restated Declaration of Covenants, Conditions and Restrictions... "This proposal assumes that the copy of the CC&R's included with Mr. Wissmann's August 13, 2002, letter to this office was properly recorded and is valid and enforceable, that there have been no amendments to those CC&R's other than the change to the member approval requirement for amendments referenced in Mr. Wissmann's letter, that the property described in the CC&R's (Lots 1 through 57 of Riverside County Tract 11049) accurately reflects the lots that constitute the Association, that the members of the Association own their lots in fee and that the Association owns the common area lots in fee. The Association will be responsible for obtaining the approvals needed to amend the CC&R's. We will prepare a written ballot for the Association's use in attempting to obtain membership approval..."
2012	The original 1921 Forest Service Coert Dubois design Cabin on Lot 33, the old (lot 19) is purchased. After 91 years, cabin can only claim 4 owners.
2013	Annual membership meeting is held. Discussion was made about the Granite Springs pipeline that runs to a spigot on Mactecklewood. The well is non-potable water that has in recent years been used by some shareholders during drought conditions for irrigation (i.e., by driving a truck up to the spigot and filling barrels, etc.). We have had a 10-year permit to use pipeline at a cost of $58.00 a year. Pat Maloney, Member-At-Large meets with Ranger Heidi Hogan who indicated that the price would go up to $292.00 this year with 1.9% per year annual increases. In addition, the well must be maintained, including installation of a water meter, annual maintenance costs, and environmental impact report ($1,100.).
2013	Due to the high costs associated, the recommendation was made to allow the well to revert back to the National Forest. Bob Wissmann discussed historical aspects of well and transition to Fern Valley Water. Ms. Judy a member of SM, Inc. made a motion to research with knowledgeable lawyer to see if there was any compelling reason not to abandon...

Saunders Meadow Timeline

2014	February 19th SM, Inc. writes to Forest Service in regards to Granite Springs Pipeline, Water Bill for Collection dated 11/12/13. "...We attempted to contact someone to discuss the billing we received for water usage etc...We have not used this spring since our water system was renewed and taken over by Fern Valley Water District sometime in 1995. At the September 2013 general membership meeting, a vote showed general consensus to abandon the spring. The Board was given approval to investigate and decide whether to renew the use of the spring. At the November 2013 board meeting, we voted not to renew the special use permit or any upkeep of the spring and let it revert entirely to the Forest Service..." February 25th, Ranger Heidi Hoggan writes back to SM, Inc. "I received a letter from you to the Recreation Officer John Ladley in regards to the bill for the spring and pipeline under US Forest Service – Special Use Permit...I have not heard from you since September 2013 – I am glad you were able to come to a decision! In regards to the annual bill, bills are sent out automatically to remind permittees to pay rent which is due prior to the use period...Since I had not heard of your decision to close, the permit is still considered issued...There are a few steps that need to occur in order to officially close your permit, and cease billing for annual rent: 1. You must restore the site...cut off the spring at the pipeline so that the water returns to the land at the spring site. The pipe can be left in place to avoid ground disturbance. 2. You must inform me that site has been restored so that I can inspect. I recommend that you take photos of your work; this is in your best interest... 3. I can then cancel the current bill and issue a final bill... 4. Once the corrected bill has been paid, I will close the permit and annual billings will cease. August 31st, Annual Membership meeting is held for SM, Inc. Present members vote to allow the well to revert back to the National Forest after 92 years of having a Special Use Water Permit...ending a wonderful relationship with the Forest Service of 95 years started back in 1920. Saunders Meadow, Inc., (Tahquitz Summer Home Improvement Association) can claim the honor of being the nation's oldest association that participated in the exchange process and continues to follow the 1915 Forest Service guild lines in keeping with Waughs, Carhart and Dubois original principles. Out of the originally, 59 lots, only 57 remain, (two lots were used to expand trails and roads). Two cabins remain authentic to their 1939-1940 designs, (lot #26 and #27). Two were rebuilt using their original designs, (lot #34 and #17) One remains authentic to its 1921-24 Coert Dubois plan, (27160 Saunders Meadow Rd. on lot #33) This cabin qualifies to be registered as a State and National Historic Place after 94 years of existence while maintaining its original integrity. The rest of the Tracts cabins were beautifully modernized and upgraded. All other current cabins blend perfectly with nature and continue the Forest Service tradition of Tract and cabin Design started back in 1920. Saunders Meadow community is truly a beautiful "Place Without Fences".
2015	Dr. Robert Reyes and Patrick Kennedy publish, "Saunders Meadow A Place without Fences – Idyllwild, California" A Historic Synopsis of The Term Occupancy Permit Act of 1915 – National Forest Special Use-Summer Home Recreation Program.

Bibliographic References

Alfano, Sam. "Forest Service Outdoor Recreation Management: A Historical Perspective." Paper presented at the Pacific Southwest Region Recreation Academy at West Valley College, Saratoga, California, March 18, 1995.

Anonymous. "1920s Recreation in Relation to National Forest Management" (unpublished manuscript, 1980) on file with the USDA Forest Service, Region 5.

Anonymous. "A Thematic Study of Recreation Residences in the Pacific Southwest Region" (unpublished manuscript, 1990), on file with the USDA Forest Service, Pacific Southwest Region.

Anonymous. "Recreation and Special Use Administration Guide" (unpublished manuscript, 1924), on file with the USDA Forest Service, Region 5.

Anonymous. "Vacations Made Easy: How Uncle Sam Inites the Family out to His Place in the Country" *Sunset: The Pacific Monthly*, August, 34–38, 71–72.

Back, Earl. "Recreation Facilities: A Personal History of Their Development in the National Forests of California" (unpublished manuscript, 1967), on file with the USDA Forest Service, Region 5.

Bellomy, M.D., "National Forest Summer Homes." *American Forests*, September 1956, 21, 51.

Berg, Donald James. "Second Homes on the National Forests: Changing Patterns and Values of Recreational Land Use in California" (master's thesis, University of California, 1976).

Carr, Ethan and Steve McNiel. "The Cultural Landscape of Mineral King, Sequoia & Kings Canyon National Parks: Determination of Eligibility for the National Register of Historic Places. National Park Service, Denver Service Center" (unpublished manuscript, 1999), on file with the USDA Forest Service, Pacific Southwest Region, Vallejo, CA.

Cleator, Fred W. "Summer Homes in the National Forests of Oregon and Washington" (pamphlet, 1932), on file with the USDA Forest Service, Region 6.

Concraft, T. "Summer Home Sites in the National Forests" *Saturday Evening Post* Vol. 202 (1930): 214.

Dodd, Douglas W. "Recreation Residence Historical Overview of Residences on Los Padres National Forest" (unpublished manuscript, 1967), on file with the USDA Forest Service.

Dubois, Coert. "1916 Summer Homes on the National Forest." Presented in *Sixth Biennial Report of the State Forester of the State of California*, 47–50. Sacramento: California State Printing Office, 1925.

Gallou, Helen Blasdale. "Lower Emerald Bay Tract Number Two: A History of a Forest Service Summer Home Area in the Eldorado National Forest, Lake Tahoe, California 1932-1976." Forest Service study, 1976.

Gallup, Aaron A. "Historic Architectural Survey Report for Big Bear Bridge Replacement Project in Highway 18 at Big Bear Dam, Big Bear Lake, San Bernardino County, CA. Office of Environmental Analysis, Department of Transportation, Sacramento, CA" (unpublished manuscript, 1989), on file with the USDA Forest Service, Region 5.

Graves, Henry S. "Instructions Regarding Term Occupancy Permits." USDA, FS. Washington, DC: Government Printing Office. 4pp.

Headley, Donn. "Angeles National Forest Administration History" (unpublished manuscript, 1991), on file with the USDA Forest Service, Angeles National Forest, Arcadia, CA.

McNiel, Steve. "A Programmatic Approach for Identifying and Evaluating Recreation Redidences on the Angeles National Forest, Region 5" (unpublished manuscript, 1994), on file with the USDA Forest Service, Angeles National Forest, Arcadia, CA.

Oppel, A.F. "Summer Homesites and Public Campgrounds in the New State Forests." *North Woods*, July/August 1923, 26–28.

Palmer, Lex and Alexandra C. Cole. "Historic Structure and National Register Eligibility Study for Tenured Recreation Residences within the Santa Ynez Recreation Tract, Los Padres National Forest" (unpublished manuscript, 1998), on file with USDA Forest Service, Los Padres National Forest, Goleta, CA.

Pinchot, Gifford. "Report of the Forester for 1905." Presented in *Annual Reports, Department of Agriculture.* Washington, DC: Government Printing Office, 1905.

Potter, Albert F. "1917 Report of the Forester." Presented in *Annual Reports of the Department of Agriculture.* Washington, DC: Government Printing Office, 1917.

Sherman, E.A. "Use of the National Forests of the West For Public Recreation." Proceedings of the Society of American Foresters, Vol. XI, No.3 (July 1916), pp. 293-296.

Singer, Caroline, "Shop-Girl's Summer Home," *Sunset: The Pacific Monthly*, August 1918, 34–36.

Supernwicz, Dana and Steve McNiel, "A Programmatic Approach for Identifying and Evaluating Recreation Residences on the Eldorado National Forest and Angeles National Forest" (unpublished manuscript, 1992), on file with the USDA Forest Service, Region 5.

Supernowicz, Dana and Lamonte Richford, "Contextual History for Recreation Residences in the Pacific Southwest Region. In USDA, FS, Pacific Southwest Region. A Thematic Study of Recreation Residences in the Pacific Southwest Region" (unpublished manuscript, 1987), on file with the USDA Forest Service, Region 5, Vallejo, CA.

Sweeley, Frank M. "Major Factors for Consideration in National Forest Recreation in Region 5" (unpublished manuscript, 1937), on file with the USDA Forest Service, Region 5, Vallejo, CA.

Thorn, H.D. "Homesites in the National Forest," *Field and Stream*, April 1928, 117–118.

Tweed, William C. "Recreation Site Planning and Improvement in National Forests, 1891-1942." (1980) USDA, FS, FS-354. Washington, D.C.: Government Printing Office. 29pp.

Tweed, William C., Laura E. Souilliere, and Henry G. Law, "National Park Service Rustic Architecture: 1916-1942" (unpublished manuscript, 1977), on file with the USDA Forest Service, Region 5.

Tweed, Willian C. "A History Of Outdoor Recreation Development In National Forests, 1891-1942." (1989) USDA, FS, Clemson University Department of Parks, Recreation and Tourism Management Publishing, on file.

USDA, FS, n.d. Region 4 Suggested Designs for Summer Homes. Ogden, USDA, Forest Service.
USDA, FS, 1969 Second Homes in the U.S. Government Printing Office, Washington, D.C.

USDA, FS, 1905-1990 Summer Home-Recreation. Records on file in the historic archives Supervisor's Office. Tahoe National Forest, Nevada City, CA

USDA, FS, 2002 Public Lands and Private Recreation Enterprise: Policy Issue from a Historical Perspective. General Technical Report on file Washington, D.C.

USDA, FS, 1940 Forest Outings by Thirty Foresters. Lord, R. ed. Washington, D.C.: US Government Printing Office

About the Author

Dr. Robert Reyes has been a cabin owner for many years both in New Mexico and California. He is a historian for the Idyllwild Area Historic Society and resided in a 1921 Forest Service cabin in the San Jacinto mountain range on the San Bernardino National Forest, in the mountain town of Idyllwild, California, established in the 1800s.

He currently lives in Laguna Woods, California.

Index

A

Adams, Ansel, 182, 257
advertising, 42-44, 77-80. *See also* promotions
A-Frame Plans, 49-50, 142
Aguirre, Martin, 228
Alabama, 135-136
Aladdin Readi-Cut Homes, 45
Alamanor Improvement Association, 110
Alaska Region, 50, 138-143
Alvin Meadow, 253
American Association for the Advancement of Science (AAAS), 9
American campground look, 4-5, 45-48
American River Summer Home Owners Association, 60
American Society of Landscape Architects (ASLA), 4, 17, 20-21
Anderson (inspector), 99
Angeles National Forest, 11, 42, 61-63, 106-112
Anthony Lakes Homeowners Association, 117
The Appraisal Foundation, 37
Arapaho National Forest, 90
architecture and plans for cabins
construction guidelines, 29, 82-86
cost and materials, 109-110
designs, 4-5, 41-50, 109-110
plans, 141-143, 168
in Region 3, 94-95
in Saunders Meadow, 156-161, 266-271
Arizona, 93-96
Arkansas, 135-136
Army Corps of Engineers, 104-105
Arrance, Helen, 201, 203, 204
Arvanitis, Theodosius, 189-190
Association of Car Dealers, 62
AstroCamp, 257
Atencio, Ernie, 280
automobile campgrounds, 19, 23, 25, 62-63
Axtens, S.A., 90

B

Banning Idyllwild Road, 239
Barr, Jim, 155
Barrett, L.A., 109
Barton Flats Cabin Owners Association, 110
Bear Creek Lake, 136
Belden, C. Selden, 175, 268-269
Best Bet & Krieger, 217
Betts, Richard, 37-38
Big Bear Lake, 11
Big Santa Anita Canyon, 106
Big Santa Anita Canyon Improvement Association, 60
Big Santa Anita Canyon Permittees Association, 110
Blanchard, Norman, 109-110
Borst, C.A., 183
Branching Pattern Tracts, 51-52
Brannon, Edgar, 73
Bridge Tract Cabin Owners Association, 110
Bridgeport Forest Homeowners Association, 100
Bridger-Teton National Forest, 97-103
bridges, 59-60
brochures, 117, 119, 173, 248
Brocklehurst, Ray, 181, 187, 191-194, 204, 208, 228
Brooklyn Lake, 91
Brudin, John, 208
Bub Smith and Son, 213
Bubb, Berdie, 229
Bubb, Harry G., 204, 206, 229
Bucharan, E.Y., 238
Buck, C.J., 116
Bumble Bee Summer Home Association, 110
Bungalow Hotel, 250
Bureau of Land Management, 105
Burns, Bobbie, 155

C

Cabin Fee Act, 39
cabin kits and plans. *See* architecture and plans for cabins
Cabin Users Fee Fairness Act (CUFFA), 38
Cahuilla tribe, 147, 234-236, 238, 262
Calderon, Ed, 228-229
California, 110-113. *See also* Idyllwild; Region 5; Tahquitz entries
California Ranch House style, 110
Camp Idyllwild, 253
Camp Mcclellan Improvement Association, 110
Camp Sierra Improvement Association, 110
car campgrounds, 19, 23, 25, 62-63
Carhart, Arthur H., 4, 19-21, 23, 45, 89, 225, 264-265, 279
Casa Loma Recreational Homeowners Association, 111
Central Forests, 107
Certificates of Corporation, 187
Chad (ranger), 242
Chattahoochee-Oconee National Forest, 136
Chenoweth, Helen, 36
Cherokee National Forest, 136
Chinook Pass, 118
Chippewa National Forest, 138
Cibola National Forest, 95
Civil Works Administration, 64
Civilian Conservation Corps (CCC), 27, 64, 93, 175-178, 253-256
Clapp, Earle, 26
Clayton, Ruth, 98
Cleator, Frederick William, 45, 116-117, 119-134, 264-265, 279
Cleveland, Grover, 239
Cleveland National Forest, 41, 63, 106-114, 239
Cliff, Edward, 34
coalitions of homeowners associations, 37-39
codes of conduct, 117, 130-131
Colorado, 88-92
Columbine (tract association), 95
commerce, 238-239, 257-258. *See also* hotels; stores
congressional funding, 20-26
construction, 29, 82-86, 124-126
Contemporary Two-Story Cabin Plan, 49-50
Coolidge, Calvin, 23
Copeland, Royal S., 26
Copeland Report, 26-27, 254
Coronado National Forest, 95
Cox, Pendleton, and Swan, 188
Cox, Swan, and Carpenter, 193
Craftsman Bungalow Company, 45

Crawford, Joseph, 238
Crescent Lake Homeowners Association, 117
Cruz, Paul E., 88
Cruzado, Antonio, 235
Crystal Crag Water & Development Association, 111
Curvilinear Pattern Tracts, 51-52
Custer National Forest, 52

D
Daniel Boone National Forest, 136
Day, Doris, 184, 257
Deadman's Flat Tract, 60
Dean, Melissa, 93
Deissler, R.T., 209
DeMille, Cecil B., 150, 249
Dendritic Pattern Tracts, 5152
Depression. *See* Great Depression
Deschutes National Forest, 117-118, 124
Desert Sun School, 174, 249, 257
design and development of cabins and tracts, 41-53
Diamond Lake, 131
Diamond Lake Homeowners Association, 118
Diamond Match Company, 45
Dickinson, George, 157, 246-249
Dingell-Johnson Act, 138, 140
Disney, Walt, 62, 108
Districts. *See* Regions
Domenigoni, Angelo, 148, 236-237
Domenigoni Flats, 150-151
Dougherty, John D., 189
Dubois, Coert, 4, 43, 45, 48, 109, 156, 162, 225, 241, 262-265, 271, 279
Durham, R.O., 152, 181

E
Eagles Nest, 111
East Coast summer homes, 48
East Florence cabin, 142
East Lakeview Water Association, 111
East Mcvity Bay Summer Homes, 138
East Shore Silver Lake Improvement Association, 111
East Silver Lake Improvement Association, 111
Eastern Region, 136-138
Echo Lakes Association, 111
Echo Summit Permittees Association, 111
economy of towns, 238-239, 257-258. *See also* hotels; stores
Eisenstadt, Alfred, 257
El Yunque National Forest, 136
Eldorado National Forest, 42-43, 50, 60, 107, 110-112
electricity, 60, 157, 159, 248, 262, 267-268
Elk Lake, 132
Elliot, J.D., 175
Emergency Conservation Work Act (ECWA), 26, 253
Emerson, Claudius Lee, 248, 252
Emerson, Zelma, 248
Emerson Hall, 248, 251
E.S. Babcock and Sons, Inc., 216
Everhart family, 191-193, 200

F
Falls Tract, 111
Farmers Home Administration (FMHA), 218-220
Federal Aid in Sport Fish Restoration Act, 138, 140
fees, 33-39, 128-129
Fern Valley, 60, 248
Fern Valley Water District (FVWD), 182, 209-221, 227, 264
finances, 20-26, 64, 69-71
fire protection
and the associations, 59
camp fire extinguishing, 120
campers and permittees beneficial, 69
and campsite building, 99
and the Civilian Conservation Corps, 254-255
fire hydrants, 215
funding, 21
guidelines for permittees, 2
prevention, 28, 151
in San Jacinto - Idyllwild, 241-242, 244
in Saunders Meadow, 175, 179-182, 209-211
fireplaces, 44, 47, 109, 161, 268, 276
fishing, 41, 90, 94, 99, 107-108, 150-153, 156, 280
Flathead National Forest, 50, 52
flooding, 4
Florida, 135-136
Forest Reserve Act, 237
forest reserves, 8-14, 105, 150, 237, 280. *See also specific national forests*
Forest Service
and architecture, 45-46
automobiles, 245
decentralized management, 55
history of, 7-11
letter to future permittee, 114
moratorium on summer homes, 35-36, 65
and the mountaintop communities, 233
and National Park Service, 21
and permit fees, 33
permit renewals, 55-57
public outcry against, 15-16
ranger building, 22
regulations for summer home tracts, 24-25
required cabin improvements, 160-161
Summer Home Policy, 87
and the Tahquitz Tract Assoc., 183
timeline, 288-290
tract guidelines, 145, 151, 214
Forest Service Rectangular Plan, 48
Forest Service Use Book, 1-3
Fromme, Rudo L., 139
Fuller Creek, 60
funding, 20-26, 64, 69-71
furniture, 43, 268-269, 272-276
Future-Use Determination, 35-36

G
Gable-ELL Plan, 48-49
Gallaher, Hugh M., 208
gasoline stations, 89
General Construction Standards (1934), 82-86
General Land Office (GLO), 8, 10, 105
Georgia, 135-136
Gibson, James, 108-109
Gifford Pinchot National Forest, 118
Gila Wilderness, 93
Gilman, John C., 183
Glacier National Park Hotel Lobby, 22
Godden, 99
Golden Elephant, 155
government control, 8, 105

Govt Mineral Springs Cabin Association, 118
Grand Coulee, 105
Graves, Henry S., 1, 10-11, 15, 55, 67-71, 280
Graystone San Jose Tract, 50
Great Depression, 26-27, 61, 64, 174, 248-249, 254
Greeley, Horace, 236, 282
Greeley, William B., 20-24
Grid Pattern Tracts, 51-52
Gridiron Pattern Tracts, 51-52
Grosvenor, John R., 50, 90, 94-95, 109
guidelines and regulations, 1-3, 18, 24-25, 29-31, 36, 64-65, 82-86, 116-117, 124-126, 129-130, 145, 151, 160-161, 171, 214

H

Haas, Richard G., 156
Hall, Milton Sanders, 148, 237-238
Hannahs, George, 147-148, 150, 239
Hannahs, Sarah, 239
Hapeman, Clark, 227
Happy Top Summer Homes, 90
Harlowe, Aurelia, 204-205
Harlowe Family, 145, 181, 191-192, 201, 208
Harmon, R.U., 75
Hass, Richard, 262-263
Hastings, Doc, 39
Hawaii. *See* Region 5
Hawk (engineer), 201
Hays, Jeff, 218-219
Hayter, Holly, 155
headquarters of national forests, 120
health. *See* sanitation
Hearst, Melissa, 97
Hedrick, C.J., 203
Hedrick, Cloa, 204-205, 207
Hedrick, Frank, 204
Hedrick, Fred, 209
Hedrick, Jewel, 209
Hedrick family, 201, 206-208
Henly, Ralph C., 263
Herman Gulch Homeowners Association, 90
Hetch Hetchy Valley, 15-16
hiking, 90, 94
Hill, Farrer, and Burrill Law Firm, 193
Hise, Laura, 136
historic cabin application for National Register, 260-282
Hitchings, Diane, 88
Hogan, Heidi, 224
Hogue, Ada M., 161-162, 167, 169-170
Hogue, Howard O., 161
Hogue cabin, 168
Holcomb, Hal, 156, 161, 174, 255, 263, 268
Hollywood, 249
Holy Ghost Canyon, 95
Homeowners Division (HD), 34, 60
Homestake Valley Tract, 91
Homestead Acts, 8-10, 137, 236-237
homesteading, 236-238
Horne, Thomas, 213-214
hotels
in Alaska, 139
allowed, 10
Bungalow Hotel, 250
encouraged by Forest Service, 89
Glacier National Park Hotel, 22
marketing maps, 75
permit fees, 33
permits, 41, 68, 98
regulations, 2
Strawberry Valley Hotel, 239
Hough, Frank B., 9
Houston, David F., 1, 41, 55
Humboldt National Forest, 100
Hume Lake, 111
Humphrey, Leigh, 145, 181, 228
Hunt, David E., 211-212
hunting, 41, 90, 94, 99, 107-108, 156, 280
Huntington Lake, 111

I

Ice House Canyon, 111
Idaho, 74-87, 97-103. *See also* Region 1
Idaho Panhandle National Forest, 49-50, 76
Idyllwild. *See also* San Bernardino National Forest; Saunders Meadow; *Tahquitz entries*
and the Civilian Conservation Corps, 253-256
conference center, 249
currently, 258
economic benefits from permittees, 179
Emerson's vision, 252
forest rangers, 240-245
and the Forest Service, 7, 233
growth and development, 246-252
historic cabin application for National Register, 260-282
history, 238-240
and Hollywood, 249
permittees as beneficial, 179
post-WWII era, 257-258
recreation, 150-151, 157
roads, 240
schools, 257
under snow, 252
storm (1938), 175
timeline, 291-297
town hall, 161
tracts, 60, 63, 109
Idyllwild Area Historical Society archives (IAHS), 226
Idyllwild Golf Club, 157, 174
Idyllwild Inn, 246-250
Idyllwild Mountain Park Tracts, 247
Idyllwild Pines Camp, 251
Idyllwild Sanatorium, 239, 246
Idyllwild School of Music and The Arts (ISOMATA), 257
Idyllwild Town Crier, 195, 222-223, 255
Illinois, 136-138
Indiana, 136-138
Indians, 97, 137, 147, 234-236, 238, 262
Intermountain Region, 97-103
Inyo National Forest, 107, 111-112
Iowa, 136-138
Irregular Cabin Plan, 49-50

J

Joe (Ranger), 151-152
Johnson, 192
Jones, Elwood, 150-152, 154-160, 180, 228-230
Jones, Hattie, 157-158
Jones, H.D., 179
Jones, Horace B., 157-158
Jones, John B., 157-158, 180, 186, 190, 205-207, 209, 213-214, 229
Jones, John M., 207
Jones, Loraine, 158
Jones, Mark, 145, 180, 215-216, 218, 226, 230
Jones, Marston, 157-158
Jones, Naomi Cory, 228
Jones family, 158, 181
Jordan, Frank M., 188-189
June Lake Permittees Association, 111

K

Kansas, 88-92
Keen, John and Mary, 150, 239
Keen House, 60, 150, 239, 255
Kennedy, Patrick, 226, 264
Kentucky, 135-136
Kings Canyon National Park, 105
Kistachie National Forest, 136
Klamath National Forest, 107-108
Kneipp, Leon F., 20, 23, 25
Kowalchuk, Marlene, 204
Kowalchuk, Raymond, 201, 203-204
Kyle Canyon Summer Homes Association, 100

L

L Plan, 48-49
Ladley, John, 224
Lake Alpine Improvement Association, 111
Lake Arrowhead, 60
Lake Kathleen cabin, 142
Lake Kirkwood Association, 111
Lake Mary, 111
Lake Mead National Recreation Area, 105
Lake Of The Woods, 118
Lake Quinault, 118
Lake Tahoe Basin Management Unit, 107
Lake Wenatchee Summer Homes, 118
Lakeshore Tracts, 51-52
Lakeview Water Improvement Tract, 111
Lambrou, Mary G., 190
land exchange, 3-4, 35, 56-57, 65, 145, 151, 181-193, 206, 225, 228, 264
Land Grant Acts, 137
landscape engineers, 19-21
landscaping, 17-21, 53, 85-86, 126-128
Lassen National Forest, 107-108, 111-112
Lassen Volcanic National Park, 105, 110
Layman Association, 111
Leach, Willis, 204
leases, 1, 3, 11, 33-35, 41-42, 55-57
Leopold, Aldo, 93
Lewis and Clark National Forest, 49
Lewitsky, Bella, 257
Lily Creek, 60, 248
Lily Rock, 234-235
Lincoln National Forest, 96
Lindley, Walter, 239
Linear Pattern Tracts, 51-52
Log Cabin Plan, 48-49
logging, 13, 67, 69, 98, 146-149, 237-239
Los Angeles Small Home Plan Bureau, 43
Los Padres National Forest, 106-107, 112
lot design, 53
Louisiana, 135-136
Lower Emerald Bay, 111
lumber mills, 67, 98

M

MacDonald, Archie, 152, 155, 159-160
MacDonald, Jim, 155
Macteckelwood, 152-153, 212, 224
magazine promotions, 44-45
Maher, Edward J., 109-110
Maine, 136-138
Maloney, Pat, 224
map of typical recreation area, 132
Marion Forks Summer Homes, 118
Marshall, Robert, 26-27
Master-Craft Cabin Company, 45
Maxwell, Ernie and Betty, 255
Medicine Bow National Forest, 91
Mendocino National Forest, 107-108
Metcalf Cabin Owners Association, 111
Metolius River Forest Homeowners Association, 118
Michigan, 136-138
Miller, Char, 39, 73
Miller, O.E., 204
mills, 67, 98
Mineral King, 105
Mineral Springs Leasing Act, 9
Minnesota, 136-138
Minnich, Sam and Mildred, 148, 174, 227
Minter, Brian, 188
Mission 66, 30
Mississippi, 135-136
Missouri, 136-138
Mitchell family, 193-194
Modoc National Forest, 107-108
Montana, 74-87. *See also* Region 1
Montgomery, James C., 208, 264
Moore, Kathleen, 97
Morris, Rita, 242, 245
Mother Lodge style, 110
Mount Baker Lodge, 116
Mount Baker-Snoqualmie National Forest, 118
Mount Hood National Forest, 122, 134
Mount Laguna Improvement Association, 111
Muir, John, 14

N

Nash-Boulden, Steven A., 109, 160, 162, 167, 169, 241
National Defense Authorization Act, 39
National Forest Circular (1941), 92
National Forest Homeowners (NFH) organization, 36-39, 60
National Forest Manual, 24
National Forest Permittees group, 60
National Forest Recreation Association (NFRA), 34, 60
national forests. *See specific names*
National Industrial Recovery Act, 26, 64
national park look, 4-5
National Park Service, 16-17, 21, 30, 105
National Register of Historic Places
generally, 4, 259-260, 282-283
application form sample, 260-282
benefits of listing, 283-284
criteria for inclusion, 260, 283
frequently asked questions, 282-287
grant money, 285
information sources, 286-287
modifications, remodeling, and renovations, 285-286
and property value, 285
restrictions of listing, 284-285
tax credits, 285
National Wilderness Preservation System, 93
Native Americans. *See* Indians
Nebraska, 88-92
Neste, Brudin, and Stone, 188, 195-196, 207-212
Nevada, 97-103

New Deal, 26-27, 75, 93, 253
New Hampshire, 136-138
New Mexico, 93-96
Newell, Martin, 155
North Carolina, 135-136
North Dakota, 74-87. *See also* Region 1
Northern Forests, 107-108
Northern Region. *See* Region 1

O

Ocala National Forest, 136
Occupancy Act. *See* Term Occupancy Permit Act of 1915
Odell Lake Homeowners Association, 118
Ohio, 136-138
Okanogan-Wenatchee National Forest, 118
Oklahoma, 135-136
O'Leary, Karen, 93
Olympic National Forest, 118, 123
one hundred-year lease myth, 55-57
Operation Outdoors, 30, 257
Oregon, 116-134
Organic Act, 150
Outdoor Recreation Resource Review Commission (ORRRC), 33-34
Ozark-St. Francis National Forest, 136

P

Pacific Northwest Region, 116-134
Pacific Railroad Land Grant Acts, 237
Pacific Southwest Region. *See* Region 5
Panhandle National Forest, 49-50, 76
Patterson, 190
Patton, Fred, 160
Peavey, A.J., 99
Peavey Cabins, 98-99
Pennsylvania, 136-138
permits
for businesses, 89-90
classes of permits, 68
fees, 33-39
history of, 8-11
renewals, 55-57, 129
Special Use Permit sample, 133
term length, 1, 3, 11, 33-35, 41-42, 55-57
transfers, 129
for water, 60, 224-225
Pettit Lake, 98-99
Pico, Francisco, 147-148, 236-237
Pico, Pio and Ruth, 161, 235
Pike National Forest, 90
Pike's Peak, 89
Pillsbury, Connie Jones, 145, 150, 156, 226-227, 230
Pinchot, Gifford, 1, 13-16, 21, 41, 73, 243
Pine Creek Tract Improvement Association, 112
Pinecrest Lower Strawberry Lake Tract Home Owners, 60
Pinecrest Permittees Association, 112
pioneers, 7, 10, 147, 236-238, 243
plans. *See* architecture and plans for cabins
Plumas National Forest, 107-108, 111
Poats, Lem, 161, 266, 268
Polique Canyon Association, 112
Porter Fork, 100
Potter, Albert, 281
Prairie Creek Homeowners Association, 112
Presley, Elvis, 184, 257
Priest Lake Permittee's Association, 76
private ownership, 4, 35, 56, 135, 137, 145, 151, 200. *See also* land exchange
promotions, 42-45, 62, 77-80, 100-103, 119, 281
public domain lands, 1, 8, 105-106
Public Land Law Review Commission (PLLRC), 34-36
Pumphrey, Douglas, 213

R

Radial Pattern Tracts, 51-52
Rainbow Canyon, 100
Raker, John E., 11, 15
Raker Act, 15
ranches, 74, 89
ranger stations, 22, 26, 109-110, 240, 254
rangers
and associations, 60
in the San Bernardino forest, 244-245
in the San Jacinto forest, 241-245
and the Tahquitz Tract, 151-152
recreation, public interest in, 13-16
Recreation Residence Policy, 36
Rectangular Plan, 48-49
Rectilinear Pattern, 51-52
Region 1, 3, 50, 52, 74-87
Region 2, 3, 88-92
Region 3, 93-96
Region 4, 3, 97-103
Region 5, 3, 23-24, 29-35, 42-48, 60-69, 104-115
Region 6, 3, 116-134
Region 7, 135
Region 8, 135-136
Region 9, 136-138
Region 10, 50, 138-143
regulations. *See* guidelines and regulations
renewals of permits, 55-57, 129
Residence Application Letter, 167
Residence Permit Regulations, 171
Residence Tract Planning Guide (1935), 81
resorts
Disney, 108
Idyllwild, 246, 255
Mt. Baker Lodge, 116-117
permit fees, 33
permits, 1-2, 27-28, 41-42, 65, 68, 89
Tahquitz Meadow Improvement Association, 196
and the Term Occupancy Permit Act, 150
visitors increased, 74
Reyes, Robert, 226, 264
Ricker, Wayne C., 204
Ridgeline Pattern, 51-52, 152
Rimrock Cabin Owners Assoc, 118
roads
and the associations, 59
and the Civilian Conservation Corps, 93, 254-255, 263
condition of, 148
difficulty traveling, 148
in District 2, 88
and the Forest Service manual, 24-26
funding, 64, 70, 76
in Idyllwild, 238-240
improved access to tracts, 106
log barriers, 108
in the San Bernardino National Forest, 243
in Saunders Meadow, 175, 197,

206, 208, 211, 231, 263
Robbins, Royal, 235
Robertson, Dale, 36
Rocky Mountain Region. *See* Region 2
Rodriguez Cabrillo, Juan, 235
Rogue River National Forest, 118
Roosevelt, Franklin Delano, 26-28, 253
Roosevelt, Theodore, 41, 239
Routt National Forest, 92
Rutledge, Ralph M., 184-185, 189
Ryan, James, 99

S

St. Francis National Forest, 137
Salmon National Forest, 99-100
Salt Creek Summer Homes, 112
San Bernardino National Forest, 11, 24-25, 50-52, 60-63, 104-112, 162, 179, 184, 225, 233-236, 239-245, 254-259
San Isabel National Forest, 89
San Jacinto forest rangers, 241-245
San Jacinto Forest Reserve, 239, 246
San Jacinto - Idyllwild Transportation Company, 239
San Juan Summer Home Tract, 114, 115
sanatoriums, 10-11, 239, 246
sanitation, 2, 29, 59, 91, 210. *See also* toilets
Santa Ana River Cabin Association, 112
Santa Fe National Forest, 95-96
Santa Lucia Improvement Association, 112
Sapp, Bill, 104
Saunders, Amasa, 148-149
Saunders Meadow. *See also Tahquitz entries*
clubhouse and golf course, 174
Desert Sun School, 249
early history of, 148-151
historic cabin, 260-282
incorporation, 184-193, 199, 209
perseverance and community service, 146
Saunders Meadow Lodge, 173
Saunders Meadow Timeline, 298-357
Sauser, James, 116
saw mills, 67, 98
Sawtooth National Recreation Area, 98-99
Scharf, Robert M., 191-192
Scherman, Anton, 147-149
Schonebaum, Judy, 145, 224
schools, 64, 70, 148, 174, 182, 184, 249, 257
Schulze, Brandon, 74
Sears homebuilding plans, 45
Sequoia National Forest, 107, 111
Sequoia National Park, 105
Seven Pines Cabin Owners Association, 112
Shermann, E.A., 17, 19
Shevlin Pine Company, 43
Shoemaker, Theodore, 88-89
Sierra Club, 108
Sierra National Forest, 107, 110-111
Silcox, Ferdinand A., 27
Silver Lake Homeowners Association, 112
Simpson, Jim, 155
Sinatra, Frank, Jr., 184, 257
Six Rivers National Forest, 107-108
Smith (Representative from Oregon), 36
Smith, Brandon, 74
Smith, Robert B., 257-258
Smith, Verne, 186
Smoker's Code, 117, 131
Snoqualmie National Forest, 118
Snowcrest Heights Improvement Association, 112
Sons of May, 151-155
South, Perry, 116
South Carolina, 135-136
South Dakota, 74-87, 88-92. *See also* Region 1
South Silver Lake Homeowners Association, 112
Southern Forests, 106-107
Southern Region, 135-136
Southwestern Region, 93-96
Spaulding, Richard, 263-264
Special Use Applications, 115, 165-166
Special Use Permit (sample), 133
Special Use Permit Act. *See* Term Occupancy Permit Act of 1915
Special Use Residence Permit, 170
Special Use Summer Home program, 8-11, 16, 35-36, 65, 104-110. *See also specific tracts*
Spradling, Oliver, 155
Spring Creek Tract Association, Inc., 112
Stahlman Summer Home Association, 118
Stanislaus National Forest, 60, 107, 110-112
states' rights, 105
Sternberg, Harvey, 257
Stockton, Albert and Arlene, 201-204
Stockton, et al v. Saunders Meadow, Inc., 204
Stone Cabin Plan, 49-50
stores, 1, 33, 41, 89, 98, 175, 237
Strauss, Levi, 236
Strawberry Valley Hotel, 239
Strong and Dickinson, 157, 246-249
Stuart, Robert, 24-27
summer homes. *See* Special Use Summer Home program
"Summer Homes in the National Forests of Oregon and Washington," 119-134
Sundry Civil Appropriations Act, 9, 60
Sunset, 44-45
"Survey of Toilet situation on Tahquitz Tract, San Jacinto Mountain," 176
Swan, D. Richard, 187-188, 190, 192-193, 198-201

T

Tahoe National Forest, 62, 107, 111-112
Tahquitz Lodge, 60, 150, 239, 255
Tahquitz Meadow Improvement Association, 3, 145, 159-160, 163-166, 186-189, 193, 196, 204-205
Tahquitz Pines, 249
Tahquitz Rock, 146
Tahquitz Saunders Meadow Tract, 3, 49, 52, 151-153, 178, 248, 255, 266
Tahquitz Special Use Summer Home Tract
annexation into Fern Valley Water District, 212-223
assessor parcel map, 210
boundary lawsuit and subdivision, 193-212
cabins, 156-159
closure, 226-232
development, 159-178

documentation, 145
the Great Depression, 174
Indians, 147
land exchange, 184-193
loggers, 147-149
present day, 225-226
recreation, 150-151
Saunders Meadow, 146
Tahquitz Meadow Improvement Association, 159-173
Tahquitz Tract, 151-153, 178
taxation lawsuits, 179
termination of special use water permit, 224-225
water conservation, 180-183
water maps, 177-178
World War II, 179-180
Tahquitz Tract Association, 60, 183
Talmage, Edwin L., 189
Tameler, Karl L., 184, 187, 189
taxation of permittees, 179
Teanaway Recreational Tract Association, 118
Tecklenborg, Ray H., 152, 155-157, 159-160, 175
Tennessee, 135-136
term length. *See* leases
Term Occupancy Permit Act of 1915
in Alaska, 138, 140
approval of, 11
benefits of, 67-71
in California, 61-65
case study, 145-232
discontinuation of, 31
implementation of, 17-31
as response to public backlash, 16
summary, 1-5
thirty-year permits discontinued, 33
Terminable Permits Act, 9
Terry, Zeb, 155
Texas, 135-136
Thomas Canyon Cabin Owners Association, Inc., 100
Thompson and Colgate, 207
Tidwell, Tom, 39
Timeless Heritage, 93
toilets, 21, 25-26, 62, 176, 216, 263, 267-269
Toiyabe National Forest, 100
Tongass National Forest, 142
tract associations, 59-60
tract designs, 50-53, 152
trails, 67, 89, 152-153, 234, 238, 243. *See also* roads; tract patterns
transfers, 129
Trappers Lake, 89
Trinity National Forest, 107-108, 112
Turkey Flat (tract association), 95
Tuttle, "Tut," 155
Twaroski, Jim, 135-136
Tweed, William C., 46, 64

U

Umpqua National Forest, 118, 131
Upper Emerald Bay Cabinowners Association, 112
Upper Rogue River Cabinowners Association, 118
Upper Truckee Tract Association, 112
Utah, 97-103

V

Vermont, 136-138
Virginia, 135-136
Viscaino, Sebastian, 235
visitors, number of
in 1913, 11
in the 1920s, 19, 23
in 1931, 99
in the 1940s, 28-29, 65, 257-258
in the 1950s, 30, 257-258
in 1961, 34

W

Wallowa-Whitman National Forest, 117
Walt Disney Enterprises, 108
Ward, James, 205, 208
Wasatch-Cache National Forest, 100
Washington (state), 116-134
water
permits, 60, 196, 224-225
and Saunders Meadow
annexation into Fern Valley Water Dist., 212-223
application for water use, 165
conservation, 180-183
increased need, 150
permit, 196, 224-225
residents set up water system, 153
tank (1969), 188
water development, 159-161, 174-178
water meters and fees, 185
Water Spring Box, 157
Watkins, John, 217
Waugh, Frank A., 4, 17-18, 45, 69, 225, 264-265, 279
Webb, Albert A., 213
Webb Associates, 215-219
Weigle, Bill, 139
Wenatchee National Forest, 118
West Virginia, 136-138
Western States Opposition, 105-106
Westward expansion, 7, 236-237
White River National Forest, 91
White River Recreation Association, 118
Whiting, Dan, 38
Whitney Portal, 112
Wiley, Cosetter C., 192, 204
Willamette National Forest, 118
Willian Kent campground, 62
Willow Canyon Homeowners Association, 95
Wilson, Meredith, 182, 257
Wilson, Woodrow, 15
Winema National Forest, 118
Winter Creed, 106
winter storm of 1938, 175
Wisconsin, 136-138
Wissman, Bob, 224, 228
Wissman, Elwood, 209, 212
Womack, Ray O., 205-209
wood, need for, 7-8
Wood, Walter, 157
World War I, 19, 61, 243
World War II, 28, 64, 69, 108, 161, 179-180, 242, 249, 255
Wrights Lake Summer Home Association, 112
Wycliffe Bible Translators, 249
Wyoming, 88-92, 97-103

Y

Yandell, Dr., 204-205
Yellowstone Timberland Reserve, 9
Yosemite Grant Act, 9
Yost, Leland, 194, 203-204
Young, Henry, McCarthy, and Mason, 201, 203-204

CPSIA information can be obtained
at www.ICGtesting.com
Printed in the USA
FSOW02n0604220916
25259FS

9 781634 139106